Dear Steve J.

To my friend and
my love!

Happy birthday.

With all my love.

# Race

**Race and Ethnicity in the American West**

SERIES EDITORS:

Albert S. Broussard
Maria Raquel Casas
Dudley Gardner
Margaret Jacobs
Delphine Red Shirt
Benson Tong

# Work

## THE RISE OF CIVIL RIGHTS
## IN THE URBAN WEST

Matthew C. Whitaker

UNIVERSITY OF NEBRASKA PRESS
LINCOLN & LONDON

Publication of this book was made
possible in part by a grant from the
Arizona Humanities Council and the
Virginia Faulkner Fund, established in
memory of Virginia Faulkner, editor in
chief of the University of Nebraska Press.

Arizona Humanities Council

♾

Library of Congress Cataloging-
in-Publication Data
Whitaker, Matthew C.
Race work : the rise of civil rights in
the urban West / Matthew C. Whitaker.
p. cm.—(Race and ethnicity in the
American West)
Includes bibliographical references and
index.
ISBN-13: 978-0-8032-4821-2 (cloth : alk.
paper)
ISBN-10: 0-8032-4821-0 (cloth : alk. paper)
1. Ragsdale, Lincoln Johnson, 1926–1995.
2. Ragsdale, Eleanor Odell Dickey, 1926–
1998.   3. African Americans—Civil rights
—Arizona—Phoenix—History—20th century.
4. Civil rights movements—Arizona—Phoe-
nix—History—20th century.   5. African
Americans in the professions—Arizona—
Phoenix—History—20th century.   6. African
American civil rights workers—Arizona—
Phoenix—Biography.   7. Phoenix (Ariz.)—
Race relations—History—20th century.
I. Title. II. Series.
F819.P57W47 2005
323'.092'279173—dc22
2005009410

For Doris, Covey, Gidget, Anastacia, and Jackson Whitaker . . .
The past is prologue to our future.

# CONTENTS

# ILLUSTRATIONS

TABLES

## ACKNOWLEDGMENTS

*Race Work*, like most books, is the product of a collaborative process. Indeed, this book would not have been possible without the assistance of numerous scholars, colleagues, archivists, librarians, family members, and friends. My interest in writing about African Americans and the struggle for racial equality in Phoenix was first encouraged and cultivated by several outstanding historians during my master's work in the Western History Program at Arizona State University. Wanda A. Hendricks, now at the University of South Carolina–Columbia, Albert L. Hurtado, now at the University of Oklahoma, and Bradford Luckingham provided guidance and support. Their substantive interest in my intellectual and professional growth was matched only by their collegiality and infectious passion for historical inquiry. This book was first conceived as a doctoral dissertation during my graduate studies in the Comparative Black History Program at Michigan State University in East Lansing. A number of individuals at Michigan State helped facilitate my research and writing of this biographical account of the black freedom struggle in Phoenix. As a result, I have cultivated myriad scholarly relationships and incurred many debts of gratitude while completing this book. Darlene Clark Hine, the historian virtuoso and adviser extraordinaire, championed this study from its infancy. Her willingness to offer "constructive and compassionate criticism" throughout the entire writing process was invaluable. I am particularly indebted to her and Wilma King, now at the University of Missouri–Columbia, for their scholarly and professional counsel and for the many times they permitted me to monopolize their seminar discussions and office hours with unsolicited talk of the dynamism of African American culture and community in the American West. It is also a tremendous personal pleasure for me to acknowledge Laurant Dubois, Leslie Moch, Richard W. Thomas, and Linda Werbish. Their patience, wisdom, and generosity never ceased to amaze me.

A number of individuals throughout the academy assisted me in authoring this book. I am very grateful to the many historians of American western history and African American western history who encouraged me, talked to me about my project, and were willing to share their time, ideas, and references. Sincere thanks are due to Anne M. Butler, Elizabeth Jameson, Clyde A. Milner, Donald J. Pisani, Glenda Riley, Charles E. Rankin, Vicki Ruiz, Gretchen Lemke-Santangelo, and Ona Siporin. The trail-blazing work of Albert S. Broussard at Texas A&M University in College Station, Quintard Taylor Jr. at the University of Washington, and Roland G. Coleman at the University of Utah helped inspire and shape my interest in this topic. Their insight, support, and generosity have enhanced the quality of this work and taught me a great deal about mentorship. Albert Broussard and Quintard Taylor, in particular, read and commented on several conference papers that evolved into chapters in this book. They offered many suggestions and counseled me to place the lives of the Ragsdales and their activities into the broader context of African American history, the history of the civil rights movement, and American western history. I must extend a special thank-you to Richard E. Harris, who authored the first book about African Americans in Arizona and who, at one hundred years old, is still researching, writing, and offering his encyclopedic knowledge of black history to young historians like me.

Various institutions were instrumental in the completion of this book. Many thanks go to the staff of the Hayden Library at Arizona State University. I wish to extend a heartfelt thanks to the archival staff, especially Patricia Etter and Chris Marin, of the Department of Manuscripts and Special Collections at the Hayden Library at Arizona State University; the Arizona Historical Society Library and Archive, Central Division, in Tempe, most notably Mary Melcher, Dawn Nave, and Jean Reynolds; the Arizona and Southwest Collections at Arizona State University; the Arizona Historical Foundation at Arizona State University; the Government Documents Division at Arizona State University; and the Phoenix Public Library. The archival staff at the History and Archives Division of the Arizona State Capitol in Phoenix were quite gracious in answering my many questions and allowing me to review documents, primarily old newspapers, that were ill-suited for public scrutiny. Other individuals and institutions that contributed to the completion of this project include the Planning Department of the City of Phoenix and Princess Crump, Calvin C. Goode, and Tommie Williams of the George Washington Carver Museum and Cultural Center in Phoenix, the Library of Michigan in Lansing, the Michigan Historical Collection at the University of Michigan in Ann Arbor, the Department of Manuscripts and Archives at the Oklahoma State

Capitol in Oklahoma City, and the Oklahoma Historical Society in Oklahoma City. This enterprise benefited from the financial support of the Martin Luther King–Cesar Chavez–Rosa Parks Fellowship at Michigan State University, Michigan State University's Comparative Black History Fellow Research Travel Grant, the Western History Association, and the Department of History and College of Liberal Arts and Sciences at Arizona State University.

Many other people who helped me during my research and writing deserve mention as well. Barbara Trapido-Lurie and Patricia Gober of the Department of Geography at Arizona State University and Remy Autz, GIS Education Coordinator for the City of Phoenix, provided wonderful assistance with the production of maps and legends. I will always be grateful for the superb effort that Barbara Jardee rendered as she transcribed many of my oral interviews. In their characteristically generous and brilliant ways, my colleagues Catherine Kaplan (and her editorial alter ego, "Angry Man") and Rachel Koopmans offered valuable critiques of draft chapters. Graduate students Laurie Arnold, Scott Bowman, Brian Collier, Lauren Kientz, and John Scheuer all aided in the project by offering valuable insights and fresh ideas. I am immensely appreciative for the support of the Ragsdale family, specifically Lincoln Ragsdale Jr., Emily Ragsdale, Gwendolyn Ragsdale Madrid, Hartwell Ragsdale Jr., and Hartwell Ragsdale III. Their willingness to share their time, recollections, and resources, as well as rare family photographs, newspaper clippings, and oral interview transcripts, made this book exceedingly richer in detail than it would have been in the absence of their support. I must also thank Judis Andrews, George B. Brooks Sr., Clovis Campbell Sr., William D. Dickey, Herbert Ely, Michael Johnson, Ed King, Calvin C. Goode, Georgie Goode, Cody Williams, and Travis Williams for welcoming me into their businesses and homes to conduct oral interviews. Their illuminating accounts humanize statistics and other "privileged" sources. To demonstrate my appreciation, I have therefore endeavored to present their words in full and in context, allowing them to tell their own stories.

This book would not have been completed without the encouragement and camaraderie of my colleagues and peers: Stephen K. Batalden, Lara Collins, Edward Escobar, Susan E. Gray, Gayle Gullett, Rita Hallows, Camille Irwin, Neil Lester, Beth Luey, Kyle Longley, Suzanne Rios, Arturo Rosales, Mary Logan Rothschild, Chris

Smith, Noel J. Stowe, Philip R. VanderMeer, Norma Villa, Jannelle Warren-Finley, and Angela Waziyatawin Wilson. I would like to add a special note of thanks to Thomas J. Davis, Peter Iverson, Brooks D. Simpson, and Chris Smith, whose unwavering support of me, my work, and my family is unsurpassed. A heartfelt thank-you to Elizabeth A. S. Demers, an outstanding editor; Gary Dunham; Robert Burchfield; and the two anonymous readers for the University of Nebraska Press. Thank-you as well to my friends, peers, and several alumni of the Comparative Black History Program at Michigan State: Dawne Curry, Eric Duke, Ernestine Jenkins, Hilary Jones, Jacqueline McLeod, Mary Mwiandi, and Kristie Rutz-Robbins. Words cannot express how appreciative I am for the support of new and longtime friends such as Tom Broderson, Mary Ruth Hackett, Alix Hart, Carol Coles Henry, Kathy Ivory, Alonzo Jones, Gina Lang, Charles Mitchell, Sheri Mitchell, and Mary Radcliffe. Moreover, the unyielding backing of "Chef" Evan J. Harris, my friend in life and big brother in spirit, and of my friends Dale DeMann, Robert J. Hackett Jr., Jason B. Harris, John L. Jones, Jeremy I. Levitt, and Michael A. Smart helped sustain my confidence, direction, and sense of humor with their unconditional support, enthusiasm, and optimism.

My sister, Mahlika Hopwood, offered her cool eye for coherence and clarity. I must thank my grandmother, Doris V. Whitaker, whose wisdom and unparalleled strength serve as constant reminders of my responsibility to those who preceded me and to those who will follow. It is because of my mother, Covey L. Whitaker, the first historian I ever knew, that I became aware of the inescapable power of history. Thank-you "Ma," you are my inspiration. I also thank my daughter, Anastacia Ami, and my son, Jackson Asantè, for their smiles and sparkling eyes. This project required me to spend far too much time away from them. They have been, and will always be, however, blessings and constant sources of inspiration. An immeasurable debt of gratitude is owed to my wife and eternal partner, Gidget M. Whitaker. Her patience and unyielding support of my dreams, studies, and career are unmatched. You are my love.

**Race** Work

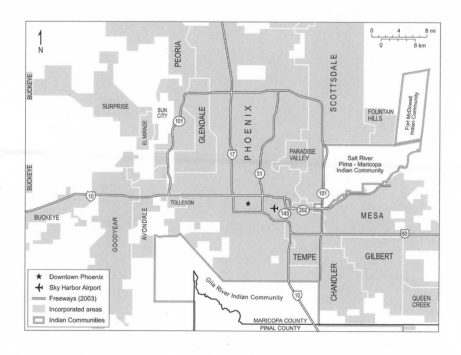

The Greater Phoenix Metropolitan Area, 2000.
*Source*: Barbara Trapido-Lurie and
Patricia Gober, Department of Geography,
Arizona State University, Tempe.

# Introduction

*The Quest for Racial Equality in Phoenix*

ON FRIDAY, JUNE 16, 1995, amid blistering desert heat of over 100 degrees, scores of ordinary citizens and some of the most influential leaders in Phoenix, Arizona, and across the nation gathered to celebrate the life and mourn the loss of Dr. Lincoln Johnson Ragsdale Sr., one of the city's wealthiest and most dynamic leaders. They assembled at the Universal Memorial Chapel at 1100 East Jefferson Street, a location that once stood at the bustling epicenter of the African American community in Phoenix. Among the many who braved the torrid heat to pay their respects to Ragsdale's widow, Eleanor Dickey Ragsdale, and the rest of the Ragsdale family were some of the most celebrated African American leaders in the nation. Leon Sullivan, a close friend and a key figure in the anti-apartheid movement and the founder of Opportunities Industrialization Centers (OIC), International Foundation of Education and Self-Help (IFESH), and Progress Non-profit Charitable Trust, was on hand to deliver Ragsdale's eulogy. Earl Graves, the millionaire publisher of *Black Enterprise Magazine*, was present to give tribute. Local civil rights legends Clovis Campbell Sr., George B. Brooks, Herbert L. Ely, and the Reverend Warren H. Stewart, among others, also came to say good-bye to their confidant and fellow activist.[1]

The distinguished congregation that amassed in downtown Phoenix that day did so to honor one of most commanding and compelling individuals in Phoenix's history. Indeed, Lincoln Ragsdale was among the first African Americans to be trained as a combat pilot during World War II, an extremely successful mortician and businessman in a city that afforded black men and women very little economic upward mobility, and a key leader of the post–World War II black freedom struggle in Arizona. Although Ragsdale's wealth and business acumen were routinely noted in the Phoenix media by the end of his life, he was an activist at his core, the quintessential "race man." That is to say that Ragsdale devoted much of his time, training, work, and resources to the reclamation and social, economic, political, and cultural advancement of people of African descent. This, he believed, was his calling and responsibility—to help reconfigure American society into one that would provide black people with the opportunity to maximize their own potential and succeed or fail by their own merits. "I am a crusader for racial justice," he declared just before he died, "and I will be to the day I die."[2]

On Thursday, May 14, 1998, just three years after Lincoln Ragsdale passed away, Eleanor Dickey Ragsdale was honored at her funeral at the Universal Memorial Chapel. The chapel, owned and operated by the Ragsdale family since 1945, was and is in many ways a reflection of Eleanor Ragsdale's warm, elegant, and cultured persona. As an equally distinguished cast of characters descended upon the chapel to attend her memorial services, including Sullivan and many of the dignitaries who attended Lincoln's funeral, they were greeted by rare paintings that adorned the complex's walls and by precious sculptures and busts that were carefully placed throughout the foyer, adjacent offices, and sanctuary. The illustrious gathering came not simply to salute the deceased wife of one the region's most celebrated leaders, they did so to honor someone who was an eminent figure in her own right. Eleanor Ragsdale was a graduate of Cheyney University in Pennsylvania, the oldest historically black college and university in the nation, an accomplished educator, an effective businesswoman, and a formidable civil rights leader. Like her husband, Eleanor, though well known by many as an affluent socialite, earned her local celebrity by positioning herself early on as a civil rights pioneer and advocate for black culture and community. She was a classic "race woman." Eleanor was wholly committed to the social, economic, political, and cultural betterment of people of African descent. Like Lincoln, she believed that this was not only her purpose but her duty. She, too, was devoted to eradicating racism and "uplifting" people of African descent who suffered from the exigencies of socioeconomic subordination and cultural deprivation.[3]

Lincoln and Eleanor Ragsdale, as black professional people, believed that it was their responsibility to aid in the advancement of people of African descent who were less fortunate than they were. They acquired their devotion to this ethic of "race work" undergirded by professional pursuits through familial and community traditions. Lincoln was a third-generation mortician and entrepreneur, and Eleanor was a third-generation educator and business owner. African Americans have had a long history of producing and sustaining professional leaders who have, in turn, redistributed their social and economic capital in black communities. A vital aspect of this black professional tradition called for African American communities to support the career specialists they helped produce, as long as these professionals distinguished themselves as advocates for black people. This practice was intended to, among other things, ensure the long-term survival and advancement of African Americans in a society that offered little, if any, meaningful and sustained outside assistance. This legacy equipped the Ragsdales with motivation to prosper. It also enveloped them with high hopes from a larger black community that expected them to aid in their betterment.[4]

Eleanor's status as a professional "race woman" differed from Lincoln's position as a professional "race man" by virtue of her substantive commitment to gender equality. She understood that the fight for black liberation necessarily required a parallel if not intertwined struggle for gender equality. For Eleanor, being a "race woman," or engaging in race work, never meant sacrificing her commitment to gender equality. Although she willingly and strategically subordinated gender issues to racial issues at times or sometimes fought for racial equality and gender equality independently, she always understood, even as many of her black male peers could or would not, that advocating for the advancement of black people, or "the race," meant working for the enrichment of black men and women. Together, Lincoln and Eleanor Ragsdale crusaded for racial and gender equality for fifty years. Lincoln and Eleanor Ragsdale's all-encompassing commitment to black progress and prosperity in postwar Phoenix helped make him the city's leading "race man" and her its leading "race woman." These labels, and their importance in Phoenix, grew out of their long-term devotion to the work to which they had set their hands—their efforts to liberate people of African descent from the web of white supremacy, their race work.[5]

Nearly fifty years before the death of Lincoln Ragsdale, he and Eleanor descended upon Phoenix, an isolated, somewhat desolate, and entirely racially segregated city, in search of freedom and opportunity. Few would have imagined that their migration would ultimately help transform an entire city and, ostensibly, a nation forever. Between 1945 and 1995, fired with a passion for racial equality, Lincoln and Eleanor Ragsdale drew upon an arsenal of social justice weapons in the battle for civil rights in Phoenix. They helped dismantle an apartheid-like system in what is presently the fifth largest city in the United States. The Ragsdales and other western activists, though geographically isolated from the civil rights movement in the American South, were not strangers to white supremacy and black resistance. They were roused by years of racial discrimination, World War II, and America's promise of democracy and were sustained by a swelling African American population. They were also buoyed by the burgeoning postwar liberalism of a number of white western leaders. Armed with their experiences, hope, and passion, and aided by sympathetic white Phoenicians, the Ragsdales led the way in securing victories for racial justice in Phoenix, sometimes in advance of national milestones in civil rights.[6]

Between 1945 and 1995 America's black freedom struggle peaked, and many African Americans made social, economic, and political gains as a result of the civil rights movement and its legacy. Through an aggressive coalition of organizations, activists fought de jure and de facto racial segregation. They attacked segregation in the courts and through direct-action protests such as sit-ins, boycotts, and other forms of civil disobedience. In the face of this onslaught, and despite persistent white resistance, legal segregation and disfranchisement collapsed. Although racism remained and African Americans lagged behind their white counterparts economically and politically, blacks experienced unprecedented improvements in their socioeconomic mobility.[7]

The Phoenician movement and activism throughout the West, as Quintard Taylor Jr. has argued, "paralleled the movement East of the Mississippi with regard to strategy, tactics, and objectives." Nevertheless, the western movement took place in an environment where black people were often not the largest minority. In Phoenix, due to the city's small African American population, black leaders were compelled to form alliances with progressive whites and Mexican Americans. As a result, the multiracial coalitions that were formed "pushed civil rights beyond black and white." The diversity of these alliances infused the Phoenician movement with a level of social capital, economic strength, and optimism that rarely existed in the South or even in the Northwest. The optimism and determination of the Ragsdales, and that of other activists, produced many of the region's early civil rights victories. As early as 1951, white Phoenician attorney and civil rights activist William Mahoney proclaimed that "the die is cast in the South or in an old city like New York or Chicago, but we here [in Phoenix] are present for creation. We're making a society where the die isn't cast. It can be for good or ill."[8]

Although white supremacy and racial segregation existed in Phoenix from its birth, the city's racial etiquette was less violent than that found in southern cities. "The difference [in Phoenix]," argued John Barber, an early black Phoenician, "was that they didn't lynch you." The Ragsdales and other activists therefore believed that Phoenix held the potential to be more responsive than its southern counterparts to calls for racial justice. Their assessment of the city's racial etiquette was sustained and productive. Indeed, in 1953 Eleanor Ragsdale played a leading role in desegregating Phoenix's Encanto District, the city's most affluent and racially segregated neighborhood. Also in 1953, the Ragsdales helped desegregate Phoenix schools one year before the landmark *Brown v. Board of Education* decision of 1954. Lincoln Ragsdale, along with black activist George Brooks, led the way in desegregating many of Phoenix's most influential corporations as early as 1962, the same year James Meredith desegregated the University of Mississippi with federal support and two years before the U.S. Equal Employment Opportunity Commission was established. In 1963, the same year that Medgar Evers was assassinated in Mississippi for his attempt to rally support for racial justice, Lincoln Ragsdale positioned himself as one of the cornerstones of a political campaign that wrested Phoenix city government out of the hands of an elite group of conservative white men. Lincoln and Eleanor Ragsdale fought for proportional allocation of government contracts to minority-owned businesses during the 1970s, and by the 1990s they were aiding in the nationally recognized, hard-fought campaign to establish Martin Luther King Jr. Day as a paid holiday in Arizona. Throughout all of their efforts, the Ragsdales were clever and potent, and their history demonstrates that no lacuna in effective African American leadership existed in Phoenix.[9]

This study examines the Ragsdale family history and how their familial traditions of entrepreneurship, professionalism, activism, and race work served to form their activist identity and ultimately placed them in a position to help desegregate Phoenix. It also underscores the ability of the Ragsdales and their peers to capitalize on the success of the movement. By 1998 the Ragsdales and their allies had worked to improve race relations in Phoenix, and people of African descent generally benefited from greater socioeconomic opportunities. The Ragsdales, by virtue of their activism and faithful devotion to racial inclusion, are also credited with helping to initiate the city's surging interest in diversity and multiculturalism. *Race Work* uses the lives of the Ragsdales to frame, view, and pursue themes of domination, resistance, interracial coalition building, race, gender, and place against the backdrop of the civil rights and post–civil rights eras.[10]

Although it focuses on flamboyant characters, the book is not merely a study of their lives. It is, in essence, an integrated biography that analyzes African Americans' quest for freedom in Phoenix, the degree to which they attained it, and their drive to give that freedom meaning. Thus this work concentrates on "making history and biography reinforce each other," as the lives of the Ragsdales are powerful symbols of black leadership, professionalism, entrepreneurship, activism, problems, and progress in African American history, American western history, and American history in general during the post–World War II era.[11] *Race Work* also endeavors to situate the black Phoenician struggle for freedom and equality in the larger framework of a regional history that defines the West as a place rather than a process. Ultimately, the purpose of this work is to present a new chapter in the history of the civil rights movement, American race relations, African Americans, and the American West. The lives and legacies of Lincoln and Eleanor Ragsdale stand at the center of this heretofore unwritten history.[12]

Like African Americans throughout the nation, black Phoenicians, led by activists such as the Ragsdales, organized to confront virtually all aspects of segregation between 1946 and 1965. Furthermore, between 1965 and 1998 the Ragsdales and their supporters fought to make further advances in education, job training, political representation, socioeconomic mobility, and racial diversity in the public and private sectors. Black Phoenicians rarely received support and attention from the leaders of the national movement and were left largely to their own devices to battle racism and white supremacy. The black freedom struggle benefited greatly from the courage, audacity, and creativity of local leaders like the Ragsdales. Endowed with these character traits, in addition to ambition and keen intellects, Lincoln and Eleanor Ragsdale redefined black leadership and respectability in Phoenix. Their ability to combat white supremacy and negotiate economic, legal, and political reform was unprecedented in the city.[13]

Prominent Phoenix attorney and fellow activist Herbert Ely argues that one "cannot emphasize enough" the importance of Lincoln Ragsdale. As an intelligent, well-spoken black crusader for equal rights, "Lincoln did things that had never been done in Phoenix," he maintains. "Lincoln was fearless. He always had a demeanor about him and a stature about him, and he made people understand that he was a business man. He wanted them to understand that he could compete with them at their level, and he was absolutely successful in that." George Brooks has declared that all races, ethnicities, and religions in Phoenix "owe Lincoln Ragsdale a debt of gratitude that they do not have enough time to pay." Brooks argues that Lincoln, aided by Eleanor, helped lead the effort that established a legal precedent for the desegregation of America's schools, and as a result, the two helped make "Phoenix and all American cities [more] inclusive cities." "Without him," he asserts, Phoenix, and perhaps the nation, "would still be on its way."[14]

The Ragsdales' history, their personal achievements, and the social and economic advances they helped bring to Phoenix rival most stories of professional activism in post–World War II America. Like Andrew Manis in *"A Fire You Can't Put Out": The Civil Rights Life of Birmingham's Reverend Fred Shuttlesworth*, I admit that I am sympathetic to the Ragsdales as people and to their positions as leaders of a significant local movement with national implications. Like Manis, I believe that "no historian is free of bias." Historian Peter Novic captured the complexity of objectivity well when he likened it to "nailing jelly to the wall." Despite the difficulties associated with neutrality, historians can be evenhanded in their analysis. I have endeavored to be fair yet critical in my examination of the Ragsdales. To this end, *Race Work* confronts multiple tensions within the Ragsdale family, including frictions that stemmed from Lincoln's authoritarian persona and his tendency to privilege work and service over spending time with his family, particularly with his children. The book will also illuminate the disquiet that emerged as a by-product of the African American community's needs and expectations vis-à-vis the Ragsdales' status as an elite black family. It will examine other strains as well, including the uneasy relationship between upstart and more seasoned activists, traditionalists and militants, male and female leaders, and African Americans and Mexican Americans in Phoenix.[15]

Black Phoenicians have never been the largest "minority" in the city. Although Phoenix had few "original-entry ethnic enclaves," Mexican Americans are perhaps the only minority group present in substantive numbers from the city's birth in 1870. They quickly became the largest racial minority in Phoenix, and as early as World War II, the number of Mexican Americans greatly exceeded the number of African Americans in the city. Like African Americans, Mexican Americans have struggled against white supremacy. Seldom, however, have these groups formed multiracial coalitions that stood in opposition to racial oppression. Ironically, multiracial coalition building in Phoenix was practiced primarily by blacks and progressive whites. Necessarily, therefore, this book offers a critical analysis of the relationship between African Americans and Mexican Americans and between African Americans and white Americans in the struggle for racial equality. Lincoln and Eleanor Ragsdale, particularly in the final years of their lives, championed greater interaction among Chicanos and African Americans. Lincoln Ragsdale, in fact, was a member of a relatively small group of local leaders who chose to do so. The Ragsdales demonstrated early on that they understood the American West, especially the Southwest, to be a harbinger for a new racial dynamic that would eventually engulf the entire nation. They knew that as the Chicano and Latino majority grew and the proportion of the African American population declined, black people would have to devise new ways of successfully negotiating the challenges of racial and ethnic divisions. *Race Work* portrays the Southwest as being something of a meeting ground between the cultures of the Old South and Mexico and examines how African Americans, by virtue of their small numbers, were obligated to devise unique survival strategies, which included substantial coalition building, to advance in this dissimilar racial order.[16]

Like many local leaders who greatly influenced the course of the

African American freedom struggle, the Ragsdales' history has been overshadowed by the more noted legacies of postwar leaders such as Ella Baker, Fannie Lou Hamer, Martin Luther King Jr., and Malcolm X (El Hajj Malik El Shabazz). Lincoln and Eleanor Ragsdale, however, are among the most unsung of the leading protagonists of the American civil rights movement. Without the support of Lincoln and Eleanor Ragsdale, Phoenix's high schools may not have been desegregated in 1953, and its elementary schools would not have been desegregated early in 1954 (before *Brown*). The U.S. Supreme Court may not have been able to use the Phoenix ruling as a precedent in the *Brown* ruling of 1954, and arguably the first landmark victory of the civil rights movement might have been postponed for quite some time and America's schools desegregated much later. This alone makes the Ragsdales' story worthy of inquiry. Moreover, their story is an irrepressible drama that I have strived to reveal and interpret with clarity and balance.[17]

Relatively few historians have written about local "race men" and "race women" in the American West, particularly the Southwest. Generally, the study of the history of African Americans in the post–World War II American West has garnered little attention. The absence of a substantial body of literature has left a scholarly vacuum in the field of black western history, which has played a key role in cloaking the history of highly influential local leaders such as the Ragsdales.[18]

The American West has long been narrowly labeled as a region with few if any African Americans and virtually no black history. This obscures the diverse nature of the western United States. Until the 1960s, academic and popular views of the American West were dominated by the work of historian Frederick Jackson Turner. He posited that rugged Anglo American pioneers, fighting to subdue an ever-expanding western frontier, ushered in the taming of the wilderness, civilization, and a process of self-redefinition. The "Turner thesis" argued that this process produced what we now consider to be "Americans," an egalitarian people who champion democratic values that continue to shape the United States.[19] This thesis embraced stereotypes already rooted in American popular culture: pious pioneers, tough outlaws, barbaric Indians, chivalrous white men, and virtuous white women. It was eventually reinforced by western paintings, novels, and, most important, movies and television programs that cemented into American consciousness, as no historical work could, the image of white settlers as "conquerors who superimposed their will on a vast, virtually uninhabited virgin land." In this interpretation, "African Americans were not considered an indigenous group, and they were not conquerors." Black people, therefore, "had no place in the region's historical saga"[20]

Seeking to fill this lacuna and advance interpretive analyses that illuminate not only black history but American western history, many scholars have opened new doors leading to the development of a more inclusive and sophisticated American history.[21] They have done so by examining the special experiences of arguably one of the American West's most marginalized minorities. Contrary to a once widely held belief that the American West is defined by its being devoid of, among other things, "Negroes," African Americans have always been, despite their relatively small numbers, a fundamental piece of the social, economic, and political fabric that is the West, particularly the urban West. Beginning in 1528 with the arrival of the Moroccan Esteban de Dorantes in Texas, the first of many Spanish-speaking blacks, African Americans were populating the region. By 1880 the earliest English-speaking blacks had moved west as slaves, free farmers, fur trappers, or servants, creating the nucleus of post–Civil War communities. Thousands of African Americans later migrated to the high plains, while others, such as the legendary Nat Love, drove cattle up the Chisholm Trail or served on remote army outposts. By the 1900s black westerners had been a part of the region for nearly four hundred years.[22]

Above all, the history of African Americans in the West is a story of urban life and "the struggle for racial equality," for black Americans in the West have lived primarily in cities that discriminated against, subjugated, and sometimes terrorized them. Reflecting this fact, it is important to give substantive attention to the twentieth-century black West. Indeed, World Wars I and II, as well as the industries that were created to support them, greatly improved the prospect of good jobs and a freer life for African Americans in the West. Black populations in the western United States increased tenfold as a result of this wave of migration. This movement brought highly influential leaders such as the Ragsdales to western cities like Phoenix. The influx of black professional people helped intensify the region's civil rights movement, and this heightened agitation eventually paved the way for black success in today's western politics and surging interest in multiculturalism.[23]

African American progress in the West, however, has always been achieved amid omnipresent racial discrimination and systematic oppression. Black women have born a triple burden of racial, sexual, and economic exploitation. A combination of Euro-American social Darwinism, Protestant ethics, exploitation, and "frontier conditions," in conflict with the ever-increasing numbers of free blacks, Asians, and Latinos who were looked upon as being "un-American," produced a region ripe for disharmony and racial discord. Moreover, the borderlands, which experienced heightened cross-cultural collisions and contact during and after the Mexican War of conquest in 1846 and the Mexican Revolution of 1910, witnessed a plethora of peoples populate the region. Anglo-Americans began to enter towns of present-day Texas, New Mexico, Arizona, and California. They were joined by Mexicans who migrated north to cities such as Santa Fe, Albuquerque, Tucson, Los Angeles, and San Diego. Asian Americans came to the region primarily through western seaports to settle in cities along the West Coast, such as Seattle, San Francisco, Los Angeles, and, to a lesser extent, Phoenix.[24]

African Americans moved to the region predominantly from southern states and areas such as Mississippi, Louisiana, Texas, and southern Oklahoma. As southwestern cities emerged, they became more alluring to Anglo settlers, and as "they assumed power in the regional centers of the Southwest," Bradford Luckingham has argued, they exploited the various races and ethnicities "to help them realize their goals, including economic growth, political control, and social and cultural prominence." "Having achieved a dominant position in each community" by 1920, Luckingham writes, "the Anglos dictated the terms" of the ethnic and racial arrangement, which invariably called for the subjugation of racial minorities and certain ethnicities by any means necessary.[25] The American South, North, and East had no monopoly on terrorism, mob violence, private and public segregation, or racialized and gendered economic inequality. Though the racial etiquette in the West was generally less rigid, by 1946 most white westerners systematically denied blacks equal access to employment, education, health care, and housing. Despite adversities, African Americans, as they have often done, resisted mistreatment and shaped their designs on independence into individual action and an organized movement to secure socioeconomic opportunity and equality. Leading the way in African Americans' efforts to secure their rights in Arizona were Lincoln and Eleanor Ragsdale.[26]

Lincoln relocated to Phoenix in 1946, and Eleanor moved to the city in 1947. The two met in 1947, and by 1949 they were married, just as Lincoln's career as entrepreneur and activist and Eleanor's career as teacher and activist were being launched.[27] After taking up permanent residence in Phoenix, it became clear to the Ragsdales immediately that the "Valley of the Sun," as it has come to be called, was not the "desert oasis" free from discontent and anguish that it was marketed as being. Popular opinion has always held that Phoenix has offered newcomers opportunity to enjoy freedom from racial tensions and antagonisms of more densely populated cities. Celebrated western poetry, novels, and films bear witness to this fact. In 1940, as World War II escalated, the population of the Phoenix metropolitan area was 86,638, of whom 4,263 were African American. Phoenix was a relatively small city when the Ragsdales arrived. Thus there was a level of logic in the prevailing assumptions that African Americans would be able to enjoy more mobility and less discrimination in Phoenix. Generally, however, Phoenix's race relations mirrored those in most American cities. The Ragsdales, therefore, if they had entertained any notions of the existence of a more racially tolerant American West, were compelled to abandon such ideas quickly.[28]

White and black migrants to Phoenix brought with them cultural attitudes about race that they attempted to adapt and negotiate after establishing themselves in the city. Concepts of race and ethnicity were only modified insofar as they would validate preconceived notions. Black Phoenicians were viewed as inferior beings by most nonblack Phoenicians. One historian overstated this case when he went so far as to say that many Mexican Americans and indigenous peoples, prior to the Chicano and American Indian movements of the 1960s and 1970s, viewed African Americans in Phoenix as a means to obtain acceptance by the dominant white society. Robert Nimmons argues that "ideally, if a Mexican-American or Indian could prove himself to be equal, or at least somewhat equal, to the member of the larger society, then he would be considered socially equal. Therefore, because of this natural ambition to succeed within the social order, the Mexican and Indian people developed deeply entrenched hostile feelings toward their Negro neighbors."[29] Although this claim is grossly exaggerated and incorporates extremely problematic vestiges of social Darwinism, the fact remains that black Phoenicians' dark skin placed them in a subordinate status lower and unlike any occupied by other racial or ethnic minorities.[30]

Like the majority of whites in American cities, Phoenix's founders and ruling white elite supported systematic campaigns to create a flourishing community "run by Anglos, for Anglos."[31] Many of the city's founders were Anglo, had southern roots, and harbored many of the antiblack attitudes that dominated race relations in the Reconstruction and Jim Crow South. John William "Jack" Swilling, a former Confederate soldier and deserter, Arizona prospector, farmer, and speculator, has been credited with surveying and laying the foundation for what is now Phoenix. Swilling, perhaps with the input of one or more of his fellow prospectors, christened the community Phoenix after the mythical bird that rose from its own ashes. As Luckingham writes, "it seemed an appropriate symbol of life rising anew from the remains of the past," as "it was hoped that the Phoenix community would build upon the ruins of the ancient Hohokam civilization," upon whose surviving irrigation system the city's water networks were built.[32]

The city was incorporated in 1870. Nestled at the bottom and surrounded by a series of upper Sonora Desert mountain ranges, such as South Mountain, Camelback Mountain, and the Estella, Superstition, and San Tan mountains, the Valley soon became a western outpost of white supremacy and racial inequality. The white male founders of Phoenix quickly imported mechanisms from states such as Texas, Oklahoma, and Arkansas, which formed the gestalt of a racial caste system, defining race relations and socioeconomic mobility in Phoenix throughout the twentieth century. De facto segregation in the city existed from its birth. African Americans were systematically locked out of the dominant Euro-American society in Phoenix, as they were segregated from the Euro-American community in restaurants, theaters, housing, hospitals, hotels, swimming pools, buses, social clubs, and other places of public accommodation. Black Phoenicians, in turn, established their own parallel sets of institutions that serviced the African American community.[33]

De jure segregation was implemented in the Arizona Territory in 1864, when an antimiscegenation law prohibiting marriages between "Whites, Negroes, Mulattos, and Mongolians" was passed. The law was amended in 1877 to include Indians. Children of such marriages possessed no legal rights of inheritance. De jure segregation was encoded again by the territory's white supremacist leaders during the first decade of the twentieth century. On March 17, 1909, the territorial legislature passed a law allowing Arizona school districts to segregate students of African descent from pupils of European ancestry. Arizona's fledgling state constitution of 1912 also designated "interracial" marriages unlawful. Reflecting local bigotry, Ku Klux Klan chapters were organized around the state in 1917. Furthermore, by 1926 the meticulously constructed Phoenix residential PalmCroft District and its Euro-American homeowners created and maintained restrictive covenants limiting the sale of PalmCroft real estate to whites only. Lincoln and Eleanor Ragsdale were the first African Americans to integrate Phoenix's all-white communities in northern Phoenix in 1952.[34]

The economic, social, and political isolation black Phoenicians experienced amplified not only the effects of institutional racism but also the negative effects of the Great Depression in the 1930s and demobilization after World War II in the 1940s. Being the last to be hired and the first to be fired affected black Phoenicians in many of the same ways in which it affected African Americans at large. The majority of black Phoenicians attended separate and unequal schools; worked in low-wage, nonmanagerial, labor-intensive occupations; lived in geographically segregated, substandard housing; and suffered physically as a result of there being few health care providers who administered to the black community. Before the arrival of the Ragsdales and the coalescence of a streamlined, professional civil rights establishment, systematic resistance to oppression was waged by prominent individual leaders and progressive community activists. In 1919 Samuel Bayless and C. Credille formed the Phoenix Advancement League (PAL) to combat racial injustice. To fight employment discrimination, James L. Davis, Sidney Scott, H. D. Simpson, and others founded the Phoenix Protection League (PPL) in 1931. The pistons that drove all organized acts, community building, and resistance were local black churches and the Arizona Federation of Colored Women's Clubs, which owned and operated, as early as 1915, many of the halls in the city in which black people could assemble.[35]

World War II ushered in a new chapter in Phoenix's history, as the number of professional African Americans in Phoenix increased.

Between 1940 and 1960 the number of black Phoenicians increased from 4,263 to 20,919, while the total number of Phoenicians approached 450,000. The percentage of African Americans in Phoenix during this period, however, actually decreased from 6.5 to 4.8 percent of the total population. Nevertheless, the growing number of blacks in the area, in addition to persistent racial and gender inequality, gave rise to ideological, political, and sometimes violent confrontations between black and white Phoenicians seeking equality and opportunity and white Phoenicians who fought to maintain their socioeconomic domination. Black Phoenicians, led by people such as the Ragsdales, fought to make Phoenix a more racially tolerant and inclusive city.[36]

The campaign for civil rights in Arizona was largely a grassroots movement, but key battles were won at the ballot box, in court, and in the state legislature. The Ragsdales worked to support change at each level. In the 1940s Lincoln and Eleanor Ragsdale became members of the local chapter of the National Association for the Advancement of Colored People (NAACP) and the Phoenix Urban League (PUL). The Ragsdales were also among the founders of the Greater Phoenix Council for Civic Unity (GPCCU). Established in the 1940s, the GPCCU worked to eliminate "discrimination in Phoenix and surrounding communities" and to "cooperate with local, state, and national groups working toward the same ends." The NAACP, GPCCU, and PUL, with the help of the Ragsdales, were instrumental in forcing the desegregation of Phoenix's public schools as early as 1953. Lincoln Ragsdale also joined with six other local leaders in 1963 to form the Phoenix's Action Citizens Committee (ACT) political campaign. ACT sought to get its members elected to the Phoenix City Council. Its platform called for a public accommodations bill, open housing, and job opportunities for minorities.[37]

Despite limited gains brought about by the GI Bill and other postwar opportunities, racial discrimination continued, and incidents of police brutality became more frequent. Activists continued to combat these inequalities and injustices with nonviolent protest throughout the 1960s. The majority of organizers in the Phoenician movement were African American or Euro-American. Despite being the "majority minority" in Phoenix and subject to many of the oppressive offenses of white supremacy, a relatively small number of Mexican Americans joined forces with black and white activists in the civil rights movement. The failure of Mexican Americans and African Americans to forge substantive coalitions during this decisive era of social and political change profoundly affected the relationship between these two groups throughout the remainder of the twentieth century. Seemingly content to fight a war against white supremacy and inequality on two fronts, both groups sacrificed a measure of their collective social, political, and economic capital at the altar of cultural defensiveness, ideological conflict, and avarice.[38]

The organizing efforts and fund-raising capabilities of black women provided the foundation of the Phoenician movement. As early as 1915 the Arizona Federation of Colored Women's Clubs (AFCWC) held meetings and supervised the activities of many of Arizona's smaller grassroots organizations. In 1927 the AFCWC erected the Phyllis Wheatley Community Center on the corner of Fourteenth and Jefferson streets. The center continued to serve in its umbrella capacity as late as the early 1970s. Until the 1970s, halls owned and operated by black women's clubs and organizations were among the few places in the Valley that permitted blacks to convene for social services and political gatherings.[39]

Eleanor Ragsdale, like black women throughout the African diaspora, balanced multiple agendas while endeavoring to realize her personal goals and those of her family and community. Early on, she nurtured her own professional career as an educator. Compelled to choose between her career and the needs of her husband and the prosperity of her family's business, however, she soon elected to give up her career to join Lincoln in the administration of their enterprises. Eleanor participated side by side with Lincoln in the movement while rearing their four children and responding to the unique concerns of local black women in ways that Lincoln could or perhaps would not. For his part, Lincoln devoted a great deal of time and energy to fashioning a reputation as an aggressive, uncompromising advocate for integration and racial equality, not gender equality. The black freedom struggle, he believed, was largely an effort to retake black men's right to compete on a fair and equal basis for the position of protector, breadwinner, and architect of their family's future. Lincoln's aggressive methods for reclaiming and demonstrating this stolen "manhood" were indicative of a type of masculinity that blacks in the South, with its history of violence and terrorism, could rarely display. Lincoln Ragsdale, perhaps more than most blacks, understood that the West's more fluid race relations created a vacuum for a more brash and enterprising black leadership. His ability to be more audacious in his activism, without the threat of mass acts of violent retribution against the black community, gave him freedom to resist in ways that were perhaps uniquely western.[40]

Women in Phoenix, like women nationwide, formed the foundation of the entire civil rights movement. Subjected to racism, sexism, and often poverty, black women fought for racial liberation while displaying a certain level of toleration for the sexism of black men. This is especially true of the 1960s, which, according to Darlene Clark Hine, was in many ways a "decade of testosterone," an era marked by the often zealous efforts of activists and historians to reclaim what they perceived to be usurped black male masculinity.[41] Operating in this masculinist climate, female activists like Eleanor Ragsdale were nevertheless able to play a leading role in ushering in some social, economic, and political progress. Although activists worked to make significant strides and leaders such as Lincoln Ragsdale squared off in negotiations with whites, advancement during the 1960s was sluggish. Black people continued to fare far worse than their white counterparts. President Lyndon B. Johnson's Great Society eradicated some of the lingering legal barriers facing African Americans. Among other things, it created programs that assisted black children and young adults seeking a college education, while reaffirming black citizenship rights and destroying legal barriers to the ballot box.[42]

The 1964 Civil Rights Act and the 1965 Voting Rights Act are examples of such measures. The majority of African Americans continued to lag behind, and issues such as education, economic opportunity, and police brutality remained. Although measures like restrictive covenants were legally eradicated, redlining by real estate companies made it virtually impossible for African Americans to buy homes in areas to their liking. Job discrimination also prevented them from securing employment, and limited educational opportunities made it difficult for black people to compete for well-paying jobs. High unemployment, substandard housing, and poor educational opportunities prompted many younger, more militant organizers to call for more aggressive protests seeking an end to gradualism. Peaceful, incremental change remained the goal of veteran members of the movement like Lincoln and Eleanor Ragsdale. Calls for nonviolence and patience were increasingly ignored by 1970. Organizations such as the Student Non-Violent Coordinating Committee (SNCC), the Congress of Racial Equality (CORE), and the Black Panther Party pushed for an immediate end to police brutality and a redistribution of local and national resources. This new militancy eventually led to violence and destruction in Phoenix, as riots erupted in the city's African American and Mexican American neighborhoods during the 1960s.[43]

By 1970, as Lincoln Ragsdale began to relinquish his position as perhaps the most commanding civil rights activist Phoenix had ever known, more militant leaders emerged with new perspectives on race and equality. Younger, more militant black activists began to regard Ragsdale not as a progressive activist with a decidedly radical disposition but as a member of the establishment. He and Eleanor at this time were among the wealthiest African Americans in the Southwest. They counted among their friends and associates some of the most influential people in Phoenix and the nation. Lincoln Ragsdale's successful business career now garnered his full attention. He came to view financial independence and economic success as the goal for which African Americans should strive. By the 1970s and 1980s he thought that legal reform had done virtually all it could for African Americans. Lincoln believed that economic inequality was the principal problem for African Americans as the 1980s drew near.[44]

Although Lincoln Ragsdale's dedication to the betterment of African Americans never waned, many in the black community viewed his "work-within-the-system" approach to black empowerment with skepticism. Ragsdale's apparent traditional integrationist approach to racial healing conflicted with the neo-separatist ideologies of many young African Americans. Many militant activists by the 1980s began to look upon the Ragsdales not as "race leaders" but as wealthy blacks whose economic goals, concerns, and responsibilities were in conflict with those of poor and working-class blacks. In a period when the most thunderous voices of race reform called for the fundamental restructuring of America's capitalist system, Lincoln Ragsdale continued to preach the virtues of the free market, entrepreneurship, and competition. Many African Americans were closing ranks while the Ragsdales continued to advocate multiculturalism. Had leaders like the Ragsdales not established a history of winning major concessions, the tensions between affluent black people and the masses might have exploded into full-blown intraracial class conflict.[45]

As acrimonious as the critiques of leaders like Lincoln Ragsdale may have been at the time, they did highlight the volatile and vexing question of class and economics in the black freedom struggle. Ragsdale succeeded in helping to orchestrate the destruction of segregation in Phoenix and the nation but failed to foresee the long-term implications of the economic divide between African Americans and Euro-Americans. He, like many of his generation and social class, did not conceive of the extent to which the interconnectedness of race, class, and gender would continue to menace black Americans. Assessing the successes and failures of the civil rights movement, Lincoln Ragsdale at sixty-nine years of age admitted that his generation of activists underestimated the importance of economic equality. The battle for financial stability is "where we lost" he confessed. "It's about education and money now," he maintained. "If you don't get the two you're in trouble."[46]

By the 1990s, as Lincoln's and Eleanor's lives neared their ends, America hosted the largest number of middle-class African Americans in its history; however, more African Americans were living at or below the poverty line than at any other time. The number of black elected officials reached unprecedented highs, while hate crimes rose dramatically and a neoconservative white backlash enveloped the country. Middle-class and wealthy African Americans found employment in suburban communities, while the black working class faced squalid living conditions, myriad health crises, violence, poor schools, and joblessness in urban areas.[47]

The Ragsdales' legacy speaks to a profound dilemma that faced African Americans during the last decade of the twentieth century. The Ragsdales dedicated most of their lives to fighting racial discrimination and inequality. During these years they tallied an impressive list of victories along the way, victories that helped bring about an era of unparalleled freedom and opportunity for many African Americans. The Ragsdales were among the first generation of black people to enjoy this new freedom and opportunity. Even as the Ragsdales and other leaders relished their successes, however, many lamented the fact that the majority of blacks were mired in poverty. Persistent racial discrimination, joblessness, severely limited educational opportunities, poor health, unprecedented urban violence, and the hopelessness associated with these conditions were all directly related to more than three hundred years of white supremacy in America.[48]

Many argued that as the socioeconomic and physical distance between middle-class and poor black people grew, an ideological breech within the African American community emerged, as it did in other communities, including the white community. Professional advancement and racial uplift had previously intersected. Black leaders, many working-class blacks believed, could never rise above the condition of the majority of blacks. By the 1980s, however, many affluent blacks chose to sacrifice the bond between achievement and cultural responsibility at the alter of personal gain and class solidarity. Some pundits argued that toward the end of their lives, the Ragsdales, like many wealthy African Americans, had undermined the balance between personal advancement and the well-being of the race. Working-class and militant blacks accused the Ragsdales of being more concerned with their own financial status than with justice for the majority of black people. Ultimately, therefore, their "success" has been judged, within African American communities, not only by their race work on behalf of African Americans during the height of the movement but also by the degree to which they interacted with and served the poor and black working classes toward the end of their lives.[49]

Despite the disquiet bred by class conflict and changes in ideology and leadership, the contributions to civil rights by leaders like the Ragsdales are on par with those of most other black professional activists in American history. Lincoln Ragsdale's influence ultimately reached the White House, as he served as an adviser to President Ronald Reagan on small and minority business ownership during the 1980s.[50]

*Race Work* demonstrates that the Ragsdales, through their entrepreneurship and work, played a critical role in defining an effective Phoenician movement that was similar to and yet distinct from the larger civil rights movement. Lincoln Ragsdale's bold and confrontational leadership exploited the West's fluid race relations to fashion a career that was both unabashed and creative, when many of his southern contemporaries were under constant threat of terrorism and a more violent version of massive white resistance. The tremendous accomplishments of the civil rights movement and leaders like the Ragsdales, however, did not end racial inequality or usher in true socioeconomic integration. Nonetheless, the Ragsdales and their fellow insurgents dealt racism and discrimination a serious blow.[51] Their race work was intended to advance the overall well-being of black people. Whenever they discovered de jure and de facto segregation and the social, economic, and political inequality that resulted, they fought back with creativity and zest. Lincoln and Eleanor Ragsdale rose to the occasion, and because of their efforts, by the year 2000 the Valley of the Sun became a much brighter place.[52]

# Part One

Power Concedes Nothing without Demand

# Chapter 1

## The Black Professional Tradition

> One of the distinguishing characteristics of the black professional class is
> its service to people whom the larger society perceived to be marginal and
> peripheral by virtue of their race and subordinate in socioeconomic and
> political status.
>
> Darlene Clark Hine, *Speak Truth to Power*

LINCOLN AND ELEANOR RAGSDALE were born into the black
professional class. Although they were reared in different regions of
the country, East and West, their shared experience as beneficiaries of
the black professional tradition influenced the course of their lives together. Lincoln and Eleanor inherited inextricably linked traditions of
leadership and service to their community, which endowed them with
an incentive to achieve and expectations to assist in the advancement
of African Americans. To prepare for their lives as stewards of the
black community, they were educated and grounded in the exigencies
of professional work and race work. The Ragsdales were taught that
black professionals were compelled to play leading roles in African
Americans' struggle for civil rights.[1]

Ever since the Thirteenth Amendment to the U.S. Constitution abolished slavery in 1865, black Americans have fought to secure their
citizenship rights. Aspects of this adaptable and rigorous fight for
freedom necessarily encompassed the attainment of educational and
financial capital that was crucial for betterment of black communities.[2] These voluminous resources included the procurement of land,
the creation of academic establishments, the provision of health care

services, and the administration of religious and secular institutions. African Americans also organized businesses such as funeral homes, banks, insurance companies, and newspapers.[3]

Striving to develop political power, black people secured and guarded the right to vote. This involved the support of the Civil Rights Act of 1866, which enabled blacks to participate in organized politics; the Fourteenth Amendment of 1868, which reaffirmed state and federal citizenship for persons born or naturalized in the United States; and the Fifteenth Amendment of 1870, which guaranteed that no American would be denied the right to vote on the basis of race. All of this occurred during Reconstruction, a period when the first postslavery generation of southern black people competed for economic and political power to give meaning to their freedom and to battle the venomous response of most whites to African American liberty.[4]

Following the Civil War, many southern whites, enraged and embarrassed by their loss in the Civil War, were headstrong in their desire to restore their hegemony. Following the compromise of 1877, white supremacy reigned in the former Confederacy, with a less noxious form shrouding the North. What remained, however, was the legacy of the Thirteenth, Fourteenth, and Fifteenth amendments. The rights that these measures afforded were not dead. They needed only to be resuscitated and enforced. In the interim, a cadre of black professional Reconstruction leaders endeavored to do so.[5]

Southern whites erected barriers to thwart black autonomy. "Black Codes," as they have come to be known, were instituted throughout the region to limit the areas in which blacks could purchase or rent property. Vagrancy laws imposed heavy penalties designed to force African Americans to return to work on plantations from which they had been recently liberated. Blacks were not permitted to testify in court, except in cases involving other African Americans. Southern whites levied fines against black people for alleged seditious speeches, insulting gestures or acts, absence from work, violating curfews, and possessing firearms. In addition to enduring systematic oppression, blacks also had their freedom assaulted by white terrorist organizations. The prototype of these groups was the Ku Klux Klan, first organized in 1866 in Pulaski, Tennessee.[6]

Throughout the last decades of the nineteenth century and well into the second half of the twentieth century, white supremacists in the South constructed a society that was split in two, separate and unequal. Supported by silence, indifference, and northern industrialists' use of race to prevent the formation of interracial alliances, white supremacy reigned. Social Darwinism was the prevailing "scientific" ideology of the time, and it presumed that people of African descent were genetically inferior, beastly, and lascivious. Traditional prejudices were, therefore, reinforced with the measure of scientific legitimacy. African Americans were discriminated against and segregated as a result. Under the ruling climate of social Darwinism and supercilious American imperialism, it was in essence open season on black people. They were lynched, raped, fleeced, and mocked with impunity. During the late nineteenth and early twentieth centuries blacks had reached what Rayford Logan has christened the "nadir" of African American history.[7]

The black professional class rose out of this racialized disorder as a result of discrimination and segregation. They cultivated institutions that promoted their well-being and advancement. The first generation of black professional leaders played a key role in preparing future generations for life in a white supremacist society. The astuteness and determination of African American leaders of earlier generations enabled them to better evaluate the needs of black communities. With the advantage of hindsight, argues historian Darlene Clark Hine, "the third generation of black professionals, especially in the 1930s, 40s, and 50s, fashioned appropriate resistance strategies and an oppositional consciousness required to launch the social transformation that generated the educational, medical, legal, cultural, and sexual rights movements of our age."[8] This is precisely what the first and second generations of Ragsdales in Oklahoma and the Dickeys in Pennsylvania did for Lincoln and Eleanor, respectively. The seeds were planted for their careers as professional activists long before they were born, just as a small desert outpost became a city named Phoenix.[9]

The Ragsdale tradition of professionalism, service, and activism started with William Ragsdale Sr. A pioneer businessman in a city named Muskogee in Indian Territory (later Muskogee, Oklahoma), Lincoln Ragsdale's paternal grandfather was born in Alma, Arkansas, in 1871 and moved to Muskogee during his late teens or early twenties. There he met a schoolteacher and fellow Arkansas native, Malinda Haes. Haes was very active in several benevolent and activist organizations in their community. The two were soon married and immediately set out to position themselves as a force in their community.

William wanted to establish himself in business, and with a Mr. Baily, he founded a livery stable, the Creek Livery Barn, in 1889. In 1890 George W. Davis succeeded Bailey at Creek Livery Barn and formed a partnership with William Ragsdale. The livery was well equipped with all the new styles of carriages and wagons and a fine stock of driving and saddle horses. Carriages were furnished for funerals, weddings, parties, and balls.[10]

During the turbulent 1890s African Americans struggled to rebound from the ostensible end of Reconstruction, while most Euro-Americans rallied around the banner of white supremacy.[11] Economic instability and decline engulfed the nation. The panic of 1893 inspired what became a serious depression, and in 1896 the U.S. Supreme Court established the practice of Jim Crow racial segregation as the law of the land in its landmark *Plessy v. Ferguson* ruling.[12]

This climate of intense racial oppression and naked white supremacy often culminated in some of the worst incidents of violence in American history. This violence was constant, but it had peaks of intensity. Race riots of epic proportions unfolded in South Carolina and in Wilmington, North Carolina, in 1898. The number of lynchings escalated, as did the rape of black women by white men. African Americans displayed their opposition to this treatment and to the reigning political structure by "voting with their feet." As early as 1865 thousands of black people elected to "quit" the South by migrating to other regions of the United States. Although the majority of black people remained in the South, by 1890 scores of black migrants had relocated in cities such as Nickodemus, Kansas; Muskogee; and Phoenix. William Ragsdale was among the first generation of African Americans to migrate to Muskogee, and by 1890 he had laid the groundwork for a future in business that would last for four generations.[13]

Life in prestatehood Oklahoma following the Civil War was extremely difficult regardless of one's race. African Americans, however, were among the hardest hit and most displaced by the Civil War and the undermining of Reconstruction. The majority of settlers who migrated to Oklahoma between 1877 and 1900 were destitute or had only nominal means. Most black newcomers and their neighbors built makeshift homes. Roscoe Dungee, an early black Oklahoma migrant, found that "most everybody lived in dugouts." He recalled that "enterprising" settlers such as the Ragsdales sometimes built two- and

three-room houses, which prompted some of their neighbors to believe that they were a "little out of the ordinary."[14] As progress came
with the passage of time, African Americans, like others in the region,
began to erect frame structures, streamline farming, and create communities in which various religious, social, political, and occupational
activities emerged.[15]

Although agriculture continued to provide the most opportunities for employment in what is now Oklahoma around 1900, cities
such as Muskogee, Guthrie, Ardmore, and Oklahoma City boasted
black-owned barbershops, blacksmiths, cafès, grocery stores, hotels,
laundries, and mortuaries. Thomas Edwards, an undertaker who established himself in Oklahoma City in 1891, remembered a professional class of black doctors, lawyers, dentists, teachers, clergymen,
and real estate salesmen, in addition to a vibrant working class in
African American communities throughout the territory.[16] The town
of Muskogee, in particular, proudly boasted of its preeminence in
hosting robust black businesses, while other towns and cities laid solid
foundations for such famous business districts as Second Street in Oklahoma City and Greenwood Avenue, otherwise know as the "Black
Wall Street," in Tulsa. African Americans maintained almost twenty-
four highly competitive businesses in Muskogee by 1905, including
an amusement park, a bank, a butcher shop, a clothing store, and a
stable for horse and buggy rentals. Although most black businesses
were small ventures, their owners rendered valuable service to those
excluded from many white establishments.[17]

William Ragsdale and George W. Davis were highly respected
within their community for their strict integrity. Since Ragsdale was so
well equipped with horses and carriages needed for funerals, friends
suggested that he go into the undertaking business. He pondered that
suggestion and concluded that it was a worthwhile endeavor. In 1896
Ragsdale founded the Home Undertaking Company of Muskogee.
He elected not to use the Ragsdale name in the title of his business.
As a sometimes outspoken individual and an emerging professional
black man in his local community, Ragsdale's success would have
been perceived as a threat to the existing racial order.[18]

Many African Americans believed that explicit promotion of their
successes would invite violent retaliation from whites seeking to keep
them dependent and deferential. In fact, one of William Ragsdale's
sons, William Ragsdale Jr., was lynched by the Ku Klux Klan in 1926.

William Jr. challenged the racial protocol of the community by becoming president of the NAACP in Oklahoma and by serving black and white people while working as a taxi driver. Lincoln Ragsdale argued that despite white supremacist efforts to intimidate blacks through lynchings and other violence, blacks were undaunted in their efforts to give meaning to their freedom.[19] "It didn't put fear [in us]," he asserted, "it put aggressiveness in us that we're going to have to work it through the system. You can't work it with a gun because you can't out-shoot white folks. There are more white folks than black folks. So you have to work it intellectually, hard work, saving your money. . . . You have to out-smart him."[20]

African Americans in early Oklahoma, especially black entrepreneurs and leaders such as William Ragsdale Sr., were faced with the sobering realities of Jim Crow and white supremacy, and the socioeconomic challenges they posed, from the moment Oklahoma became a state in 1907. The state's first legislature moved quickly to legalize racial segregation. It did not adopt sweeping and stringent segregation provisions, but it did introduce Jim Crow segregation in public transportation. African Americans were segregated in railroad cars and waiting rooms. Places of public accommodation were ordered to have a racial designation posted in a "conspicuous place." The law also made it illegal for anyone "to use, occupy or remain in any waiting room, toilet, or any water tank in any passenger depot, set apart [to] which he does not belong" in areas of public transportation.[21] The Oklahoma legislature, enabled by the state's constitution, also adopted a policy of racially segregated schools, and it banned interracial marriages. School segregation had been practiced in Oklahoma before statehood, and the new law simply maintained a common practice. Unlike prestatehood school segregation, however, the constitutionally backed law mandated that the state provide separate schools for black and white children to be administered on an equal basis with "like accommodations." Most whites in Oklahoma, like most whites in other states that encoded the separate but equal doctrine, supported the "separate" part of the clause but routinely ignored the "equal" provision. Violations of the law regulating school segregation were misdemeanors, while infractions of the interracial marriage statute were felonies, a clear reflection of the strong opposition to mixed marriages and ideas of racial equality among most whites.[22]

Like William Jr., blacks in Oklahoma resisted their racial subordination. They were active in organizations such as the NAACP and were extremely vocal and direct in their opposition to white supremacy in the state. Members of one equal rights group blamed the prejudice in early Oklahoma on whites who were "busy educating their children to hate us and to believe that we are low, degraded, and vicious because our skins are dark. Nor do they make any exception of those of us whom they have made about as white as themselves, their eyes many times blue and their hair straight. We are all 'niggers' together. Our wives, sisters, and daughters are either 'nigger' wenches or 'nigger' bitches and have no rights that white people have to respect."[23]

Despite the efforts of African American activists, racial segregation remained very much a part of the socioeconomic landscape of Oklahoma during the Ragsdales' rise to distinction. The isolation it sired made it extremely difficult for most blacks to meet the most basic of their needs. It did not, however, shatter their collective pride, cultural identity, ability to produce effective leaders, and capacity to prosper within the confines of a white supremacist system. Black newspapers, ministers, lawyers, doctors, and everyday folk played key roles in alleviating some of the negative effects of Jim Crow on black communities. Morticians such as William Ragsdale Sr. and his progeny also took on key leadership positions in African American communities. As entrepreneurs, humanitarians, and "race workers," they helped shape the viewpoints and influence the actions of their patrons. They refused to stand by idly while blacks were tyrannized and rendered marginal and dependent. Their efforts, with the help of others, provided lessons in self-efficacy, ingenuity, and racial pride.[24]

It did not take long for William Ragsdale Sr. to become visible in his community as a businessman and advocate for black people who were on the move. Unwilling and unable to conceal his business and leadership acumen, William Sr. decided to change the name of his business from the Home Undertaking Company to Ragsdale Mortuary. By 1910 the business progressed from one relying on horse-drawn transportation to a completely motorized fleet of vehicles. Shortly afterward, William met schoolteacher Malinda Haes. After a brief courtship, they were married and on their way to starting a family. They would eventually have two daughters, Beatrice and Celestine, and six sons, William Jr., Louis, Howard, Vernon, Theodore, and Hartwell. Like their father, five sons became undertakers. Upon the death of William Ragsdale Sr. in 1921, Hartwell took his place at the helm of the family business in Muskogee. Other Ragsdale mortuaries were eventually established in Taft, Bristow, and Ardmore, Oklahoma.[25]

Scattered across Oklahoma, the Ragsdales' mortuaries firmly established the family as part of the black professional class. Teachers, attorneys, and physicians did not monopolize the black professional class throughout the United States, and Oklahoma was no exception. Although the undertaking business, unlike education, medicine, and law, did not qualify as one of the traditional professions, it was an enterprise in which a person could participate for gain in an activity often engaged in by amateurs. By virtue of their training, skill, service, and limited numbers, morticians were elevated to the status of professionals in the minds of many. African Americans, who had highly restricted access to training in traditional professions at this time, were particularly prone to accord morticians professional status. Undertakers were among the few expert and accomplished individuals in black communities whose careers opened doors to substantial wealth, authority, and opportunities for representative leadership.[26] In 1899 W. E. B. DuBois, renowned scholar and a founder of the NAACP, argued that black morticians constituted a solid, upwardly mobile segment of the African American community. "In no branch of business, save one," he insisted, "has the Negro evinced so much push, taste and enterprise."[27]

Booker T. Washington, champion of industrial education, founder of both the Tuskegee Institute in Alabama and the National Negro Business League, and chief DuBois antagonist, agreed. He stated in 1889 that it was "a curious fact that with the exception of that of caterer there is no business in which Negroes seem to be more numerously engaged or one in which they have been more uniformly successful."[28] Innovations in body preparations, coffins and caskets, embalming procedures, and methods of training and certification, along with the expansion of the funeral market, helped make the funeral industry a viable enterprise. This, coupled with the fact that black funeral directors tapped into an exclusive, ever-expanding market base, propelled the funeral industry into a potentially lucrative business for many black entrepreneurs. A decent burial has always been considered to be a mark of status by Americans generally. Thus undertaking held the potential to yield high profits for morticians, and black morticians sought to capitalize on this promise.[29]

Black undertakers helped create a funeral industry that had a steady configuration along race lines throughout the first few decades of the twentieth century. Their service to African Americans has given rise to one of the most unique relationships between business leaders and their clients in American history. Undertakers, though providing a necessary service in the preparation and interment of the dead, did much more than that for black people living in a segregated society. Indeed, Michael A. Plater posits that "funeral service was a profitable industry that African Americans engaged in without white competition, and as a result generated large amounts of capital."[30]

Funeral directors, in turn, redistributed tremendous amounts of this capital in African American communities. Moreover, because funeral service was a church-sanctioned ritual and the industry had enormous economic influence in the community, morticians evolved into major power brokers in early-twentieth-century African American communities. For example, in their businesses, black undertakers provided chapels and assembly halls for various functions and mass meetings, as well as office space for African American organizations. Meeting in places owned by black funeral home directors, Plater maintains, "meant that the fraternal orders did not have to use their capital for building construction costs or lose capital outside the community by renting from white landlords." Funeral businesses strengthened the economic base of the black community by allowing individuals and institutions to channel their resources into an enterprise that would support black educational, religious, and civil rights organizations.[31]

Morticians reached elite status in black and white communities, according to Plater, by exploiting financial segregation to attain political integration. The elite status of funeral directors such as William Ragsdale Sr. and his heirs and their willingness to be at the forefront of movements to improve the conditions of black people provide an illuminating story about black culture and its internal power structure. The ability of morticians to rise to elite status within their communities, for example, was directly related to their understanding of the importance of African American death rituals. They capitalized on this knowledge and provided black communities funeral services that complemented their cultural traditions. As Plater argues, they became specialists at utilizing ethnicity to publicize their businesses. Morticians employed African American traditions, the black church, and black folklore to create an environment that catered to the wants and needs of black communities. They offered services that white funeral directors were either unwilling or unable to provide. At a basic level, they simply exploited a fundamental principle of supply and demand.[32]

Black people throughout the African diaspora have placed a tremendous amount of importance on death rites. People of African descent, particularly in the United States, have valued death ceremonies primarily because of their ability to transform and enhance the status of individuals who were often disinherited by society while they lived. For many black people, extravagant and sometimes costly funerals are deemed necessary as meaningful proclamations of the deceased's intrinsic value. Joseph Holloway posits that these death rites and what they symbolized were cultural retentions, or "Africanisms," originating from African death customs.[33] The Bakongo of West Africa, for instance, practiced grand burial rituals to acquire the spiritual support and protection of their ancestors. They paid tribute to the dead while employing elaborate funeral ceremonies to empower the living. Morticians also wielded considerable power because blacks placed a great deal of importance on funeral services, ceremonies denied them during slavery and often prohibitively expensive and elusive in freedom.[34]

Funeral directors also secured wealth and status because the majority of African Americans who needed their services were not prepared to bargain with them on an equal basis. Most black people were poor and had few alternatives, and many were unschooled in the art of negotiation. Furthermore, African Americans were forced to buy the services of black funeral directors if they wanted to be buried in a manner reflecting their cultural cosmology. In short, black funeral directors, including the Ragsdales, sometimes exploited their customers' socioeconomic condition and culture for financial and political gain. Often sheltered from the negative effects of racial economic isolation and well suited to make use of their entrepreneurial niche, black funeral directors were able to nurture their sometimes powerful hunger for power and prestige. Despite their gracious manner and devoted service toward their clients, for example, they were more often than not shrewd, hustling, and imaginative entrepreneurs.[35]

R. C. Scott, a contemporary of William Ragsdale Sr.'s and a prominent mortician in Richmond, Virginia, between 1890 and 1940, stated that undertakers usually adhered to the moral doctrine of "charity yes," but "charity tempered with prudence."[36] Undertakers capitalized on black American culture to create community solidarity and provide a monetary foundation for economic development for themselves and their communities. Cultivating social roles within the community beyond simply providing funeral services, they were also business and social leaders. Although African Americans often had few if any alternatives, black communities supported this symbiotic relationship by consistently funneling cash into the funeral industry via services such as transportation fees, meeting space rentals, and insurance organizations.[37]

Following in his father's footsteps, Hartwell Ragsdale had established himself in the family as a skilled mortician by the early 1920s. In addition to inheriting his father's business acumen and expertise in undertaking, Hartwell also acquired many of the social burdens that William Sr. had come to know. Hartwell took the helm of the family business at the height of one of the most vitriolic periods in the twentieth century. Despite the reformist impulse of the Progressive Era, fueled in large part by African American calls for equality and justice and by the democratic ideals trumpeted as the United States engaged in the war against Germany, most white Americans clung to social Darwinism and white supremacy. Whites were seeking to maintain their socioeconomic privilege, and blacks were determined to move forward. These parallel and inextricably linked struggles often sparked fierce competition for jobs and resources between 1917 and 1921. Whites reacted with contempt and violence to demands by black people for fairer treatment and equal opportunities. This intense competition, exacerbated by intensified white racism and nativism during and following World War I, wrought tremendous conflict and suffering throughout the United States.[38]

During this period many "native" white Americans became increasingly convinced that nonwhite "natives," particularly but not limited to African Americans, placed "Anglo Saxon ethnic purity" and privilege in significant danger. Many Protestant whites lashed out against African, Jewish, and Catholic Americans, as well as nonnative white immigrants. Seeking aid and encouragement, many whites joined organizations that stressed racial, national, and religious pride. Millions of white Americans joined the revived Ku Klux Klan in the 1920s. White Americans' crusade to reassert their socioeconomic supremacy and privilege and the determination of African Americans to demand equality and economic opportunity set the stage for violent confrontations across the country. Between 1917 and the summer of 1919, East St. Louis, Illinois; Houston, Texas; and Elaine, Arkansas exploded with racial violence.[39]

Perhaps the most violent and costly disturbance occurred in Tulsa, Oklahoma, the location of Hartwell's first effort to expand the family mortuary business. On May 30, 1921, thousands of white men and women, many deputized by the local police, descended upon the Greenwood section of Tulsa. Despite the efforts of many African Americans to resist this attack, the killing mob looted, plundered, and ultimately burned the neighborhood to the ground. Whites in Tulsa maintained, falsely, that a local black man named Dick Rowland had raped a white female elevator operator the previous day and that his purported crime ignited the allegedly justified fury of the white mob.

The pretext of a black man's rape of a white woman had long been used to justify the violence and terrorism whites perpetrated on African Americans. Behind the fabrication of the rape myth often lay whites' desire to maintain white privilege and control and to eliminate black socioeconomic competition. To protect Rowland, who was later found innocent, blacks had assembled at the courthouse jail, where white men also gathered. Furious words were exchanged, and shooting erupted. Several men, black and white, died in the disorder that followed.[40]

African American men retreated to the predominantly black neighborhood of Greenwood to protect their families and homes. Hartwell Ragsdale happened to be in Tulsa on that day, working at the family's new mortuary. As he became aware of the chaos that was rapidly approaching the black business district located on Greenwood Avenue, he tried to gather as many of his belongings as possible before the violence reached his business. Hartwell left the mortuary and narrowly escaped what might have been an untimely death just as the enraged white mob approached the Ragsdale Mortuary. He ran with whatever wares he could salvage to a nearby train station, where he stowed himself away in a train car that was already in the process of making a swift departure from the embattled city.[41]

By the time Hartwell had fled, the National Guard had arrived after being ordered to the scene by Governor James A. Robertson to retrieve Rowland from the jail and transport him to an undisclosed location. By the morning of June 1, upward of five hundred white men had accosted nearly one thousand black men near or in the Greenwood area. Armed white men in some seventy automobiles patrolled African American residential neighborhoods. Almost fifty armed African Americans defended themselves in a black church near the edge of Greenwood, as a mob of angry whites approached them. The whites set fire to the church as they advanced. As the blacks inside ran, they were shot on the spot. Over two thousand African Americans scrambled to a convention hall, as more fires were set throughout the black enclave.

Forty square blocks and over one thousand Greenwood businesses, churches, homes, and schools were burned to the ground. White men went so far as to drop incendiary devices on Greenwood. More than three hundred African Americans and twenty whites died and as many as six thousand African Americans were herded into detention camps in what was arguably the most pernicious example of domestic terrorism in American history until the Oklahoma City bombing on April 19, 1995.[42]

In the aftermath of the riot, Hartwell escaped on a train to Wichita, Kansas. He remained in Wichita for a brief time, while he and many other blacks who had escaped the violence waited until things had settled down in Oklahoma, particularly in Tulsa, before they returned. When blacks did return, they were greeted by images of a racial enclave that had been utterly decimated. Hartwell returned to Muskogee in the fall of 1921, where he tried to secure more information about the extent of the damage in Tulsa and the status of his mortuary. He learned quickly that the mortuary went up in flames along with nearly every other business in Greenwood. Like other blacks who had lived or worked in Tulsa, he was faced with the staggering reality that most black institutions and homes in Greenwood had been decimated. Most blacks set out to rebuild almost immediately, but they were faced with a daunting task. Despite their best efforts to reconstruct their lives, families, and community, blacks in Tulsa were never able to resuscitate the vibrancy and dynamism that existed in Greenwood before the riot. Hartwell did reconstruct the Ragsdale Mortuary in Tulsa, however, and despite maintaining his permanent residence in Muskogee, he played a key role in facilitating the rebuilding process that did occur in Tulsa.[43]

Just after the riot, Hartwell met, courted, and married a school-teacher by the name of Onlia Violet Perkins. Their marriage produced two sons, Hartwell Jr. and Lincoln. Lincoln Johnson Ragsdale was born on July 27, 1926. Onlia Ragsdale gave birth to Lincoln on the edge of town where his grandmother lived. The family remained in Muskogee until 1930, when they moved to Ardmore, where they settled at 803 E. Main Street. Once the family became settled in their new surroundings, Hartwell established the Ragsdale Mortuary in Ardmore. This business was the foundation upon which Hartwell and Onlia would cultivate their careers as entrepreneurs and activists in Oklahoma. Not only did they possess a desire to succeed in business, both Hartwell and Onlia believed they had a duty to support black communities.[44]

As a child, Lincoln Ragsdale was taught that black people had a "responsibility to the community, to yourself, to your family, and to your race." When it came to community activities, Hartwell and Onlia were "always involved."[45] Onlia was president of the Oklahoma chapter of the National Association of Colored Women (NACW). Created in 1896, the NACW has been regarded by many scholars as America's foremost African American women's organization throughout the first twenty-five years of the twentieth century. Black women throughout American history have struggled to combat negative stereotypes that depicted them as licentious, irresponsible, and intellectually inferior. They have been faced with the challenge of fighting racism, sexism, and economic subordination.[46] "In defense of themselves" and all African Americans, black women organized clubs at the local and state levels to battle the forces that conspired against them. The NACW operated as an umbrella organization to which a network of state and local clubs were affiliated. These organizations, like some of their early-to-mid-nineteenth-century predecessors, promoted personal cultivation and community uplift through charity, professional development, and political activism. Their motto was "lift as we climb," and their agendas were defined by a commitment to education, economic independence, political activity, and health care. The NACW was organized, in part, to fight a racist, sexist society that sought to demean and marginalize black womanhood.[47] "The creation of the National Association of Colored Women," argues Wanda A. Hendricks, "was both an affirmation of their efforts and a method of organizing women's clubs nationwide in the struggle for voting rights and health and educational programs for women and their communities."[48]

Being the wife of a successful businessman provided Onlia flexibility that eluded most black women. Lincoln Ragsdale remembered his mother being "one of the few educated ladies who was able to retire from school teaching at a young age."[49] Indeed, although Onlia stayed devoted to her club activity, at thirty years old she decided to quit teaching school to assist Hartwell in the family funeral home. She helped maintain the company's records; promoted and advertised the company through local institutions, primarily black churches and social clubs; and offered guidance and companionship to grieving friends and family for whom the Ragsdale Mortuary was providing service. Onlia certainly had more than her share of familial, organizational, and occupational responsibilities. Lincoln, however, remembered her having "time to do a lot of things." It is unlikely that Onlia had a great deal of time and even less likely that she chose to "retire" for conventional reasons.[50]

When Onlia left teaching in 1930, the Great Depression had transformed a prosperous American society into a nation reeling in an economic tailspin. In this environment, few Americans were spared financial troubles, and African Americans, including the black professional class, were often the hardest hit. The Ragsdales seemed to have avoided the kind of financial despair that plagued most African Americans. Lincoln maintained that during the Depression, he "grew up in an environment that was personally secure, but in an area of poor surroundings. As a successful mortician [his father] managed well, and, partly because of the type of business he operated and the traditions surrounding it, even during the Depression there was always plenty of food available. Our being in Oklahoma, in a more rural setting, made it easier to manage during hard times than for those who lived in larger cities."[51] Like most Americans, however, the Ragsdales' financial stability was substantially undermined by the Great Depression.

Under these circumstances, it is much more plausible that Onlia left her teaching career to help maintain the mortuary's solvency. The effects of the Great Depression were not entirely lost on Lincoln, as he recalled his parents having to "raise money to send [their] kids to school."[52] Onlia "was the first in her family to earn a college degree," Lincoln recalled, "so education was seen as a very important aspect of success" in the Ragsdale home. Achievement in school was expected from an early age, and Lincoln and his siblings were expected to "make it happen no matter what." The Ragsdale children were taught that in order to be successful, "you have to do what you've got to do."[53]

Doing what they had to do also involved living in a segregated society dominated by white supremacy and racial discrimination. Lincoln Ragsdale's firsthand knowledge of the childhood home and his cognizance of the Tulsa riot and related racial incidents in Oklahoma history led him to believe that Oklahoma was in many ways as segregated and tolerant of racist beliefs and policies as any state in the Union. Ragsdale recalled that in 1907, in fact, "Governor William 'Bill' Murray, referred to as 'snuff-dipping' or 'tobacco chewing Murray' by many blacks, played a key role in institutionalizing Jim Crow in Oklahoma." Governor Murray, he argued, "made it illegal for blacks to use white folks' telephones. He encouraged cities and towns to be all white and all black. We had towns like Henrietta, Durant, and Norman, Oklahoma [that he hoped to make all-white]. In fact, he worked to have the University of Oklahoma built in Norman, Oklahoma, because it was a town where blacks weren't allowed to spend the night."[54]

In the early years after Oklahoma became a state, Norman instituted an ordinance that made it illegal for African Americans to spend the night in town or to be out at night without the permission or sponsorship of local whites. Murray maneuvered to place the university in Norman to "protect the white folks" from blacks, Ragsdale maintained. Most white people "were so bad in that town," he remembered, that "if you drove your car through the town, to show respect [to whites] you had to take your hat off." When Ragsdale and other African Americans would drive through Norman during the day, the majority of them would "automatically" take their hat off if they had one on, because if they did not, "the police would stop you." These kinds of rites of racial subordination permeated the social landscape of Oklahoma during Lincoln's young life, and they played key roles in forming Lincoln's oppositional consciousness.[55]

White supremacy and the inequality and violence it often spawned angered Lincoln at an early age. When as a twelve-year-old he was told stories about his uncle William being murdered by the Ku Klux Klan, he was mortified and infuriated. His indignation was exacerbated by occasional reminders of this tragedy as he came of age. "After hearing about my uncle's lynching all my life," he revealed, "my displeasure became a subtle rage." Lincoln worked hard to avoid becoming bitter, but at times it was difficult. "You push [resentment] back," he conceded, "but it's always there." Lincoln chose to overcome his anger and frustration by using them as fuel to fire his personal passion for black empowerment and liberation. This required vigilance on the part of African Americans, he contended, because "you're always proving something. You're always pushing. You're always fighting." The lynching of his uncle did not stop his family from participating in organizations seeking to protect and advance black people. Lincoln's uncle Theodore "Ted" Ragsdale succeeded William Ragsdale Jr. as the president of the Oklahoma NAACP in the 1930s.[56]

By 1930 Theodore Ragsdale and the NAACP were still working to repair the black community of Tulsa after the riot of 1921 and to hold those who participated in the destruction of the Greenwood section accountable. Moreover, the lynching of blacks continued in the state, which prompted many leaders and organizations, especially Theodore and the NAACP, to intensify their efforts to call attention to the injustice. Antilynching committees were formed, and black and white leaders routinely petitioned their elected representatives to pass a law that would hold lynchers, and those who harbored them, accountable for the crime of murder. Their efforts to create an antilynching law at the state and national levels failed, however. Nevertheless, the NAACP, governors Lee Cruce and J. B. A. Robertson, the progressive Oklahoma Interracial Commission, and the Association of Southern Women for Prevention of Lynching contributed to the curtailment of mob violence in Oklahoma, as evidenced by the state's last recorded lynching in 1931.[57]

In the 1930s Lincoln also completed primary school and entered secondary school at Douglass High School in Ardmore. During these years he became enamored of aviation. Only a few airplanes were accessible in Ardmore, Lincoln believed, and one of them was owned by an "older, stately fellow." This airplane, as he recalled, was old and resembled a crop duster. The owner of the plane hired a friend of the Ragsdales, a Mr. Jones, to serve as his copilot in business, which was presumably crop dusting. After Jones learned how to fly the airplane, he became quite well known in Ardmore's black community as a pilot. Lincoln remembered him flying past his home "every day going back and forth with his goggles hanging down." He sported "leather jackets" and "a beautiful white scarf." Lincoln was duly impressed when he saw Jones adorned in his flying regalia. Jones died in a tragic automobile accident near Biloxi, Mississippi, not long after becoming an experienced pilot. Lincoln's father was contracted to handle the funeral arrangements and was dispatched to Biloxi to recover Jones's body. When Hartwell returned to Ardmore with the body, the city's rumor mill was circulating outlandish stories about Jones dying in a dramatic plane crash. People in Ardmore were "cautious about flying" for quite some time as a result.[58]

Lincoln knew the truth surrounding Jones's death and continued to cultivate his interested in aviation. Occasionally a pilot from the Oklahoma Ford Tri-motor Company would fly his airplane to Ardmore to provide rides around the city for $1.00. The Ragsdales looked forward to the pilot's visits with great eagerness. Lincoln's father would escort him and an equally excited Hartwell Jr. to the airplane to help load the boys into the craft. After watching his sons enjoy their ride across the Ardmore sky, he would step aboard and enjoy his own midair escape. He told the boys that he preferred to fly separately because he did not want the plane "to go down and kill" them, leaving nobody "to take care of your mother." The area "didn't even have an airport," Lincoln recalled. The airplanes "landed in the field in a place that was flat and level."[59]

Hartwell Sr. made his sons pay for their flights over Ardmore themselves with money they had earned. He entertained them, while also teaching them the value of money and the nature of entrepreneurship. Hartwell Sr. would buy two sets of newspapers distributed by black publishers, each for $1.00. He would then give the newspapers, publications such as the *Pittsburgh Courier* and the *Chicago Defender*, to his sons. If they each sold all of their newspapers, they could make up to $1.00. Their $1.00 allowance and their trip across the Oklahoma sky were earned.[60]

Lincoln Ragsdale took great pride in devising creative ways of earning his own money and became an adept entrepreneur at an early age. Hartwell Jr. remembered Lincoln as "always being an advanced person," particularly when it came to developing ways to earn money, and recalled that "when Lincoln was about twelve years old he started his own business." Lincoln built a makeshift "tin building on Main Street in Ardmore" to house black newspapers that he was now purchasing with the funds he was earning from his father. Lincoln began "buying black newspapers from all over the nation" and selling them to people from his makeshift stand and his family's mortuaries, to which he paid a small commission, and through mail order. He also began selling cosmetics to black women after he realized how much money his mother spent purchasing her own. He bought the cosmetics that his mother used by way of mail order through a company named Longe, based in Nashville, Tennessee. He sold them after school in his stopgap retail outlet on Main Street and in his family's home. Lincoln's eclectic array of wares also included record albums. As his business interests grew, he hired Hartwell Jr. to assist him. Hartwell Jr. was primarily responsible for the acquisition, through postal delivery, and distribution of the various albums they sold, which included music by Duke Ellington and Louis Armstrong.

By the time Lincoln was thirteen years old, Hartwell Jr. maintains, Lincoln had learned how to "turn a nickel" and earn money by understanding his community's needs and wants and by figuring out creative and profitable ways of meeting those needs and desires. He was an entrepreneur and leader in the making, and as the 1930s rolled around, he was uniquely positioned to learn from a generation of African Americans who began to engage in more vocal and coordinated efforts to promote black self-determination, entrepreneurship, and race-conscious activism.[61]

The early 1930s ushered in a decade of change for the Ragsdales and all African Americans. Major developments inaugurated a new era of black political participation and economic nationalism. In 1930 the NAACP successfully blocked the appointment of white supremacist John J. Parker to the Supreme Court, while Fannie Peck created the Detroit Housewives' League (DHL), which promoted black economic nationalism. In 1933 President Franklin D. Roosevelt organized the Federal Council on Negro Affairs, or the "Black Cabinet," led by Mary McLeod Bethune. Elijah Muhammad became the leader of the Nation of Islam in 1934. In 1936 Roosevelt was reelected with the overwhelming support of African Americans, and in 1937 William Hastie was selected as the first African American federal judge.[62]

When World War II erupted in 1939, Lincoln was in high school. In addition to committing himself to completing his schoolwork, he continued to assist in the family business and earn money by selling newspapers and record albums. Like his mother, Lincoln primarily helped keep track of business records and circulate promotional materials. He also performed maintenance on the mortuary's various offices and galleries. When black men were brought to Fort Leavenworth, Kansas, to work for the war effort, Lincoln, the budding entrepreneur, made the trip to sell his merchandise to the soldiers. It was at this point that Lincoln first heard rumors that the federal government was contemplating the creation of a flying school for black soldiers. This news, coupled with his interest in aviation, set Lincoln's spirits ablaze. He was not alone. When the rumors became reality on January 16, 1941, newspapers, including all of the major black periodicals, trumpeted the historic news. On this day the U.S. War Department announced the creation of a training facility for black pilots in Tuskegee, Alabama. They would become the 99th Pursuit Squadron, the 332nd Fighter Group, and the 477th Bombardment Group, better known as the Tuskegee Airmen.[63]

Every week the black press "would tell about their progress," Lincoln recalled. The resulting enthusiasm within the black community made the sales of black newspapers increase dramatically. Lincoln was still selling the *Pittsburgh Courier* and the *Chicago Defender* and was now earning up to $5.00 a week. "I made a lot of money," he remembered. He charged "a nickel a paper" and "ten cents for the out of town papers, and they cost a nickel apiece to deliver" to a home or an office. His ready access to the latest news about the Tuskegee Airmen kept him tuned in to the progress of the black soldiers being trained in Tuskegee.[64]

Although the idea appealed to Lincoln, becoming a Tuskegee Airman was not his specific goal. Lincoln would later say that "I wanted to be a pilot because I wanted to prove something." He did not possess an arbitrary desire to fly. "The papers said that blacks could not do it," he recalled. "I wanted to prove that we could do it. We [as a nation] were very segregated. The army was segregated. The navy was segregated. We couldn't use any of the facilities. We were treated as second-class citizens, but the only way to change something is to prove that you can do something."[65] Lincoln was interested in pursuing an education beyond high school, and he was encouraged to do so.

The often unspoken qualification of this support was the expectation that Lincoln would use whatever privileges and authority his education bore for the betterment of African Americans. He looked upon a career in the military, specifically the U.S. Army Air Corps, as an opportunity to secure the education he desired while also fighting the myth of black inferiority. Academically, however, he was not sufficiently prepared to pursue an education after high school, whether it was in the military or elsewhere. He nevertheless determined that a military career would help him begin to acquire the education, training, respect, and authority he knew he would need to build upon his family's tradition of entrepreneurship, service, and leadership.[66]

Although Lincoln applied himself in high school and was awarded good grades, he did not perform well on military or college entrance examinations. He cited his segregated education in a deprived school as the reason for his performance. "Due to the fact that the high school was segregated" and unequal, he recalled, his training in mathematics and English was limited. Moreover, many of the students at his school lacked training in basic health and what the dominant society established as proper social protocol. "A lot of us had not had social graces taught to us," Ragsdale remembered. "The teachers spent a lot of time teaching us cleanliness, how to eat, cook, nutrition, and all of those things." In a regular school day, Lincoln and his classmates would spend "two hours a day just [learning] how to be people" and three hours a day doing schoolwork.[67] As a member of the black professional class, he was surely exposed to this group's prevailing "social graces," which included informal and sometimes formal training in customs of courtesy and interpersonal protocol. It is plausible that many of his classmates, by virtue of their impoverished socioeconomic status, were not. Whatever the case may have been, Lincoln suggested that he could have benefited from a more challenging curriculum and fewer lessons in manners and decorum.[68]

Lincoln and many of his fellow students at Douglass High School were fortunate enough to have at least one teacher, H. F. Wilson, who sacrificed his time, and no doubt money, to help them strengthen their knowledge of math and English, in addition to social proprieties and the requisite survival strategies that black people needed to negotiate effectively in what Lincoln Ragsdale described as a "Negrophobic" society. Wilson, Ragsdale's favorite high school instructor, worked to maximize his students' formal and informal education. He was always looking out for opportunities that would allow his students to better themselves academically, personally, and professionally. Wilson believed, for example, that World War II provided many of his students with an opportunity to advance themselves by joining the armed services. He also thought that for those African Americans who did not want to join the military, the war still offered many a chance to capitalize on some of the educational and economic prospects that the war mobilization effort created. He initiated an intensive after-school program to prepare a small group of students to take and pass the military and college entrance examinations. He organized a body of "about seven" students who met in his home three nights a week. "We would stay there for an hour and a half," Lincoln recalled. Wilson instructed them in "trigonometry," in "basic English," and "how to read statements" and understand their meaning.[69] Lincoln took advantage of his opportunity to make up for lost ground and excelled in his after-school study.

Lincoln graduated from Douglass High School in 1944, and with the help of Wilson and his remedial studies, he believed he was prepared to take advantage of any opportunity that presented itself. Attending college appealed to him, but the immediate future for Lincoln was in the skies. The opportunity to fly, defend his country, and destroy the myth of the inferior and unpatriotic "Negro" was to him a chance of a lifetime. Rising to the status of an elite air corps officer was his immediate goal.[70]

While Lincoln Ragsdale was writing his own chapter in the long history of black entrepreneurship and activism in Oklahoma, another family, which would eventually unite with the Ragsdales, was building upon its own history of hard work and industry. Like the Ragsdales, the Dickeys' history of educated professional leadership began nearly a hundred years ago, when William Dickey, born in Thomasville, Georgia, around 1894, and Estelle Odell, born in Gloucester, Virginia, around 1902, enrolled in Hampton Institute in Hampton, Virginia. Hampton, which lies on the peninsula between the James and York rivers at the mouth of the Chesapeake Bay, was founded by General Samuel Chapman Armstrong in 1868 during Reconstruction as a normal school primarily for the industrial education of African Americans. His intent was to establish a school to "prepare colored teachers for southern schools; teachers who can make a living out of their schools, and, after being started, support themselves through augmenting their low salaries with money earned through manual skills learned at the school." Armstrong aimed to develop a cadre of self-sufficient, thrifty, contented African American teachers and leaders who would be willing and able to attend to the social and economic needs of other blacks while negotiating, and in many cases accommodating, the prevailing social order characterized by white supremacy and racial inequality.[71]

William graduated from Hampton in 1915, and Estelle earned her college degree around 1918. After graduating from Hampton, Estelle became a teacher, which is what most black women who completed their college education at the institute did. She returned to Gloucester, where she taught at Locus Grove Elementary School. She excelled in her new profession and was made principal of Locus Grove within the first few years of her appointment. Estelle hailed from a family of teachers who were deeply involved in the education of black youth. Estelle's maternal great aunt, her youngest brother, and several of her cousins were teachers. Eleanor Ragsdale would later remark that teaching "was sort of second nature in the [Dickey] family."[72] When the students, teachers, and administrators of Locus Grove were dismissed for summer vacation in 1918, Estelle journeyed to Philadelphia to enjoy the summer with some of her Hampton friends. During her respite in Philadelphia, one of her friends introduced her to William, who was also vacationing in Philadelphia. Estelle was pleased to learned that William was a fellow Hampton alumnus, and although he graduated from the institute earlier than she, they both shared fond memories of their days at school.

William had worked as a specialist in gun manufacturing for Remington Arms in Georgia before becoming a sergeant in the U.S. Army. He had just returned from serving on the front lines of some of the most ferocious battles in France during World War I when he met Estelle. They spent much of their time together during the summer of 1918, until William returned to France and Estelle returned to Locus Grove during the fall of that year. Estelle and William continued to communicate and "court each other," despite being an ocean apart for nearly twelve months.[73]

William returned to the United States during January 1920. He decided not to go back to Georgia because he believed the state offered few opportunities for employment. No matter where he looked, it seemed, he found it very difficult to secure work. By the spring of 1920 he interviewed for and was offered a position as superintendent of the fifty-two-acre Eden Cemetery in a small town named Collingdale, Pennsylvania, on the outskirts of North Philadelphia. He accepted the position. Not long after securing what was considered by many, especially within the town's small black community, to be a secure, middle-class job, he decided to propose marriage to Estelle. She accepted his proposal, and they were married during the summer of 1920. William spent the next several years constructing a three-story house, complete with an attic and full basement, on a connecting property adjacent to the burial grounds of the Eden Cemetery. The family resided there from 1926 until 1938. A few years after their house was completed, Estelle gave birth to Eleanor Odell, on February 23, 1926. William and Estelle Dickey had three other children; another daughter, Gwendolyn, and two sons, Earle and William Jr.[74]

William Dickey earned enough money as superintendent of the Eden Cemetery to provide a secure economic environment for Eleanor and her siblings. Once Estelle married William and moved to Collingdale, she retired from teaching and became a full-time homemaker. She nevertheless augmented her demanding home schedule with a fair amount of social work and her work as a Sunday school teacher at her family's local African Methodist Episcopal (AME) church. Unlike Hartwell Ragsdale Sr., William was not an entrepreneur or seasoned civil rights activist, but he was considered to be a leader and member of the black professional class by virtue of his education and administrative position at the Eden Cemetery. Like the Ragsdales, however, the Dickeys endeavored to instruct their children early on that professional and middle-class blacks must seek excellence and achievement in education, must devote themselves to a skilled occupation, and must commit themselves to race work in the interest of improving the overall status of African Americans.[75]

Although growing up with the pressures that came with being part of the black middle class, Eleanor enjoyed her childhood. She had no recollections of enduring the many indignities that Lincoln Ragsdale experienced as a young black person in a state heavily influenced by Jim Crow segregation and intense racial hostilities. Eleanor often recalled the fun times she had with Gwendolyn, Earle, and William Jr. Some of her happiest childhood days, she remembered, were "spent in a beautiful flower garden playing hide and seek with her brothers and sister behind the tall tombstones" in the Eden Cemetery where William Sr. worked. She attended an elementary school near Eden, where she read avidly. Unlike her future husband, Eleanor attended a racially integrated school of predominantly middle-class children who did not suffer from ill-equipped classrooms or overextended faculty, and she enjoyed school. The school's lack of a common eating area may have irritated some of her peers and their parents, as all of the students had to make their own accommodations for lunch, but the

Dickey children came to love their daily walk home for lunch through the cemetery grounds, where they would often see their father at work. "I did not realize until many years later how fortunate we were as a family to have that kind of togetherness," Eleanor recalled. "That was a special time."[76]

During her teen years, Eleanor attended Darby High School. Like Lincoln, Eleanor's parents and extended family intensified their efforts during her high school years to teach her that achievement and duty to family and race were the criteria by which her success as an individual would be calculated. By virtue of her being black and female, however, Eleanor's initiation into the black professional class emerged along a different trajectory. Unlike Lincoln, Eleanor learned that her status in society was not only defined by her being an African American professional but a woman as well. Stephanie J. Shaw argues that black female would-be leaders like Eleanor Ragsdale faced an array of constraints in their lives because of private-sphere responsibilities bestowed upon them as women. At the same time, she posits, they were entrusted to assume crucial public obligations because of the needs of African Americans.[77]

Historically, to meet these needs black communities formulated a social construction of gender that was consciously devised to empower black women, especially working women, to transcend the pernicious effects of racism, sexism, and economic marginalization. Black women learned early on that mediating these ostensibly competing traditions was both obligatory and arduous. To raise the probability of their achievement, Shaw maintains, "interested persons generated a process that encouraged these women to take responsibility for their own futures and simultaneously to become agents of social change. The process produced some notable leaders among black women and had far-reaching consequences in and beyond African American communities."[78]

The primary "interested persons" in Eleanor's life were her immediate family and members of her local church. They provided what appears to have been a relatively quiet home life undergirded and sustained by black institutions and black culture. Eleanor devoted a great deal of time to reading and attending church services with her family but was always mindful of the overall status of black people in relation to whites and what challenges and responsibilities this dubious relationship held for her. Her recollections of race relations in

Collingdale, unlike the aggravated memories of many blacks subjected to the prejudice and racism of the time, were atypical and somewhat innocuous. Coming of age in a northern community, perhaps, can be cited as the reason for her developing memories devoid of the many of the overt racial indignities that Lincoln endured in Oklahoma. Eleanor maintained that "in the little community in which I lived, we just happened to be the only colored family. So, straight through elementary school, each of my two brothers and my sister and I were the only colored child in each of our classes." Darby High School boasted a larger black student population than Eleanor's elementary school, but African Americans still represented a small minority at the institution.[79]

Despite growing up in a northern town with some integrated institutions, Eleanor was astute enough to comprehend the nature and significance of the social construction of race in America. She was aware that she lived "an extremely isolated type of life." Her family knew they "were of a colored race" and that their "outsider" experience "was integrated in the school system" with caution. The Dickeys lived "in a community that was black," and on Sundays they went "to a black church" where Sunday school and their "social life was with blacks." Eleanor came to cherish her memories of interacting with the black communities of Collingdale and Darby.[80]

With regard to de facto and de jure racial segregation, however, she believed that those affected by it "just grow up and accept that [it exists] because that is all you know." Unlike Lincoln, she never felt oppressed by white citizens in the towns in which she grew up. One of the few institutional manifestations of racial prejudice in Eleanor's youth was the "colored section" in the movie theater near her family's home. As a young person, however, she did not concern herself much with white prejudice or with what white people were doing or thinking. Eleanor was largely interested in what was happening in other black communities, and she spent little time thinking about the often odious nature of racial segregation. She stated that "I always felt that reading the black newspaper [in town] was the most wonderful thing in the world, because that is where you found out [about] what was happening among black people."[81]

To Eleanor, much of the news she read about in African American newspapers was something of which to be proud. She recalled that "when [African American congressman] Adam Clayton Powell came to speak in Philadelphia, we just made a big holiday of it." She and other blacks in Philadelphia were happy "just to be able to sit and look at that beautiful man and listen to his elocution." Not withstanding de facto racial segregation, Eleanor's experiences as a young black woman in Pennsylvania were in some ways different than Lincoln's life as a young black man in Oklahoma. The ubiquitous nature of racial segregation and terrorism that the Ragsdales faced in Oklahoma was somewhat alien to the Dickeys. Both families, however, knew that race mattered, it was simply a matter of degree.[82]

While Eleanor was attending Darby High School between 1939 and 1943, she became more active in her family's AME church, joined organizations that protested racial inequality, evolved into an outspoken proponent of black self-determination and self-sufficiency, and distinguished herself as an outstanding student. Eleanor was baptized at age twelve, and she continued to be devoted to religious education throughout her teenage years. Her family went to church every Sunday. "The Sunday school was the backbone of the [black] community in Darby," she reminisced, "so I went to Sunday school every Sunday morning and Sunday service every Sunday afternoon."[83]

By the time Eleanor enrolled in Darby High School, she, like her mother, had become a Sunday school teacher. In a very short time she "ran all of the little programs for the children, like Children's Days, Easter [plays], and Christmas [pageants]," at her church. She became increasingly aware of issues that were important to most African Americans, such as political participation and representation, the negative effects of racial segregation, and the kind of racial violence that terrorized African Americans in other parts of the country. In 1940 she joined the recently established NAACP Youth Council in Darby to fight racial injustice. Eleanor quickly became one of the most effective members of the organization and an imposing member of its debate team. "I remember going around to other NAACP Youth Councils in the area for debates," she recalled. Her team won often, and she was considered to be the club's best debater.[84]

She enrolled in college preparatory courses at Darby High School and outperformed many of her peers in advanced courses in English, literature, and mathematics. She was very proud of her record and believed herself to be "fortunate to finish in the upper quartile" of her class. She was equally pleased with her 1943 school yearbook, in which her English and literature teacher inscribed, "you must go to college, it is for your kind." Although her parents were members of the black middle class, able to take care of the family's most basic needs and provide a modicum of conveniences, their prospects of being able to pay for Eleanor to attend college were meager. During her senior year in high school, she realized that her "parents could not afford" to send her to college. As her graduation day drew near, Eleanor learned that a schoolteacher in the Philadelphia school system who had been informed of her intellectual acumen and academic achievements encouraged her mother to assist Eleanor in applying for a college scholarship. Eleanor and her mother completed and submitted the application expeditiously. They waited patiently until her graduation day to find out whether she would be awarded the fellowship.[85]

Eleanor graduated from Darby High School during the spring of 1943. She was recognized for her hard work and sagacity, and on the day of her graduation she was awarded the Richard Humphries Foundation Academic Scholarship to attend college at the predominantly black Cheyney State Teacher's College, now Cheyney University, in Pennsylvania. During the fall of 1943 she enrolled in the historic institution that was established for the express purpose of providing qualified black people with an opportunity to earn a higher education. Eleanor went to Cheyney to further her education and her socialization into a culture of racial restoration. Indeed, most black colleges endeavored to produce future generations of community leaders. The universities were not simply erected to provide their students with a formal education. Their goal was not merely to promote professional advancement and financial gain but racial uplift and cultural enhancement. Struggling under the yoke of racial oppression, black communities required their professional people also to pursue positive changes in African Americans' health, social conditions, economic opportunities, and political standing. Black communities considered devotion to racial reform and philanthropy to be a bedrock principle upon which a traditional higher education should be built.[86]

Black women such as Eleanor were expected to adhere to a higher standard of personal refinement than black men of equal standing. In addition to preparing themselves to be at once professional people, agents for social change, and gatekeepers for African American families, communities, and culture, black women were compelled to defend themselves against racist and sexist attacks against their respectability and physical and emotional well-being. The purpose of black female education went far beyond the classroom and involved more than economic independence. To be sure, black women were encouraged to seek financial stability, but as Shaw indicates, black parents wanted their daughters to use their intellectual training and their resulting employment, working class or professional, paid or unpaid, in a manner that would support their families and aid their communities.[87] Their success was gauged by their faithfulness to black community codes of service, sacrifice, and respectability.

Thus black women led the way in educating the unschooled, caring for the sick, aiding children in need, and protesting discrimination and sexual harassment. They did these things not only to excel in a particular vocation or to embrace a rewarding niche in the world of philanthropy but to advance black communities and, ostensibly, freedom and democracy. The safety, health, welfare, and prosperity of black women in America, and by extension all African Americans, were inextricably linked to their roles as key agents for social change. The well-being of black people depended upon the efficacy of their women.[88]

Cheyney State prepared African American women to be teachers and leaders in black communities. In this capacity, the institution was instrumental in shaping the lives of its students. Eleanor was a recipient of this legacy. She was also pursuing a dream in studying to become a teacher. As early as elementary school, she aspired to be an educator. "I remember in the eighth grade writing in an ethics course," she recalled, "the question was 'what do you want to be when you grow up?' At age thirteen I was saying I wanted to be a teacher, and giving the reasons why. I could travel in the summer, and if I married I would be home with my children. That didn't materialize later, but at least that was the original thought."[89]

At the time of Eleanor's training, Cheyney was one of fourteen state teachers' colleges in Pennsylvania. Founded in 1837 as the Quaker School for Colored Youths, it is the oldest historically black college in the United States. Richard Humphries, a Quaker and outspoken supporter of black education, willed a $10,000 endowment upon his death for the construction of an institution of higher learning to educate children of African descent. Located first in Philadelphia, the institution was moved to its present location in Cheyney, Pennsylvania, in 1903. A Quaker board of managers had administered the institution for eight decades when it was purchased by the state of Pennsylvania in 1922.[90]

In 1983 the college became part of the newly formed State System of Higher Education and was renamed Cheyney University of Pennsylvania. The institution, situated on 275 acres of rolling hillsides in the southeastern quarter of the state, stands as the earliest representation of an institutional commitment to the education of people of African descent in the United States. There are more than 7,100 Cheyney alumni throughout the United States, including 5,100 in Pennsylvania. Although there were many state teachers' colleges in Pennsylvania by the time Eleanor enrolled, Cheyney was the only predominantly black college. What distinguished it from other historically black colleges and universities at the time of Eleanor's studies were its president and faculty. Leslie Pinckney Hill, a black Phi Beta Kappa from Harvard University, was the college's president, and its teaching positions were overwhelmingly occupied by black women. Most of these teachers were graduates of storied institutions such as Vassar, Wellesley, and Antioch. Eleanor remembers them being "the kind of women who had dedicated their lives to education."[91]

Eleanor enjoyed the camaraderie among her classmates and made many friends. She remembered with a bit of revelry that she joined the campus chapter of the Woman's Christian Temperance Union (WCTU) to form bonds and express her opposition to vices such as smoking and drinking. She also worked in the college library to earn spending money that helped defray the cost of her occasional trips to Philadelphia. Eleanor completed her bachelor of science degree in education in 1947 and earned an elementary teaching certificate. She did well enough in her studies to be offered a graduate school fellowship.

Although she found the idea of living in the U.S. capital alluring, she declined a master's degree fellowship at Howard University to travel over two thousand miles to Phoenix for her first teaching job. This decision proved to be a critical one, as she would soon find herself at the center of one of the most important local movements in the American Southwest. When she made her initial decision to move to Phoenix, however, her mind was not focused on the "race problem" or civil rights. Eleanor was simply happy and eager to be entering a new stage in her life. She was "excited" when she was given the assignment of teaching a first-grade classroom at Paul Laurence Dunbar Elementary School in Phoenix. Dunbar was one of two segregated elementary schools established in Phoenix for black children during the second and third decades of the twentieth century. Part of Phoenix Elementary School District Number One, the school was adjacent to Block 41, which was bounded by Jackson, Madison, Fifth, and Sixth streets.[92]

Eleanor was not surprised that she was offered positions only in segregated schools. Institutions such as Cheyney prepared their students for an educational system greatly influenced by Jim Crow segregation. Eleanor's administrators and teachers at Cheyney routinely reminded her and her peers that they would be recruited almost exclusively by black schools. For instance, when Eleanor was completing her student teaching in Westchester, Pennsylvania, her psychology teacher overheard her and some of her classmates discussing what they thought it would be like to instruct a classroom of white students. The teacher told them in no uncertain terms that as black teachers, they should not "expect to teach in a integrated school, because your opportunities are going to lie in segregated ones—which, of course proved to be true," Eleanor recalled with exasperated amusement.[93]

Phoenix was an attractive destination because Eleanor had relatives who lived in the city. Her paternal uncle Thomas Dickey Sr. and his wife, Mayme Dickey, as well as her paternal uncle Lloyd Dickey Jr., had migrated to Phoenix from the East Coast in the early 1920s. Thomas Dickey Sr. owned and operated a drugstore in the segregated black community, and Lloyd Dickey Jr. was principal of the segregated Booker T. Washington School. Although Philadelphia had just increased teachers' salaries to $2,000 a year, the excitement of relocating and reuniting with family members in Phoenix, in addition to earning more money, convinced Eleanor to make the trip instead of enrolling in graduate school. Elementary School District Number One in Phoenix "was paying teachers $2,470 for a teaching year" she recalled. Eleanor figured that the additional $470 she would earn at Dunbar "would pay her way" to Phoenix.[94]

Eleanor remembered being "fully prepared for teaching" at a segregated school for black children. Although she claimed that she "didn't think in terms of color," she probably had a good idea of what was going to be expected of her and what unique challenges awaited her students. "I knew that the school was all colored, and I had done my practice teaching in a colored situation back in Pennsylvania." Eleanor firmly believed that she was prepared to meet potential challenges because of the instruction received at Cheyney. She recalled the lessons she learned from observing and listening to Lesley Hill and "all of the university's faculty of color." Moreover, her "background in being one of the few black children in every community [she] lived in, integrating [her] elementary school in Collingdale, studying in mixed situation throughout high school in Darby," and her "experience at the all-black Cheyney University," she believed, "fully prepared" her for what she had to face in Phoenix.[95]

Unlike her mostly fond memories of the school systems in Collingdale and Darby, her memories of the segregated school system in Phoenix were quite different. When Eleanor arrived in Phoenix, she remembered the city being a place where the racial divide was clearly marked and rarely crossed. Historian Dean E. Smith describes Phoenix as an area that was "all settled by ex-Confederates" who were determined to build Phoenix in the Southern image. "They came flooding out here after the Civil War," he posits, "and they brought prejudices with them."[96]

These prejudices were systematically sewn into the social, economic, and political fabric of the city, and the Phoenix public school system was no exception. The Euro-American-dominated administrative hierarchy of the public school system greatly affected virtually all decisions made in the district along race lines. The superintendent and other school administrators presided over the entire district, including white and black schools. The Phoenix public school system attempted to create an illusion that no racial hierarchy existed by staffing all of the African American schools with black teachers and administrators and paying black teachers and white teachers equal salaries.[97]

Lincoln argued much later that despite the manufactured facade of a race-neutral public school system, black educators and students were treated in a degrading and unequal manner. Although black and white teachers were paid equally, black teachers taught at segregated black schools that were routinely underfunded and marginalized within the district. Although *Plessy v. Ferguson* provided for "separate but equal" institutions for white and black people, whites who dominated public institutions rarely provided for equal facilities for African Americans. In addition to institutional racism, African American educators also had to deal with the condescending color consciousness of white educators.

Lincoln Ragsdale remembered being called "colored, negro and negroes." "They called us that to make us feel very inferior, along with that word 'black,' " he argued. "Black" had been associated with negatives except when it came to finance, Ragsdale maintained. "Normally you would think of black sheep, black night, black Tuesday"—all negative, he argued. Ragsdale acknowledged the fact that many African Americans have chosen to refer to themselves as black in recent decades, but he believed they did so "just to get over the fear of the name." "Africans did not associate [with] the word black" he declared, suggesting that African Americans and their kinsmen and women in diaspora should not.[98]

It took Ragsdale "a long time to accept that word," opting in later years to refer to himself as "African American," a term he described as being "universally accepted" in America. He believed that the term "black" obscures the many differences among people of African descent. He argued that in "talking to white folks you can't classify all white people the same. You can't say Germans are the same as the English." Ragsdale suggested that many people chose to use the terms "European" and "Orientals" while making some generalizations "because there are certain similarities."[99] He believed most people chose to use the label "African American" because it reflects the unity and diversity of people of African descent.

What links African Americans to other blacks throughout the African diaspora, Ragsdale believed, are some of their cultural characteristics and physical features. The biggest thing blacks have in common, he asserted, is "oppression." Generally, however, he provided for nuances in identity among people of African descent based largely upon nationality. "After all," he posited, "a black growing up in New York is different from a black growing up in Mississippi, the Bahamas, [or] Haiti." "A Haitian would certainly not feel exactly as we [African Americans] feel about white people and race." In Brazil, where the population consists primarily of people of African descent, he maintained, "they have a different feeling about 'white people' than we have because their experiences are different."[100]

"My experience in the U.S., like most African Americans," Ragsdale offered, "has been a very negative one." Despite sharing a history of oppression in Western and non-Western societies profoundly affected by white supremacist principles and practices such as colonialism, slavery, and Jim Crow, Ragsdale believed that the unique and protracted history of enslavement, de facto segregation, "Negrophobia," and white supremacy, as well as the relatively small percentage of people of African descent in the United States, has made race relations and life for black people in America distinct and more hazardous.[101]

By the late 1940s Lincoln and Eleanor had left their homes in Oklahoma and Pennsylvania to pursue careers in the military and education, respectively. Their pursuits would bring them together in what was still considered by many to be a relatively unknown, remote desert community. Soon, however, Eleanor and Lincoln would know quite a bit about the city in which they would live for the rest of their lives. They would witness firsthand the retrograde nature of race relations in the city, a place being marketed as a "desert oasis" overflowing with opportunity. Lincoln and Eleanor took very little time to determine that Phoenix and its race relations were as dangerous to the overall well-being of black people as any place they had known. The schoolteacher and would-be fighter pilot were disappointed with the status of the African American community when they arrived, and they would utilize their formal and informal training as professionals and activists to bring about change.[102]

For the majority of black Phoenicians, the Great Depression intensified an already tormented existence. The number of African Americans in Phoenix more than tripled between 1920 and 1940. The vast majority were new migrants from the American South who were poor and uneducated. Black people were forced to the periphery of an already socioeconomically depressed community, as they were denied equal opportunity to quality education and employment. Even in starvation black people faced discrimination, for in few areas was aid forthcoming on a nonracial basis. During the Depression years it was found that "the average black family in Phoenix was living under crowded conditions in a poorly furnished home." Federal census workers noted that there were "only a few modern homes, and many wooden shacks, trailers, tents, sheds, and abandoned stores" in the African American community. They also reported that "most homes are one to four room structures without benefit of running water or sewerage."[103]

Black men in Phoenix who had once found jobs in the unskilled labor market and black women who had worked as domestics in the homes of white Phoenicians now found it difficult to secure even these low-paying jobs. Increasingly, rank-and-file black Phoenicians were faced with competing for jobs against mobile white job hunters who were considered to be inherently more qualified. Madge Johnson Copeland, a local black entrepreneur and political activist, argued that many white Phoenicians feared the presence of black men in their homes and offices and often refused them employment opportunities as groundsmen or domestic workers.[104] As a result, African American men had fewer job opportunities than black women in Phoenix.

Not only were African American men denied white collar jobs because of their race, but they were refused many other employment opportunities as well. Copeland noted that "[black] men were always far behind [black] women in employment. Far, far behind. They had to accept very menial jobs. Some of them worked in garages, which didn't mean mechanic, but they had to keep the place clean and be a helper for the mechanics."[105] A small number of black men found jobs in hotels as butlers and doormen, but these prospects were strictly limited. John Barber, who migrated to Phoenix on December 20, 1918, recalled his experience in Phoenix during the 1930s: "When the Depression hit, things were pretty bad around here until Roosevelt helped to get things straightened out. I got a job on the PWA [Public Works Administration] in 1934, getting $35 a week. Wasn't that some money!"[106]

Although the Great Depression was a time of intense deprivation for black Phoenicians and most African Americans, it was also a period in which black people made inroads in art, music, sports, and drama. The Works Progress Administration (WPA), for example, provided financial support for a number of artists whose work would greatly influence American culture, inspiring the Chicago Renaissance and the growth in popularity of jazz music. All of this occurred while racism and discrimination raged on in American society. The New Deal stimulated some economic healing. More important, however, by World War II the New Deal had helped to establish the United States as a powerful national state with political coalitions that had coalesced to mount formidable dissent to the prevailing racial order. African Americans saw their participation in the federal government increase; black social scientists like E. Franklin Frazier and Charles S. Johnson influenced social policy; and the NAACP organized a successful fight against discrimination in government programs and, led by Charles Hamilton Houston, stepped up its attack on segregation and black political disfranchisement. Black women such as Ella Baker continued to support the NAACP through critical fund-raising activities, but they also participated in and organized other reform associations, such as the Young Women's Christian Association (YWCA) and the DHL.[107]

To address racial inequality and discrimination in labor, the Committee for Industrial Organization (CIO) was formed in 1935 as an interracial labor union (it changed its name in 1938 to the Congress of Industrial Organizations). Black and white Communist Americans such as Hosea Hudson, Al Murphy, Angelo Herndon, Clyde Johnson, and Ruby Bates mounted campaigns against social and racial inequality. They fought, for instance, for the freedom of the "Scottsboro Boys" in Scottsboro, Alabama, nine young black men falsely convicted of raping two white women. This era ushered in improvements in black political participation and the fluorescence of black culture, but it also revealed the extent to which white supremacy was woven into the fabric of American society.[108]

Lincoln and Eleanor took up residence in a city where white supremacy and all that it engendered were as pronounced as in any place in the country. Longtime resident John Barber believed that Phoenix "wasn't much different than in the South. The difference here was that they didn't lynch you."[109] Historian Shirley J. Roberts suggests that Phoenix was a city "where differentiation between the white and colored races" seemed to be "an accepted fact." Eleanor and Lincoln would not accept the racism and discrimination that separated the Phoenix community. Although they had experienced racial discrimination and separatism early in their lives, legal segregation in Lincoln's case and de facto segregation in Eleanor's, their families did not expect them to accept it and do nothing to fight it. On the contrary, they inherited familial traditions of professional activism and service that stood in direct opposition to such ideologies. They were reared in families of professional people who worked to eradicate discrimination and strengthen black communities.[110]

Black professionals such as the Ragsdales and Dickeys emerged as a response to racial oppression and through individual ambition and achievement. As a result, these professionals created institutions that fortified and cultivated their status. Black families like the Ragsdales and Dickeys paved the way for the financial success and political effectiveness of third-generation leaders such as Lincoln and Eleanor, enabling them to evaluate and respond to the needs of blacks, particularly the need to develop effective strategies to resist white supremacy.

Lincoln's and Eleanor's families nurtured their ability to use their talents to cultivate and deploy such strategies. By 1946 Lincoln and Eleanor Ragsdale brought their ambitions, talents, and commitment to black advancement to Phoenix, and soon thereafter the city would never be the same.

# Chapter 2

## Tuskegee, World War II, and the New Black Activism

In fighting fascism and Nazism, America had to stand before the whole world in favor of racial tolerance and . . . racial democracy.

Gunnar Myrdal, *An American Dilemma*

ON DECEMBER 7, 1941, the Japanese attack on Pearl Harbor ended years of America's questionable "neutrality" during World War II. It propelled the United States immediately into a climactic event that changed the nation forever. America's participation in the war also altered its global status, making it the world's wealthiest industrialized military power. The impact of America's involvement in World War II on African Americans is complex. On the one hand, the war ushered in a period of unprecedented progress in black employment, mobility, and professional activism. On the other hand, America's crusade in the name of freedom and democracy in World War II failed to reach millions of its black citizens at home. White supremacy and racial discrimination flourished in the United States during the war. African Americans such as Lincoln Ragsdale joined the armed services to fight America's fascist enemies while resisting white supremacy and their own subordinate status at home.

Prior to the bombing of Pearl Harbor, African Americans responded to the escalating conflict by supporting Ethiopia's fight against the Italian invasion. Ethiopia was the world's sole independent nation genuinely controlled by black Africans. The Ethiopian-Italian conflict demonstrated to African Americans the ways in which fascism and racism were interconnected. This rekindled the keen interest in the links between Africans' struggles against colonialism and African Americans' fight for freedom and democracy within the United States that black Americans had demonstrated ever since the Spanish Civil War (1936–39).[1] The military service rendered by black American soldiers later in World War II, therefore, was inspired by their condemnation of fascism and American racism. At home, African Americans responded to the challenge of white supremacy and the lack of opportunity in several ways. Like Lincoln and Eleanor Ragsdale, black people migrated in large numbers to western cities such as Phoenix, Los Angeles, and San Francisco, taking advantage of career opportunities created by war mobilization and the increased demand for everything from shipbuilding and aircraft production to health care, housing, schools, and teachers. African American soldiers fought against fascism abroad and returned to America and civilian life to play pivotal roles in the ensuing change.

Led by individuals such as Lincoln and Eleanor Ragsdale, black people established and restructured protest organizations that formed the backbone of the modern civil rights movement. When whites responded to their efforts to give meaning to freedom and democracy by reinforcing Jim Crow conventions, black activists reinvented themselves. Out of this insurgent revival grew a new black activism rooted in greater political participation. Lincoln Ragsdale's experiences during the World War II era illuminate the problems and progress that marked this riotous period. The experience that would most profoundly influence Ragsdale's life during this era was his tenure in the military, culminating with his graduation from the Tuskegee Army Air Corps Flying School in Tuskegee, Alabama.[2]

To understand Lincoln and Eleanor Ragsdales' significance as business and civil rights leaders in Phoenix after World War II, one must grasp the importance of the war in shaping their views of democracy and freedom and the necessity of African Americans to fight for them more urgently at home. A new generation of black Americans became soldiers during World War II, and many, such as Lincoln Ragsdale, would come forth from the war with a fortified awareness of who they were and a renewed dedication to fight for African American equality. Unlike World War I, more black soldiers had earned their high school and college diplomas by World War II. Many more black servicemen and women, particularly those from professional, activist backgrounds like Lincoln's, were proud, self-confident, and aware of their own value and dignity as human beings and Americans. For thousands of black servicemen, the armed services offered them their first exposure to a world free of legal segregation. For Lincoln and many others serving in the military during World War II, the conflict inspired them, their families, and their friends to raise critical questions about America's racial order.[3]

After finishing his after-school studies and secondary education at Douglass High School in Ardmore, Lincoln took the air corps entrance exam in Oklahoma. He enlisted on July 14, 1944. Lincoln immediately prepared to be assigned to a training installation and relocated. Despite his hard work and practice, he failed the written examination the first two times he took it. After finally passing the written portion of the test, he then "flunked the physical." At five feet six and a half inches tall and weighing 130 pounds, Ragsdale was not a large, muscular, imposing man. Generally, however, he was healthy and in good condition. He had no reason to believe he would have trouble passing the routine physical examination. "My eyes were good, my depth perception was good," he recalled, "everything was good except my pulse."[4]

Ragsdale's average standing heart rate was around 150. When he was instructed to jump up and down, his heart rate would climb to 200. He was told by the test administrators that he was "going to flunk this thing again" if he could not maintain a lower heart rate during increased physical activity. Ragsdale was informed that one more failed attempt would bring about his dismissal. Concerned, Ragsdale consulted a doctor who prescribed a sedative to help him relax. When he took the test again, his standing heart rate "was beating about 50." After he jumped up and down for a short period of time again, his heart rate registered 80. This conspicuous improvement in his heart rate gave the examiner pause. The test administrator believed it was "better than perfect." This dramatic change made it necessary for Ragsdale to take the test yet again. The next time his heart rate was recorded at 45. Confused and no doubt exasperated, the examiner reluctantly gave Ragsdale a passing grade.[5]

After finally completing his examination in Oklahoma, Ragsdale relocated briefly to Howard University in Washington DC. At the time, Howard and Wilberforce universities were the only "Negro" universities offering reserve officer training. As the war escalated and the likelihood of black pilot training increased, the Roosevelt administration considered the schools to be pools from which to recruit air corps officer candidates. Ragsdale's temporary stop in the nation's capital ushered in a series of sobering events. While stationed at Howard, Ragsdale was not present to accept and sign for his air corps certified recruitment letter ordering him to report to basic training. Since he was not present, Ragsdale recalled, "they didn't give it to anybody." After some searching, they eventually solicited the support of his mother, who gave the air corps representatives his address in Washington.[6]

Soon after, a cohort of military police (MPs) brandishing "guns and big sticks" arrived at Ragsdale's residence in Washington announcing that they were going to take him to jail. When he asked the MPs what he did to warrant the arrest, they told him that he had failed to report for service. The MPs took him to the military base at Fort Meade, Maryland. It is not clear whether he was subjected to any disciplinary action. Once at Fort Meade, Ragsdale received a number of required inoculations and for ten days prepared for another transfer. As a "preaviation cadet," he was ordered to escort ten men south to the military base in Biloxi, Mississippi. He and the recruits boarded a train at Fort Meade and headed south, stopping briefly in St. Louis. There, the black recruits were not met by what Ragsdale described as traditional "southern hospitality." Rather, they were met by southern white hostility and Jim Crow segregation.[7]

An official at the train station told Ragsdale and the rest of his party that they could not ride the Pullman train and that they had to remove themselves. Irritated, Ragsdale reminded the official that he and the other recruits had purchased tickets to ride the train and that they had every intention to do so. An argument ensued between the two, which resulted in Ragsdale and his entire cohort being thrown off the train. As he threw them off, the train controller bellowed, "No Negro is going to be riding on this train to Mississippi."[8] Ragsdale, realizing that the group was going to arrive in Mississippi behind schedule, phoned the base in Biloxi to inform his commander that as "Negroes," the group was denied access to Pullman trains. Ragsdale was told that it made no difference that they were military personnel. Racial segregation penetrated every segment of society, and the air corps provided no special protections. The administrator who received Ragsdale's call was not concerned about the indignities and problems the recruits faced. "Look here, nigger," the officer barked, "you better be on that train and get down here the best way you can, right now, wherever they put you."[9] After a day and a half of waiting, the men managed to secure transportation. Ragsdale and his group were most likely made to wait until a train became available with few if any whites on board. Many black soldiers were forced to wait until trains and buses had been loaded with white soldiers before they were permitted to board.[10]

They arrived at Keesler field in Biloxi and were housed in a segregated section of the base called the "KK." In the segregated bivouacs of the KK, Ragsdale went through three months of basic training and a battery of examinations. What Ragsdale remembered most about his introduction to the military was not the physical challenge of basic training or the cerebral demands of the tests. What stood out in his mind was the unequal and demeaning nature of military segregation. Black soldiers were banned from almost all of the places where white soldiers trained and relaxed. African American soldiers were not allowed to enter a military club to dine or drink. "[When] we wanted a beer," Ragsdale recalled, "we went to the window and asked for it. White guys walked inside. We had to stay on the outside to get it."[11] Despite this unequal treatment, many black soldiers made the most of the opportunities to better themselves. For example, "many of the brothers, blacks, who came to the induction station to get basic training couldn't read and write," Ragsdale asserted. "The good thing" about their military experience, however, was that it "made them go to school."[12]

There were around five hundred preaviation cadets in Biloxi when Ragsdale arrived. "They eliminated, of the five hundred of us, about four hundred and fifty," he remembered.[13] Having succeeded in his training, Ragsdale was one of a relatively small number of recruits who were given the opportunity to attend officer training. He and the other remaining preaviation cadets were relocated to Tuskegee Flying School to receive pilot training. At Tuskegee, Ragsdale underwent intense instruction and myriad psychological challenges. Cadets at Tuskegee were subjected to the rigors of pilot training and the frustrations of being black in an institution dominated by white leaders who possessed deep-seated notions of white supremacy. During one of his first days at Tuskegee, in fact, one of Ragsdale's commanding officers told him and his fellow trainees to "look at the person to the left and to the right, because at the end of the program they won't be here with you."[14] Indeed, most cadets did not complete the program. Dogged by an overwhelming military ethos, intense competition, internal military politics, and institutional racism, successful cadets had to possess a cornucopia of laudable character traits, including intellectual acumen, strong interpersonal communication skills, and strength of will. Lincoln Ragsdale Jr. remembered his father telling him that over the years, "there were a lot of people that started out in the program," but through natural and coerced attrition, "only so many people" graduated from Tuskegee Flying School.[15]

Despite the military establishment's lingering opposition to black people rising to the status of officer, it was pressured by black leaders and prompted by the urgency of war to create the program. The first class of thirteen flying cadets of the 99th Pursuit Squadron began its training at Tuskegee on July 19, 1941. The black press labeled the men the Lonely Eagles because of their small numbers and segregated status. They were trained in four phases: preflight, primary flight, basic military flight, and advanced military flight training. The instruction was provided primarily by white military personnel, with the exception of physical education and a limited amount of primary flight instruction, which were taught by Tuskegee Flying School chief C. Alfred Anderson. Cadets received their preflight education in a dormitory on the Tuskegee campus and their primary training on Tuskegee's Morton Field. Their basic and advanced training were scheduled to be conducted on Army Field, which was under construction during the summer of 1941. If a cadet was one of the few who successfully completed the four stages of training, he would receive his pilot's wings and a commission as an officer in the U.S. Army Air Corps.[16]

Reeling from the Japanese attack on Pearl Harbor, the air corps intensified its training at Tuskegee Flying School. Late in 1941 the air corps transferred black fighter plane mechanics and specialists from Maxwell Air Force Base in Montgomery, Alabama, to the airfield in Tuskegee and gave them rank. Five nonflying cadets also received commissions. These men were joined by the first class of black preaviation cadets at Tuskegee. The soldiers were housed in a bathhouse and in makeshift tarpaulin shelters supported only by mud and muck in what became known as Tent City.[17] Eight out of the first thirteen cadets were dismissed from the program, failing in at least one level before basic flight training. Most of the cadets who washed out could not handle the psychological stress associated with their service and training. The cadets were supervised primarily by white southern flight instructors, and many cadets were not oriented to military discipline and the intensity of military drilling. Most of the cadets, especially those from the North, clashed with white southern officers who used abusive, racially derogatory language. Some enlisted men, such as a cadet by the name of Jimmy Moore, eventually succumbed to the constant abuse. Moore endured the harsh environment through most of his training. He eventually "snapped," however, and lashed out verbally at a white superior officer who hit him with a barrage of racial slurs, causing Moore to wash out one day before his graduation.[18]

The first class of Tuskegee cadets only produced five graduates in March 1942: Capt. Benjamin O. Davis Jr., George S. Roberts, Lemuel Custis, Charles De Bow, and Mac Ross. Davis, the first black graduate of West Point in the twentieth century, was the son of Benjamin O. Davis Sr., who was the only senior black officer in the army and was promoted to the rank of brigadier general by President Roosevelt in 1941. Between March and September 1942, thirty-three pilots received their wings. They were soon followed by more commissioned officers eager to see action. Once they were given the opportunity to fight, the Tuskegee Airmen proved themselves to be quite proficient in battle.[19]

The 99th Pursuit Squadron was deployed to North Africa in April 1943, where it flew its first combat mission against the island of Pantelleria on June 2, 1943. Benjamin O. Davis Jr., who had been promoted to colonel, was placed in command of the 332nd Fighter Group when it was dispatched to Italy in January 1944. Davis, like his father, would later rise to the rank of brigadier general. The Tuskegee fighters escorted bombers and took part in many other missions. The 332nd was instrumental in sinking an enemy destroyer off the Istrian peninsula, and it protected the 15th Air Corps bombers in important attacks on the oil fields of Romania. Under Davis's command, the fighter group won the admiration of African Americans throughout the United States and the respect of many officials in the air corps. The Tuskegee Airmen flew more than 15,500 sorties and completed 1,578 missions. They escorted heavy bombers into Germany's Rhineland in 200 separate missions without losing one fighter to enemy fire. They destroyed 409 enemy aircraft, sank one enemy destroyer, and eliminated myriad ground installations with strafing runs. On January 27, 1944, the 99th shot down five enemy aircraft is less than four minutes, despite being outnumbered nearly two to one. The soldiers were revered and honored for their valor. In recognition of their service to their country, the Tuskegee Airmen collected 150 Distinguished Flying Crosses, one Legion of Merit, one Silver Star, fourteen Bronze Stars, and 744 Air Medals.[20]

Despite their heroism in battle and their service at home, black soldiers routinely suffered from low morale and frustrations born of racial discrimination. The military's segregationist and white supremacist policies relegated the majority of the one million African Americans who served during World War II to auxiliary units in transportation and engineering corps. Throughout the South, black soldiers were refused service in places of public accommodation where German prisoners of war were often dining and enjoying the good life.[21] World War II veteran Dempsey Travis remembered German prisoners being "free to move around the camp, unlike black soldiers who were restricted. The Germans walked right into the doggone places like any white American. We were wearin' the same uniform, but we were excluded."[22] In a "whites only" waiting room in a railroad station in Kentucky, three black soldiers were beaten by civilian policemen for not deferring to white women when ordered to do so. An African American soldier had his eyes gouged out by a white policeman in an altercation in South Carolina, and in Durham, North Carolina, a white bus driver was found not guilty of murder after he killed a black soldier following an argument in July 1944.[23]

Military bases offered little sanctuary from Jim Crow and white racism. Many commanding officers banned from their bases the black newspapers that Lincoln had earned money selling, and some resorted to burning them. Military markets were segregated and distributed inferior wares to black soldiers, and officers' clubs and entertainment facilities were segregated. The cadets at Tuskegee tried to make the best of their segregated environment. Black entertainers such as Lena Horne, Duke Ellington, and Cab Calloway would visit and entertain the servicemen occasionally, to what Ragsdale described as their "utter delight." Joe Louis, the celebrated heavyweight boxing champion, visited Tuskegee during the spring of 1945. He toured the facility, spoke with Lincoln and the other cadets about the significance of their service, and signed autographs. Military bases in the American West placed black soldiers, unlike Mexican American or American Indian soldiers, in separate units or confined them to labor roles. Due to racial segregation and their small numbers, African American troops found few sources of entertainment on the base. Moreover, since most bases were in predominantly white rural areas, black soldiers had even fewer options when they left their stations. Many military authorities encouraged segregation in surrounding cities. Lawrence B. de Graaf has demonstrated that in San Bernardino, California, white business owners posted "We Cater to White Trade Only" signs by 1944.[24] When the Japanese attacked Pearl Harbor, a twenty-two-year-old sailor named Dorie Miller pulled his captain to safety under heavy enemy fire, commandeered a machine gun, and having never before fired a gun, shot down at least two and perhaps as many as six enemy aircraft. Miller was awarded the Navy Cross for his heroism but was subsequently placed back in his former position as a mess attendant without promotion.[25]

Racial segregation during World War II affected black soldiers and civilians alike. African Americans were excluded from many defense industries during the first years of the war. The effects of this practice were most striking in the American West, where a large allocation of government contracts were awarded. Western states received over half of the defense contracts to build ships and aircraft. The San Francisco Bay Area led the way in shipbuilding, while southern California became the leader in air craft construction. In Phoenix, World War II ignited an economic boom and unprecedented population growth, which led to the establishment of several high-profile military bases in the area. Named after noted Phoenician and World War I pilot Frank Luke Jr., Luke Air Field, now Luke Air Force Base, opened in June 1941. Mesa Military Airport, now Williams Air Force base, opened its doors in January 1942 and was named after an army air corps pilot. The creation of these installations bought at least six thousand jobs to the Phoenix area and funneled millions of dollars into the local economy.[26]

Following the attack on Pearl Harbor, more airfields were opened in the Greater Phoenix Metropolitan Area. Thunderbird II, a primary aviation training school, was established north of Scottsdale in June 1942, and Litchfield Naval Air Facility, a research and development center, became operational in October 1943. American and foreign cadets flocked to these Valley of the Sun military complexes by the thousands.[27] As World War II drew to a close, Luke Air Field, for instance, was the largest advanced aviation training school in the world. By 1945, 13,500 pilots received their wings from Luke Air Field. Off-duty white troops in the area found Phoenix to be "the desert's greatest oasis." They packed every obtainable structure, including makeshift accommodations constructed at the Arizona State University (ASU) fairgrounds. Many white soldiers described their military experience in positive terms and remembered the Phoenix community for its warm hospitality. Black soldiers, however, did not benefit from the boom in the defense industry during the early years of the war.[28]

While white workers found jobs in aircraft factories, shipyards, and other defense industries, African Americans were routinely left behind. Defense industries would hire black people only in menial labor positions, even if they were qualified for more skilled jobs. In shipyards, African American women engaged in scaling (cleaning), sweeping, and painting work, and Chinese women performed electrical work, while white women held welding jobs, which were considered to be the easiest positions.[29] Most predominantly white American Federation of Labor (AFL) unions prevented their employers from hiring African American workers who were not members of the labor establishment. The president of North American Aviation articulated the position of many white business and labor leaders of the time, declaring that "regardless of their training as aircraft workers, we will not employ Negroes. It is against our policy."[30] A top oil company official refused to hire African Americans, arguing that the drilling and producing of oil wells was a "white man's job" and was "going to stay that way."[31] The federal government did nothing to discourage these discriminatory practices. In its own training and placement programs, the United States Employment Service (USES) filled "whites only" requests for employers and deferred to the social mores of local communities. Many USES employees themselves believed that African Americans were best suited for custodial labor. In a gross example of institutional racism, the primary USES training facility in Inglewood, California, deemed any African American presence on the streets after dark to be cause for arrest.[32]

African American leaders demanded substantive changes and an end to segregation in the armed services. Discrimination in defense industries found a formidable adversary in A. Philip Randolph, president of the Brotherhood of Sleeping Car Porters. Randolph had been working with a coalition that opposed the government's discriminatory practices. This coalition called upon African Americans to march on Washington in protest of institutional racism in the federal government. The March on Washington Movement (MOWM) became the largest grassroots movement of African Americans in twenty years.[33] The threats of Randolph and the MOWM pressured President Roosevelt to issue Executive Order 8802, creating the Fair Employment Practices Committee (FEPC) in June 1941. The FEPC investigated complaints of job discrimination and tried to arbitrate such disputes. The agency had limited success. Thanks to the federal government and western industrialists who were now compelled to yield to government and private pressures, western unions began to open their doors to African Americans, and black people were able to secure skilled positions in coastal shipyards and factories.[34]

Nonetheless, segregation and racism in the military continued, and officials vigorously resisted demands for change. The black press and leaders like Randolph, however, were undaunted. The black press had long been an outspoken supporter of U.S. participation in the war, while criticizing American racism. On January 31, 1942, the *Pittsburgh Courier* published a letter to Robert Vann, the editor, which had a powerful impact on the course of African American history.[35] In his letter, James C. Thompson of Wichita, Kansas, shared his hope that African Americans "keep defense and victory in the forefront so that we don't lose sight of our fight for true democracy at home."[36] He argued that if the Allied nations evoked the "V for Victory" sign to rally them in opposition to aggression, slavery, and tyranny, then black Americans should embrace the "double V," victory over fascism abroad and victory over white supremacy at home. The *Courier* took Thompson's concept and coined it "Double V" for "Double Victory."[37] The Double V concept and slogan were soon adopted by all of the black press and civil rights leaders and organizations.[38]

The Double V campaign inspired black leaders and organizations to intensify their protests of inequality in the military. Randolph, Walter White of the NAACP, T. Arnold Hill and Lester Granger of the National Urban League (NUL), New York congressman Adam Clayton Powell Jr., Robert Vann, and Mabel K. Staupers of the National Association of Colored Graduate Nurses (NACGN) led the way.[39] Together, with other leaders and organizations, they mobilized African American workers, women's groups, college students, and interracial alliances to resist inequality. When America's leaders were working hard to present the nation as a beacon of freedom and democracy to the world, these leaders forced government and military officials to confront the contradictions inherent in their professed ideals and practices. White supremacy endured throughout the war, but the efforts of black leaders and protest organizations, coupled with the military's need for workers, slowly reduced the pervasiveness of segregation and inequality.[40]

Black soldiers themselves demanded equal treatment, and although most of them attempted to secure equal treatment without breaking military discipline, their dissatisfaction inspired by white malevolence and unequal treatment sometimes aroused heated and violent confrontations with whites. Their efforts included peaceful attempts to desegregate officers' clubs and organized protests of racial discriminatory military justice. For example, over three hundred American sailors were killed by an explosion in Port Chicago north of San Francisco on July 17, 1944. Of the 320 men who lost their lives, 202 were black ammunition loaders. Following the incident, 328 of the surviving black soldiers were relocated to another ship to load ammunition; 258 of the soldiers protested and were summarily arrested. Fifty of the soldiers were cited as leaders of what has come to be known as the Port Chicago Mutiny. They were charged, convicted, and, despite a brief filed in their defense by the NAACP's Thurgood Marshall, sentenced to prison terms as long as fifteen years.[41]

With the number white and black troops increasing on the city's surrounding military bases, Phoenix was inundated with young men looking to spend money, find entertainment, and enlist the companionship of local women during their down time. As historian Philip VanderMeer has argued, "rowdiness became a problem in Phoenix, as in all nearby towns."[42] Race only complicated these conditions, and armed confrontations involving white and black troops erupted often. As the war raged on, black soldiers increasingly responded violently to white admonitions, coercion, and brutality. On one such occasion, off-duty African American soldiers from the 364th Infantry Regiment stationed at Papago Park in Phoenix were involved in a violent incident in a "colored neighborhood" they often visited.[43]

On Thanksgiving night 1942, one of the black soldiers struck a black woman over the head with a bottle following an argument in a Phoenix cafè. An MP attempted to arrest the soldier, but he resisted

with a knife. When the MP shot and wounded the soldier, black servicemen protested. MPs soon rounded up about 150 black soldiers at
random, most of whom had nothing to do with the incident, to return
them to Papago Park. Buses were secured to transport the group, but
before the soldiers could be transported back to base, they became
inflamed and broke ranks when a jeep full of armed blacks appeared.
A "lone shot from somewhere" was fired, according to accounts;
the source of the shot was never determined, but it ignited a riot.[44]
"This does it," an observer shouted, "now all hell will pop." Soldiers
disbursed randomly as handguns, rifles, and high-caliber automatic
weapons furiously "snapped and barked." A "hunt" for everyone
who may have been involved ensued.[45]

Phoenix's law enforcement authorities quickly summoned all available police officers and ordered them to join the MPs in apprehending
the suspects. Twenty-eight blocks were cordoned off and searched.
Several of the "hunted" soldiers hid in the homes of friends in the area.
To "flush them out," the MPs mounted armored personnel carriers.
An anonymous observer later recalled that "they'd roll up in front
of these homes and with the loudspeaker they had on these vehicles,
they'd call on him to surrender. If he didn't come out, they'd start
potting the house with these fifty-caliber machine guns that just made
a hole you could stick your fist through."[46] Before the tumultuous ordeal ended, three men died and eleven were wounded. Most of the 180
men arrested and jailed were soon released, but some of those who
bore arms during the riot were eventually court-martialed and sent
to military prisons. This chapter in Phoenix's history demonstrated
the injustice and brutality with which the military treated its black
soldiers and the commitment of African American soldiers to resist
such treatment.[47]

Despite the many obstacles that stood in his way, in November
1945, at the age of nineteen, Lincoln Ragsdale was commissioned
as a second lieutenant in the U.S. Army Air Corps. Proud of their
son's achievements, his parents drove all the way from Muskogee to
Tuskegee to attend his graduation ceremonies. During their visit to
Alabama, their joy was offset by realities of southern race relations.
As Lincoln recalled, "I was feeling pretty good about the graduation
and so I drove my parents' car, a 1940 Buick, off the base alone one
day and took it to a service station. The attendant was white, and I
asked him to look under the hood and service the car. I guess I must

have sounded arrogant to him. I was a cadet captain, the head of my class, and I was used to barking out orders. He wasn't used to hearing a black man talk like that." [48] Although Ragsdale's pride and burgeoning propensity to "bark out" orders probably offended the attendant on a basic level, his audacity and willingness to challenge white supremacy played a more substantial role in what transpired next. [49]

"I think the attendant called the police because when I pulled away from the station, a police car began to follow me. I picked up speed, and the guys in the police car picked up speed. I turned off on a little road to see if they would still follow me, and they did. I stopped the car, and they stopped, and three men got out of the car." Ragsdale, while "blinded by the pitch darkness of a rainy November night in Alabama, heard the cold steel click of a shotgun being cocked" and a belligerent police officer yelling "let's get that nigger!" They charged Ragsdale, and in seconds "they knocked me down and one of them started kicking me in the head. Reeling and aching from three officers' brutal kicks to my face and body, I was made to lay face down in the thick clay-like mud of a deserted field in the outskirts of Tuskegee, Alabama. The only thing that saved me was [that] it was really muddy, and my face was caked over with mud so [the officers] didn't really hurt me." As one of the officers prepared to fire his shotgun into the overpowered and prone Ragsdale, another one of the policemen said, "Naw, he's got a military uniform on. Let's just scare him." They continued to beat Ragsdale for several more minutes until they apparently tired of the assault. Ragsdale was left alone, beaten and bruised on a muddy back road outside Tuskegee on that dark, rainy November night. The affair left him terrorized and afraid. "I was scared," he remembered, "more scared than I've ever been in my life." At that point in his life, Ragsdale recalled, it was the closet he had ever come to death. [50]

Beaten and bullied, Ragsdale returned to base and remained there for the rest of graduation week. "That is what fear can do to you," he said. "My mother was hysterical when she found out what had happened to me." Still haunted by the "bitter memories" of the lynching of her brother-in-law in Muskogee twenty years earlier, Ragsdale's mother feared for her son's life. [51] Despite being beaten without provocation, Ragsdale was not surprised by the attack. Such an incident, he argued, was commonplace in the Deep South during this era. "We knew that was something to be anticipated," he maintained. "It was typical." [52] What did astonish him, however, was the extent to which the racial injustices of the Deep South extended thousands of miles west to Phoenix, where he was relocated within weeks of his brutal brush with Alabama police officers and death. Ragsdale was not thrilled at the idea of making the move to Phoenix, as he recalled reading an old city directory that proudly promoted Phoenix as "a modern town of 40,000 people, and the best kind of people too. A very small percentage of Mexicans, Negroes or foreigners."[53]

A couple of weeks later, just before Christmas in 1945, Ragsdale was one of eleven Tuskegee graduates assigned to Luke Air Field in Arizona. The group was relocated as a part of an experimental integrated gunnery team. This project was one of several test cases that influenced President Harry S. Truman's desegregation of the U.S. military through Executive Order 9981 in 1948. During World War II, before Luke Air Field was integrated, many African American servicemen had trained at the segregated Fort Huachuca military installation in the southern Arizona Sonoran Desert. Fort Huachuca had the largest concentration of black soldiers in the nation after the army elected in 1942 to establish the U.S. 93rd Infantry Division by combining the 25th, 368th, and 369th regiments with various field companies and battalions. It had been home to the all-black 9th and 10th cavalries, known also as the Buffalo Soldiers, who, after being organized by an act of Congress in July 1866, protected settlers; subdued Mexican revolutionaries, indigenous peoples, outlaw gunfighters, and cattle thieves; and patrolled the U.S.-Mexican border during World War I. During World War II Fort Huachuca was enlarged to quarter fourteen thousand soldiers, who constituted the only all-black division in the U.S. Army. The Buffalo Soldiers had been led by white officers; the 93rd, however, had nearly three hundred African American officers. By December 1942 the 32nd and 33rd companies of the Women's Army Corps (WAC) had joined the men of the 93rd in the Sonoran Desert. These women served as postal clerks, stenographers, switchboard operators, truck drivers, and typists, freeing the men from these duties for combat.[54]

Because he was commissioned after World War II, Ragsdale never had the opportunity to fly a military combat mission, but during his four-month stay at Luke Air Field, he continued to engage a different kind of enemy at home. All of the eleven Tuskegee officers stationed at Luke Air Field were paired off with white roommates. With regard to race relations, "Phoenix was unquestionably the Mississippi of the West," Ragsdale believed. When Ragsdale arrived in the "Mississippi of the West," he was assigned to live with a white captain from the Mississippi of the Deep South. His roommate proved to be unaccommodating and disagreeable. Ragsdale's relationship with his roommate, however, would teach him a great deal about how most white people knew little about black people and how that ignorance often generated faulty perceptions, ill-will, and racist behavior.[55]

Ragsdale recalled that his southern roommate "didn't come to the room until late that first night." When he arrived, he was incredulous. "When he saw me," Ragsdale recounted, "he couldn't believe it. He said, 'Who are you staying with nigger?' I said I was staying with him, and he stormed out of the room. He didn't sleep in the room that night, and he complained to his superiors that I shouldn't be with him; that there were other rooms available. None of us knew about Truman's integration experiment. We were as confused and upset as the white officers. It wasn't until April when I went back to Tuskegee that I learned about the experiment."[56]

Ragsdale never forgot the humiliation he experienced as a black officer at Luke Air Field. White airmen refused to salute him and conspired to harass him throughout his stay. On one occasion, Ragsdale's roommate filled a balloon with water and placed it in Ragsdale's bed. "I didn't notice it when I went to bed," Ragsdale recalled, "but I rolled over on to it and woke up immediately. I was soaked and my bed was soaked. He couldn't do much more harassing than that though. He outranked me, but I was still an officer." Ragsdale's roommate treated him with a modicum of respect only once during his entire stay, immediately after the two had joined together to place first in a target competition. "I was the wingman and we had one other wingman," Ragsdale remembered. "My roommate flew in the middle and led the formation in the competition. After we had shot our bullets and had landed, he was feeling real happy about how well we had done, and he came up to me and slapped me on my back."[57] After two months of living together, Ragsdale and his roommate began exchanging small talk. "He was not an ignorant man by any means," Ragsdale recalled of his roommate, "but he wasn't informed racially. We talked a lot about the [white and black] races. I had never been around white people very much, and he had never been around black people. We were both ignorant and reluctant to get too close."[58]

During one of their conversations, the captain told Ragsdale something that made him "shake his head in disbelief" for the rest of his life. "There was a bathroom where we were living," Ragsdale recalls, "and often when we were showering I'd look up and catch him staring at my body. I wondered why he was staring." After a couple of months the Mississippi native told Ragsdale what had caused him to stare. The captain told Ragsdale that "back in Mississippi, his church and family had told him that all niggers had tails." "He was staring at me to see if I had a tail," Ragsdale declared. "I guess to the white man's mind back then it was only logical: We came from Africa, just like the baboons and monkeys, and we had black skin, just like the baboons and monkeys, and we had kinky hair, just like the baboons and monkeys. So naturally, we had tails, just like the baboons and monkeys."[59]

Ragsdale credited World War II and his tenure in the military for inspiring him to work toward eradicating such ignorance. Whether or not the captain had actually believed that black people had tails mattered less to Ragsdale than the extent to which America had produced racial ideologies that sometimes bordered on the insane. World War II and the Double V campaign propelled Ragsdale into a lifetime of work on behalf of civil and human rights.[60] Lincoln Ragsdale Jr. thought this experience led his father to believe he could do anything. Lincoln Sr. was a trained pilot of the P51, the fastest single-engine airplane in the world at the time. With an engine built by Rolls Royce, it was the largest piston-driven airplane in the world as well. The P51 was the first piston airplane to break the sound barrier at seven hundred miles an hour.[61] To Lincoln Ragsdale, his ability to navigate the P51 was symbolic of the ability of black people to overcome the many adversities they faced.

Ragsdale's ability to serve a white military administration while preparing himself to use his training for his own purposes later on also reveals his early willingness to work with people across race lines in the interest of advancing his own personal agenda and some of the objectives of the larger African American community. He understood that as his military career developed, his service would give him almost instant legitimacy in future business enterprises and political activities. Americans showered respect and almost instant credibility on those who served in the military during World War II, and servicemen who sought political or economic power benefited substantially from having served in the conflict. In fact, Ragsdale stated that it was the military "Tuskegee experience" that gave him direction. "It gave me a whole new self-image," he maintained. He "remembered when we [Tuskegee Airmen] used to walk through black neighborhoods right after the war, and little kids would run up to us and touch our uniforms. 'Mister, can you really fly an airplane?' they'd ask. The Tuskegee Airmen gave blacks a reason to be proud," and it also gave Ragsdale incentive to believe that he could achieve much more.[62]

World War II and the fight to preserve democracy abroad fueled a massive effort by black people in America to make good on the promise of democracy at home. Ragsdale argued that although the attitudes of whites did not change, when the Tuskegee Airmen came back home the attitude of blacks did. "If you're told over and over again that you're not worth anything, and you don't have any contact with the people who are telling you that, then there's no way to disprove what they're saying. You start to believe what they say is true. But the Tuskegee Airmen disproved it, and men like Joe Louis and Jesse Owens disproved it. Those men were signals to our race that we were equal to whites."[63] The collective effort of African Americans culminated in the issuing of Executive Order 8802 by President Roosevelt, the victory over the all-white primary in the Supreme Court's *Smith v. Allwright* ruling in 1944, and the successful campaign led by Mabel K. Staupers to end formal discrimination against black nurses in the military in 1945.[64]

World War II had a significant impact on the African American West. The region's black population grew by 443,000, or 33 percent, during the 1940s. The largest urban regions hosted increases in the African American population ranging from 798 percent in San Francisco to 168 percent in Los Angeles. Increases were not as striking in the Hawaiian Islands and the Southwest, but cities in these areas did witness an increase in the number of black residents.[65] Black Phoenicians saw their numbers surge from 4,263 in 1940 to 5,217 in 1950.[66] The growing populations ushered in social, economic, and political change, and as a result of desegregation in defense industries, employment opportunities increased somewhat as well. Four states— Oklahoma, Texas, Louisiana, and Arkansas—produced the majority of black migrants to the West. Fifty-three percent of the migrants were women, most of whom were married. As historian Quintard Taylor Jr. has indicated, "many migrants followed hot, dusty stretches of U.S. Highways 80 and 60 and Route 66, made famous by the Dust

Bowl migration a decade earlier, across Texas, New Mexico, and Arizona."[67]

Since most hotels and other places of public accommodation were off-limits to African Americans, black migrants shared driving responsibilities and camped on the roadside. Black Americans also relied on the hospitality of other black people, staying in the homes of African Americans throughout their journey in Amarillo, Albuquerque, Flagstaff, and Phoenix. Once black migrants made it to the West Coast, some were finally able to secure skilled work. Executive Order 8802 and the Fair Employment Practices Commission (FEPC) aided some blacks and gave them access to jobs in the region's shipyards and factories. Western African Americans, along with the rest of the nation, celebrated V-E Day in 1945. Their optimism, however, was tempered by the reality of postwar cutbacks.[68]

As World War II drew to a close, western industrialists and the federal government were downsizing war-related production and jobs. Many of the limited economic gains that black westerners had made eroded in the face of postwar reductions. Cities such as Los Angeles, Oakland, and Portland, for example, hosted a large population of out-of-work African Americans. San Francisco and Seattle, on the other hand, suffered no significant economic downturn. In the Southwest, African Americans had virtually no access to skilled jobs, and they continued to work primarily as field laborers or domestics. Both prior to and after World War II, black people in the American West were generally expected to remain subordinated in socioeconomic status. White supremacy and Jim Crow in the American West were most salient in southwestern cities like Phoenix. Though not as rigid, volatile, and capricious, race relations in this region most resembled those of the American South.[69]

The segregation of black students in schools was also pervasive during this period, particularly in the Southwest. Local-option segregation in states like Arizona endured.[70] Acts of violence to keep black people "in their place" during this era occurred often. In the Southwest, fears of black men raping white women ignited the Beaumont, Texas, riot of 1943. During this melee, two African Americans were lynched, over fifty people were injured, and many businesses were looted and set ablaze. Police brutality became an important issue during this period. In the Los Angeles "zoot suit riot" of June 1943, police officers singled out Mexican Americans and African Americans for physical abuse. Dressed in sporty suits, Mexican Americans and Africans Americans were targeted for arrest, beatings, and other forms of persecution at the hands of police officers and off-duty military servicemen. The media, dominated by whites, exacerbated racial tensions by producing coverage of the controversy that bordered on the theatrical. Ultimately, the racist and violent behavior of the police during the 1940s, building upon a long history of racist transgressions by those enforcing the law, gave African Americans and other minorities further reason to distrust law enforcement officers. This set the stage for poor relations between minorities and the police for decades to come.[71]

African American migrants brought with them a race consciousness and a desire for positive change. Pressured by black activists, for example, the California legislature was considering bills to outlaw racial discrimination in workplaces and public accommodation by 1943. In Denver, black protesters eliminated legal segregation in theaters. Victories over job discrimination and Jim Crow were more elusive in the Southwest. In Phoenix, segregation continued to arrest the socioeconomic mobility of African Americans. As oppressive as Jim Crow segregation and racial discrimination in the workplace were, however, the residential segregation that accompanied black western migration often proved to be the most critical problem. In cities like Phoenix, whose prewar African American population had been small, World War II created distinctive neighborhoods marked by low living standards, poor health, and socioeconomic isolation. This "ghettoization" was the result of Euro-American discrimination in the form of "restrictive covenants" that barred the occupation or use of property by certain racial groups.[72]

During World War II few African Americans could secure decent housing as a result of racial marginalization and economic subordination. In 1946 the Federal Housing Administration (FHA), against the protests of the NAACP, financed the construction of homes in residential districts in Arizona that openly discriminated in the sale of real estate properties. FHA officials claimed that it was unconstitutional to force realty agents and contractors to integrate African Americans into white neighborhoods. Black applicants who sought and could afford housing outside predominantly black neighborhoods either were given the run around, flatly rejected, or served with court injunctions. Most black military veterans who relocated to Phoenix also confronted housing shortages. For instance, eighty-five homeless African American veterans were forced to move into an abandoned Civilian Conservation Corps (CCC) camp near South Mountain Park in South Phoenix when they were unable to find affordable housing elsewhere in the city. The circumscription of African American socioeconomic mobility extended to virtually every facet of black life. In 1946, for example, black Phoenician veterans Elihu A. English and Jiles Davis petitioned the Arizona Corporation Commission for permission to start their own taxicab company. The commission predictably rejected their request, arguing that another cab company was not needed, despite the fact that the Phoenix Yellow Cab Company, the only other cab company in the city, refused to transport black people in its cars.[73]

As historian Lawrence de Graaf has argued, "one of the most significant impacts of World War II on African Americans was on their attitudes. Many became more aware of the discrepancies between America's professed ideals and its practices, and of their ability to bring about change. African Americans in the West reflected this increased assertiveness."[74] African Americans were angered by the poor treatment they endured and the lack of opportunities that many of them faced as they endeavored to improve their lives. Black veterans such as the ones who had no choice but to seek refuge in a deserted CCC camp in Phoenix were particularly petulant. The heightened confidence that many of them developed as soldiers, however, and their collective decision to no longer accept unequal treatment were essential to the development of the modern civil rights movement. Black military personnel were particularly affected. Would-be leaders like Ragsdale played a substantial role in the growth of protest organizations. The American West was a participant in a national trend that witnessed the number of NAACP branches triple and its membership increase over eightfold between 1940 and 1946.[75]

The NUL, which Ragsdale would eventually join, also played a critical role in the advancement of African Americans. The many ad hoc black and multiracial organizations that protested various forms of discrimination represent one of the most conspicuous manifestations of wartime activism. Unlike the NAACP, these groups organized marches and picket lines. World War II also sparked an increase in black political participation. Historian Darlene Clark Hine has maintained that one of the most notable "black victories" occurred in Texas, where the NAACP in 1944 successfully petitioned the U.S.

Supreme Court to nullify the all-white primary, which had effectively disenfranchised black voters in Texas.[76]

World War II also influenced white racial attitudes. African Americans, members of the press, and various government officials argued that the war for democracy necessarily involved the destruction of racial barriers. Their efforts often coalesced into unrivaled interracial cooperation. In 1943, for example, activists of various racial and ethnic backgrounds in Los Angeles established the Council on Civic Unity, which championed interracial understanding and contested racial injustice. The group was duplicated in several western cities. In Phoenix, a similar organization would be founded in the late 1940s.[77]

Ultimately, the Double V campaign proved to be bittersweet—sweet because many socioeconomic advances were made; bitter because, despite gains, African Americans continued to be subjected to economic oppression and segregation in schools, places of public accommodation, and residential areas. Military desegregation, even though it was not put into effect until the Korean War, and the development of the civil rights movement were perhaps the most significant advances. The African American vote, America's budding fidelity with emerging nations, and the rise of the civil rights movement facilitated the desegregation of the military. A Communist coup in Czechoslovakia in February 1948 re-ignited tensions between the United States and the Soviet Union. Many leaders in both countries believed a war between the superpowers was imminent. U.S. military leaders, however, were concerned because African Americans had already voiced their opposition to serving yet again in a racially segregated army. In response to President Truman's resuscitation of the draft, A. Philip Randolph once again posed the threat of massive black resistance.[78]

In 1947 Randolph formed the League for Non-violent Civil Disobedience Against Military Segregation, and in 1948, through this organization, he warned America that African Americans would not comply with a racially segregated draft. From his pulpit and seat in the U.S. Congress, the outspoken Adam Clayton Powell Jr. championed Randolph's stance, proclaiming that the U.S. did not have enough jails to accommodate all of the African Americans who would refuse to serve. On June 24, 1948, pressures mounted as the Soviet Union instituted a military blockade on West Berlin. Truman, viewing this as a precursor to war and scrambling to rally support for his reelection campaign, issued Executive Order 9981 desegregating the military. The air force was the first branch of the military and the first federal agency to integrate, five years before the landmark *Brown v. Board of Education* decision. Following the issue of Executive Order 9981, Randolph and Grant Reynolds, cochairs of the League for Nonviolent Civil Disobedience Against Military Segregation, dissolved the organization and canceled all protests against the military and federal government.[79]

If African Americans' successes against segregation in the federal government gave them reason to celebrate, the sobering reality of racial inequality in postwar America gave them pause. When the war came to an end, the 332nd came home to segregated reception centers and local separation stations. There were no New York ticker-tape parades, such as those given in honor of black soldiers who served in World War I. Black soldiers and veterans were not embraced like their white counterparts. All were subjected to the strictures of racial segregation, and many suffered physical abuse at the hands of angry white mobs. There were numerous instances of attacks on black soldiers and their families, particularly in the South.[80]

In Walton County, Georgia, an honorably discharged black soldier was involved in a fight with a white man who had been making sexual advances toward the soldier's wife. The World War II veteran was arrested and jailed without medical attention, while the white assailant was taken to the hospital. Shortly afterward, a mob of whites, enraged at the soldier's defiance, stormed his jail cell and took him to an isolated area where his wife and another African American couple were being held prisoners. All four of them were tortured and brutally lynched. Although the NAACP attempted to intervene and successfully secured a grand jury, no one involved in the lynchings was ever brought to justice.[81]

The impact of World War II on black westerners was considerable. Despite postwar cutbacks and persistent racial inequality, World War II and the industries that were created to support it improved the prospect of good jobs and a freer life for African Americans in the American West. As a result, large numbers of African Americans migrated to the West, increasing black populations in the region. This migration furnished many of the leaders and participants in the region's burgeoning civil rights movement. It also paved the way for African American success in western businesses and politics. World

War II ended unqualified discrimination in some areas, and throughout most of the West, African Americans were no longer relegated
to unskilled labor positions. In southwestern cities such as Phoenix,
however, white supremacy continued to reign, and blacks lagged behind their counterparts in other parts of the West and across the
nation. Over one million black people migrated from the South to
western states, including California, Washington, Colorado, and Arizona, ushering in more vocal black presence in politics.[82] As early
as 1948 African Americans' political power influenced presidential
elections, as both Republicans and Democrats included limited civil
rights measures as part of their agendas. World War II also paved the
way for African American leaders who sometimes greatly influenced
race relations and the course of American history.[83]

In some cases black westerners would achieve national recognition as politicians, lawyers, entertainers, or athletes. Jackie Robinson, for example, who grew up in California and attended the University of California at Los Angeles, was to many people a symbol
of African American progress and potential.[84] Often, however, local
leaders unknown outside of their communities played critical roles
in black progress at the local level. African Americans and Latinos
elected Gus Garcia and George Sutton to the San Antonio, Texas,
school board in 1948.[85] Sutton was the first black elected official in
Texas since the nineteenth century. In Arizona in 1944, Hayzel B.
Daniels and Carl Sims became the first blacks to serve in the state's
legislature. Black Phoenicians organized systematic support networks
to foster social, economic, political, and cultural enhancement. They
established churches to provide spiritual support. Secular institutions
were formed to heighten educational and intellectual development,
improve medical care, and cultivate camaraderie among the black
population.[86]

De facto and de jure segregation limited the mobility of black
Phoenicians and held them within the boundaries of their communities. Although confined, African Americans fought to overcome
educational inequalities, labor problems, and ostracism from the
larger, more economically secure Euro-American population. Simultaneously, black Phoenicians sought to retain their racial and cultural
identity within their own neighborhoods, and though not immune
to class consciousness and sexism, African Americans were able to
flourish within their boundaries while being rendered "second-class"

citizens in the larger community dominated by whites. After World War II, Lincoln and Eleanor Ragsdale would settle permanently in Phoenix and set out almost immediately to improve the status of blacks in Phoenix and to fight black marginalization in the city.[87]

After his stint in the military, Lincoln Ragsdale brought his business, activist, and military background to Phoenix. He knew then that he could succeed and compete in a society that had been telling him that he was "nothing." As a result of his service during World War II, Lincoln, like many black service personnel and their supporters, decided that he was not going back to "business as usual." The personal transformation that Lincoln experienced and the partnership he would form with Eleanor, coupled with the international, national, and regional forces that the war unleashed, helped lay the foundation for the civil rights movement in Phoenix. Lincoln and Eleanor Ragsdale became acquainted with the local community and established themselves as leading entrepreneurs and proponents of racial equality. It did not take long for their presence to be felt. After extensive combat training during World War II, Lincoln Ragsdale, with Eleanor's help, set out to fight three of the most insidious racial problems in Phoenix: school and residential segregation and black Phoenician economic isolation.[88]

# Chapter 3

## Mobilization, Agitation, and Protest

I want to congratulate you for doing your bit to make the world safe for
democracy and unsafe for hypocrisy.

A. Philip Randolph, *Messenger*, December 1, 1948

LINCOLN AND ELEANOR RAGSDALE were among a historic group
of black migrants who moved west in search of opportunity during
World War II. They brought with them tempered optimism, and they
were determined to capitalize on the meager gains made by African
Americans during the war years. The Ragsdales' personal success and
service to the black community during the postwar years placed them
among the most influential leaders in Phoenix. Between 1947 and
1954 their efforts, and the work of other activists, culminated in the
destruction of residential and school segregation in Phoenix.

After Lincoln Ragsdale graduated from Tuskegee and completed
gunnery training at Luke Air Field in 1947, he relocated to nearby
Phoenix. He brought with him a distinguished military record, cunning, ambition, and brashness. One of the first things Ragsdale did
when he settled in the Valley of the Sun was to meet Eleanor Dickey,
the woman who would eventually be regarded by many as the black
"First Lady" of Phoenix. Just before Lincoln was honorably discharged from the military, he was introduced to the recently certified schoolteacher. Eleanor arrived by train near Luke Air Field from
Pennsylvania in 1947. She had arranged to live with her uncle Thomas
Dickey Sr. and his wife, Mayme Dickey, as she began teaching at Dun-

bar Elementary School. In a series of events that had all of the airs of a calculated effort, Thomas Dickey Sr. and Thomas Dickey Jr. collaborated to bring the ambitious young soldier and idealistic young teacher together.[1]

Thomas Dickey Jr., Eleanor's first cousin, had returned to Phoenix in 1946 from his service in the U.S. Army during World War II. He met a young, confident, articulate Lincoln Ragsdale at "one of the many social events given at the home of Fred and Emily Crump Williams" in the city. Dickey and Ragsdale became good friends. Soon afterward, Dickey told Ragsdale that he had a "beautiful cousin coming to town to teach school and showed Lincoln a photo of Eleanor." Ragsdale was impressed by Dickey's description of his cousin and the photograph. He decided to join the matchmaker when he made his way to the train station to receive Eleanor. Ragsdale was at the train station when Eleanor disembarked, and he believed it was "love at first sight." Eleanor thought highly of Lincoln, and the two began a courtship that would soon culminate in marriage.[2]

While Lincoln and Eleanor's relationship deepened, black Phoenicians and African Americans across the nation entered a critical period in their history. Their entry into a new era, marked by the end of World War II and demobilization, brought the reality of white supremacy and racial inequality to the forefront of local and national news.[3] This inequality gave birth to spirited dissent by black and white Phoenicians after World War II. On one such occasion, the Communist Party of America (CPA) responded to this inequality. Stepping into a leadership vacuum created largely by the PUL's and NAACP's reservations about fighting racial inequality in the streets rather than in the courts, the CPA led a protest at a Phoenix Woolworth's store that discriminated against African Americans.[4] On Friday, May 17, 1946, Morris Graham, of the black-owned-and-operated *Arizona Sun*, reported that "a picket line of about 15 Negro and white people marched before the Phoenix Woolworth store protesting its discrimination policies." Woolworth's did not "allow Negroes at its food counter" and did not "hire any Negro clerks." The picketers' signs reminded whites that "Negroes had fought a recent war for democracy, but were denied democracy in their own country." Some proclaimed that their picket line was the "Frontline for Democracy," while others carried signs that included statements such as "Woolworth's Pays Low Wages—Its Workers Are Not Unionized"; "We Fought for Democracy Overseas,

Yet Can't Eat in Woolworth's"; "Arizona Needs Fair Employment Practice Law"; and "Arizona Needs Civil Rights Law." The CPA distributed flyers that called for the end to discrimination at lunch counters; for the hiring of "Negro Girls" as clerks in proportion to the black population; for Woolworth's to allow its workers to unionize; and for new American civil rights laws.[5]

Despite the CPA's hands-on approach, the PUL and the Phoenix branch of the NAACP received much more public attention and support from those who championed change. At a rally at East Lake Park on July 4, 1946, the NAACP again voiced its desire to push for change through the courts. It also verbally criticized the discriminatory practices of Woolworth's and called for civil rights laws in Arizona.[6] The NAACP officially assailed the practices of Woolworth's in a decree that described the NAACP "as protesting the un-American, undemocratic, pro-Fascist actions of the Woolworth store in its policy of not serving meals to Negroes at their lunch counters, notwithstanding they will serve them at the merchandise counters."[7] Months later the PUL protested a sign that read: "This Entrance for Colored," which hung in a modest downtown restaurant. The duplicitous manager of the eatery professed that he "meant no harm by displaying the sign." According to the manager, the sign "was only to inform the colored people that they could come inside and eat, since the custom had been to feed them standing up on the outside for many years."[8]

Although the Servicemen's Readjustment Act of 1944 (the GI Bill) and other postwar opportunities ushered in limited economic gains, racial discrimination continued to arrest the socioeconomic development of black Phoenicians. Police brutality emerged as a serious issue, while racial tensions worsened after the military riot of 1942, a disorder in which tanks and other military weapons were deployed in the city's streets. Organizational and grassroots leaders confronted these persistent problems by reorganizing the PUL and the NAACP. The Phoenix NAACP, under the leadership of James L. Davis, stepped up its campaigns to address racial discrimination. Leaders such as Davis, many of them members of the black professional class, were not always confronted with the harshest indignities that poverty, discrimination, and segregation engendered. Nevertheless, they were affected by the most salient exigencies of white supremacy. Lincoln Ragsdale, for example, always maintained that white people in Phoenix were "just as bigoted" as most whites in the South and that all black

Phoenicians were adversely affected as a result. To him, race relations in Phoenix were not complicated. White supremacy ruled; "they had signs in many places, 'Mexicans and Negroes not welcomed.'" Most black professionals, although they willingly distinguished themselves from poor blacks along class lines, believed that financially successful black people could not rise above the condition of their race. Many believed their success was inextricably linked to the success of the entire black community.[9]

Bradford Luckingham argues that conditions for African Americans in Phoenix following World War II "were generally deplorable." The majority of black Phoenicians lived at or below the poverty line in segregated neighborhoods dotted by substandard housing and economic isolation. The vast majority of black Phoenicians rented their homes or apartments; over 50 percent "resided in dwellings without running water or bathrooms."[10] Unsanitary conditions and inadequate nutrition created acute health concerns, and with the exception of a limited amount of educational attainment, African Americans in Phoenix were generally at the bottom of most socioeconomic indices. Most of these conditions were fostered and intensified by the inability of black people to make inroads in the labor market. African Americans in Phoenix, unlike their counterparts on the West Coast and in other regions of the country, were excluded from white unions until the 1950s.[11]

Despite the obstacles they faced, black Phoenicians continued to develop their own community and institutions, as they had since the second half of the nineteenth century. African Americans in the Valley frequented the Ramona and Westside theaters, where they watched films with all-black casts. Musician and disc jockey Curtis Grey provided music and news of interest to black Phoenicians on the KPHO radio station. The Miss Bronze Arizona pageant proved to be a popular event, and Zeta Phi Beta and Delta Sigma Theta sororities presented "outstanding women" of the community awards and sponsored charitable events. Eleanor Ragsdale became an active member of the Phoenix chapter of Delta Sigma Theta. Fraternities such as Lincoln Ragsdale's own Sigma Pi Phi sponsored local programming and social events. Local leaders and groups worked diligently to enhance the black community's cultural and political awareness.[12]

Occasionally, these individuals and organizations hosted nationally recognized African American leaders. Roy Wilkins, future executive director of the NAACP, visited Phoenix in September 1946. During his stay he was accommodated in the home of local educator Roy Lee and entertained at the Phyllis Wheatley Community Center. Wade Hammond, administrator of the Arizona Voter's League (AVL), often took it upon himself to speak out in defense of black Phoenicians. In return, influential whites occasionally offered him and other blacks political appointments and job opportunities. The fact that such tokenism benefited a relatively small number of middle-class black Phoenicians was not lost on the AVL or the state's largest and most influential black newspaper. The AVL, declared the black-owned *Arizona Sun*, would not "sponsor candidates who practice buying Negro voters with a slice of watermelon and red soda-pops."[13]

Even though black Phoenicians worked to strengthen their community, they labored against the backdrop of socioeconomic isolation and racial discrimination. By the late 1940s black and white activists organized to combat institutional racism. Historian Mary Melcher posits that some whites, "motivated by a deep aversion to segregation, strove to understand racial oppression and identify with the blacks who suffered under it." Though somewhat romantic in her appraisal of whites' motivations, Melcher was more astute in suggesting that whites such as attorney William P. Mahoney Jr. and physician Fred Holmes "could not duplicate the tragic, bitter memories of someone like Ragsdale, yet they were equally determined to challenge segregation in Phoenix."[14]

In 1947 Holmes invited Lewis Wirth, a scholar from the University of Chicago, to speak about race relations. About three hundred Phoenicians, blacks and whites, attended the event. After the lecture, members of the assembly worked to lay the foundation for one of the most progressive organizations in Phoenix history. Their drive culminated in the creation of the GPCCU in 1948.

Modeled after the Los Angeles Council on Civic Unity, founded in 1943, the GPCCU was a middle-class, multiracial organization. The GPCCU hired John Lassoe, a student of Wirth's, to direct the group. Within a year it boasted a membership of more than four hundred people. The GPCCU pledged to "foster and promote understanding" and positive relations among people of various racial, religious, and social backgrounds and to work to eliminate "discrimination in Phoenix and surrounding communities, and to cooperate with local, state, and national groups working toward the same ends." It sought to "achieve these ends by means of education, consultation, cooperative planning and voluntary group action" and by encouraging the "inclusion of the representatives of minority groups in all endeavors having to do with community activities and planning." Few of these groups, however, including the GPCCU, openly challenged restrictive covenants or specific employers and unions.[15]

African American activists Thomasena and J. Eugene Grigsby were among the many blacks who joined the GPCCU, having migrated to Phoenix in 1946, when Eugene accepted a teaching position at the all-black Carver High School. Reactionary white supremacists in Phoenix bemoaned the activities of the Grigsbys and their fellow activists Mahoney and Holmes. Many patrons of Mahoney's law practice opted to take their business elsewhere as a result of his participation in groups such as the NAACP, PUL, and GPCCU. Despite pressure to desert their African American comrades, some whites continued to protest. Mahoney recalled that in 1947, when renowned black vocalist and friend Dorothy Maynor was visiting the Mahoney family, he came face to face with segregation and discrimination. Prior to selecting a restaurant to dine at, Mahoney did "a little checking" and to his surprise learned that all the best restaurants he contacted in Phoenix refused to serve Maynor. Angry and disgusted, Mahoney phoned Holmes in an attempt to locate another prospective restaurant. Cudia's, a restaurant owned by Salvatore P. D. Cudia, was recommended and was described by Holmes as a "fine place." A cantankerous yet progressive person in his own right, Cudia assured Mahoney that "no Ku Klux Klan son-of-a-bitch is going to tell me who I can or cannot serve. Come on out." Mahoney and his guest welcomed the spirited gesture and enjoyed a "delightful dinner featured right in the middle of the dining room." As a result of the dedication displayed by Mahoney and other white progressives, many blacks protested in earnest, side by side with whites. Thomasena Grigsby likens their collaboration to "yeast in bread"; when mixed together, things began to click.[16]

Lincoln and Eleanor Ragsdale joined the GPCCU and the local chapter of the NAACP during the winter of 1948, the same year that President Truman issued Executive Order 9981 desegregating the U.S. military, just as their businesses were being launched. The couple would play an active role in the GPCCU's fight against racial injustice in Phoenix. Friend and fellow activist Herbert Ely became the president of the GPCCU and quickly established a lifelong friendship with the Ragsdales. Ely moved to Arizona because he "wanted to make a contribution" to the field of racial equality in America. "I probably didn't have the guts to move South," he recalled, "but I fell in love with the West, and obviously I saw an opportunity as a young lawyer interested also in providing a good living and providing an opportunity to handle constitutional law cases." The main reason he chose to move to Phoenix, he remembered, "was because Phoenix was at a crossroads in terms of its racial inequality" and "was one step removed" from a typical segregated southern community. "So it was where I wanted to make my mark in that field."[17]

Ely and the Ragsdales objected to segregation in schools, residential areas, housing, and places of public accommodation. "When I came to town," Ely maintained, "north of Van Buren, north of McDowell, blacks could not get into restaurants and could not go into places of public accommodation. Certainly there were very few, if any, hotels or motels of any merit that would allow them in. This needed to be changed. There were other problems, obviously in housing patterns and in employment, but the focus was on public accommodations because that was so patent." Ely wasted little time in becoming involved in the GPCCU and other organizations as well. He "became legal counsel not as an occupation, but as an avocation," for the American Civil Liberties Union (ACLU).

The ACLU, however, was not really involved in discrimination cases. That was primarily the province of the GPCCU, which did not act through legal cases but mainly relied on boycotts and other public pressures. The GPCCU did contribute to important legal actions, however, by soliciting financial and political support of the NAACP's official legal campaigns against segregation. Ely eventually became legal counsel and vice president of the NAACP. Lincoln and Eleanor had a potent ally in Ely, an attorney who specialized in constitutional law and progressive politics.[18]

While Lincoln and Eleanor became involved in the desegregation movement in Phoenix, they also worked hard to lay the foundation for financial success. Lincoln established himself with the money he earned while serving in the military. During his tenure in the service Ragsdale set aside portions of his stipend and sent it to his mother for safekeeping. Indeed, "while in the service," he remembered, "I put as much money into savings as possible—to the extent that I sometimes went without meals or managed on a very meager amount of food—

so that I would have the money to start a business when the time was right."[19]

Once he was discharged, Ragsdale retrieved the money his mother had been placing in a savings account for him. Building upon his family's history in the funeral industry, Lincoln decided to open a mortuary in Phoenix. In the fall of 1947 Lincoln's father and his brother, Hartwell Jr., joined him to lend their support. Their goal was to provide African Americans and Mexican Americans funeral services that were administered professionally and with care. Above all, Lincoln Ragsdale wanted to create a successful business, and he had reason to believe that the Phoenix community offered a unique opportunity. As he saw it, he had found a niche in the Valley that would bring him and his family financial success.[20]

Ragsdale planned to capitalize on the racial segregation that blanketed the city by offering funeral services to those who were refused such service by white businesses. Lincoln Ragsdale Jr. notes that his father "thought he would have the opportunity [to] bury the blacks and the Hispanics in the area, considering it was a segregated society." African Americans and Mexican Americans were the largest minorities in Phoenix, and both groups experienced the damaging effects of racial subjugation. In 1947 there were nearly fifty-two hundred African Americans and sixteen thousand Mexican Americans in Phoenix. Lincoln Ragsdale believed he would have a lock on the patronage of both of these groups and believed that the Phoenix community "was a good market base."[21] The fact that Ragsdale elected to exploit the white supremacist system that discriminated against him and other minorities for financial gain was not lost on him. He was, after all, a member of a long line of businesspeople who benefited from America's racial caste system.

It appears that Ragsdale did not see any potential contradiction between his business practices and his belief in a "color blind" society. He knew he was engaging in an industry that lacked white competition and realized that he would probably reap large amounts of capital in return. This was an issue that many black business leaders dealt with at the time. Many, however, reconciled their position as both exploiter and benefactor by redistributing portions of their income to the black community. This capital, in turn, supported charitable efforts in the black community and antidiscrimination efforts.[22]

Ragsdale's first step in erecting his mortuary was finding and purchasing the land upon which he would build. Using his savings, Ragsdale purchased the land he desired at Eleventh and Jefferson streets in downtown Phoenix. Buying the land, however, was not his toughest challenge. Securing a loan for the building itself was much harder. Whites controlled the local banks, and they routinely denied loans to blacks. Despite his service during World War II, Ragsdale was no exception. As a result, he had a difficult time securing the necessary loans to underwrite his venture. "None of the banks would loan me one red nickel," Ragsdale remembered. He owned the land he needed but did not have the financial support to build anything on it. "He went to all the banks in the area, and they wouldn't give him a loan," Lincoln Jr. recalled. Bank administrators would have him fill out stacks of paperwork without having any intention of lending him the money he needed. His applications were always denied. One banking official went so far as to say that "they'll never give him a loan." It was their policy to "never give a black man a loan." "Eventually he had exhausted all of his opportunities and all [of] his resources." He had no one else to appeal to. Ragsdale was not one to accept racial discrimination and failure. If he was going to be turned away, he would never go quietly. William "Bill" Dickey, Ragsdale's future brother-in-law, stated that "Lincoln Ragsdale was a dynamo, a person with energy." He went back to the last bank that would not finance his mortuary, sat in the lobby, and said, "I'm gonna stay here until you all decide to lend me some money." [23]

Ragsdale did leave the bank eventually, without obtaining a loan. Feeling dejected and humiliated, he wandered out onto the sidewalk adjacent to the bank and stood there for hours "pondering what to do next." A man who worked in a nearby office building walked by Ragsdale several times that day. Each time he noticed a despondent Ragsdale standing on the street corner as if he had no place to go. Finally, on the way back from his lunch, the man stopped and asked Ragsdale why he had been standing in the same spot all day. Ragsdale told him his story. The stranger invited Ragsdale up to his office, which was adjacent to the corner upon which Ragsdale stood. Ragsdale was escorted to the office of E. Harry Herrscher. [24]

Once in Herrscher's office, Ragsdale realized that his new acquaintance was an architect. The Good Samaritan told Ragsdale he empathized with him and shared with him his own struggle to overcome adversity. The Grecian immigrant told Ragsdale that when he came to the United States, he was penniless and hungry. The kindness of a black teacher who took him in, however, saved his life. After a lengthy conversation, the architect agreed to lend Ragsdale $35,000 of his own money in exchange for the contract to build his mortuary. Ragsdale agreed to pay him back over a ten-year period. He would eventually pay him back in five years. Ragsdale had finally obtained his financing and in the process secured the services of a man who proved to be one of Phoenix's premier architects.

Although Ragsdale had purchased the necessary land, secured financing, and obtained an architect, he not yet earned his funeral director's license. Hartwell Jr. came to Phoenix to help construct and administer the mortuary until Lincoln had gone to mortuary school and obtained his license. Hartwell Jr. had already attended mortuary school while Lincoln was in the air corps. Although Hartwell Sr. graduated from Worsham College of Embalming in Chicago, Hartwell Jr. had attended mortuary school in San Francisco. He returned briefly to Oklahoma after completing mortuary school and moved to Phoenix shortly thereafter. When he arrived in Phoenix, Hartwell was a licensed funeral director in California, Oklahoma, and Arizona.[25]

Lincoln and Hartwell worked diligently throughout December 1948 to ensure that the mortuary was completed promptly and opened with flare. During this time Lincoln also proposed marriage to Eleanor, who promptly accepted. They planned to be wed during the spring of 1949. Although Lincoln was extremely pleased with his engagement, he could focus on very little except on the imminent opening of his first "serious" business. Lincoln alerted the local media of the start-up of his new mortuary, and he shared the news with local African American leaders and institutions throughout the black community. On January 7, 1948, the *Arizona Sun* reported that "Arizona's Finest Negro Mortuary" was scheduled to open on January 9, 1948.

The new Ragsdale mortuary was named The Chapel in the Valley. Eleanor Ragsdale recalled that Lincoln phoned her the day before the opening of the mortuary and said, "Miss Dickey, would you come and be one of my hostesses for the opening of my funeral home?" Eleanor "did so gladly." She remembered the opening of The Chapel in the Valley as being one of the most important events in the black community that year and one of the most significant of their lives. When Ragsdale opened his mortuary, black Phoenicians did not simply gain an undertaker, they acquired an institution that would meet multiple needs. Moreover, the Ragsdales created an institution that would enable the couple's activism and upward mobility for the rest of their lives.[26] The *Arizona Sun* noted that the opening of The Chapel in the Valley marked "a great step in this community for Negro people by providing a building and service equal to the best in the country, where a dignified memorial service can be held."[27]

While simultaneously opening The Chapel in the Valley and working toward graduating magna cum laude from the California College of Mortuary Science in Los Angeles, Lincoln Ragsdale followed in the family profession. He became the second member of the third generation of Ragsdales to receive his funeral director's license. Ragsdale was also accepted to ASU, located in the Phoenix suburb of Tempe, where he planned to major in business management. During this time Ragsdale intensified his activism in the city's emerging black freedom struggle. He remembered being "persuaded" by the NAACP to enroll in the all-white Lamson Business School in central Phoenix, rather than ASU, to "integrate it." None of the school's students were black, he recalled, and because the school's "operators were using federal money" to administer it, he and the NAACP believed that the institution was bound by federal law to take steps to diversify its student population. Ragsdale enrolled without incident and completed a certificate program in business administration and income tax in June 1952. His willingness to enroll in Lamson at the behest of the NAACP endeared him to the organization's leaders, and Ragsdale soon found himself well on his way to the top leadership ranks of the organization.[28]

By 1952 Ragsdale had also become a notary public and a licensed commercial pilot. Ragsdale's flying license was extremely valuable to his business and the black community. On July 2, 1948, the *Arizona Sun* announced the Ragsdale mortuary was the first funeral home to furnish airplane service to black Phoenicians. This allowed African Americans, in what was still regarded by most people as an obscure southwestern town, to return the remains of their family members to their hometowns in other states for interment. It also enabled relatives of black Phoenicians in other states to travel to Phoenix to attend funeral services of relatives who had migrated to the Valley. The Ragsdales' charter service flew its first flight to Omaha, Nebraska, on June 29, 1948. Lincoln's schedule was becoming increasingly busy. To assist him and Hartwell Jr. with the administration of the business, Lincoln's brother, Wallace C. Ragsdale, moved to Phoenix at the completion of his degree in mortuary science to assist in the business.[29]

During 1949 the lives of Lincoln Ragsdale and Eleanor Dickey underwent significant changes. Lincoln and Eleanor's courtship culminated in their marriage on May 29, 1949, in The Chapel of the Valley, and thus began a unique partnership characterized by love, productivity, protest, and pragmatism. Eleanor wanted to marry a man who possessed a "pioneering spirit" and someone "who was not boring."[30] She got her wish.

Lincoln and Eleanor's marriage "set in motion events that forever changed the history of the city and state." Their partnership would help secure victories for racial justice in Phoenix, sometimes in advance of national milestones in civil rights.[31] Changes also occurred in The Chapel in the Valley. The transformations had nothing to do with the success of the business. Its standard funeral home functions, charter flight service, meeting rooms for local organizations, and space for community events such as weddings, charitable events, and political gatherings made it an instant community center. Living conditions for the Ragsdales were becoming too strained and congested. Hartwell Jr. had recently married Hazel Williams, expanding the family and bringing another person to live in the chapel's two adjoining apartments. "There were too many people" trying to carve out a living from The Chapel in the Valley, Lincoln Jr. recalled. "They couldn't sustain two families out of the funeral home." To pursue their own dreams and business interests, Hartwell Jr. and Hazel decided to move to San Diego, California. Hartwell Jr. eventually opened his own funeral business, the Anderson-Ragsdale Mortuary.[32]

Lincoln Ragsdale remained in Phoenix and became the sole administrator of The Chapel in the Valley. He moved forward with his plan, which, as he described it, was to "provide service through the funeral industry for the people in the [minority] community." He worked to secure the patronage of African Americans and Mexican Americans. Ragsdale soon discovered that many "Hispanics considered themselves white," however, and that "they patronized the white funeral homes." Religion, rather than race, may have a played a major role in Mexican Americans frequenting white funeral homes. Many of the white funeral homes that they went to may have been administered by Catholics, and inasmuch as most Mexican Americans in Phoenix were Catholic, they may have chosen to use white-owned mortuaries because of their religious beliefs.

Regardless, the market that Ragsdale thought was probably as high as 35 percent of his potential business "dwindled down to about 4 percent." This dynamic, posits Lincoln Jr., "made it much more of a challenge to maintain cash flow in the business." Always looking to tap into a potential source of revenue, Lincoln decided to enter the insurance and real estate market. He secured a license to sell insurance and a real estate broker's license. Ragsdale again targeted the African American and Mexican American communities for his latest ventures. This time, however, African Americans were his primary target group.[33]

Black people continued to migrate to the city from southern states, where many had performed agricultural work. Phoenix's cotton and citrus industries attracted many of these laborers. Ragsdale offered these migrants low-cost burial insurance, which, according to Lincoln Jr., was one of the few "investments in their future they could make."[34] Most black migrants could not afford much in the way of health care, but most managed to save enough money to buy inexpensive insurance policies.

Insurance policies enabled black people to have elegant funeral ceremonies that provided a stark contrast to their spartan lives. That which they could not attain in life, black cultural tradition gave in death. Ragsdale's efforts were not entirely altruistic. He was exploiting the poor economic and social status of migrant labor as well. Ragsdale also saw a void in the housing market for blacks in Phoenix, and he soon entered the real estate business. When he elected to do so, housing opportunities for black Phoenicians were limited to the economically and politically isolated area of South Phoenix.

Some blacks could afford property throughout Phoenix but could not purchase housing in the exclusively white areas that made up most of the city. To help alleviate this problem, in 1946 the Progressive Builders Association, a company owned and operated by black builders J. S. Jones and D. W. Williams, began building affordable, attractive homes on parcels of land extending from Sixteenth to Fourteenth streets between Broadway and Rosier roads in the budding black enclaves of South Phoenix. In 1950 Ragsdale founded the Ragsdale Realty and Insurance Agency. In doing so he planned to capitalize on Phoenix's restricted housing market by offering new opportunities in commerce and real estate to African Americans.[35]

Ragsdale's new enterprises pulled him in many directions, and he soon figured out that he needed help in administering the family businesses. During the first year of the Ragsdales' marriage, Lincoln managed to keep things together. Emily Ragsdale, the youngest child of Lincoln and Eleanor, explained that by her parents' second year as husband and wife, Lincoln needed Eleanor "to come work with him, because he knew that he wouldn't be able to continue the business without her help and support." Eleanor continued to teach for as long as she could, but by the end of 1950 she "ended up coming to work in the mortuary and helping to build the business." "My husband asked me to please come work with him in the business rather than go back to teach," Eleanor recalled. "I was devastated. I loved the work. In fact, I had fun with those first-grade children. Teaching them reading was always my favorite subject, and I would usually have four reading groups, because reading to me was a very intense and important program. I really hated to give it up, but of course I did as he requested." Eleanor obtained her insurance license and was involved in every aspect of the Ragsdale Realty and Insurance Agency.

During this period Eleanor also became pregnant with the couple's first child. Between 1951 and 1957 the Ragsdales would have four children, three girls and one boy. Eleanor referred to them as her "stair-step family," as Elizabeth Estell, Gwendolyn Onlia, Lincoln Johnson Jr., and Emily were born virtually one after the other. Lincoln Sr. was not the only member of the family with a demanding schedule. Eleanor's many obligations placed her at the center of their growing family and their budding enterprises.[36]

Although Lincoln Ragsdale has received the majority of the credit for the family's business acumen and legacy of activism, Eleanor was an influential leader in her own right. Her influence on Lincoln and her ability to tap into specific resources in the black community, particularly resources generated by black women, are difficult to overstate. For example, Eleanor joined the local graduate chapter of the Delta Sigma Theta sorority during the spring of 1948. Founded in 1913, the predominantly black sorority was incorporated in 1930 at Howard University to promote academic excellence and to provide assistance primarily to black individuals, organizations, and institutions that worked for the overall advancement of African American communities. As a member of Phoenix's chapter of Delta Sigma Theta, Eleanor helped raise much-needed funds to help defray the costs of a wide variety of desegregation litigation involving everything from public accommodations to public schools.[37]

Eleanor Ragsdale also became a charter member of the Phoenix chapter of The LINKS, Inc. Founded in 1946 in Philadelphia, The LINKS is a predominantly black organization of female role models, mentors, activists, and volunteers who plan and direct programs to empower young people to become cultured, professional activists in their communities. Through The LINKS, Eleanor was able not only to raise money but also marshal the enthusiastic support of many young African American women who wanted to aid in the black freedom struggle in Phoenix. She also joined the YWCA in 1946 and was quickly named to the organization's board. The YWCA's leadership was eager to solicit the support of an active, professional black woman who would serve as a liaison and goodwill ambassador to the black community, which had recently forced the desegregation of the institution in Phoenix. Eleanor did not concern herself a great deal with why she was appointed to the board. Instead, she used her new position to organize groups of black women, create literacy programs for black youths and adults, speak out in favor of social integration, and create an informal activist coalition of black and white women who sought to end racial segregation in Phoenix.[38]

The organizing efforts and fund-raising capabilities of black women provided the foundation of the civil rights movement. Eleanor, like black women throughout American history, balanced multiple agendas while endeavoring to realize her personal goals and those of her family and community. As early as 1952 she was raising children, administering her family's businesses, participating in Phoenix's surging civil rights movement, supporting institutions such as the Phyllis Wheatley Community Center, and responding to the unique concerns of black women in ways that Lincoln could or perhaps would not. She devoted a great deal of her time negotiating political partnerships with their clients and associates—black churches in Phoenix and across the country and, most important, black women's clubs and voluntary associations.[39]

Eleanor's work in the real estate industry led to the desegregation of one of Phoenix's most discriminatory neighborhoods. With their growing family, wealth, experience in real estate, and connections in the construction industry, Eleanor and Lincoln decided to seek housing outside of the mortuary complex not long after they were married. In 1950 the couple built a duplex at 1110 East Jefferson Street and moved into one of its units. The duplex was located across the street from Phoenix's East Lake Park, a few miles east of downtown Phoenix. Lincoln remembered the area around East Lake Park as "the nicest neighborhood we had in Phoenix that was available to blacks." The Ragsdales lived in the home on East Jefferson Street for a couple of years. During that time Eleanor gave birth to their first child, Elizabeth Estelle, on December 4, 1951. Eleanor became pregnant with their second child, Gwendolyn Onlia, in 1953. That summer, with their ever-expanding family, the Ragsdales decided to sell their home on Jefferson Street in order to purchase a larger one.[40]

The Ragsdales set their sights on a home located at 1606 West Thomas Road in an all-white, well-to-do North Phoenix neighborhood near the city's Encanto Park. The Ragsdales were riding a wave of financial success and opted to reward themselves and their growing family with a larger, more expensive home. Lincoln and Eleanor were faced with a major problem, however, and it had nothing to do with being able to afford the home. African Americans and other racial minorities were barred from the Encanto District, which bordered the historic PalmCroft District, which was also notorious for being an affluent, "whites only" neighborhood.

People of color were banned because realtors and most Encanto residents believed their presence would undermine the community's stability and property values. The Encanto and PalmCroft subdivisions, and the all-white neighborhoods surrounding them, had barred racial minorities for decades. As early as 1924 the Phoenix Real Estate Board (PREB) adopted the new code of ethics of the National Association of Real Estate Boards. The PREB ordered Phoenix realtors to comply with Article 34 of the national code, which stated that they "never be instrumental in introducing into a neighborhood members of any race or nationality, or any individuals detrimental to property values in that neighborhood." Any realtor willing to break this code was subjected to stiff penalties by the association.[41]

Dwight B. Heard, a New England business leader who migrated to Chicago, then on to Phoenix in 1895, played a critical role in establishing the restricted Encanto-PalmCroft neighborhoods. Heard used his Machiavellian entrepreneurial skills to establish the Dwight B. Heard

Investment Company, the most powerful real estate brokerage firm in early Phoenix, and he became a powerful player in the economic, political, and social development of the city. Heard not only operated his real estate business, he also owned the *Arizona Republican*, one of the city's most influential newspapers, and the Bartlett-Heard Land and Cattle Company. Herbert Ely stated that the "newspaper and the business community," led by individuals such as Heard, "were absolutely opposed to the notion" of changing the status quo.[42]

The *Arizona Republican* quickly became "the dominant force in the community," Ely maintained, and it represented white power and privilege from the beginning. Heard wielded his formidable authority in politics and other aspects of Phoenix and Arizonan life. He has been credited with being the driving force behind the construction of Phoenix's Central Avenue Bridge, South Mountain Park, and other landmarks in the city. A friend of President Theodore Roosevelt's, he also played a pivotal role in the construction of the Roosevelt Dam. In addition to being active in the Episcopal Church, the YWCA, and the Boy Scouts of America and a strong benefactor of the University of Arizona, Heard provided land for what is now Phoenix's distinguished Heard Museum.[43]

Heard's PalmCroft subdivision, heralded as "a high-class development" upon completion, was established in 1926 after his company bought eighty acres of land from the estate of James W. Doris. Bound by West McDowell Road, North Fifteenth Avenue, West Thomas Road, and North Seventh Avenue, Heard split the parcel into two forty-acre plats. The eastern forty acres were the first to be developed. Advertisements for PalmCroft asked, "Why is PalmCroft the ideal?" The "contemplated palm bordered winding drives" and its "quiet and clean" location, which was "only five minutes by auto from downtown," made it ideal, the advertisement offered. Costs ranged from $850 to $5,000 for the most opulent homes. Heard affectionately referred to his picturesque PalmCroft home as the "Casa Blanca."[44]

What PalmCroft's brochures did not reveal were the race restrictions that prohibited the sale of property in the subdivision to "those having perceptible strains of Mexican, Spanish, Asiatic, Negro or Indian blood." Indeed, as early as 1924 the PREB, believing that these groups would undermine the community's stability and property values, ordered realtors to deny them access to the PalmCroft properties. The creation of Heard's PalmCroft subdivision helped firmly root an unequal racial hierarchy in Phoenix. It helped relegate black people to the periphery of Phoenix's inner circle of socioeconomic elite by separating African Americans from substantive interactions and dealings with those whites who collectively controlled the means of production and distribution in Phoenix. Even those African Americans who could afford to buy a home in the PalmCroft area were refused.[45]

Heard was instrumental in the economic growth of Phoenix and the surrounding valley and in the introduction and maintenance of racial segregation and white supremacy in Phoenix until well into the second half of the twentieth century. Black Phoenicians were spurned by a restricted neighborhood that housed many of the community's most influential people, a neighborhood that Heard constructed. Heard did little, if anything, to challenge exclusionary practices based on race perpetrated by the PREB and the National Association of Real Estate Boards.

Heard's silence and indifference on the issue of racial segregation were in many ways as detrimental to minorities as the vitriolic words and violent actions of the Ku Klux Klan. Restrictive race policies and the silent support or submission of powerful people like Heard prevented blacks from moving into the PalmCroft subdivision. More important, it kept African Americans out of the pipeline that, in theory, would ultimately lead to substantive economic and political power.[46]

Heard, heralded as "Arizona's greatest citizen" while also being rumored to have been the Exalted Cyclops of the Phoenix chapter of the Ku Klux Klan, may have intentionally established a racially restrictive community and secretly held more covert racial animosities. In fact, the Klan staged rallies, mass meetings, and marches in support of local candidates, most notably for Heard himself, who was a Republican candidate for governor in 1924. Whether Heard was a card-carrying member of the Klan will most likely remain unsubstantiated, but what is certain is that Heard, whether by neglect or design, contributed to the maintenance of a white supremacist system and racial prejudice in Phoenix.[47]

As early as the 1920s, and certainly by the late 1940s, therefore, a large number of Phoenix white male boosters, realtors, political leaders, and business owners, through overt action and tacit compliance, firmly rooted the pillars of racial segregation and caste. Hallie Q. Brown, the noted African American educator and national president of the Federation of Colored Women's Clubs, was compelled to purchase her winter home some four miles east of Phoenix because African Americans were denied access to property in Phoenix's affluent white neighborhoods. This area was marketed as "the first restricted district for colored people ever offered for sale in America."[48]

In response to being segregated from whites residentially, black Phoenicians formed their own neighborhoods. As early as 1911 John E. Lewis, an African American businessman, purchased a building on West Washington Street from Frank Shirley and created the Lewis Apartments. Lewis provided living accommodations for African American migrants who were denied the opportunity to stay in white-owned establishments. Lewis, who was also co-owner of the Fashion Square Barber Shop with Shirley, labeled his lodge a "hotel for colored people," while noting that all the finer hotels and rooming houses catered exclusively to white people. "There are a few cheap places where a colored man can find accommodations," Shirley stated, "but there are many colored men who do not care to patronize such places, both because the accommodations are poor and because of the low class of humanity often met there." Realtor Marshall Shelton subdivided tracts of land on Van Buren Street, and by 1930 he had created an exclusive black amusement park, pool, and dance pavilion. As a result, the two black residential neighborhoods already in existence gradually expanded. One concentration extended southward from Washington Street to Buckeye Road and eastward from Central Avenue to Sixteenth Street. The second was located in southwestern Phoenix in the area bounded by Seventh and Seventeenth avenues, extending from Madison Street to south of Buckeye Road.[49]

Between 1920 and 1950 the majority of black Phoenicians were immigrants from highly segregated sections of the rural South. Many of these newcomers had never shared the same neighborhoods with whites and were not inclined to do so in their new home. Moreover, a large portion of these migrants were poor and did not possess the funds to live anywhere but in the most inexpensive areas of the city, the economically depressed and politically estranged black neighborhoods. Regardless of their financial status, some African Americans simply wished to remain in the black community for ideological and cultural reasons.[50]

During the years 1930 to 1950 socioeconomic conditions in Phoenix deteriorated to the lowest point since Reconstruction, when black residential areas became noted for "illegal games of chance," "illicit drugs," "liquor," and "sexual favors." Many local law enforcement officers labeled African American neighborhoods "notorious dark-towns" or "Nigger Towns" and routinely referred to their low-stakes dice games, an activity that landed many blacks in jail, as "African golf" or "Harlem polo." Black Phoenicians who could afford to leave the "notorious darktowns" were refused mortgages for homes in white neighborhoods by white-owned loan companies for fear of losing licenses and "their white customers." As a former educator, Eleanor Ragsdale was primarily concerned with the inability of black teachers to find standard, affordable housing. "I was absolutely ap-palled at the housing conditions for [black] teachers," she declared. "This was part of my incentive for getting into real estate sales. I was determined to find, list, and sell properties" to black teachers who had difficulty finding homes. Eleanor's efforts made it possible for "many [black] teachers to move out of cubbyhole types of apartments, and rented situations, into their own homes."[51]

Restrictive covenants and racial segregation in the Encanto District and similar neighborhoods found a cunning adversary in Eleanor Ragsdale. She used her knowledge of the real estate market and ex-ploited the underdeveloped color competency of many whites. As a real estate broker, she knew what homes were for sale and their pur-chase price. Eleanor found the home that she and Lincoln wanted to purchase at 1606 West Thomas Road in the restricted Encanto Dis-trict. The home on West Thomas Road, far from the African American enclaves in South Phoenix, came to her attention early. Eleanor was able to enter the home and view it carefully and patiently. The agents who admitted her presumed she was white. As a very fair skinned African American woman who spoke precise English, she was able to view homes that most black people could not. "My mother could have passed for white if she wanted to," Emily Ragsdale posits, "but she was black and would not have done that." Eleanor slipped into the home and never mentioned her race. She simply let the white agents' rigid sense of color and race work against them. Eleanor figured that when she "moved in with her little black children and her black hus-band," they would know that she and her family "were black." The only glimpse Lincoln was able to get of the home was at night as Eleanor drove him down the alley behind the home.[52]

Since Eleanor spent her childhood years in integrated Pennsylvania communities, she had no qualms about the move and becoming the

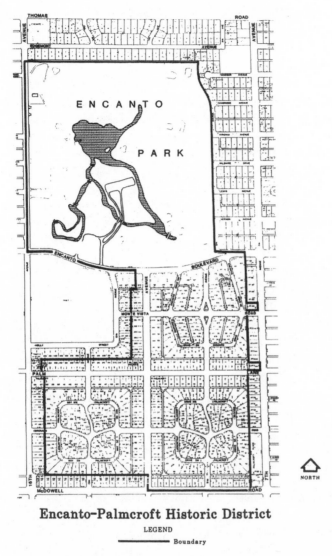

NORTH

## Encanto-Palmcroft Historic District
### LEGEND
———————————— Boundary

PREPARED BY THE PHOENIX HISTORIC PRESERVATION COMMISSION

Original PalmCroft-Encanto District Plat, 1940. *Source*: U.S. Department of the Interior, National Park Service, in Cooperation with the Phoenix Historic Preservation Commission. Encanto-PalmCroft Historic District Publication (National Register of Historic Places Inventory-Nomination Form, Continuation Sheet 81, Item no. 8), 3.

first and only black family to live north of Thomas Road in Phoenix. Lincoln Ragsdale had always lived in segregated communities, and Eleanor was not sure if he was willing and able to make this kind of move. She consulted with him, and he responded by saying that he wanted her to be happy and that she should "go ahead and buy the house if you like it." When she was not permitted to purchase the home, she circumvented the restrictive covenant that barred them. Eleanor had a white friend purchase the home, and when the contract was still in escrow, the friend transferred the title to the Ragsdales. Although they had acquired the house they wanted to buy, their problems were far from over.[53]

When they arrived to move into their new home, Lincoln Ragsdale remembered, the realtors "wouldn't let me in." This was the beginning of a relationship between the neighborhood's residents and the Ragsdales that was fraught with discord. Journalist Lori K. Baker writes that "although the Ragsdales lived in the house for seventeen years and raised four children there, relations with neighbors remained icy at best." "Within a month of their move," three members of a neighborhood "improvement" committee rang the Ragsdales' doorbell. When Eleanor and Lincoln answered, they were greeted by one of their neighbors who told them that "we know you're not going to be happy here." As Eleanor stood there holding Gwendolyn, who was born just weeks earlier, the committee proceeded to offer to buy the Ragsdales' home if the family would be willing to move. The Ragsdales refused to sell.[54]

Following this encounter, the harassment worsened. One morning the family awoke to find the word "nigger" spray painted on their home in "two-foot-high black letters." Lincoln refused to remove the racial epitaph because he "wanted to make sure that the white folks knew where the Nigga lived." Eleanor and Lincoln, through what historian Robin D. G. Kelley describes as "infrapolitics," resisted the guardians of white residential purity. By refusing to remove the racial epitaph on their home, the Ragsdales flaunted their presence in a previously all-white neighborhood. By demonstrating their determination and courage, the Ragsdales transformed the humiliation of white despotism into a declaration of dignity. In the process, they alerted their neighbors of their distinction and self-respect.[55]

The family was terrorized by threatening phone calls: "Move out, nigger," the callers demanded. Harassing Lincoln Ragsdale in partic-

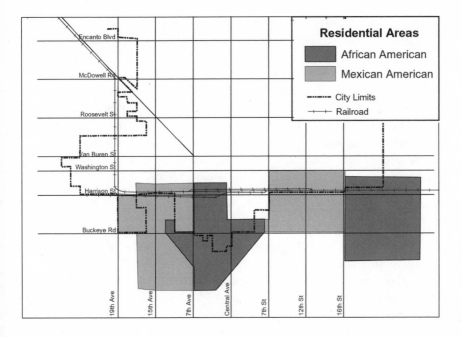

Distribution of black population in
Phoenix, 1940. *Source*: Remy Autz,
Geographic Information Services, City
of Phoenix.

ular appears to have been a rite of passage for new police officers who patrolled the neighborhood. Lincoln was routinely stopped in his Cadillac sedan late in the evening on the way home from work. "I looked suspicious to them," he recalled, "and all I had to do to look suspicious was to be a black man driving a Cadillac. When I'd see the police coming with their lights, I'd get my [evidence] of ownership out and prepare to show it to them, and my driver's license." The police officer would interrogate Ragsdale: "What are you doing here, *boy*? Where are *you* going? It was always *boy*," Ragsdale recalled with a hint of acrimony. "Here were these guys just out of high school calling me '*boy*.'"[56]

Breaking the color barrier in the Encanto District was not enough for Eleanor Ragsdale. She repeated the process that had worked for them in the Encanto District for other black families. "Again, because my mother was light skinned," Lincoln Jr. observed, "she was able to engineer the purchase of homes in white neighborhoods with the intent to resell them to a black person." These black families were often treated poorly by their white neighbors as well, but Eleanor's actions successfully ended the exclusion of black people from Phoenix's most exclusive and influential communities.[57]

Although Eleanor took a leading role in combating racial segregation and injustice, Lincoln was the more outspoken and dynamic of the two. More often than not, Lincoln took on the more visible, official, and traditionally masculine leadership positions within the civil rights establishment. These positions, according to historian Harvard Sitkoff, helped black men regain self-confidence and a sense of manhood usurped by a racist society that was determined to emasculate them. The extent to which Eleanor has received much less attention than Lincoln is perhaps an accurate reflection of the fact that many historians, through the overuse of the "manhood" analogy, have "failed to consider the impact of the movement on black women's consciousness" and to recognize the contributions of women such as Eleanor Ragsdale to the movement.[58]

Like many black women, Eleanor probably accepted secondary roles in an effort to present a "united front to white authorities," and she may have simply deferred to Lincoln, the more aggressive of the two, when aggression and audacity were necessary. Nevertheless, given the nature of patriarchy, she was no doubt relegated to auxiliary roles within the civil rights movement as well. As Anne

Standley posits, "the argument that men were the principal leaders of the civil rights movement is not wholly inaccurate . . . sexism and authoritarian views of leadership prevented women from assuming command of any of the movement organizations." Yet women like Eleanor Ragsdale "exerted enormous influence," both informally as "dedicated participants" and formally as members of organizations such as the NAACP and GPCCU. Whether serving as a primary leader or as an enabler, Eleanor's participation was key.[59]

In addition to desegregating Phoenix's all-white neighborhoods long before the U.S. Congress passed the Fair Housing Act outlawing restrictive covenants in 1968, Eleanor and Lincoln were also instrumental in forcing the desegregation of Phoenix's public secondary schools in 1953 and the city's public elementary schools months before the May 17, 1954, landmark Supreme Court decision, *Brown v. Board of Education*. Unlike in the South, racial segregation at Arizona's colleges and universities has never been a fiercely contested issue. Nevertheless, as early as 1909 many white Phoenicians supported leaders such as Dwight B. Heard, James H. McClintock, H. A. Hughes, and Floyd B. Christy in calling for stricter racial etiquette in Phoenix. In response, Fran Smith, a local black resident, wrote to the *Arizona Republican* in 1915 that "there is more race hatred right here in Phoenix to the square inch than in any city I have lived in."[60]

Campaigns against school segregation occurred during the first decade of the twentieth century. In March 1909 the territorial legislature passed a law permitting school segregation. This move both surprised and angered the black community. The vast majority of whites in the territory supported the measure, with the exception of the governor, Joseph H. Kibbey, who swiftly vetoed it. When he refused to sign the bill and sent it back to the legislature, he attached a memo that characterized the reactionary move as "utterly ridiculous, un-Christian, and inhuman." He stated that "it would be unfair that pupils of the African race should be given accommodations and facilities for a common school education, less effective, less complete, less convenient or less pleasant so far as the accessories of the school and its operations are concerned than those accorded pupils of the white race in the same school district; and the bill in terms contemplates nothing less."[61] Nevertheless, Kibbey did not oppose segregation solely on moral grounds, he opposed it primarily for economic reasons. Kibbey did not agree with allocating additional funds necessary to produce African American schools that were equal in every way to white schools. Many business owners with black and white employees resented spending funds for this purpose as well.

The territorial legislature overrode Kibbey's veto, and segregation became legal on March 17, 1909. Benjamin B. Moeur, chairman of the convention convened in 1910 to draft Arizona's constitution for statehood, angrily bemoaned the antisegregationist rhetoric of Governor Kibbey and his supporters when he stated: "You gentleman can do what you please, but I for one, won't send my children to school with the niggers, and I will fight sending them until I die!" Moeur, whose name is respectfully inscribed on buildings throughout Arizona, was the state's leading advocate for racial separatism, emphatically calling for "complete and total segregation."[62]

William P. Crump, a local African American businessman, responded to the legislation by stating that "from the organization of the territory to the present time the children of all classes of its cosmopolitan citizenship have gone to school together and there has been no friction or trouble of any kind, and as a result there is not a community in America where the relations of the black and white are more amicable and peaceful than Phoenix." Some whites supported the efforts of black Phoenicians, but those who did were in the minority, and although few Arizona districts adopted segregated schools, Phoenix did, linking itself to a long list of American cities that sought to maintain white supremacy by denying black people the opportunity to receive a quality education.[63]

In August 1910 Maricopa County district attorney George Bullard stated that African American residents favored segregation in the schools, indicating to him that their children would not get an even break with whites in integrated schools and that they would be ostracized. In response to this move to segregate black people educationally, the African American community formed delegations led by Crump, J. T. Williams, Lucy B. Craig, and others. Crump disputed Bullard's claim that black people wanted separate facilities. He countered by noting that "98 percent of the African Americans he knew in Phoenix bitterly resented the policy [of segregation]." Crump stated:

> We do not oppose it from any desire for social equality, for
> that is foreign to our thoughts. We fight it because it is a

step backward; because there are not enough colored children here to enable them to establish a fully equipped school; because it is an injustice to take money of all taxpayers to establish ward schools and then force the colored children to walk two miles to school while their property is taxed to provide ward schools for all other children. I wish to deny emphatically that there has been a revulsion of feeling among colored people themselves in favor of segregation. There may be a stray colored person or two who have drifted in from Texas or Arkansas who may have the idea that they would prefer separate schools. This is because they do not know any better.[64]

In rejecting social equality but insisting upon equal protection under the law, Crump and several other black leaders endorsed the philosophy of Booker T. Washington, the most prominent African American leader of the time. Like Washington, Crump supported the idea that in "purely social" matters, black and white Phoenicians could "be as separate as the fingers, yet one as the hand in all things essential to mutual progress." Washington would later visit Phoenix on September 22, 1911. During his stay he met with local black leaders and denounced the desire to seek social integration as "folly." Washington called for hard work and self-discipline, stating that "just in preparation as we learn to dignify labor in this generation, will we lay the foundation on which to rise and grow in what the world calls the higher and more important things in life."[65]

What Washington and Crump did in conceding black people's civil and political subjugation in return for limited economic mobility was to allow white people to use segregation as a means of systematizing discrimination and inequality. Following the teachings of Washington, Crump was able to maintain his position as the axis between the races, but in doing so, he weighted down the boots he so strongly advised the majority of black Phoenicians pull themselves up by. Crump was willing to temporarily accept second-class citizenship, political sterility, and social invisibility in hopes of acquiring economic viability. In spite of African American objections and protests, segregated schools became a reality in Phoenix. In September 1910 sixteen black students were forced to walk two miles across the Southern Pacific and Santa Fe railroad tracks to Douglass High School to study under the instruction of black principal J. T. Williams and black teacher Lucy B. Craig. Undaunted, however, African Americans, and the small group of white people who supported them, continued to organize and develop strategies for countering steps taken to force them into second-class citizenship.[66]

In 1910 Samuel F. Bayless, a local black merchant, filed suit against the segregation of African American children in Douglass High School. Former governor Joseph H. Kibbey represented Bayless as his attorney. Bayless won an injunction that allowed African American children in grades one through four to attend their neighborhood schools. In 1912 the ruling was overturned, and all African American children were forced to attend separate schools. Many whites were undaunted in their opposition to African Americans' opposition to segregated schools. White separatists continued to attack African Americans verbally in the local press, and often their aspersions were paternalistic and threatening in tone. On October 12, 1912, the *Arizona Democrat* wrote: "The Negroes who are responsible for allowing a mass meeting to protest against the segregation law are doing their race a great injury. The colored people in Arizona are nicely treated, and we suggest that they conduct themselves in such a manner that this kindly feeling will continue."[67]

Most black students attended classes in a makeshift building located on the campus of Phoenix Union High School located on Van Buren and First streets in downtown Phoenix. On September 15, 1923, the school was moved to a frame and brick structure at Ninth and Jefferson streets. This site was larger and provided space for athletics, a science room, and a library. On August 18, 1925, the school board passed a resolution to purchase from the city of Phoenix approximately 4.87 acres of land at 415 East Grant Street as a site for a high school for students of the "African race" at a cost of $11,000. On December 21, 1925, Pierson and Johnson, the lowest bidder at about $110,000, was awarded the construction contract for the Colored High School building. The building was completed on September 16, 1926. In 1943 the name of the school was changed from Phoenix Colored High School to the George Washington Carver High School, in honor of the noted African American scientist.[68]

Due to lack of proper funding, Carver High School quickly deteriorated and found itself in terrible condition when new principal W. A. Robinson was hired in 1945. "The high school had no library, no music equipment, no modern home economics, no shop equipment, and no art equipment," Robinson recalled. With regard to athletic equipment, the school possessed only "worn-out parts of football and basketball uniforms marked with the names of other schools in the system." Under Robinson's leadership, Carver improved. He stressed excellence and black pride. Meager improvements in the school's infrastructure brought the school "up somewhere near the legal requirement that a segregated Negro high school be as good as the segregated white schools," Robinson remarked.[69]

Nevertheless, Robinson argued, Carver still offered "a separate but unequal education." Despite its problems, the principal believed, Carver had dedicated, capable, and committed teachers. Although most of its students lacked resources, Carver produced graduates who became successful citizens and leaders in the Phoenix community. Carver became the center of much activity in the black community. Its auditorium offered a community meeting room, while its administrators supervised a number of programs and expositions. Carver provided evening education for adults, and its sports teams were routinely among the top in the state. Even though the school had its positive features, it continued to lack the financial and material resources its white counterparts had and was thus unequal.[70]

Irene McClellan King, a prominent African American teacher and leader in Phoenix's history, migrated with her family to Laveen, Arizona, in 1920. McClellan remembered the injustice of Arizona's educational system and why she and others chose to fight it: "I fought [segregated and unequal] education for years because I resented it. I had to come [a much longer way] to High School in an old Chevy, and the whites had a school bus. They would pass by us and laugh."[71]

Between 1940 and 1950 protests against segregation in schools and public accommodations intensified. In 1945 educator Opal Ellis led five other Phoenix Carver High School students in a sit-in for thirty minutes, on six Sundays in a row, at a coffee shop at Central Avenue and Adams Street that refused to serve blacks. The following year, about fifteen black and white people marched in front of Phoenix's downtown Woolworth's store. The placards they carried brought out the fact that blacks had fought a recent war for democracy but were denied democracy in their own country. Most white Phoenicians were loath to change their outlook or behavior, but black activists were often greeted by a small yet encouraging group of whites who supported their goals. "You're right, keep up the good work," some would shout to black activists who were protesting segregated facilities in downtown Phoenix, while other whites yelled, "Don't worry I won't go in there either," to black activists as they marched on Woolworth's. Much of this activity reflected the initial hope and optimism that marked the postwar years. In 1947, for example, the PUL began sponsoring a Sunday morning broadcast on KOY radio "for the purpose of creating better social and economic conditions for Negroes and better understanding between races."[72]

On October 8, 1948, an interracial group representing the NAACP and other organizations formed a picket line to protest Phoenix's segregated Rialto Theater. Lincoln and Eleanor Ragsdale were among the protesters. This put them at the forefront of the emerging Phoenician movement, and it demonstrated to Phoenicians across race lines that the Ragsdales were not simply concerned with their personal economic well-being but with the overall welfare of the black community. Seven days later, the Ragsdales accompanied renowned actor and vocalist Paul Robeson as he spoke out against racialized social and economic inequality at the Phoenix Union High School auditorium.[73]

Despite opposition, Lincoln and Eleanor Ragsdale supported leaders such as Robeson, and they played key roles in bringing the issue of school desegregation squarely to the forefront of public discourse. In addition to serving in the GPCCU, the couple joined the Arizona Council for Civil Unity (ACCU), a statewide organization modeled after the GPCCU. Both of these groups targeted Phoenix's schools for desegregation in their original 1948 charters. By the winter of 1948 Lincoln and Eleanor Ragsdale had become powerful members of the GPCCU and ACCU. By the spring of 1950 Lincoln had been elected president of the ACCU. Under Lincoln's leadership, the ACCU joined with the GPCCU, NAACP, PUL, and other state and local organizations to press for school desegregation. Lincoln and Eleanor Ragsdale helped raise the first $5,000 the GPCCU needed to sue the state in a heated battle for school integration. Lincoln described the ACCU as a "group that tried to persuade people to do the right thing."[74]

Lincoln and Eleanor Ragsdale were intimately involved in raising money on behalf of the NAACP to challenge school segregation in Phoenix. As chairman of the local NAACP's Legal and Educational Defense Fund, Ragsdale canvassed the community soliciting the community's financial support. In October 1951 he spoke out in favor of a systemic attack on school segregation. That month, at an NAACP mass meeting in the recreational building at East Lake Park, Ragsdale took the stage and "made a fervent plea" to a large crowd to make financial sacrifices in order to give "financial support to the cause; that their children and generations to come may benefit in equal education and opportunities." Ragsdale's appeals resulted in the collection of $3,066.05 that evening. He also secured another $1,180 in pledges.[75]

Tapping into every potential source of financial support, Ragsdale succeeded in persuading legendary conservative politician Barry Goldwater to donate $500 to the city's NAACP to help in the struggle to desegregate Phoenix's schools. Goldwater saw what the Ragsdales were doing in the community and decided to support some of their efforts while seeking their opinion in matters that concerned the "race question." Ironically, the conservative politician "was a great inspiration" to Lincoln and Eleanor, and the three became good friends. Lincoln remembered Goldwater asking "questions about how we felt about certain things and we'd try to give him a very honest appraisal of it." Despite Goldwater's reputation and record as someone who stood in opposition to racial equality and African American rights, Lincoln believed he may have been judged too harshly.[76]

"Goldwater was perceived as being a racist," Ragsdale stated, but he also "helped make Tuskegee Airman Chappie James a four star general while he was in the Senate. Goldwater was the one [who] gave us five hundred dollars to fight for school integration. He was the one that gave another four or five hundred dollars to help save the Urban League when it was closing down. So Goldwater . . . what he said and what he did [sometimes] may [have] been totally different."[77] Goldwater's local independent campaign to be elected on a Charter Government ticket may have had something to do with his interaction with black leaders like the Ragsdales. Goldwater's opponent, the popular Sylvanus "Breezy" Boyer, was the first highly visible black person to run for the Phoenix City Council. Although Boyer posed no serious threat to Goldwater's bid, agreeable collaboration with black leaders certainly did not hurt the conservative politician's career. Goldwater considered himself to be fair and impartial when it came to matters of race, and Lincoln Ragsdale suggested that Goldwater never indicated that he believed that he an Eleanor were inferior because they were black.

"Although Goldwater's future opposition to the 1964 Civil Rights

Act [a law prohibiting discrimination in public accommodations and in employment] had offered reason to suspect his commitment to civil right," historian Peter Iverson argues, "Goldwater contended his vote on the legislation had been dictated by his commitment to state's rights." He became angry when his position on federal intervention in matters regarding African American equality and opportunity was perceived as racist or opportunist. Goldwater's "silence on issues involving race," however, "was interpreted as assent to reactionary white intransigence against long-standing African American grievances." Notwithstanding Goldwater's relationship with Ragsdale, he rarely dealt directly with the small African American community in his home state, and this did not win him favor among many blacks, nor did his inexperience with blacks help him deal effectively with one of the major issues of the era. Moreover, the fact that his Goldwater's Department Store failed to employ any African Americans at the time did not endear him to many black Phoenicians or civil rights activists. [78]

By 1951 Lincoln held important positions in virtually every major civil rights organization in the city, and he and Eleanor had begun to cultivate relationships with some of the most powerful leaders in Phoenix. At the forefront of the civil rights establishment, they operated in the eye of Phoenix's protest storm. In April 1951 Lincoln was elected to the GPCCU board of directors, along with Alberta Garcia, Dr. J. O. Grimes, and Ruth Robbins. Later that year Lincoln and Eleanor, with undisclosed assistance from a small cadre of conservative white leaders such as Goldwater, helped the GPCCU and other civil rights groups successfully lobby the legislature to obtain a statute giving area school boards the option to desegregate voluntarily.

Not surprisingly, the measure lacked teeth and was not easily enforceable. White legislators and Phoenix law enforcement officials were not willing to support the measure. Although most Arizona cities desegregated their schools voluntarily, the Phoenix public school system refused to do so. Lincoln believed that Arizona's educational system and Phoenix's decision to remain segregated were designed to "humiliate" black children and "teach them that they were inferior." The long-term effect of this treatment, Lincoln argued, was to control African Americans and keep them "subservient." If a person is "beaten down and called a nigger often enough," he asserted, "he begins to believe it. This is what the system [in] Arizona did." [79]

Working with black Arizona legislators Hayzel B. Daniels and Carl Sims and whites such as attorneys Herb Ely, Herbert Finn, and William P. Mahoney Jr., the Ragsdales responded to the recalcitrance of the Phoenix public school system by pressuring the Arizona courts into outlawing racial segregation. In June 1952 Daniels, Mahoney, and Finn filed a lawsuit on behalf of plaintiffs Robert B. Phillips Jr., Tolly Williams, and David Clark, three black children seeking admission to Phoenix Union High School. The suit named members of the school's governing board as defendants. Financed by the NAACP, GPCCU, ACCU, and the Ragsdales, the attorneys successfully argued the case against school segregation in the Maricopa County Superior Court. Their arguments were based upon reasoning used in recent California cases that attacked Mexican American school segregation. Lawyers in the California cases argued that the school board's segregation of students on the basis of race was an "unconstitutional delegation of legislative power." In 1953, in a landmark decision, Superior Court Judge Fred C. Struckmeyer handed down the first legal opinion in the United States declaring school segregation unconstitutional. Struckmeyer ruled that Arizona's school segregation laws were invalid because they constituted an unconstitutional delegation of powers by the legislature to subordinate bodies.[80]

Struckmeyer declared that "if the legislation can confer upon the school board the arbitrary power to segregate pupils of African ancestry from pupils of Caucasian ancestry, then the same right must exist to segregate pupils of French, German, Chinese, Spanish, or other ancestry; and if such unlimited and unrestricted power can be exercised on the basis of ancestry, it can be exercised on such a purely whimsical basis as the color of hair, eyes, or for any other reason as pure fancy might dictate." After delivering the decision, Struckmeyer proclaimed that "a half century of intolerance is enough." Eleanor Ragsdale remembered sitting in the courtroom, after participating in a contentious struggle to desegregate the city's education system, the day Struckmeyer rendered his decision. "I felt it was a giant step in the right direction," she recalled.[81] Many Phoenix Union High School board members—including its president, Dr. Trevor G. Brown; Frank Haze Burch; Dr. Norman A. Ross; and Hay Hyde—wanted to appeal the decision. In the end, the group decided that the U.S. Supreme Court would probably outlaw school segregation nationwide and therefore voted to adhere to Struckmeyer's ruling.

Daniels and Finn, aided by a powerful legal precedent and financial help from leaders like the Ragsdales, filed a lawsuit against Wilson Elementary School District in Phoenix in 1953, just months after Struckmeyer's initial ruling. Judge Charles E. Bernstein ruled in this case that segregation in elementary schools was unconstitutional. Like the members of the Phoenix Union High School board, Wilson's board members abided by the court's decision. Largely ignored by historians of the larger movement to desegregate America's schools, Phoenix, in the words of Mahoney, is nothing more than "a footnote" in the historical literature that examines the *Brown v. Board of Education* decision of 1954. The Supreme Court requested a copy of the Phoenix ruling, but failed, inexplicably, to acknowledge the important role it played in the national ruling against segregated schools.[82]

The first casualty of school desegregation was Carver High School. Closed in 1953, its 481 students were directed to schools in their residential zones, primarily Phoenix Union High School and South Mountain High School. Students in Phoenix's elementary schools were also instructed to report to schools in their neighborhoods. Demographics, residential patterns, and economics all contributed to an educational system that was far from integrated. White students remained in predominantly white schools, while minorities found themselves again in underfunded minority neighborhood schools. Some black children ended up in former predominantly Mexican American schools, while some Mexican American children found themselves in former predominantly black schools. Only a small group of black Phoenicians resided in white school precincts. The Ragsdales were among this small group. Elizabeth Ragsdale, in fact, was the first black child to be admitted to previously all-white Clarendon School in Phoenix.[83]

W. A. Robinson, Carver's former principal, had conflicted views about the practicality of school desegregation. He believed that, in principle, integration was in some ways more favorable than the former pattern of complete segregation in the schools. Nonetheless, Robinson argued that Phoenicians maintained "a sort of belief that desegregation can be carried out successfully without greatly disturbing the former pattern of school attendance and teacher employment."[84] Like many African Americans, Robinson also was concerned about the possible negative effects of desegregation in black communities. Segregation allowed blacks to create their own institutions that catered to African Americans in ways that white institutions would or could not. Leaders like Robinson wanted to know how black children would be treated in all-white schools. If desegregation meant that black children would have to learn while being ostracized, mocked, terrorized, beaten, and humiliated, many black people wondered how efficacious such an education would be.[85]

Robinson argued that black students "who were lifted suddenly out of the security of their own schools and placed in a new, uncertain, and insecure situation" would be subjected to undue emotional strains. He offered the example of a recent dance at a newly integrated Phoenix school. "Mixed dancing couples were called off the floor and told that mixed dancing was not permitted," he stated. School officials subsequently decided that the action "should not have been done," but "the harm to a budding friendly acceptance," Robinson asserted, "had been done." He believed that there were "still situations occurring in classrooms and in school activities in both elementary and high schools which the Negro students handle with awkwardness and frustration." One American history textbook, Robinson noted, "still in use in the high school treats Negro slavery in America as a benevolent institution in which Negroes were happy and gay; calls the abolitionists trouble-making meddlers; implies that the Union soldiers were cowards; and completely discredits the Negro legislators and congressmen during Reconstruction. The school libraries have been taking no Negro periodicals or newspapers and have, in most cases, few, if any references favorable to Negroes in America."[86]

Desegregation did little, if anything, to improve the financial condition of schools in black communities. While whites maintained the same neighborhood schools and strong tax bases, black schools had to continue to rely on the support of communities that rested on the brink of poverty. W. A. Robinson did not believe African Americans were ready for desegregation, and he did not lend much support to leaders like Lincoln Ragsdale. Lincoln believed Robinson wanted desegregation to happen eventually, "but the question would be timing; was it the right time for it?" Lincoln stated that in some ways, Robinson believed that Ragsdale and his fellow activists would be "hurting the people more than we'd help them."[87]

The poor treatment that the Ragsdale children received while attending predominantly white schools in the elite north end of the city appeared to confirm Robinson's suspicions. Elizabeth Ragsdale endured countless indignities at the hands of white children at the predominantly white schools she attended. One afternoon she came home from her elementary school and told her mother that someone had called her a "tar baby." Elizabeth surely knew that this was an insult and an attack on her physical appearance. Nevertheless, she asked her mother what that phrase meant. Eleanor was left with the arduous task of having to allay the potentially damaging effects of white supremacist ideology and discrimination. "To soothe Elizabeth," Lori K. Baker writes, Eleanor told her that "tar baby" was a mean-spirited reference to her brown skin and that her skin was, in fact, unique and lovely. Eleanor told her that life was like a flower garden: "You need many colors to make it beautiful." Eleanor's comforting words calmed Elizabeth and helped her as she moved through grade school, but her high school memories proved to be even more bitter. One of a few black children in a predominantly white school, Elizabeth was isolated and was never asked to dance at any school function, such as homecoming or prom.[88]

All of the Ragsdale children suffered from the negative effects of isolation, racial persecution, and their parents' high-profile lives in a plethora of ways. They were on the front lines of their parents' integration efforts, and as a result they felt the sting of white supremacy directly and more often then their peers in Phoenix's predominantly black neighborhoods. The Ragsdale children were regularly denied service and expelled from places of public accommodation near their home. They were not permitted to buy ice cream at the upscale Mary Coyle's ice cream parlor one block east of their home. They often told Lincoln and Eleanor, "They won't sell me a hamburger in there daddy" or "They won't let me have a drink here mommy," after trying in vain to purchase a meal or quench their thirst at a local cafè.

Eleanor worked very hard to not let the racism that surrounded them affect her children. "My mother was very stern about the concept of her children becoming racist or being sensitive about the color issue," Emily Ragsdale recalls. "My mother never allowed my father to use the words black or white around the home. When they talked about [race] issues they said 'B' or 'W'" instead of black or white. Emily Ragsdale argues that her mother and father understood the salience and significance of race and believed it was necessary to break the color line in housing in Phoenix. As a result, "they were forerunners to [integrate] into neighborhoods that blacks were not allowed." It added "extra pressure to us kids," she maintains, but "we didn't really know any different. While living in an overwhelmingly white neighborhood and going to predominantly white schools, we were treated differently, often quite poorly, but we definitely knew that, you know, we were the only ones who looked like us."[89]

Lincoln Jr. believes that after a certain age, the Ragsdale children knew that their harassment and estrangement were a direct result of white racism and their parents' roles as leaders and activists. Sometimes white teachers were hostile to the Ragsdale children because they believed that Lincoln "was doing something that he shouldn't be doing." Lincoln and Eleanor often feared for the safety of their children and instructed them to be extremely careful with whom they chose to speak and interact. For Lincoln Jr., his parents' instructions "don't take candy from strangers" took on added meaning. If he would have taken candy from a stranger, "it might have been the last candy bar I might have eaten," he maintained, not only because he might have been "taken advantage of or molested" but also because "there might have been some other issues" at work. He believed that some of his parents' white enemies might have wanted to poison him in an effort to harm their family and curtail his parents' race work. Lincoln Jr. recalled that he also had to be concerned about his safety because he may have fallen victim to "the Klan, or some other white supremacy group." He was aware that he "might have been a victim" of terrorism and of his father's aggressive, highly visible leadership and his mother's more discrete but uncompromising agitation.[90]

The Ragsdale children were isolated, discriminated against, and in at least one case damaged by the cruel nature of their treatment. Indeed, Lincoln Jr. believes that Elizabeth Ragsdale ultimately paid the price for racial integration and justice with her emotional stability. Her childhood frustrations wrought by racial persecution and social isolation would ultimately lead to her emotional undoing. She would be diagnosed as manic depressive, placed on lithium, and institutionalized by age twenty-seven.

Despite the negative effects of racism in Phoenix and the Ragsdales' race work, Lincoln Jr., Emily, and Gwendolyn Ragsdale believe that their parents' activism was necessary and productive. Each cites the desegregation of Phoenix's restricted neighborhoods and public school system as major milestones in the history of the city and the civil rights movement. Lincoln Jr. has suggested that such achievements are rarely secured without sacrifice and pain. It was important for his parents to take risks in the interest of black progress and prosperity.

Victories against de jure and de facto segregation did not come without a price. At the same time that they were pressuring Phoenix to serve as a major model for school desegregation, the Ragsdales were exposing their family to racially inspired attacks that would weigh heavily on the family's emotional and eventually financial stability.

Despite the Ragsdales' efforts and sacrifices, and although Phoenix established a precedent with its ground-breaking ruling on school desegregation, black Phoenicians continued to experience poor living conditions during the 1950s. Most housing and public facilities continued to be off-limits to blacks, and occupational discrimination remained omnipresent.[91] In an effort to secure national attention to pressure more whites in Phoenix to confront inequality "once the limelight fell on them," Lincoln Ragsdale and Thomasena Grigsby worked to expose the socioeconomic condition of blacks in Phoenix to the entire nation. Grigsby and her husband, J. Eugene, moved to Phoenix in the mid-1940s and quickly became involved in Phoenix's black community and the struggle for racial equality. The Grigsbys were teachers, and both found positions in the city's black schools. Eugene Grigsby, an artist trained by the legendary Hale Woodruff at New York University, would later become a highly celebrated professor of art at ASU. When Phoenix's Carver High School hired Grigsby in 1945, many in the black community were delighted to see him become a member of the school's faculty. "In view of the unusual successes which have been achieved in art circles in America by colored artists and the fine opportunities open to Colored artists both in Commercial and Fine arts," the *Arizona Sun* wrote, "it is gratifying that colored pupils with talent in Phoenix will have the opportunity to study under Mr. J. Eugene Grigsby." Grigsby majored in art and theater staging under Hale Woodruff, one of America's most renowned muralists. A graduate of Morehouse, Grigsby earned his master's of art education at Ohio State University. He also spent a year at the American Artist's School in New York and studied at l'Ecole des Beaux Arts de Marseilles in France.[92]

Supplementing her work with the GPCCU, PUL, and NAACP with editorials in several national black periodicals, Thomasena Grigsby spoke out against injustice in Phoenix. After being asked by Lincoln Ragsdale to comment on the white veterans' cemetery in the Valley in 1952, Grigsby wrote an article for the *Chicago Defender*. In the polemic piece, Grigsby explained how Ragsdale's mortuary was holding the body of Thomas Reed, a black serviceman killed in Korea, whose family wanted him buried with his fellow white veterans in Greenwood Cemetery. Grigsby argued that "to talk about that in Phoenix alone wasn't going to do it. The white newspapers weren't concerned about it particularly. The only thing you could do was to get this out of the community. Remember Phoenix has always been a tourist town. People who come to a tourist town want to feel it's peaceful, restful, etc. If they get the idea that this is going on in Phoenix, they might begin to question this [discrimination]." An editorial in the *Arizona Sun* stated that "Reed was good enough to fight in combat duty alongside white boys, why can't they be buried side by side?"[93] Grigsby's and Ragsdale's campaign on behalf of Reed was successful, as in the end Reed's body was interred in the previously exclusively white veterans' cemetery.

Ragsdale's enlistment of Grigsby and her pen began the slow process of desegregating Phoenix's cemeteries. The desegregation of Phoenix's cemeteries, however, simply contributed to long-standing racial tensions and the poor state of race relations in the city. In Phoenix, declared Ragsdale, "not only is the Negro segregated while alive, but even when he is dead, when he goes to his final resting place, and to the sod. Every cemetery in Phoenix has some form of discrimination, either racial or religious. As one man told us, 'So shall you live. So shall you die. Segregated.'"[94]

Religious leaders also contributed to racial discrimination in the city. The Catholic Church, according to Ragsdale, refused to allow his mortuary to handle any funerals. "The Catholic Church was bitterly opposed to us burying Hispanics," he remembered. "We had one fellow who had lived within a block of the mortuary, a Mexican fellow. The family called us to serve them. We picked up the body, but the priest at the Roman Catholic Immaculate Heart Church on Ninth Street and Washington refused to let us have the services there" until the services were handled by a white-owned mortuary. "Let me repeat this," Ragsdale stated, "the Catholic white priest of the Catholic Mexican church refused to have the services when the body was brought from a black undertaker."[95]

Reactionary white supremacists in Phoenix bemoaned the activities of the Ragsdales and Grigsbys and their fellow activists Mahoney and Holmes. In fact, many local whites boycotted Mahoney's law practice and loudly proclaimed their opposition to his support of civil rights. Despite pressure to desert their African American comrades in struggle, whites like Mahoney continued to protest.[96]

Eleanor Ragsdale and Thomasena Grigsby, like many black women in Phoenix, continued to do a great deal of fund-raising and organizing for the city's major civil rights organizations. They had a tremendous amount of help from black women such as Madge Johnson Copeland. Copeland migrated to Phoenix from Louisiana with her husband, Clarence, in 1919. By the late 1950s she had become a successful entrepreneur, an active participant in the Phoenician movement, and a close friend and ally of Eleanor Ragsdale's. At this time, Phoenix was still "very prejudiced," she recalled, and as a result, African American social and economic mobility continued to be extremely circumscribed.[97] Copeland operated a beauty shop that boasted a large clientele and employed six hairstylists. Black female grassroots activists gathered at Copeland's shop regularly to discuss protest strategies and to devise ways of pooling their resources to assist those who had been fired from a job or who had been evicted from their home by a white person who objected to their agitation. Copeland, in particular, proved to be a skilled grassroots organizer. She, with the help of Eleanor, "routinely brought baskets of food to shut-ins and helped elderly neighbors in her black South Phoenix neighborhood."[98]

Copeland provided shelter and warm meals for soldiers stationed at nearby army air corps installations. After establishing herself as a skilled registrar and active political agent, she eventually became the first permanent deputy county recorder in Arizona, a post she held from 1947 to 1961. A lifelong supporter of the Democratic Party, Copeland devoted much of her life to working for the party, which she believed "really helped the poor." Copeland describes her allegiance in these terms: "I really launched out into the political field because I saw how the Democratic Party would help the poor people. I knew the Republicans were always for the rich, and the Democrats really were down to earth. I worked very hard at registration and on campaigning, anything to help the Democratic Party. They helped the poor, and I'm always for the underdog, someone who really needs it."[99]

Unlike Copeland, Eleanor Ragsdale's political allegiances were more malleable. Eleanor was a registered Democrat throughout the 1950s and 1960s, but by 1970 she switched to the Republican Party "just for the hell of it." She and Lincoln, who was a lifelong Democrat, believed that each party put forth good and bad ideas about improving education, opportunities for small businesses, and advances in health care. Neither party, they believed, demonstrated any substantive concern for the well-being of African Americans. According to Lincoln Ragsdale Jr., his parents wanted to "keep an eye on both parties, and pressure both parties from within to address issues that were important to black people." At a basic level, Eleanor "felt as if one should know both sides of the issues, and one should have literature in their home from both points of view." Eleanor Ragsdale and Madge Copeland, notwithstanding their distinct political points of view, worked together throughout the late 1950s to counter white opposition to desegregation efforts by participating in and funding grassroots activism, such as sit-ins, picket lines, and marches, and philanthropic efforts, such as fund-raisers for displaced blacks and civil rights workers.[100]

For black Phoenicians, World War II and the industries that were created to support it improved the prospect of good jobs and a freer life for them in the American West. Nonetheless, postwar labor reductions exacerbated by racial inequality and discrimination offset the promise of a better life. African Americans continued to migrate to the West, however. Joining other blacks in their move to cities like Phoenix were people such as the Ragsdales, who became participants and eventually leaders in the region's budding civil rights movement. Their activities paved the way for future African American success in business as well as legal and political reform. The Ragsdales infused the black community in Phoenix with a sense of righteous indignation and urgency with regard to race relations. The couple capitalized on the modest gains made by African Americans during World War II and used their personal success to improve their lives while also servicing the black community. In the process, they became one of the most influential black families in the American West. Between 1947 and 1954 their efforts, and the work of many other activists, culminated in the destruction of, among other things, residential and school segregation in Phoenix.[101]

Lincoln Ragsdale was trained to defeat American enemies who threatened freedom and democracy during World War II, but he and Eleanor proved to be quite adept at "shooting down racism" and tyranny at home. Their critical contribution to the black freedom struggle in Phoenix during these years provided the basis for one of the most important court cases in American history, *Brown v. Board of Education*. Between 1947 and 1954 activists in Phoenix propelled the city into a period of progressive organizing highlighted by increased national and international awareness. The cold war cast a shadow over the efforts of black activists and the budding struggle for black freedom. While national and international leaders such as Paul Robeson and W. E. B. DuBois came under attack, local leaders in Phoenix were also affected by the "Red Scare." Progressive but gradualist organizations such as the NAACP and the GPCCU pursued their goals within the ideological and legal constraints of the nation. They were, however, able to secure some major victories. The civil rights movement would soon broaden ideologically and strategically. This transformation would create a more dynamic, intense, and effective challenge to white racism. Lincoln and Eleanor Ragsdale continued to be at the forefront of this movement.[102]

Beginning as early as the late 1950s, these newspapers published editorials that criticized the Ragsdales' roles in leading local civil rights protests. Such tactics were deemed threatening to the power and privilege of the state's white majority. If it was not enough to undermine racial equality and impair black upward mobility by resisting civil rights legislation, during the spring of 1960 the *Phoenix Gazette* published a cartoon with a character called "Hambone" that portrayed a stereotypical black man who embodied illiteracy, irresponsibility, and buffoonery. Phoenix's black press responded to the cartoon by arguing that black people "of all ages and walks of life are violently opposed" to the image and that Hambone "is the very image held by the majority group which prevents the Negro from getting a job, being upgraded, living out of the ghetto, or selecting a restaurant."[3]

Leading Arizona citizens also voiced their opposition to civil rights. In 1960 Governor Paul Fannin called protest marches and sit-ins "un-American." That same year Phoenix residents Gen. Edwin A. Walker of the U.S. Air Force and leading physician Billy Hargis suggested that civil rights agitation was a threat to the foundations of the "American way of life." Prominent Phoenix attorney Merle Hanson proclaimed that neither the Phoenix City Council nor the state legislature had the authority to adopt statutes that would ensure the civil rights of black Phoenicians. By 1960, as the rhetoric and military actions of the United States and Soviet Union escalated the cold war and intensified the "Red Scare," Arizona's Department of Justice began to investigate Phoenix activists and their organizations for Communist infiltration. The hiring of Richard Harris, the *Arizona Republic*'s first black reporter, in December 1960 marked a slight turn in the manner in which the local media addressed issues of racial equality and civil rights. Although Harris often struggled to be heard and treated fairly at the *Republic*, he used his position whenever he could to refute negative images of African Americans and to serve as a liaison between the black community and his white co-workers and administrators.[4]

Despite the "massive resistance" of whites in much of the nation, desegregation often occurred without incident in the Southwest. Activists in Phoenix such as Eleanor and Lincoln Ragsdale, however, still confronted racial discrimination and inequality. De facto segregation emerged as one of the primary obstacles to black social, economic, and political progress in the wake of *Brown*. Specifically, education, housing, and employment continued to pose major problems for black

Phoenicians. By 1960 the African American population in Phoenix reached 20,919, up from 4,263 in 1940. Nevertheless, between 1940 and 1960 the percentage of African Americans in Phoenix decreased from 6.5 to 4.8 percent of the total population. The PUL reported that at least 95 percent of black Phoenicians continued to live south of Van Buren Street in the worst housing areas in the city. "Of the 21,000 Negroes in Phoenix," the organization reported, "19,000 live in 9 of the city's 92 census tracts, with 7 of these south of the Southern Pacific Railroad tracks. Three of these seven tracts contain roughly one-half of the city's Negro population."[5] The Ragsdales were among a handful of middle-class and affluent black families who managed to secure housing in North Phoenix. A Phoenix resident noted that in South Phoenix in 1960, "in almost every instance in education, employment, and housing, the minority-group members are suffering some degree of deprivation, not necessarily civil rights deprivation, but less schooling, less employment, and more crowded housing." These substandard schools, low-paying jobs, and discriminatory real estate patterns led to black isolation and poverty.[6]

Housing opportunities for African Americans increased in Phoenix during the 1950s, but they continued to be restricted primarily to the south side of the city.[7] J. S. Jones and D. W. Williams of the Progressive Builders Association made some progress in building many of the most attractive homes for black Phoenicians on the city's south side, while Jones, Travis Williams (D. W. Williams's son), and real estate magnate Clyde Webb built homes in the Park South subdivision. These homes were marketed primarily to black middle-class and professional people, however. Poor black Phoenicians continued to endure squalid living conditions. "Most blacks were too poor to qualify to buy homes," Webb recalled.[8]

Black churches, as they had often done, continued to play a pivotal role in creating a more inclusive city. Church leaders and other civil rights activists frequently assembled at local churches to organize protests. Tanner Chapel AME Church (an institution that Eleanor's family helped establish and maintain) and the First Institutional Baptist Church, named the First Colored Baptist Church until 1951, provided financial support and leadership training. Dr. Robert B. Phillips and his wife, Louise Phillips, for instance, were members of the First Institutional Baptist Church, where they worked diligently as leaders of the church and the NAACP, particularly in the battles for better housing for minorities and the integration of Phoenix's public schools.[9]

Lincoln and Eleanor, though completely immersed in civil rights activities at the local level, found time to nurture their business interests and political contacts at the national level. During this period the Ragsdales began to work more closely with other leaders who had similar objectives. Thus the 1950s and early 1960s can be thought of as an era of interracial collaboration, marked by the Ragsdales' increasing awareness of the need to build coalitions across racial lines, at both the local and national levels, to fashion a more effective Phoenician movement in a city where black people constituted a fraction of the population. In mid-July 1960 the Ragsdales boarded their Cesna 172 airplane on a trip to cultivate their personal and professional relationships. The *Arizona Sun* reported that the Ragsdales "scanned the U.S. during a three-week business and pleasure sojourn." Their itinerary and hosts included the Illinois State Funeral Directors and Embalming Convention at the Conrad Hilton Hotel in Chicago and a short visit with members of the Dickey family in Cleveland, including Roosevelt Dickey, a member of the Ohio Fair Employment Committee, and Thomas Dickey Jr., Cleveland Urban League director of housing.[10]

The Ragsdales also made stops in Detroit, where they were the guests of Charles S. Diggs Sr., president of the Detroit Mutual Life Assurance Company and father of Congressman Charles S. Diggs Jr. of Michigan; Philadelphia, where they spent time with Eleanor's parents; and Washington DC, where they discussed civil rights and protest strategies with black congressmen, including Diggs and Adam Clayton Powell Jr. of New York, and with white congressional leaders such as John Rhodes and Stewart Udall of Arizona. Before they returned to Phoenix, the Ragsdales visited North Carolina Mutual Insurance Company; William Hale, president-elect of predominantly black Langston University; and A. G. Gaston, president of the Booker T. Washington Life Insurance Company. The following summer Lincoln took to the air again, as he flew to Oklahoma to present the funds for a scholarship that the Langston University Development Foundation offered to undergraduate students.[11]

In August 1960 Lincoln Ragsdale joined black builder J. S. Jones in Tucson as guest speakers at Prince Hall Chapel AME Church and to network with many of the city's black leaders. The members of the church had invited the "two outstanding Phoenix businessmen" to deliver keynote addresses at their annual Men's Day program. Ragsdale's speech was titled "The Businessman's Responsibility to the Community and the Church," while Jones's speech was titled "Opportunities for Negroes in Arizona." Ragsdale argued that it was extremely important for black businessmen to use whatever resources they secured through their entrepreneurial efforts to aid in the socioeconomic advancement of black communities. Black businessmen must funnel a substantial amount of their profits into black institutions such as schools, churches, mutual aid societies, and other business, he maintained, because the capital they channeled into these institutions would subsidize social and political efforts to improve the general welfare of black communities. Although there were some whites who supported black businesses and civil rights activities, African Americans certainly could not depend on most whites to do so. The progress and prosperity of blacks depended on their ability to continue to form partnerships with progressive whites and other people of color, while investing in themselves and each other, and in their ability to remain connected to black churches, perhaps the only wholly autonomous institutions that blacks owned and administered that were not vulnerable to white economic power and authority.[12]

In Phoenix, Lincoln and Eleanor Ragsdale led the way in developing professional and personal relationships across race lines that would ultimately lead to civil rights victories and greater socioeconomic mobility for black Phoenicians. They also played a key role in supporting black institutions, particularly churches, as they served as centers of black insurgency and moral authority throughout the remainder of the civil rights movement. By 1960 Lincoln Ragsdale joined with Rev. George B. Brooks, leader of the Southminister Presbyterian Church, to battle informal racial segregation and black socioeconomic isolation and poverty. Southminister was one of the most powerful black churches and institutions in the city, and the two men forged one of the most colorful and effective tandems during the civil rights era. Ragsdale had become vice president of the Maricopa County branch of the NAACP. Brooks was its president. Like their counterparts who began sitting-in in Wichita, Kansas, in 1958 and in Greensboro, North Carolina, in 1960, the two leaders would eventually attack segregation in places of public accommodation. First, however, the two canvassed Phoenix neighborhoods in an effort to integrate the city's labor force.

Ragsdale and Brooks, representing the local chapter of the NAACP, were able to make good use of community resources and obtain some socioeconomic concessions.[13]

Brooks was born in South Carolina but later moved to New York, where he spent much of his childhood. A religious scholar, Brooks earned degrees from Johnson C. Smith University in North Carolina, New York Theological Seminary, and ASU. He completed his doctoral studies at San Francisco Theological Seminary. Brooks moved to Phoenix in 1953 and "was devastated" at what he found. "I expected something entirely different than [what] I saw," he remembered. Having been reared in South Carolina, Brooks was very familiar with the nature of white supremacy and racism, but he did not expect to find racism and segregation so prevalent in Phoenix. The only difference in racism in the West and in the South was its face. Brooks noted astutely that "in the South you knew where you could go and where you couldn't go. In the West, however, racists were more apt to conceal their contempt for black people." Although "whites only" and "no colored allowed" signs could be found throughout the region, they were not as common as in the South. The racial etiquette in the West was more ambiguous but no less malignant. The ambiguity of western race relations sometimes caught black people like Brooks off-guard when they moved to the region. Brooks claimed he had "become acclimated" to race relations in the South, but as he came west, "I didn't expect some of what I experienced." His expectations were altered quickly. In fact, his notion of a more equal and hospitable American West were challenged before he arrived in Phoenix.[14]

When the minister embarked upon his journey west from the South, he packed what he hoped would be enough food to sustain him during his trip. Brooks knew that African Americans were routinely refused service at places of public accommodation, or reluctantly given the worst facilities and service, and that blacks often placed their lives at risk by attempting to patronize white establishments on long journeys across the country. To avoid the humiliation of Jim Crow segregation and the threat of white violence in white-owned places of public accommodation as he made his way west, Brooks loaded his car with as many provisions as possible. "I had a big box of chicken and all kinds of stuff that I ate as I drove," Brooks recalled. As he approached Phoenix, Brooks eventually exhausted his supply of food and was forced to stop at a white-owned restaurant for a meal. To his utter dismay, he was forced to eat in the kitchen "on a flour barrel." The most disturbing thing about the restaurant was the "little girl who served me." She was a little white girl, he remembered, and "she cried because she had to serve me." It was "dehumanizing," Brooks maintained, "but that's what racism does to people. It dehumanizes them."[15]

When Brooks finally reached Phoenix, he found white supremacy and segregation omnipresent, much like Eleanor and Lincoln Ragsdale had when they arrived. He took little time in dedicating himself to fighting white supremacy and racial inequality. The *Arizona Sun* reported that Brooks blew into Phoenix "somewhat like a tornado." By the winter of 1953 Brooks had established the Southminister Presbyterian Church and was instrumental in the construction of the church's new building in South Phoenix. "From a vacant lot owned by Dr. and Mrs. Robert B. Phillips he developed the first recreational areas for boys and girls" in Phoenix, the *Arizona Sun* wrote. Also "with his guidance," Southminister "created a well baby clinic, to which came most of the babies" in South Phoenix. The *Sun* described him as "not a religious fanatic" but a person who had "deep convictions" while carrying "the atmosphere of Christian service into all his activities."[16]

Brooks took counseling courses at the Veterans Hospital in Phoenix and quickly became one of two black ministers in the city who engaged in "ministerial counseling under the sponsorship of the Maricopa Mental Health Association." His passion for racial reform and his acute leadership skills catapulted him the top ranks of the city's civil rights establishment. In addition to becoming president of the Maricopa Country branch of the NAACP, he became intimately involved with the PUL, Phoenix Ministerial Alliance, Phoenix's Social Actions Committee, the Migrant Ministry Committee of the Phoenix Council of Churches, and the city's Committee on Evangelism. Brooks also added the Phoenix Council of Churches Training Program, Phoenix Memorial Hospital Chaplaincy Committee, Institutional Representative and Neighborhood Commissioner, Boy Scouts, Cub Scouts Master, Arizona Council for Youth and Adult Programs, and the YMCA to his rèsumè. Brooks was active indeed. "In his spare time," the *Arizona Sun* wrote, Brooks was a counselor for the Arizona Presbyterian Synod.[17]

Ragsdale and Brooks met not long after the minister moved to Phoenix. Initially, Ragsdale did not think too highly of Brooks. "I thought [white people] were using him," said Ragsdale. He believed white Phoenicians encouraged Brooks's new assembly as a means of keeping African Americans out of the central Phoenix Presbyterian congregations. Ragsdale's skepticism soon faded. In fact, Brooks was married in 1954, and the ceremony was held at Ragsdale's Chapel in the Valley.[18] After the ceremony, Brooks set out to pay the minister who presided, the organist, and Lincoln and Hartwell Jr.'s limousine and driver. The Ragsdales refused to accept payment for the use of their limousine and driver. "They said you pay us when you come back from your honeymoon," Brooks recalled. He appreciated the gesture, and from that day forward Ragsdale and Brooks became friends and comrades in struggle. Brooks was particularly impressed with Ragsdale's influence and tenacity. "Lincoln, had a lot of connections," Brooks remarked. He also "had a kind of boldness about him, which for some ordinary [black] folk would have been a detriment to them." Like many black Phoenicians, "Lincoln owed the white folks money, being a businessman, but he did not allow that to keep him from doing what he needed to do to affect civil rights in Phoenix."[19]

Ragsdale and Brooks were soon spending many hours at the Ragsdale home discussing possible strategies for attacking white supremacy and racism in Phoenix. Eleanor also participated in their late-night sessions. According to Brooks, "Eleanor was very much an activist as well. She was called upon to contribute her ideas and energy to the movement. She frequently was on the picket line with her children, and she never complained. She was an activist." Lincoln and Eleanor "were tremendous," he declared. "I remember that on many days, the three of us would just be moving around in the streets talking to people about discrimination and racism in Phoenix." The Ragsdales risked quite a bit by being so outspoken, Brooks believed, because the city's white elite were watching them, especially Lincoln, and they had the power to hurt him financially. "He was a businessman, he needed his business, I was a preacher and my congregation came to church whether I was there or not, but Lincoln was a businessman. He owed money to powerful white bankers, and he had a great deal at stake."[20]

Despite being vulnerable to white financiers, Lincoln Ragsdale condemned racism and segregation with a particular disdain for white racial chauvinism and circumlocution. He was direct, audacious, and aggressive. Striving "to move into every aspect of economic life" in

Phoenix, the two leaders targeted the powerful Valley National Bank, the predecessor of Bank One of Arizona, for protest. "We had to pick out someplace to start the fight," said Ragsdale, "so you had to figure out who will you knock off first, the king or the subjects? We figured it was best to start at the top." During the fall of 1962 the fiery Ragsdale and the devout Brooks scheduled a meeting with Jim Patrick, president of Valley National Bank. Like all of Phoenix's banks, Valley National employed no black tellers at the time. At that meeting, the two leaders demanded that the bank cease its discriminatory practices and hire qualified African Americans for something other than unskilled positions. Patrick and the bank's officials refused. Ragsdale and Brooks devised an alternative plan and scheduled another meeting. Brooks remembered the meeting well: "Lincoln was brash, nasty . . . he would back him [Patrick] up into a corner and I was the good guy. I would pull him out. Then he would get belligerent again, and Lincoln would back him up again, and I would pull him out . . . that's what you call creative conflict. We didn't know it, but that's what we did." Patrick would say something like, "What can I do for *you people?*" That's when Ragsdale tried to scare Patrick. He ranted and raved, and at one point he pounded Patrick's desk with his fist in anger. "I remember hitting [Patrick's] desk so hard I thought I heard it crack," recalled Ragsdale. Brooks reports that Ragsdale would say something like, "You know goddamn well what we want," while turning to Brooks and complaining loudly that Patrick was "a bigot, a Hitler, a hater." Brooks said he would then ask Ragsdale to leave and cool down, while he would continue from a considerably stronger position.[21]

When "creative conflict" failed, Ragsdale returned to his naked aggression during the meeting. Forceful and resolute, he threatened to chain himself and other protestors to the Valley National Bank and bring five hundred people to the institution in a mass protest. Protesters had already formed long lines at the bank windows. Others clogged up lines in the bank "requesting seventy-five pennies as partial change for a dollar" while singing "We Shall Overcome." Nevertheless, Brooks thought to himself, "Oh my God, where are we going to get five hundred people?" Ragsdale's threats, coupled with the protesting that was being waged in the lobby of the bank and on the street, were more than Patrick was prepared to endure. "Patrick," said Brooks, "would just be livid." The strategy worked, and a mass protest involving five hundred people was not necessary. "It worked," argued Ragsdale, because "white people weren't used to belligerent Negroes." Soon after this meeting in 1962, Patrick hired Wilbur Hankins as the institution's first African American teller. Ragsdale and Brooks squared off with many employers in Phoenix, imploring them to hire African Americans. Not every company proved to be as easy to convince as the Valley National Bank. Phoenix's technology giant, Motorola, was steadfast in its refusal to hire blacks. Motorola operated three major plants in the Valley and employed thousands of white Phoenicians. The company's refusal to hire black Phoenicians constituted a major barrier to black advancement in a city that was becoming increasingly dependent on a technology-driven economy.[22]

On February 3, 1962, some of Phoenix's leading activists, including Ragsdale, Brooks, Hayzel B. Daniels, Herbert Ely, PUL executive director Charles F. Harlins, radio broadcaster Grace Gil-Olivarez, and businessman and former migrant worker Manuel Pena, testified before the U.S. Commission on Civil Rights in downtown Phoenix on de facto segregation and racial discrimination in the city. Created in 1957 by President Eisenhower and chaired by John A. Hannah, president of Michigan State University, the commission "served as a civil rights watchdog, with no real enforcement powers, but with considerable influence on public opinion." Hannah, who championed civil rights, came to Phoenix on the heels of his state passing one of the most progressive state constitutions in the nation. He told the city's leaders that he hoped that his experience in Michigan would help him evaluate racial discrimination in Phoenix. Hannah believed that "of all the Constitutions in the fifty states," the Michigan Constitution does "more for civil rights than has been done in any state Constitution." He cited George Romney, former governor of Michigan, who declared that Michigan's constitution "contains the most complete, the most direct and clearest expression of state policy guaranteeing human rights of any state Constitution in the country."[23]

Brooks's testimony was direct. He announced that

> racism and segregation was [sic] fiendish and undemocratic. No doubt about it, segregation has made the Negro poor. It has forced him into the slum areas, into bad schools, it's cut him off from better jobs. Segregation has built a wall of poverty around the Negro, and psychologically it's done

worse than that. There's hardly any mixing of black and white Phoenicians. In most parts of the city, a white boy can get into his early teens before he sees many Negroes. Then the ones he sees are likely to be busboys, janitors, street sweepers. He never sees educated Negroes holding responsible jobs. He isn't going to like and talk about social equality. This is bad for the Caucasian, no matter what the bigots say, but it's even worse for the Negro. He grows up in a segregated or near-segregated neighborhood. That's all he knows; segregation. He accepts it, takes if for granted in housing, employment, schools. He's conditioned to it, and for a lot of Negroes, it's a crutch, a defense against the world.[24]

In a feverish tone, Brooks declared that "the greatest problem facing the Negro in Phoenix is that of employment discrimination." There were perhaps three reasons the problem existed, he posited:

First, there is a problem of skills which are demanded by industry. Most Negroes who are seeking employment must do so without adequate technical knowledge or experience. There are certain firms that have consistently refused to hire Negroes, and this is the second point, on the pretense that the community is not yet ready for integration in the work force. Though there are some eight major firms doing business with the federal government in this area, and hiring more than 15,000 people, less than 350 of them are Negroes. The retail and service industries hire Negroes for the most part in custodial positions only. With respect to banks, insurance companies, and to a lesser extent department stores, there are few Negroes employed in anything other than menial capacities. If the absence of Negroes on such jobs is due to racial discrimination, as at least one man has charged, it is a clear violation of Arizona State Law and the Fourteenth Amendment.[25]

When Lincoln Ragsdale addressed the commission in the New Federal Building on February 3, 1962, his intent was to appeal to the commissioners' consciences and democratic principles. As he prepared to give his formal testimony, Ragsdale stated to a group of bystanders that "if we can get the political leaders, maybe even our mayor, just to say that something is wrong, 'let us do something about it; let us investigate it, at least, and recommend that we treat all Americans, all citizens of Phoenix alike, in opportunity of jobs, working conditions, and everything else,' I think that Phoenix would change abruptly." Ragsdale was confident that the evidence he brought to bear on the issue of racial discrimination and the black socioeconomic suffering it created was copious and damning. He was especially prepared to discuss the improper actions of realtors in Phoenix and to demonstrate the extent to which discrimination in the housing market undermined black upward mobility and the spirit of American documents of freedom.

When Ragsdale took the floor to address the commission, he was intense and articulate:

> With regard to housing, the significant thing to point out is that 90 percent of all the Negroes living in Phoenix live south of Van Buren Street. It is also important to note that 97 percent of all Negroes live within a radius of one mile of the railroad tracks or the riverbed. Let's take one report, census track 105. We have 4,000 Negroes that live in this area. 73% of these units are substandard, 34% of them are dilapidated; unfit for human occupancy. What has our industry done about housing for Negroes? Let's look at it. 31,000 new homes have been built by three builders in the North East Section of Phoenix, and the North West Section of Phoenix. Not one of these new houses, not one, has been sold to a Negro when it was new. Not one![26]

At this juncture, Hannah asked Ragsdale if it would "be your judgement based on your experience that there are substantial numbers of Negroes now residing in the area of concentration who could afford to purchase housing outside their area if they had equal opportunity to obtain it?" Ragsdale responded that "over 640 have qualified for and have been given FHA loans through the local office here in Phoenix. So we have 640 people to my knowledge. When black Phoenicians arrive at the FHA office in Phoenix, however, officials discovered they were Negroes and said, 'We are very sorry. There must be some mistake. We cannot make this loan.'" Other lending institutions were more direct, Ragsdale testified. He told Hannah that one lender notified the civil rights leader that his company "cannot salt and pepper the community."[27]

The few white Phoenicians who were willing to sell their homes to African Americans were ridiculed and harassed by other white people. When one white seller decided to sell his home to an African American, Ragsdale reported, "a suit was issued against him by a white real estate broker." The suit languished in court for two years. Eventually, the lawsuit was thrown out, but not without having inflicted unwarranted "mental anguish" on the seller and the buyer of the home. Herbert Ely's testimony supported Ragsdale's allegations. "Private housing in Phoenix is virtually totally restricted, particularly to Negroes in the North part of town," he stated. "If a man is financially able to buy a home in an area, then that's all that's necessary. As Mr. Ragsdale pointed out, there are 640 Negroes that have recently qualified for FHA mortgages, and I state to this Commission that with rare exception, none of them could secure such a house in the North part of town." The commission's final report on the hearing revealed what most of Phoenix's activists had already known: the city was one of the most segregated in the nation, and black Phoenicians were among the most marginalized African Americans in the nation. The commission observed that the twenty largest stores in downtown Phoenix employed a total of only twenty blacks. Only nine blacks worked in supervisory positions in the city's twelve school districts, and the four hundred–member Phoenix Police Department had only five African Americans. The commission recommended that a public accommodations statute be implemented in the city and that the Office of the Attorney General be given broader powers to punish those who violated the law, based upon recommendations made by the Arizona Civil Rights Commission. The fight for a public accommodations law in Phoenix would prove to be a heated and confrontational struggle.[28]

While activists took their concerns to the federal government, Lincoln Ragsdale continued to square off as the "bad guy" in negotiations with white leaders. He, with the help of Brooks, Eleanor, and other leaders, decided to assault the discriminatory practices of Motorola and other large companies such as Sperry Rand and General Electric. In his estimation, job discrimination was more damaging to minorities than segregation. "How can you go into places to eat or sleep when you don't have any money?" Ragsdale asked.[29] As early as 1960 he, Brooks, and other NAACP leaders started taking carloads of people to employers throughout Phoenix to apply for jobs. To demonstrate their resolve, hundreds applied. Hundreds were rejected. Many employers "were cordial but firm," Brooks remembered. "They told us, 'We are not going to hire any black folks here. We must give these jobs to parents of white engineers we want to recruit.' " [30]

The Ragsdales and Brooks were incensed. They immediately marshaled their resources to stage an all-out assault on Motorola's practices. The three leaders had observed the company's actions for months, and they decided, along with the NAACP, that it was time to act. The NAACP sent a delegation to Motorola to discuss the company's poor minority hiring record and scheduled a meeting with the president of Motorola. Black homebuilder and NAACP official Travis Williams accompanied Lincoln Ragsdale and George Brooks to the meeting. During the exchange, Williams recalled, the two leaders were cantankerous, indignant, and assertive. Initially, the group attempted to be "diplomatic." They argued that Motorola was "licensed to do business in the state of Arizona," and as Arizona residents, black Phoenicians deserved equal opportunities to compete for employment in the corporation. "We do not want to be left out," the leaders stated. Motorola's president said that the company did not intentionally leave anyone out and that it employed minorities. Soon after the president made this comment, Williams recalled, the group noticed an American Indian woman walking by the conference room. Ragsdale stood up, looked at the woman passing by, then turned back to the president and said that of the few minorities he saw, none were black. "In fact," Ragsdale quipped, "it's no wonder you don't have any blacks here, you don't know what a black person is." [31]

The group left the meeting with no concessions. It was not until Brooks was slipped a memo from the Maricopa County Welfare Department in 1962 that the leaders acquired the smoking gun they needed. The memo noted that a large electronics firm was looking for "a young woman on welfare, eighteen years of age, with a high school diploma, who must be white." Rumors had already been circulating throughout the black community that the Welfare Department was practicing blatant discrimination. Until the NAACP secured the memo, however, the rumors could not be substantiated. The Ragsdales and Brooks, with the help of Herbert Ely, investigated the matter further and determined that the NAACP had found a verifiable case of racial discrimination. The state-run employment office was, in fact, conspiring with private industry to deny black Phoenicians employment. Lincoln Ragsdale, Brooks, Ely, and the NAACP called for a meeting with the state attorney general, Robert Pickrell, and secured the full attention of the Phoenix media. At the meeting, Brooks accused the Welfare Department of "being in collusion with firms to deny black people jobs." "I was good that day," Brooks reminisced. "I got quoted." The publicity resulted in Motorola's capitulation. Soon it hired its first African American employee on the manufacturing line.[32]

Ragsdale and Brooks's tag-team efforts worked enough to open the minds, if not the wallets, of a few business owners, and it earned the two leaders, and the NAACP, respect from progressive Phoenicians—and contempt from many white people. Improvement in the overall condition of the black community was limited, however. Most city officials and white business leaders rejected urban renewal and similar federal assistance programs. The majority of influential white Phoenicians encouraged private industry, rather than government, to assist struggling minority communities. Adequate support was not forthcoming from either. With a poor economic base, black Phoenician communities continued to suffer. While activists began to make inroads in employment, many began to set their sights on eradicating segregation in public facilities. Historian Mary Melcher writes that Barbara Callahan of Phoenix's Interdenominational Ministerial Alliance organized a number of sit-ins during the summer of 1960. The protestors were inspired to act by Ezell Blair Jr., Joseph McNeil, Francis McCain, and David Richmond, black students at North Carolina Agricultural and Technical College who, on February 1, 1960, ignited the national sit-in movement at a Woolworth's lunch counter in Greensboro. The NAACP also participated in the demonstrations at Phoenix's businesses. Inspired by the events taking place in the South, young black Phoenicians followed their southern counterparts lead and staged sit-ins at lunch counters throughout the city. Many businesses did not resist. They no doubt wanted to avoid the sort of mass hysteria that had overtaken many southern states. On the other hand, some businesses flatly refused to serve African Americans.[33]

Lincoln Ragsdale stated that many of Phoenix's white restaurateurs would not even allow blacks to enter through the back of their establishments to eat or to use the bathroom. "The only bathrooms you could use downtown were [in] Phoenix City Hall, the bus station, the train station and the County Building," he recalled. Clovis Campbell

Sr., an understudy of Ragsdale's, was much more indignant in his rec-ollections. African Americans were frequently greeted by signs in local eateries proclaiming the "right to refuse anybody service," Campbell mused. "Well, you know what that meant," he exclaimed: "Nigga don't come in here."[34]

Campbell played a pivotal role in the civil rights movement in Phoenix. Born in Elizabeth, Louisiana, in 1931, he migrated to Phoe-nix in 1945. After a brief stint in the military, Campbell returned to Phoenix in 1954 and began a long career in politics, community ac-tivism, journalism, and newspaper publishing. He worked as a colum-nist for the *Arizona Sun* during the early 1960s and was elected to the Arizona state legislature in 1962. He ran a successful campaign for a seat in the state senate in 1966, becoming the first African American in Arizona to serve in this capacity. Active in the Phoenix chapter of the NAACP, Campbell protested discrimination and spoke out against racial injustice in regular editorials in the *Arizona Sun*. Campbell left the *Arizona Sun* and purchased the ailing *Arizona Informant* in 1968. Under his direction, the *Arizona Informant* quickly became the largest African American–owned newspaper in the state.[35]

By 1962 Lincoln Ragsdale was a veteran member of the Phoenician movement, and in this capacity he served as a mentor to Campbell, who worked with the Ragsdales to end segregation in education and public accommodations. Alongside the Ragsdales, Brooks, and other activists, Campbell attacked the discriminatory practices of the city's white power structure. During the early to mid-1960s, he argued, most activists were not militant enough in their approach to force the city's white leadership to address the needs of black Phoenicians. Campbell's rise, however, marked the earliest stage in the emergence of black leaders who were less concerned with integration than they were with equal opportunity, black pride, and black self-determination. Campbell relished his role as a progressive leader whose political phi-losophy was almost black nationalist in orientation. In the same way that Eleanor Ragsdale and George Brooks benefited from Lincoln Ragsdale's arrogance and audacity, Lincoln Ragsdale would benefit from Campbell's temerity and black nationalist leanings. Ragsdale prided himself on rocking the boat and calling attention to racial in-justice. Campbell, on the other hand, declared that "I didn't believe in rocking the boat, I believed in turning it over." Campbell distin-guished himself by urging black Phoenicians to open and support their own businesses, especially restaurants, and to funnel their resources back into the black community, which needed capital and financial cohesion. He also did so to encourage black Phoenicians to avoid the humiliation of being denied access to establishments outside of the black community, especially restaurants, which he considered to be among the most discriminatory places of public accommodation in the Phoenix area.[36]

William Dickey, Eleanor Ragsdale's younger brother, stated that two businesses were especially mean-spirited to black people. The Citrus Drugstore, located at Sixteenth and Van Buren streets, refused to serve blacks, and its owner, one of the most stubborn and antagonistic white proprietors in the city, often chased groups of Phoenician sit-in protestors away while bellowing racial epitaphs and issuing threats of violence. Rather than succumb to media and activist pressure to desegregate his lunch counter, the owner removed the stools altogether. At the Woolworth's store in downtown Phoenix, Dickey recalled, "you couldn't sit at the counter and have a Coke." The NAACP in Phoenix went on the offensive. Led by Eleanor and Lincoln Ragsdale, Campbell, Brooks, and W. A. Robinson, on January 27, 1962, more than one hundred black and white Phoenicians concerned with "the sad and deprived economic state" of African Americans marched in protest of Woolworth's discriminatory practices. According to Eleanor Ragsdale, "they were protesting the previously stated and definitely applied policy of Negro discrimination in clerical and sales capacities in the Woolworth Stores in the Phoenix area." Up to that point, Eleanor argued, no black person had ever been "hired to sell goods at Woolworth stores or any of the other downtown 5 & 10 cents chain stores." NAACP leaders proclaimed that they had undertaken "this method to abolish job discrimination" and would continue to "fight until the walls of discrimination in jobs opportunities come tumbling down."[37]

According to the NAACP, this march was almost thwarted when Edward Banks, editor and publisher of a local tabloid, took it upon himself to inform the Woolworth's management and Harry Ronsenzweig, president of the Downtown Merchants Association, that he planned to denigrate and discredit Lincoln Ragsdale and other activists if the march took place. Edwards threatened to make public various allegations of Lincoln's engagement in an extramarital affair. Such efforts proved to be ineffective, however, and the march proceeded. Nevertheless, unsubstantiated rumors of Lincoln's marital infidelities began

The Ragsdale family, circa 1910. Standing from left to right: Adair Ragsdale and Fred Ragsdale. Seated from left to right: Ross Ragsdale, William Ragsdale Sr., and Gus Ragsdale. Courtesy of Lincoln J. Ragsdale Jr.

The Dickey family, 1928. From left to right: Estelle Ashley Dickey, William Dickey Sr., Eleanor Dickey Ragsdale (age two), Gwendolyn Dickey, Fannie Johnson Dickey, William "Bill" Dickey Jr., and Earl Dickey. Courtesy of Lincoln J. Ragsdale Jr.

Lincoln J. Ragsdale (center) with his fellow pilots at Tuskegee Airfield, Tuskegee, Alabama, 1945. Courtesy of Lincoln J. Ragsdale Jr.

Black athletes, entertainers, and politicians often took time out to visit and support black military personnel. Celebrated boxing heavyweight champion Joe Louis visited Tuskegee, Alabama, in 1945. He signed autographs for Lincoln Ragsdale (far left) and his fellow servicemen. Courtesy of Lincoln J. Ragsdale Jr.

Lincoln J. Ragsdale Sr., 1957.
Courtesy of Lincoln J.
Ragsdale Jr.

Eleanor Dickey Ragsdale,
circa 1950. Courtesy of
Lincoln J. Ragsdale Jr.

(Above left) Hayzel B. Daniels, circa 1953. Courtesy of the George Washington Carver Museum and Cultural Center, Phoenix.

(Above) Fred C. Struckmeyer Jr., circa 1953. Courtesy of the Herb and Dorothy McLaughlin Photograph Collection, Arizona State University Libraries, Tempe.

(Left) William P. Mahoney Jr., circa 1980. Courtesy of the Arizona Collection, Department of Archives and Manuscripts, Arizona State University Libraries, Tempe.

From left to right: Lincoln Ragsdale, attorney John Van Landingham, activist J. D. Holmes, Arizona attorney general Wade Church, and Representative Hayzel B. Daniels, circa 1953. Courtesy of Lincoln J. Ragsdale Jr.

From left to right: civil rights activists Thomasena Grigsby, J. Eugene Grigsby, Sandra Wilks, and Richard Wilks, 1962. Courtesy of Lincoln J. Ragsdale Jr.

(*Above*) Christmas at the Ragsdale home at 1606 West Thomas Road in Phoenix, 1959. From left to right: Lincoln Jr., Lincoln Sr., Emily, Eleanor, Gwendolyn Onlia, and Elizabeth Estelle. Courtesy of Lincoln J. Ragsdale Jr.

(*Top right*) Black Phoenicians protest the absence of African Americans in nonmenial positions throughout the city in February 1962. One marcher bemoans the police department's poor record of hiring African Americans, while one protestor reminds onlookers that Barry Goldwater's Goldwater's Department Store employed no African American sales associates at the time. Courtesy of Lincoln J. Ragsdale Jr.

(*Bottom right*) Lincoln Ragsdale raises his right hand to encourage and direct activists who marched in opposition to racial discrimination in places of public accommodation during the spring of 1962. Courtesy of Lincoln J. Ragsdale Jr.

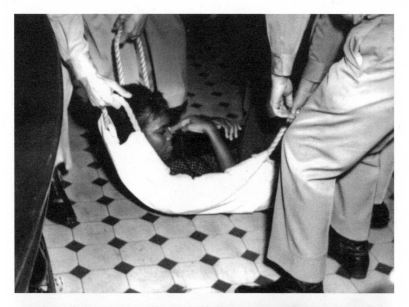

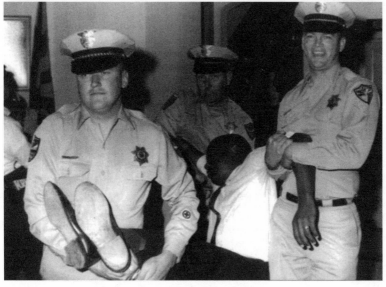

While a nonviolent sit-in took place inside the Arizona State Capitol building during the spring of 1964, this demonstrator is forcibly removed by eight Phoenix police officers after refusing to leave the protest against segregation in places of public accommodation. Courtesy of Lincoln J. Ragsdale Jr.

Lifting a sign that reads "Help Phoenix to Help Negro and Mexican Americans Educate their Children," Lincoln Ragsdale Jr. joins his parents in protest against racial discrimination, circa 1967. Courtesy of Lincoln J. Ragsdale Jr.

Lincoln Ragsdale poses with Martin Luther King Jr. in Phoenix. King visited the Valley on June 3, 1964. Courtesy of Lincoln J. Ragsdale Jr.

A proud Lincoln Ragsdale poses for a photograph in his study at the Ragsdale estate in the Phoenix suburb of Clearwater Hills, circa 1991. Courtesy of Lincoln J. Ragsdale Jr.

Eleanor and Lincoln Ragsdale, circa 1990.
Courtesy of Lincoln J. Ragsdale Jr.

Emily Ragsdale and Lincoln J. Ragsdale Jr.
represent the fourth generation of Ragsdales to
participate in the funeral home industry. They
continue to manage their family's business after
nearly sixty years of service in Phoenix. For more
than 110 years, the Ragsdales have used their
success in business to promote African American
advancement and interracial unity. Standing
from left to right: Universal staff members Joe
Ramirez, JoAnn Miguel, Kevin Weaver, Melissa
Meraz, and Manuel Villelas, 2001. Courtesy of
Universal Memorial Center, Phoenix.

to hound him around this time, and they would continue to do so throughout the remainder of his life. Protesters targeted the Woolworth's store on Washington and First streets because it had long been frequented by African Americans due to its location close to their homes and to the city bus line. The intense picketing of the store persisted for more than three weeks, when the store manager reluctantly contacted Brooks and announced that the store would hire one black salesperson. Brooks, upon recommendation from Eleanor Ragsdale, offered Doris Stoval as a potential interviewee for the new position. Stoval was chosen to interview for the position not simply because she was recommended by the movement's top leaders but also because of the sales experience she acquired while working in retail in Rochester, New York. After a long and uncomfortable interview in which she was made to "feel inferior" and unwelcome, Stoval was hired in February 1962. She became the first African American to work in sales in the Phoenix Woolworth's stores and in all of downtown Phoenix. After being hired, Stoval faced many disgruntled customers who came to the store simply to harass her. The store's management appreciated her professionalism and sales acumen, however, and eventually came to her defense by refusing to service anyone who targeted her for poor treatment.[38]

Later that year, Eleanor Ragsdale took a leading role in calling for legislation that would make racial discrimination in places of public accommodation illegal. The fight for a public accommodations bill in Phoenix would emerge as a defining moment in the Phoenician movement and for Eleanor Ragsdale. By 1962 various public accommodations bills had been defeated in the legislature twelve times, and Eleanor believed that the time had come to intensify the effort to secure one. She became more outspoken, marched often, wrote to and met with lawmakers, and continued to raise money through churches and women's associations to underwrite the activities of the NAACP, PUL, and GPCCU. One of Eleanor's most disturbing memories during this period, however, was picketing at the state capitol in 1962 to call attention to the need for a public accommodations bill. "It was the first time in my life that I had been spat upon and called ugly names," she remembered. "There were people standing on the sidelines jeering. Because my skin is fair, they called me 'White folks' nigger.' They thought that I was white, and they were wondering what I was doing standing in a picket line trying to help black people."[39]

Highly profitable establishments owned by white Phoenicians such as Barry Goldwater were not the only ones that refused to service black patrons. Several Mexican American restaurants would not serve blacks, Dickey remembered. El Rey Cafè on South Central Avenue was one of them. Fair skinned and green-eyed, Dickey, like his sister, could have passed for white or a Latino if he chose to do so. He did not. Nevertheless, he did make use of his appearance to silently subvert the prevailing racial ethos. While picketing the El Rey Cafè for its discriminatory practices, Dickey and a Latino friend decided to "sneak in" to grab a bite to eat. "Well, they didn't realize that I was black," Dickey recalled, "so we went in and sat down to have lunch." It was not long before the owner of the restaurant knew something was awry, because all of Dickey's fellow protesters started smiling and waving at him and his friend through the restaurant window. Once the proprietor was "tipped off" to Dickey being an African American, he escorted Dickey and his friend out of the eatery and closed down for lunch. Some black activists were deeply offended by the discriminatory action of some Mexican Americans. *Arizona Republic* reporter Richard Harris was shocked and angered when he witnessed some Mexican Americans laughing and jeering outside of El Rey Cafè when Dickey was removed from the restaurant. Harris and other civil rights workers expected as much from most whites, but they did not anticipate this kind of behavior from another minority group that would benefit from black agitation.[40]

The relationship between African Americans and Mexican Americans in Phoenix has a long history. The two groups have resided in the city since its birth. Both have been instrumental in the development of Phoenix. Each group was subjected to the racism of Phoenix's ruling white elite. Like black Phoenicians, Mexican American workers were exploited, underpaid, and restricted to the most menial labor. Unlike African Americans, however, Mexican Americans with fair skin and nonindigenous, "European features" were often deemed white by the dominant society. This racial dynamic afforded some Mexican Americans more socioeconomic mobility than blacks.[41]

The southern founders and early boosters of Phoenix embraced many of the antiblack attitudes that dominated race relations in the South. To the majority of whites, African Americans represented the antithesis of whiteness, while Mexican Americans, although they were deemed subordinate and inferior, were also viewed as partially European. Some Mexican Americans thought of themselves as, and were viewed as, a white ethnic group, much like the Irish or Italians. The fact that some Mexican Americans considered themselves to be a kind of ethnic group caused tension between black and Mexican American Phoenicians throughout the twentieth century. Moreover, in order to prosper politically and economically, some Mexican American business leaders adopted some of the city's prevailing racial customs.[42]

The fact that Mexican American restaurants often refused to serve blacks underscores the link between capitalism, economic competition, assimilation, white supremacy, and racial discrimination. As long as such restaurants were serving other Mexican Americans, Ragsdale stated, there was usually "no problem." When white people came to eat at some of these restaurants, however, the owners became afraid that the presence of black patrons would scare off the majority of their business: white people. Moreover, white people "would threaten the owners," Ragsdale maintained. "We won't come back if you serve these niggers," they would say. Mexican American restaurateurs did not appear to harbor any deep-seated racial animosity toward black people or the kind of "Negrophobia" that many whites did. Their decision to deny blacks access to their establishments seemed to have been inspired primarily by their desire to maintain a profitable business. Given the demographics of the city, Mexican American restaurants could ill afford to estrange white Phoenicians, who constituted the overwhelming majority of the city's residents. To remain competitive and profitable, some Mexican restaurateurs would adopt the prevailing racial mores and customs of their white clientele when white Phoenicians dined at their establishments. Nevertheless, when whites were absent from restaurants operated by some Mexican Americans, Ragsdale suggested, African Americans were treated fairly.[43]

Throughout the 1960s Phoenician activists employed strategies that were somewhat successful in slowly dismantling the apartheid-like system in the Valley of the Sun. Their efforts did not go unchallenged, however, and often activists were isolated, threatened, and physically terrorized.[44] In 1962, in response to the racist behavior of Phoenix's white power structure, the *Arizona Sun* expressed its belief that "if anyone doubts that there is discrimination against Negroes in Phoenix, he must be deaf, dumb, and blind."[45] As Lori Baker posits, the backlash against Lincoln Ragsdale's civil rights activities intensified as his profile and fortune grew. For example, by 1962 the Federal

Bureau of Investigation (FBI) had "warned him that the Minutemen, a self-named 'patriotic party,' were plotting his assassination." An FBI agent "advised him to carry a gun with him at all times." Unmoved by the threats against his life, Ragsdale did not reduce his activities. "I was young, and I didn't have much fear," he recalled.[46]

Ragsdale was an "antagonist who never hesitated to become brash or confrontational with white leaders" who treated blacks unfairly. This made him an enemy to many white Phoenicians. In addition to white hatred, Ragsdale faced black animosity as well. Some in the black community feared white retaliation in response to his bold activism. Some believed that Ragsdale's confrontational character might cause black Phoenicians more harm than good. Their fears were in many ways justified. Many southern black leaders were lynched for exhibiting behavior far less controversial than Ragsdale's. In fact, Ragsdale's aggressive methods for demonstrating his "manhood" were indicative of a type of masculinity that blacks in the South, with its history of violence and terrorism, could rarely display. Perhaps better than most blacks, Ragsdale understood that the West's more fluid race relations created a vacuum for a more confrontational and enterprising black leadership. His ability to be more audacious in his activism, without the threat of mass acts of violent retribution against the black community, gave him a freedom to resist in ways that were perhaps uniquely western.[47]

By 1962 Ragsdale had developed a reputation for being brash and confrontational. He never, however, advocated violence in the pursuit of racial equality. On the one hand, Ragsdale was among the most militant of the Phoenician movement's leaders because of his emphasis on black self-determination and economic self-sufficiency within what he hoped to be a more level socioeconomic playing field. He and Eleanor did not support integration so that black people could simply live, learn, work, and play closer to and with white people. As black parents and entrepreneurs, the Ragsdales hoped that residential integration would enable their children, and the children of other blacks, to attend schools that were generally better equipped and funded than those in segregated black neighborhoods. As proponents of residential integration, they also believed that such geographic consolidation would enable black businesses and aspiring political leaders to tap into heretofore inaccessible pools of social and financial capital that would expand the black middle class, who would in turn redistribute their newly acquired social and financial capital to black businesses and communities. The Ragsdales, like-minded "race workers," and other members of the black professional class believed that this scenario would increase the likelihood of success for individual blacks and the entire African American community.[48]

Lincoln and Eleanor Ragsdale thought that racial healing and African American progress depended upon the boldness and efficacy of black leaders. They always believed, however, that activists could be confrontational and "radical" without abandoning the concept of nonviolent resistance. To motivate black Phoenician activists to remain committed to racial equality and peaceful protest and to build upon their success in desegregating Phoenix's schools, the Valley National Bank, Motorola, and other businesses, the Ragsdales began making plans for a major civil rights rally to be held in Phoenix during the spring of 1962. The Ragsdales and Brooks solicited the support of the Phoenix Forum and extended an invitation to Martin Luther King Jr. to speak on civil rights at Phoenix Union High School on March 10, 1962. The Phoenix Forum was organized early in 1962 to give community members an opportunity to engage in dialogue and intellectual exchange about various social and political issues of local, national, and international importance.[49] Rev. George Schilling was the chairman of the forum, and its board included William P. Mahoney, W. A. Robinson, Rev. Paul Alexander, Rabbi I. Schulman, Herbert Ely, Rev. William Bostrom, and Frances Waldman. King accepted the invitation and was scheduled give a speech titled "Realizing This American Dream through Non-Violent Activity," but he later canceled the event. He changed his speaking schedule in order to attend an SCLC reception for outspoken southern activist Rev. Fred Shuttlesworth. Shuttlesworth had just been given bail upon the writ of habeas corpus issued by Supreme Court Justice Hugo Black. For three months he lay in prison on trumped-up charges relating to his civil rights activity in Alabama.[50]

In Phoenix, as in the national civil rights movement, the tension between gradualists and more aggressive leaders posed a challenge to activists like the Ragsdales. As historian Mary Melcher has indicated, Phoenix "mirrored the nation at large in the sense that the NAACP pursued a more confrontational approach than did the Urban League." Eugene Grigsby concurred, stating that although the NAACP and PUL worked together to end discrimination, the NAACP was actually the "pusher" and the "firebrand." Using different language, George Brooks likened the NAACP to "the War Department" and the PUL to "the State Department." The NAACP did the "dirty work," and the PUL, according to Melcher, "cleaned up the mess." As the NAACP and PUL fought against employment discrimination and segregated facilities, the GPCCU and the Lincoln and Eleanor Ragsdale–led ACCU worked to establish a city commission, much like the national Civil Rights Commission, to monitor and contest racial discrimination in the city. After having their pleas go unheeded for almost two years, the Phoenix City Council finally surrendered to the mounting pressure of the Ragsdales and their fellow activists. The council created the Phoenix Human Relations Commission on July 2, 1963—one month before Martin Luther King Jr.'s famous "I have a dream" speech.[51]

Fran Waldman, a Jewish activist and original member of the Phoenix Human Relations Commission, remembered that the commission investigated a number of complaints alleging racial discrimination during its first year in existence. The body had no power to force local businesses, or anyone, to integrate. The commission learned quickly that it could not rely on pressure or compassion. During the fall of 1963 the Ragsdales and other leading members of the NAACP, PUL, and GPCCU called for a law banning racial segregation in Phoenix's places of public accommodation.[52] This was not the first time activists had tried to implement such civil rights legislation in Phoenix. Their previous efforts had been met with a firestorm of opposition. The local white press supported this resistance. As early as 1956 an *Arizona Republic* editorial argued that "the way to the abolition of discriminating practices is not through law." Phoenix's ruling white administrators rejected nondiscriminatory measures every time they were proposed. In 1961 an editor for the *Arizona Republic* railed against civil rights legislation. "If there is a state in the union that doesn't need civil rights legislation," he wrote, "it is Arizona."[53]

Dan Smoot, a local television personality, went so far as to accuse outspoken black leaders like Lincoln Ragsdale of being driven by a latent desire to intermarry with white people. During his controversial television program, *Dan Smoot Reports*, the talk show host said that "Negroes are trying to lose themselves as a race completely. This is the reason why they want integration. They hope by living intimately with the whites that interracial marriages will follow. Then the Negro race will be completely lost and just light tan people will remain." During his talk show, Smoot also suggested that the NAACP was a "Red" organization that was secretly controlled by the Soviet Union and bent on undermining the "American way of life." The *Arizona Sun* reported that Smoot, once employed by the FBI to investigate Communist activity in America, was connected to various "White Citizens groups" and very adept at "psychological warfare." The newspaper attributed his ability to "plant fear in people's minds" to the days he spent "learning many tricks of the commies in brainwashing" during his "days with the FBI." The *Arizona Sun* posited that Smoot knew "that the average American white is not opposed to living on the same social level with the Negro, but through very strong traditions [perpetuated by leading citizens such as Smoot] they fear the mixing of the races and nationalities whether it be Jews, Greeks, or Italians."[54]

There were white Phoenician business owners who did voluntarily endorse antidiscrimination policies. For instance, local white utility magnate William P. Reilly persuaded a number of white restaurant owners to offer black Phoenicians unfettered access to their businesses. Most business owners were not easily swayed. Some were ideologically in tune with civil rights activists, but many more desegregated their facilities for purely economic reasons. Despite the relatively small black population in Phoenix, many business owners were losing profits as a result of boycotts supported by black and white Phoenicians. Eleanor Ragsdale recalled that by 1962, the Adams Hotel in downtown Phoenix had opened its doors to baseball star Willie Mays and his fellow black teammates after New York Giants manager Leo Durocher "raised hell." Taking a stand, Durocher threatened to remove his team from spring training in Phoenix and with it, no doubt, a great deal of tourist revenue. Mays and his teammates were an exception. Most of the time, Lincoln Ragsdale remembers, the Adams Hotel was "flagrant" in its refusal to accommodate African Americans. The Westward Ho Hotel, one of three major hotels in downtown Phoenix at the time, always denied black people access. Ragsdale recalled that he "could walk through the lobby if I had a message for [a white person to come to] the counter, but I couldn't have a seat in the place. I couldn't go to the bathroom. I couldn't have a room there."[55]

Lincoln Ragsdale, frustrated and angry after being routinely barred from white establishments and having few entertainment options, decided in 1962 to add nightclub owner and restaurateur to his expanding endeavors. William Dickey, Ragsdale's brother-in-law, remembered he and Lincoln wanting to provide somewhere for black professionals to socialize and have cocktails and something to eat, since they were barred from white-owned places of public accommodation. Although they believed that protesting racial discrimination would eventually open up more opportunities for blacks, they also believed that black people should create and maintain their own institutions to sustain and move black communities forward. When Ragsdale was moved to open his own club, Dickey remembers that black social institutions in Phoenix were limited to "maybe the [American] Legion, the Elks Club, or some of those VFW places." Ragsdale's and Dickey's associates, including the handful of black doctors, business owners, and teachers in the Valley, originally conceived of the Skyroom as a private club. Despite their desire to establish what would have amounted to an elite club of well-to-do black people, the plans evolved along a different trajectory.[56]

Ragsdale wanted to "send out applications asking people to join [the] private club," Dickey recalled. "This would be their place," Ragsdale announced. Ragsdale and his partners decided to "ask for three hundred dollars for a joining fee, and two dollars a month for dues." Dickey remembered mailing "something like one hundred and fifty applications to all the [black] professional people and so forth in town." With amusement, Dickey recalled, "we only got two back." "The brothers and sisters want some place to go," he mused, "but they don't want to spend no money." Dickey believed that the chilly response might have been linked to jealousy or class divisions within the black community. "A lot of people said, 'Well, [Ragsdale's] just trying to use us to get a club.'" Some black Phoenicians probably believed that as Ragsdale's power and influence in the community expanded, so, too, did the gap between his concurrent allegiance to civil rights and capitalism. Some may have wondered how he, as a leader of a primarily poor people, could open a club that would by virtue of its monetary requirements exclude the majority of them. Many believed that he truly relished working for the advancement of the black community, but some began to believe that he did not see himself as being *of* the black community.[57]

Despite the cold response to his membership application drive, Ragsdale decided to proceed with his plans. On July 8, 1962, Ragsdale, with the help of Dickey, opened the doors of the Century Skyroom Restaurant and Social Club to the public. The club was located on the second floor of the Ragsdale Valley Life Insurance Building. Century Skyroom was soon known for its "fine restaurant and cocktail lounge, beautiful atmosphere, and lunch and evening dining." The Century Skyroom hosted celebrated entertainers such as Duke Ellington, and before long it was regarded as "one of the top jazz clubs in the country." Reflecting on what they created, Dickey noted that "we made it beautiful. It had beautiful red carpet and a brand new grand piano." Ragsdale eventually "eliminated the idea of getting members," Dickey recalled. Ragsdale decided to "just open it as a regular club, a restaurant club."[58]

The Century Skyroom, Ragsdale's ever-expanding business interests, and his political activities made the Valley Life complex the center of a wide variety of activities. At the heart of the hustle and bustle was Ragsdale, who appeared to have endless energy. "He was a dynamo," Dickey proclaimed. The numerous offices in his complex carried on a wide range of work in several fields of business and the professions. Housed in his building were the Lyles School of Beauty, Ragsdale's Century Skyroom Restaurant and Social Club, the offices of surgeon Dr. Mason C. Reddix, Dr. John Fitt's dental practice, the offices of attorney Karl N. Stewart, Ragsdale's Valley Life Insurance Company, Right Way Printers, and Ragsdale's Home Realty and Insurance Company.[59] In addition to the very broad business community assembled at the Valley Life complex, the site also hosted political gatherings as well as dignitaries and entertainers. Early in 1963 the Valley Life building hosted luminaries from Liberia, Nigeria, and Kenya. The African officials were attending a worldwide conference in Phoenix. Lincoln and Eleanor Ragsdale were usually present when special guests visited the Valley Life complex. Often, however, Dickey ran the day-to-day operations of Ragsdale's many business interests. Executive vice president of the Ragsdale enterprises, Dickey's responsibilities, as he recalled, were "so extensive it would be difficult to describe them." Dickey kept the Ragsdales' ship afloat when the business and civil rights leaders made various trips to other states. Dickey was in charge, for instance, when the couple flew to Jackson, Mississippi, to meet James Meredith and attend Lincoln's Thirty-third Degree Mason induction ceremony.[60]

Although the Ragsdales, especially Lincoln, seemed to be extending themselves in every possible direction, their fellow activists continued to push for a public accommodations law in Phoenix throughout the spring of 1964. Progress was, as one observer put it, "agonizingly slow." The pleas of activists routinely were ignored. City leaders regularly cited Phoenix's reputation as a sanctuary, unspoiled by the kind of racial discrimination found elsewhere in the nation, particularly the South. Owning to Arizona's self-proclaimed progressive image, in 1962 Phoenix mayor Samuel Mardian stated correctly that municipal facilities in Phoenix had never been segregated. The qualification, of course, was that jails, streetcars, buses, libraries, parks, and swimming pools were never segregated by law. In the realm of de facto segregation, custom, and possible reprisals, however, Phoenix's leaders segregated African Americans as effectively as if it were mandated by law. Los Angeles attorney Loren Miller, who spent a considerable amount of time in Phoenix, stated that the city "has the reputation of being one of the most segregated cities in America. Yet it is a city which has won the designation of 'All-American' in competition with other cities, and attained national renown by desegregating schools in advance of the 1954 Supreme Court decision."[61]

Between 1962 and 1964 young blacks in Phoenix increasingly protested segregation in places of public accommodation. Blacks used sit-ins and marches on city hall and the state capitol to make the Greater Phoenix area aware of their plight. Members of the local chapter of CORE, which had recently been organized in the city, joined with older activists such as Eleanor Ragsdale in calling for an ordinance outlawing segregation in places of public accommodation. Founded in 1942 by a group of interracial pacifists in Chicago, CORE was decentralized and very democratic, unlike the NAACP. James Farmer and Bayard Rustin played key roles in developing the organization. In early March 1964 members of CORE, the NAACP, and the PUL planned a massive joint protest at the Arizona State Capitol building to force the Phoenix City Council to enact a public accommodations ordinance. The activists planned to enlist the support of black high school students, average citizens, and anyone else who wished to participate in the demonstration. The Ragsdales allowed the heads of these organizations to meet at the Valley Life complex to coordinate their efforts, and organizers used the Ragsdales' copy machine to produce hundreds of flyers and leaflets announcing their plans.[62]

On March 31, 1964, with media from around the state converging on the Arizona State Capitol building in anticipation of further civil rights activity, hundreds of African Americans from the city's high schools, colleges, churches, and civil rights organizations entered the Arizona Senate building singing "Freedom" and "We Shall Overcome." Blacks from Tucson and other areas of the state, in addition to a number of sympathetic whites, arrived on the scene to take part in the demonstration. Many protestors, including the Ragsdales, formed a human barrier around the Senate chamber and refused to let anyone in or out of the assembly until their demands were met. Governor Paul Fannin rushed to the protest with an armed police escort, but he refused to sign a petition redressing grievances over racial discrimination. In response, Eugene Grigsby, his two sons, and other activists confined themselves in the rotunda of the capitol, refusing to leave for several days. Thomasena Grigsby and other activists supplied food and water to them by sending up rations in a bucket via a makeshift pulley system. As the tensions escalated, Fannin ordered 120 state troopers to the scene to break up the human barrier, empty the rotunda, and escort the demonstrators off the premises for "disturbing the peace."[63]

In the spirit of nonviolent direct action and staunch resistance, marches and other demonstrations were peaceful and orderly. Every effort was made to prevent violence. Picketers were asked not to smoke while marching, and they were admonished to be polite and civil under all circumstances. Lincoln Ragsdale told demonstrators that "we plan to continue these marches until every trace of job discrimination is gone. We're not being antagonistic. We're simply asking our people not to support stores and politicians that discriminate. We feel that when white people know what the situation is, they will help us too."[64] Ultimately, the impasse at the capitol in March ended with no victory or concessions on the part of Fannin, Mardian, or the city of Phoenix. State troopers eventually escorted everyone away from the capitol; those who refused to leave were forced to do so. Police officers and troopers, however, were ordered to be as temperate as possible when removing demonstrators from the premises. White authorities did not want law enforcement officers to be captured on film mishandling any civil rights activists. City leaders wanted to avoid allegations of police brutality, and they did not want Phoenix's reputation as a tolerant and peaceful city to be tarnished. "After all," remarked one observer, "this is not Birmingham." Law enforcement officers lifted protestors who refused to leave the capitol onto police-issued blankets and carried them to adjacent areas, where they were instructed to leave. Few refused, but those who did were arrested and taken to jail without incident. Most were too exhausted, hungry, and thirsty to resist, and some were carried away after collapsing from fatigue.[65]

After the spring protest at the capitol, Thomasena Grigsby recalled, most black civil rights activists "came to the conclusion that the numbers of African Americans in Arizona were limited and the possibility of a large enough pressure group was at that time unobtainable. We moved in the direction of alliances between blacks, whites, and others, who believed that Martin Luther King's movement was a potent vehicle for change." Grigsby, the Ragsdales, Brooks, and other leaders worked harder to solicit the support of white leaders after the showdown with government officials on March 31, 1964. Lincoln and Eleanor Ragsdale worked particularly hard to garner the support of progressive leaders across race lines. After expanding their inner circle of white progressive activists, which already included Herbert Ely, William Mahoney Sr., Wade Church, and John Van Landingham, the Ragsdales took their case to the Human Relations Commission. Their task was difficult. Many conservative and moderate white leaders condemned the March 31 protest. They believed the movement was becoming too aggressive. Many suggested that CORE and the interracial band of activists that spearheaded the protest did themselves and the movement a disservice by protesting and forcing whites to address the issue. Local white media outlets supported this contention. Cartoonist Reg Manning, in fact, published a political cartoon in the *Arizona Republic* on April 5, 1964, that portrayed a trounced public accommodations bill clinging to life after being trampled by activists on March 31.[66]

The Ragsdales and their supporters nevertheless continued to push for a public accommodations bill. After some political maneuvering by the Human Relations Commission, a series of interracial high-profile confrontational protests at the Arizona State Capitol building, and some heated debates between the NAACP (represented by Ragsdale and Brooks) and the city council (supported by Governor Fannin and Mayor Mardian), the city council finally relented on July 16, 1964, enacting a public accommodations ordinance in Phoenix. The law made it illegal to "discriminate in places of public accommodation against any person because of race, creed, national origin, or ancestry." The Human Relations Commission created a public accommodations committee to supervise the implementation of the law. Phoenix's new ordinance came on the heels of the national Civil Rights Act passed on July 2, 1964. One year later, Arizona passed a statewide civil rights law that banned discrimination in housing, employment, voting, and public accommodations. Phoenix, like many cities elsewhere in the nation, made critical advancements in civil rights despite the relatively small number of black people in the city.[67]

The passage of the municipal and state civil rights laws, along with ensuing federal legislation, aided in the destruction of major impediments to black progress and racial equality. As a result of the Ragsdales' leadership and the activism of civil rights workers, a number of Phoenix's downtown stores integrated their workforces. Goldwater's Department Store, for example, hired a black woman as a sales clerk and announced intentions to hire blacks in upper-level positions, and Mexican American restaurants such as El Rey Café began to serve African Americans. As Bradford Luckingham argues, however, the "white problem" remained. Indeed, in early 1965 one white Phoenix business leader declared:

> You ask about the Negro problem in Phoenix. Understand now, if you want to know what I really think, I can't be quoted. I can't have the company I work for associated with what I say. If you're going to use my name, then I'll repeat the standard line—civil rights, education, tolerance, the whole bit. But as a businessman and a taxpayer, I think there's a real problem. We've got all those people down there [South Phoenix] and let's be honest about it, most of them are costing the rest of us money. They're uneducated, unskilled. You can't hire or use half of them. Their crime rate is way up. They can't pay any taxes. I'm not anti-Negro, but you wanted my opinion. Just from the standpoint of simple economics, the city would be better off without them. Another thing, with all this civil rights marching and demonstrating, how long is it going to be before some half-educated crackpot gets those people all excited and we have a first-class riot on our hands? This has nothing to do with prejudice; I'm talking straight economics and the city's image. I don't think there's any question about it; Phoenix would be better off if they weren't here.[68]

Given these kinds of sentiments, it came as no surprise to the Ragsdales and other activists that municipal and state discrimination laws were rarely enforced and that de facto segregation remained in businesses, neighborhoods, and schools. The coming of antipoverty programs helped, but job-training projects were few, and they brought additional complaints of racial discrimination. Following the civil rights hearings in Phoenix in 1962 and the fight for a public accommodations bill between 1962 and 1964, the Ragsdales led the way in organizing private groups and city leaders to address problems in black employment and socioeconomic mobility. They raised money, hosted lectures and seminars featuring experts in the fields of civil rights and public policy, and devised provisional job-training programs that were held at the Ragsdales' Valley Life complex. The Ragsdales continued to fight for equal access to Phoenix's places of public accommodation, but they began to believe, given the fact that Phoenix now had a law the banned racial discrimination in places of public accommodation, that it was crucial that African Americans be prepared to compete for and secure the kinds of jobs that would allow them to increase their standard of living and improve the institutions in their communities that welcomed their patronage. Although many leading black and white activists applauded the Ragsdales' efforts to produce a more skilled and competitive black workforce, others called Lincoln Ragsdale's attention to the absence of minorities in city government. Black leaders in particular began to believe that they needed a strong presence on the Phoenix City Council to be outspoken on issues that were important to black people, such as racial equality, education, jobs, and health care.[69]

Lincoln Ragsdale believed that serving as an elected official would be an effective way to fight for better educational, employment, and health care opportunities for blacks and in the ongoing effort to desegregate places of public accommodation. Moreover, Ragsdale believed that serving on the Phoenix City Council would enhance his ability to help shape a city government that would be more responsive to business leaders regardless of race and to all residents who desired a more open and prosperous city. He, like a great many Phoenicians, had grown tired of Phoenix's conservative, white male–dominated Charter Government Committee (CGC) machine. As Mary Melcher indicates, "prior to the mid-1960s, the CGC held a tight grip on Phoenix city elections." Formed in 1949, the CGC was supported by white

Public accommodation bill cartoon, 1964

Phoenician power brokers such as Eugene Pulliam and businessman and future political legend Barry Goldwater. The CGC, with its deep pockets and extensive networks, continually persuaded Phoenicians to support its slate in selecting candidates for mayor and city council through the 1950s. Ragsdale criticized the CGC, arguing that it catered to middle-class and wealthy whites. The fact that Ragsdale had recently entertained the idea of creating a supper club that would cater specifically to black professionals made this criticism ironic. Unlike the CGC, however, Ragsdale in his role as activist did address the needs of poor black people. He may not have been inclined to socialize with poor African Americans, but unlike most members of the CGC, he was willing to speak out and act in their defense. Ragsdale's criticism of the CGC was not simple speculation. Practically all CGC candidates were white, conservative, Republican men who lived in the affluent areas of North Phoenix.[70]

In 1963 Lincoln Ragsdale and other members of the GPCCU formed the progressive community-based Action Citizens Committee (ACT) to challenge the CGC. The ACT campaign operated independently of the GPCCU and offered a roster of candidates for mayor and city council that included Ragsdale; Richard Harless, a widely known three-term U.S. Democratic congressman and the slate's mayoral candidate; business leader Robert L. Alden; Ed Korrick, chief heir of Korrick's Department Store chain; Manuel Pena, owner of an insurance and realty company; and teachers Madelene Van Arsdell and Charles J. Farrell. The slate ran on a platform that called attention to discrimination, political elitism, crime, political favoritism, corruption, and the city's poor infrastructure. Herbert Ely, ACT's campaign manager and legal adviser, remembers the ACT committee "taking on the City of Phoenix against hostile forces." The "business community and the [*Arizona Republic*] newspaper were absolutely opposed to the notion of taking on the establishment, which included the progeny of Barry Goldwater."[71]

"Our leading candidate was Lincoln Ragsdale," Ely maintained. "He wasn't the leading vote getter, and leading is probably poor nomenclature, but [he was] the most significant candidate." Ely and activist Frances Waldman believed Ragsdale was instrumental because of the long-term implications of his candidacy. Ragsdale called attention to the fact that minorities were not represented on the city council. As one eyewitness noted, "the only areas being developed are the ones where councilmen are interested [in]. Look south of the [railroad] tracks. Nothing is being done there." Black Phoenicians and residents of South Phoenix were not represented on the city council. Lincoln Ragsdale's bid for a city council seat was an attempt to change that. Eleanor was very much a part of the ACT campaign. She registered voters, helped raise money, scheduled debates and similar events, and when Lincoln became ill and could not deliver several of his speeches, spoke on his behalf, sometimes with little or no preparation. "We didn't win," Waldman acknowledged, "but we did shake up city hall!" "We rallied this community like it had never been rallied before," Lincoln maintained. He remembered registering "more African Americans and Mexican Americans [to vote] than ever before." The ACT candidates received 49 percent of the vote and "changed the city forever" Ely boasted.[72]

Lincoln Ragsdale's participation in the ACT campaign also gave rise to increased collaboration between African American and Mexican American leaders. Throughout the campaign, Ragsdale worked closely with Manuel Pena and other members of the Mexican American Political Association (MAPA). Together, he and Pena promoted cooperation between the two communities, while calling for increased voter registration and political activism in minority communities. From 1956 through 1964 Pena and Ragsdale were members of the PUL. When he and Ragsdale helped launch the ACT campaign, they were both members of the GPCCU. Ragsdale and Pena bemoaned the lack of minority representation on the Phoenix City Council, and both leaders worked to improve educational opportunities for minorities in Phoenix.[73]

In 1965, a year after the ACT campaign, the CGC selected African American teacher Morrison Warren as a candidate on its slate. Warren integrated the CGC and broke the stranglehold affluent white men had on the council. Warren won a seat on the Phoenix City Council that year and was elected to a second term in 1967. Warren lost his seat in 1969, but Calvin C. Goode, a young black political force, was elected to the council as a CGC candidate. Goode would be elected to his seat for over two decades.[74] While making his historic run for city council to unseat Phoenix's ruling white political establishment, Ragsdale supported George Brooks's effort to ensure that black Phoenicians had full access to the ballot. During the early 1960s some white Phoenicians deliberately tried to prevent African Americans from voting.

Black activist Madge Copeland argued that members of the Young Republicans conspired to hinder black Phoenicians' ability to vote by terrorizing them in front of the polls. George Brooks recalled having to confront William Rehnquist, future U.S. Supreme Court chief justice, about his efforts to disenfranchise black voters. As black Phoenicians arrived at polling places to cast their votes, Rehnquist would sometimes appear and administer a literacy test to them. The jurist would force African Americans to read passages from the U.S. Constitution. If they were unable or unwilling to do so to his satisfaction, Rehnquist would not permit them to the cast their ballots.[75]

Brooks, who served as an election officer at Julian School, where ballots were being cast, confronted Rehnquist within sight of numerous witnesses. Brooks "told him that he was interfering with the people's right of franchise, and I was going to call the sheriff and have him arrested." Rehnquist reluctantly left without incident. This episode reminded Brooks and other leaders that there was still much work to be done in the area of civil rights in Phoenix. Despite advances, black Phoenicians continued to encounter adversity born of racism and discrimination. Economic and political gains were made but were often mitigated by persistent inequality and problems in housing, employment, education, and health care. While activists worked hard to attain substantive victories, advancement was for the most part sluggish.[76]

The Phoenician movement was relatively swift and successful at forcing the desegregation of area schools and a number of important businesses without one recorded episode of egregious violence. This distinguished it from many other local movements. By 1964, however, activists in Phoenix, not unlike their peers in other cities, were faced with the staggering reality that the legacy and preservation of white supremacy, through custom and official doctrine, still relegated blacks to the bottom of virtually every major socioeconomic category.[77]

Undaunted, Eleanor Ragsdale continued to manipulate what had become an extensive interracial network of civil rights activists and progressive women's groups, while Lincoln Ragsdale continued to organize and square off as the "bad guy" in negotiations with white leaders to produce educational and job opportunities for racial minorities in Phoenix. In an effort to maintain the movement's momentum, expose the unjust treatment of people of color in the "Mississippi of the West," and place added pressure upon the city's leadership to enforce

Phoenix's ban on de jure segregation, the Ragsdales and the NAACP extended a second invitation to Martin Luther King Jr. to speak about the issue of racism and peaceful protest in Phoenix. King accepting the invitation and visited the Valley on June 3, 1964. The occasion provided a welcomed boost for the Ragsdales and other civil rights workers. Lincoln accompanied King to a speech he gave for 450 Kiwanis at the Smokehouse Restaurant in downtown Phoenix. He then escorted King to Phoenix's Tanner Chapel AME Church, where the renowned civil rights leader urged the racially mixed congregation to "continue the struggle for justice and equality until the battle is won. We must learn to live together as brothers or we will parish together as fools." He spoke of the need for blacks and whites to work together because it is "simply the right thing to do." After King addressed the Tanner AME gathering, Lincoln Ragsdale accompanied him to the Goodwin Auditorium on the campus of ASU, where King extolled the virtues of nonviolent action before a crowd of three thousand. During the fleeting moments of his stop, King spoke of brotherhood, asking his audience to continue to struggle for justice and equality so America could "get rid of the last vestiges of segregation." "[They] throw us in jail . . . bomb our homes . . . threaten our little children," King cried out, "and as difficult as it is, we will still love [them]. This is the meaning of non-violent action."[78]

Lincoln Ragsdale escorted King to his home following the leader's speech so that the minister could meet Eleanor and their children. Eleanor recalled that encounter as an event that changed her life. She remembered King as a "warm, dedicated man" who radiated distinction. "I brought a great deal of anger and frustration to the civil rights movement" after years of disappointments and broken promises, Eleanor admitted. She could not accept "the injustice of the laws that would keep black people in a spiral of perpetual frustration and denigration, and in a system that taught us we weren't worth anything. But it was he [King] who really taught us the strength to love despite everything." King's visit to the Valley had a powerful impact on Lincoln as well. After King's visit, Emily Ragsdale remembers that her father would often listen to "tapes of Martin Luther King's speeches over and over again. I realize now, as I've gotten older, that he was building his spirit up; giving himself that spiritual lift that he needed."[79]

By the time King made his speech in Phoenix, de jure segregation was prohibited in the city. King's presence, and the spirit and force of the national civil rights establishment that he brought with him, helped dispose of the some of the last vestiges of formal racial segregation in the city. Phoenix also benefited from the passing of the 1964 Civil Rights Act and would later benefit from the 1965 Voting Rights Act. When it was passed in 1964, the Civil Rights Act represented the acme of the civil rights movement. The most salient provisions of the act prohibited discrimination in places of public accommodation and by employers of labor unions on the basis of color, race, religion, national origin, and sex. Perhaps most important, the act permitted government agencies to deny federal aid to any program allowing and practicing discrimination. Lastly, it established the Equal Employment Opportunity Commission to monitor discrimination in employment. Although the Civil Rights Act included specifications for assisting in the registration of African American voters, whites in the South often circumvented them and rendered them ineffectual. The Voting Rights Act of 1965 addressed the flaws in the Civil Rights Act by outlawing major educational requirements for voting and by empowering the attorney general to have the Civil Rights Commission assign federal registrars to enroll voters.[80]

The leadership of the Ragsdales and their allies at the local level helped end formal discrimination in employment, public accommodations, and voting in Phoenix soon after the enactment of the Civil Rights Act of 1964 and Voting Rights Act of 1965. The success of the civil rights movement and local leaders like the Ragsdales and their comrades was the result of a number of factors. The federal government played a key role in producing landmark legislation, responding to the demands of protestors, and enforcing the law at critical moments throughout the movement. Black leaders like the Ragsdales at the local level and Martin Luther King Jr. at the national level deliberately pursued strategies to provoke confrontations that would ensure government intervention and media coverage. They attacked the towering edifice that was white supremacy and socioeconomic inequality. The determination and the spirit of these leaders, the dedication of their partners, the strength of their organizations, and the trust of their constituents pressured private institutions and governmental leaders, agencies, and courts to render decisions that systematically desegregated the nation.[81]

Lincoln and Eleanor Ragsdale led the way throughout the peak years of the civil rights movement in Phoenix. Their efforts were often met with contempt and hostility. In order to overcome this massive resistance, the Ragsdales were compelled to collaborate with other civil rights activists to devise viable strategies to combat discrimination. As Mary Melcher writes, "by working together, this small band of activists, black, white, Chicano, male, female, broke down the barriers of racial discrimination and profoundly changed the political and social fabric of Phoenix." This influential group, and the Ragsdales' ability to secure resources and support from a racially diverse group of people, made the city's movement unique. Like the Ragsdales, many in this group, such as Manuel Pena, Frances Waldman, Herbert Ely, and Ed Korrick, were business and religious leaders, activists, and professionals. All of them had a passion for justice and believed that racial integration was the best way to secure it. They held prominent leadership positions within their own subgroups, while maintaining substantive networks and lines of communication with the city's white elite. These leaders formed a small yet very well connected, outspoken, and influential cluster. Although their subgroups, particularly African Americans, wielded limited institutional and mainstream power, together they constituted an influential bloc. Moreover, the support of a small number of influential progressive whites such as Robert L. Alden, Richard Harless, and Madelene Van Arsdell gave the Phoenician movement an air of legitimacy that it may not have attained had these leaders not supported it.[82]

When rallied together, Phoenix's various racial communities were able to push the ruling white elite to alter the way in which it viewed and handled race relations and issues of access and opportunity. Unlike in the South, white Phoenicians concerned with maintaining the status quo had to contend with the protests and insurgency of two peoples of color and the progressive activity of a number of local whites as well. A thirteen-year-old Lincoln Ragsdale Jr. underscored this reality when, during the spring of 1963, he marched in protest with his parents while holding a sign that implored local whites to "Help Phoenix to Help Negroes and Mexicans Educate Their Children." Led by the Ragsdales, movement organizers were compelled to view racial reform holistically, while simultaneously addressing issues that were foundational for various racial and ethnic minorities within the larger movement—desegregation, access to the ballot, anti-Semitism, and indigenous sovereignty, for example.[83]

The Ragsdales, through their work in the GPCCU, NAACP, PUL, and the ACT campaign, and through intense networking and dialogue, played a critical role in defining an effective Phoenician movement that was both similar to the larger civil rights movement yet distinct from it. Lincoln Ragsdale's bold and confrontational leadership exploited the uniquely fluid racial relations in the West to fashion a career that was both unabashed and creative, when many of his southern contemporaries were under constant threat of terrorism and a more violent version of massive white resistance. Emboldened by a more flexible racial ethos and a more racially diverse population, the Ragsdales and their partners managed to change the law and transform the ways in which black Phoenicians and civil rights were treated, when racial injustice was encoded in law and practiced by the majority of the people. The tremendous accomplishments of the civil rights movement and leaders like the Ragsdales, however, did not end racial inequality or usher in true socioeconomic integration. Nonetheless, the Ragsdales and their fellow insurgents weakened the effects of white supremacy, and in the following years the Ragsdales and their allies continued to fight racial inequality. Although they had ended de jure segregation, they quickly realized that de facto segregation and racial socioeconomic inequality were just as debilitating and often more difficult to combat. [84]

Younger, more militant activists soon took center stage in the civil rights movement, and they aimed their efforts at the economic inequality that they believed white supremacy and capitalism had produced. A fracture within the civil rights movement ensued, with older, "traditional" civil rights leaders often on one side and younger leaders calling for "Black Power" on the other. Despite the antagonisms that emerged during this transition, the Ragsdales continued to fight against racial discrimination and for greater opportunities for African Americans. They worked to produce greater educational, employment, and entrepreneurial opportunities for African Americans. The Ragsdales and their partners managed to change the law and transform the ways in which black Phoenicians and civil rights were treated. Racism and discrimination survived to be sure, but the Ragsdale's and their fellow activists dealt them a serious blow. [85]

# Chapter 5

## The Quickening

I *am* for violence if non-violence means we continue postponing a solution to the American black man's problem—just to *avoid* violence. If it must take violence to get the black man his human rights in this country, I'm *for* violence exactly as you know [other races would be] if they were flagrantly discriminated against.

Malcolm X, *The Autobiography of Malcolm X*

Rattlesnakes don't commit suicide. Ball teams don't strike themselves out. You gotta put em out!

Fred Shuttlesworth

THE YEARS BETWEEN 1964 AND 1980 introduced America to a new era in the black liberation struggle. Despite the enactment of the 1964 Civil Rights Act and the 1965 Voting Rights Act, proponents of civil rights realized that major obstacles remained. Even with the 1964 presidential victory of the progressive Lyndon Johnson over conservative senator Barry Goldwater of Arizona, the cause of civil rights and racial equality faced a number of obstacles. In Phoenix, veteran activists Lincoln and Eleanor Ragsdale were forced to deal with new barriers that many white people erected to stem the rising tide of black activism and racial integration. Many activists reasoned that new, more militant organizations and strategies were requited to overcome these hindrances. The new groups and methods that emerged, unlike their predecessors, did not focus solely on racial discrimination.[1] The new black activism put forth a profound critique of the interconnectedness of white supremacy, capitalism, and racism. By 1965 activist organizations such as the Phoenix chapters of CORE and SNCC, which was organized at the national level by Ella Baker in 1960 to acknowledge the possible need for increased militancy and confrontation in the black freedom struggle, joined the NAACP, GPCCU, and PUL in protesting the persistence of poverty and discrimination in South Phoenix. The fluidity and militancy of CORE and SNCC appealed to young activists in Phoenix who had grown tired of the Ragsdales and the more conservative NAACP. The ascension of these groups challenged the authority and activist agenda of leaders such as Lincoln and Eleanor Ragsdale, George Brooks, and Clovis Campbell Sr. These challenges marked a quickening in the Phoenician movement that culminated in intense confrontations between moderate and militant activists and between activists and those who opposed the civil rights movement.[2]

By 1966 many white Americans who opposed recent civil rights legislation spearheaded campaigns that protested or revoked such measures in states across the country. In the South, members of the Council of Federated Organizations (COFO), an alliance of workers in Mississippi, were bullied and beaten as they promoted nonviolence and integration in the workplace. On the West Coast, Californians adopted an amendment to their state constitution that revoked all legislation that banned discrimination in the sale or rental of housing and prohibited such legislation from ever being enacted in the future. The measure was later struck down by the U.S. Supreme Court. Nevertheless, its initial passing revealed the extent to which many white people opposed integration and civil rights. In Phoenix, whites who opposed the black freedom struggle and its leaders worked to undermine Lincoln and Eleanor Ragsdale financially. Prominent white financiers believed that if they damaged the Ragsdales' financial stability, the couple would no longer be able to subsidize race work that undermined white power and privilege. What happened in California and in Phoenix reflected the fact that white resistance to the civil rights movement was not simply a southern phenomenon. As whites demonstrated their objection to black insurgency through systematic subversion and violence, the Ragsdales continued to fight, and young African Americans called for more radical ways of seeking black liberation.[3]

Leaders like Stokely Carmichael (Kuame Ture) of SNCC and Malcolm X of the Nation of Islam renounced the gradualism of the SCLC and Martin Luther King Jr.'s unyielding support of interracial cooperation and nonviolence. As the tension between traditional organizations such as the SCLC and newer, more radical groups such as SNCC intensified, young activists further distanced themselves from conventional leadership. After the failed Mississippi Freedom Democratic Party (MFDP) effort of 1964, Carmichael, for example, popularized the maxim "Black Power" and in 1965 founded the Mississippi Lowndes County Freedom Organization (LCFO). This independent black political party was the first organization in the civil rights movement to use the image of the black panther as a symbol of black independence and potency. Drawing upon the imagery and symbolism of the LCFO, Huey P. Newton and Bobby Seale formed the Black Panther Party for Self-Defense in Oakland, California, in October 1966. The Black Panther Party fused black nationalism and Marxist-Leninist philosophy in an effort to supplant capitalism and eradicate racism and police brutality.[4]

SNCC and the Black Panther Party stepped into a vacuum in civil rights leadership. They appeared to offer an alternative to the traditional "work-within-the-system" approach that had been employed by groups like the NAACP. The "race problem," many activists now argued, could not be answered merely through legislation or goodwill but only through a fundamental restructuring of America's socioeconomic system. These groups were vocal and often uncompromising in their demands for equality.[5] The radicalism of leaders like Carmichael and Malcolm X and revolutionary organizations like the Black Panther Party was emblematic of the frustration and rage that pervaded black communities. In 1965, 29 percent of black households, compared to only about 8 percent of white households, lived below the poverty line. Almost 50 percent of nonwhite families lived in substandard housing compared to 18 percent of white families. Despite a drop in the number of Americans living in poverty from 38 million in 1959 to 32.7 million in 1965, the percentage of poor black people increased from 27.5 percent to 31 percent. The Ragsdales called attention to the fact that the socioeconomic status of black Phoenicians mirrored that of most African Americans, citing several community surveys that graphically detailed the depth and nature of poverty in Phoenix. Clearly, recent civil rights legislation did little if anything to address this inequality. U.S. jobs moved to the suburbs and became more technologically driven, and most middle-class whites followed, while black inner-city residents could not qualify for, or travel to, what amounted to remote, inaccessible jobs. Black communities descended further into poverty. School dropout rates exploded, crime and drug abuse became epidemic, and family structures were undermined. Sociologists Douglas S. Massey and Nancy A. Denton labeled this labyrinth of white supremacy, racial discrimination, segregation, and socioeconomic inequality "American Apartheid."[6]

Many white people and predominantly white institutions were unwilling to acknowledge and respond to the problems of black people, and most were entirely unaware of the intensity of black exasperation. This caldron of inequality, apathy, and anger propelled America into one of the most violent periods in its history. African Americans were staggered by the assassination of Malcolm X on February 14, 1965, and by the ongoing devastation in their communities, and inner cities exploded into rebellion each summer between 1965 and 1969. Watts, California, was the first city to experience some of the worst urban racial violence since World War II. African Americans in the Watts area, reeling from police brutality, high unemployment, crime, drug use, and poor health care facilities, took to the streets in revolt on August 11, 1965. During the Watts riot, Lincoln and Eleanor Ragsdale encouraged young black Phoenicians to channel their frustrations into constructive action. They did not want Phoenix to explode in the same way that Watts had. Emily Ragsdale recalls that during the riot, "my brothers and sisters were at the home on Thomas Road, and my parents were out playing their part, trying to making a difference."[7]

Despite the pleas of the Ragsdales, frustrated black Phoenicians, like their counterparts in Watts and throughout the rest of the nation, sometimes responded violently to white supremacy and their poor socioeconomic status. They occasionally rejected gradualism and what they perceived to be the obsequious maneuvering of veteran civil rights leaders such as Lincoln and Eleanor Ragsdale. At the behest of the Ragsdales, Martin Luther King Jr. pleaded in 1965 for activists in Phoenix to embrace nonviolence. King's appeals were a distant memory in the minds of young activists by 1966. Persistent racial antagonisms, economic repression, political marginalization, and increasing allegations of police brutality led to more disorder and destruction in the city. On July 25, 1967, a violent race riot erupted in the streets of Phoenix. Some in the crowd hurled firebombs into the air and fired guns at a police wagon filled with officers on East Van Buren. At the Sidney P. Osborn Project, a public housing facility, a crowd of angry, dispossessed black people, including members of CORE and SNCC, gathered to express their collective displeasure in a haze of cathartic rage.[8]

The inflamed group participated in "stoning, gunfire, and disorder in the streets." In similar communities around the nation, African Americans and other people of color were rioting. On the evening of July 26, the rioting in Phoenix exploded again near the Osborn Project. As a result, Mayor Milton Graham imposed a curfew and ordered police to enforce it. Nevertheless, rioters, whom George Brooks referred to as radical noisemakers from CORE, proceeded to burn down a house and set several police cars on fire. Brooks tried his best to calm the rioters. He stood at a street corner near the Osborn Project and listened to their grievances. "We're not going to do anything foolish in this town," he admonished, "and if you do it, you're going to have to come by me." Despite Brooks's effort to prevail upon the respect younger activists may have had for the veteran leader, rioters continued to pillage and plunder. About 280 people, including 38 "juveniles," were arrested and taken into custody. More than 376 Phoenix police officers were on duty at various times in the battle zone, while their stations elsewhere in the Valley were taken over by 190 highway patrol officers, 148 sheriff's deputies, and 64 firefighters. Despite isolated skirmishes around the city over the next few days, the curfew was retracted on July 30. Shortly after the riot, Brooks was able to convince a number of politically active young people to join him in a meeting with Mayor Graham to demand more aid for minority communities.[9]

In response to the these events, Graham, choosing to refer to the violence as a "serious civil disobedience" rather than a riot, trumpeted Phoenix's intention to provide more job training and jobs for minority groups. In a last-ditch effort to quell allegations of police brutality in Phoenix, he pledged a citywide campaign to make "community relations" a more vital function of the police force. Despite these and other promises, Phoenix's minorities continued to encounter a disproportionate amount of socioeconomic adversity in their lives. Some observers have suggested that the money Graham pledged to improve "community relations" was actually deployed to fight crime rather than poverty. Economic and political progress was made by African Americans, but any gains continued to be offset by persistent inequality and problems in housing, employment, education, and health care.[10]

CORE's participation in the riot and the pleas of the Ragsdales and other NAACP leaders forced Phoenix's leaders to act. Despite the pronouncements and protests of civil rights workers, most white Phoenicians saw the city and the entire nation as an "affluent society." The Ragsdales and their more militant progeny forced them to deal with the reality of racism and the existence of poverty. Reinforced by the efforts of the Phoenix Human Relations Commission, the Ragsdales, Brooks, Campbell, and Travis Williams began working with Mayor Graham. Recognizing both the serious issues and the fact that South Phoenix had voted strongly for the ACT campaign's candidates, Graham invited numerous community leaders to meet and work with the Phoenix City Council to devise a program that would bring opportunities to African Americans and other minorities and calm to the city's race relations. Graham, the Ragsdales, Brooks, Campbell, and Williams, in conjunction with the city's Human Relations Commission, created Leadership and Education for Advancement of Phoenix (LEAP), which functioned as a liaison between Phoenix government and federal programs created to improve conditions in urban areas. Funded with $50,000 from the city and the obligation to obtain $25,000 from private donors, LEAP quickly outgrew the expectations that African Americans and city officials had for it. In 1966 it was transformed into a city department that administered federal monies generated by President Lyndon Johnson's War on Poverty. These government-subsidized programs offered educational and employment opportunities for a limited number of minorities. The aid, activists such as Lincoln Ragsdale believed, was insufficient and arrived too slowly. They were displeased with limited job-training programs and Phoenix's dismal record of employing minorities. Activists argued that the War on Poverty in the city was "a day late and a dollar short." Indeed, despite the fact that the U.S. government had funneled $15 million into South Phoenix, minorities saw little improvement in their overall condition.[11]

A year after LEAP was created, one journalist observed that despite $15 million in new services, the "LEAP target area is more impoverished than in 1965." "People are still not working because they lack the ability to compete for work in the labor market," the reporter argued.[12] Another observer maintained that "the fact is that agency workers have been foundering in a sea of uncoordinated, limited programs that lead nowhere. All efforts have had a Band Aid effect." A July 1967 LEAP statement revealed only "52 job placements out of 250 contacts in Phoenix." At the same time, however, Phoenix continued to offer its welfare recipients benefits that were far below the national average. One observer declared that for poor people of color, "Arizona is a tough state." The vast majority of Phoenix's African Americans and Mexican Americans were underemployed, poor, and lived in substandard housing in squalid living conditions. By 1967 the 21.2-square-mile LEAP target area contained most of the blacks and Mexican Americans in the city, and "within its boundaries," the organization argued, "could be found some of the worst slums west of the Mississippi River." In July 1967 unemployment in the area was extremely high, and 30 percent of working adults residing in South Phoenix earned less than $3,000 a year, a figure that marked the poverty line at the time. One observer noted that the area "might be fairly termed a human disaster area in an affluent metropolis." Despite its many limitations, LEAP organized various neighborhood councils, operated a small-business loan program, and administered the city's Head Start and Youth Corps job programs. Nevertheless, the stark reality of the poor conditions of African Americans in the city and LEAP's limited ability to make a substantive difference in their lives demonstrated that suburban Phoenician whites experienced far more economic prosperity and mobility than did most African Americans and other people of color in core city neighborhoods.[13]

Some believed that the city was committed to doing what was necessary to promote racial healing and improve the lives of black Phoenicians. Many did not. Many whites were not convinced that groups such as LEAP and social programs that targeted racial minorities and the poor were necessary. Some simply called for more police to ensure their safety and enforce law and order. African Americans as well as whites spoke out in favor of an increased police presence and fewer social programs. Older African Americans in the city disapproved of the actions of young insurgents, whom they believed caused unnecessary disturbances. One observer argued that "eighty percent of all the kids who were making all the noise wouldn't take a job if you offered it to them, or if they did, they wouldn't work. They want to get paid, that's all."[14] Some attributed the riot to similar rebellions in Los Angeles and cities such as Newark and Detroit. Black Phoenicians, it was suggested, were simply mimicking the behavior of black people in other cities. African Americans in Phoenix, however, were not merely imitating the behavior of blacks in other cities; they were lashing out against white supremacy, poverty, and police brutality in their own communities.[15]

Having seen civil rights laws circumvented and flagrantly ignored, young members of the NAACP, CORE, and SNCC staged a series of protests between 1965 and 1967 in Phoenix. Typically about a third of the protestors, as was sometimes the case in South, were college students, teenagers, and often schoolchildren. These young protestors usually participated with the reluctant approval of their parents and school administrators. Many of these young demonstrators ignored the teachings of their elders and sometimes acted upon their own activist agenda. For example, when confronted by Phoenix authorities or others who attempted to mute the fervent calls for immediate redress of the socioeconomic problems, teenage activists often broke ranks and lashed out violently against both black and white authorities. On one occasion, young activists responded to white racial slurs and the forbearance of their older leaders by abandoning nonviolence and engaging those who taunted them in a curbside brawl. A reporter for the *Phoenix Evening Telegram* newspaper wrote that he "saw the look of shame and disgust on the faces of the older demonstrators, the NAACP faction, for the most part, as young CORE demonstrators turned what started out as an orderly protest, into a teenage rumble."[16]

The name "CORE" conjured negative images in the minds of most white Phoenicians and many older black activists as well. " 'CORE' had developed a negative connotation among local authorities, based on its aggressive tactics on the national scene," journalist Richard Harris has argued. Some white Arizona legislators went so far as to suggest that the "Black Muslims" of the Nation of Islam (NOI) were behind the protests. Elijah Muhammad, the controversial leader of the NOI, had, in fact, owned a large home in South Phoenix and supervised the NOI's mosque No. 32 in Phoenix since 1961, but there is no evidence that he or the NOI played any role in incidents involving violence during the Phoenician movement. Generally, the NOI's involvement in the struggle in Phoenix was marginal. Individual NOI members may have participated in various marches and protests, but the NOI itself rarely, if ever, sponsored any major events associated with the civil rights movement in the Valley. Elijah Muhammad usually came to Phoenix between December and March to avoid the harsh Chicago winters, which exacerbated his bronchial asthma. As historian Claude Clegg has demonstrated, "during his trips to Phoenix, he rarely left his home. Much of his time was spent entertaining visitors and directing the Chicago headquarters. Occasionally, property acquisitions and proselytizing work broke his routine." In January 1962 he delivered an address in the Phoenix Madison Square Garden that allegedly netted three hundred converts, including the entire congregation of the Mount Zion Baptist Church. By and large, however, Elijah Muhammad's visits in Phoenix were free of much of the duress associated with life in the NOI's nerve center in Chicago, and the NOI's activities in Phoenix happened infrequently and independently of the NAACP, CPCCU, PUL, CORE, and SNCC.[17]

Lincoln and Eleanor Ragsdale were not particularly fond of the NOI, despite the fact that the separatist organization's emphasis on entrepreneurship and black self-determination complemented the Ragsdales' economic black nationalist leanings. As Christians and proponents of racial integration, the couple frowned upon some of the NOI's Islamic teachings and its opposition to social integration. By 1967 the Ragsdales had also come to associate the NOI with the pro-self-defense doctrine of Malcolm X, who was gunned down two years earlier in the Audubon Ballroom in Harlem, New York. The Ragsdales, particularly Eleanor, cited Malcolm X's philosophy of self-defense as one of the major causes of impetuous behavior and unimaginative resistance among many younger activists. Despite their frustration with militant local activists, leaders such as Eleanor and Lincoln Ragsdale sought to exploit white apprehension about "radical" groups like the NOI and the gulf between traditional and more militant black leaders and organizations. Lincoln and Rev. Kermit Long, a local black Methodist minister, stated publicly that legislators must decide which group they preferred to deal with, "the NAACP, CORE, or the Black Muslims." Many whites did not care who was organizing the effort to bring civil rights and equality to Phoenix. White people who opposed black socioeconomic integration targeted all civil rights activists for intimidation and terrorist acts. These assaults prompted leaders like Lincoln Ragsdale to reevaluate the ways in which they would work toward equality and black liberation.[18]

For Lincoln Ragsdale, reconsidering his role in the civil rights movement did not simply involve choosing between traditional and militant
strategies. Indeed, unlike minister George B. Brooks, attorney Hayzel
B. Daniels, and educator W. A. Robinson, Ragsdale was a businessman who risked the financial stability of his enterprises to promote
civil rights. In fact, the more he pushed the civil rights envelope, the
more his business interests suffered. Generally speaking, by the late
1960s white Phoenicians who opposed his activist leadership stepped
up their efforts to intimidate him and undermine his success in business. Ragsdale had become the object of frequent acts of physical
intimidation and death threats, but as early as 1964 he also had to
contend with intense attempts to destroy him and Eleanor financially.
Rumors were again circulating that a confederation of racist organizations and local white Phoenicians had produced a short list of
activists in Phoenix who were being targeted for assassination. Lincoln Ragsdale's name, argues Emily Ragsdale, was at the top of the
list. The rumors came as no surprise to the Ragsdale family. "He was
in danger," Emily maintains, "but that was just the part he played. We
didn't dwell on that. We didn't dwell on the fact that he may not come
home one night." Lincoln Ragsdale's family may have been able to
ignore the danger he was in, but by 1964 the attacks on his business
and the threats against his life caused him to lose some of his desire
to maintain his position as one of the top leaders in the Phoenician
movement.[19]

By 1964 Lincoln Ragsdale had reached the crossroads of his activist
career. "I remember the hour. I remember the day," he recalled. While
leading a protest against racial discrimination at the Arizona State
Capitol building on May 20, 1964, Ragsdale received an "emergency
call" while "reading a long list of grievances" to reporters and lawmakers about the lack of educational and employment opportunities
for blacks in Phoenix. A very wealthy and influential white creditor
who had grown tired of his progressive politics and ceaseless agitation
phoned him with a threat. The lender warned Ragsdale that he was
prepared to take away three automobiles he used for his mortuary
because he was "three payments late." "I was humiliated," Ragsdale
remembered. "I couldn't talk." He walked back to the demonstration,
but he returned a changed man. It became clear to him during what
was a long walk back to the rally that despite all of the victories
he had helped secure in recent years, most black Phoenicians still

lived in poverty and that black people with some means were largely dependent on white institutions for their livelihood. Financial independence, he now believed, was the most important challenge that faced African Americans.[20] As he participated in the protest that day, Ragsdale "stood back and listened" to demonstrators sing "We Shall Overcome." Despite desegregating Phoenix's neighborhoods, schools, sectors of its job market, and places of public accommodation, what black people needed to overcome, he mused, was poverty. The majority of black Phoenicians, he argued, were "broke." Ragsdale's frustration and "humiliation" brought him to tears that afternoon. "How can you go into places to eat or sleep," he questioned, "when you don't have any money?"[21]

Ragsdale paid the creditor who threatened to confiscate his vehicles, but white leaders found other ways to undermine his family financially. Not long after Lincoln paid the lender, Eleanor Ragsdale recalled, he received more shocking news. Several black and white families notified the Ragsdales that a number of white business leaders had offered to pay their life insurance premiums, funeral expenses, and burial costs if they took their business to one of the Ragsdale's white competitors. Before the Ragsdales had received this news, they had noticed a decline in the number of their white and black clientele. They had not known what to attribute these losses to until they learned of this new effort to undermine their business and ability to compete. By the end of 1964 the Ragsdales' businesses, particularly the mortuary, were in "shambles from neglect." Besieged by white business leaders who endeavored to destroy their financial self-sufficiency and overwhelmed by the demands of race work, the Ragsdales' many battles began to take a toll on their ability to maintain profitable businesses. They were losing both white and black customers steadily. White Phoenicians always represented a fraction of their mortuary's clientele, but while the Ragsdales were at the acme of their civil rights careers between 1953 and 1964, many whites who had done business with them stopped doing so. Some of their black customers, who disliked the virtual monopoly they held over black burial in the city and Lincoln's immodest leadership style, also began to frequent their business less often.[22] It is also reasonable to suspect that many black and white patrons also avoided his services for fear of white retaliation. To get a clearer picture of his company's status, Ragsdale had another Phoenix businessperson do a feasibility study of his mortuary. "He gave me three choices," Ragsdale said: "Leave town and start fresh; stay and go broke; or change the name of my company, take down Martin Luther King's picture, and cease agitation." "Which do you think I did?" asked Ragsdale, "I did the third one."[23]

Ragsdale's decision to reduce his civil rights activities drastically ushered in a new era in his life and in the civil rights movement in Phoenix. For the next two decades Ragsdale worked largely behind the scenes for African American advancement and socioeconomic equality. He continued to support progressive causes and the NAACP financially, while also helping black Phoenicians and African Americans throughout the country by giving generous endowments to historically black colleges and universities. In addition, Ragsdale devoted a great deal of time assisting aspiring black entrepreneurs in the city. While the civil rights movement became more radicalized, Ragsdale turned most of his attention to rebuilding his business. Content to allow younger, more militant leaders with less to lose assume leadership positions in Phoenix, Ragsdale quickly went from outspoken protest leader to elder statesman and adviser to younger activists and would-be business leaders.[24]

Eleanor firmly believed that it was time for she and Lincoln to serve as mentors and advisers to younger activists who were beginning to rise in stature. Between 1946 and 1964, she recalled, the couple believed it was their time to take the lead fighting for African Americans and racial equality. She thought their professional and activist backgrounds necessitated action when faced with racial discrimination and inequality. During these years, she argued, they were, like those taking center stage by 1964, young, energetic, and endowed with the skills and wherewithal to engage in race work that was more aggressive and nuanced than their later efforts. Eleanor suggested that this was a natural progression. If African Americans were to continue to move forward, she posited, "somebody must take the risk. Somebody must be at the cutting edge, and if you are there, then that means you. If you are mature enough not to pass the buck."[25]

As the Ragsdales refashioned their leadership roles, they set out to remodel and reorganize their mortuary. Due to the poor feasibility study, however, they were not able to receive the necessary loan to finance their renovations. The bank reasoned that the percentage of black people in Phoenix was not high enough to constitute a market that would support the financial stability and expansion of their mortuary. African Americans constituted approximately 5 percent of the Phoenix population, and banks indicated that Lincoln would not be able to pay them back on the ratio of seven black people dying per thousand annually. Moreover, the fact that there was another black-owned funeral home in the city split the target market in two. Applying Martin Luther King Jr.'s integrationist philosophy to the business, the Ragsdales decided to integrate their funeral home. In 1964 they elected to change the name of the mortuary to Universal Memorial Center and rethink the way the approached their business.[26]

In addition to renaming the mortuary, Eleanor and Lincoln Ragsdale decided to integrate their staff. They hired Euro-American, Mexican American, and African American workers. Considering the reality of race relations in the city at the time, Lincoln's methodology was pragmatic and effective. He directed white people to service potential white customers, Mexican Americans to work with Mexican American patrons, and African Americans to assist African American clients. He initiated this practice, he maintained, because "you can have an ignorant, moron white person sitting at a front desk and [white] people would come in and talk to them, but if you had a well-dressed, educated black man [at a front desk], [white] people would walk in the door and just turn around and walk away." The only thing he had to do, he reasoned, was "have someone who was white there" to work with clients and make them feel comfortable. When Lincoln and Eleanor surrounded themselves with a diverse workforce, Lincoln argued, they could manufacture a business environment that would be tolerable for white, Mexican American, and black Phoenicians. By 1967, therefore, the Ragsdales' mortuary had gone from a funeral home that exploited racial prejudice and segregation to one that exploited racial prejudice and integration. The Universal Memorial Center became one of the first integrated funeral homes in the United States. By 1967 there were very few black-owned funeral homes that buried black, white, and Latino Americans.[27]

The Ragsdales' reorganization efforts were successful, and it did not take long for the Universal Memorial Center to regain its profitability. People of all races began to bring their business to the Ragsdales in larger numbers. The couple's salesmen and women, in fact, were able to attract patrons of their own race to the mortuary and secure their business, and the Ragsdales persuaded many black Phoenicians who were tempted to take their business elsewhere not to do so. Lincoln's more covert activism probably aided in the turnaround as well. As the Ragsdales reorganized their mortuary and assumed a lower profile in the civil rights movement, Lincoln stepped up his support of less politicized organizations that addressed the socioeconomic problems of black people. As a charter member of the PUL, for example, he played a key role is battling urban decay and poverty. Following the passage of state and municipal civil rights legislation and the coming of federal antipoverty programs, journalist Richard E. Harris posits, Ragsdale and the PUL assumed a unique role in the city. "Its expertise in minority affairs," Harris argues, "was welcomed by [government] agencies holding responsibilities of administering [antipoverty] funds." The PUL's executive secretary, Junius A. Bowman, "an able administrator and negotiator," worked hard to ensure that his interracial board of directors included representatives from prominent businesses and social agencies, such as Lincoln Ragsdale. The PUL employed a staff of over one hundred and created programs that dealt with job internships, housing construction, cultural enhancement, education, health care, and day care.[28]

Some of the more militant activists in Phoenix who cried out for radical changes in the socioeconomic system also worked for traditional organizations like the PUL. The PUL's intent was to use the current system to confront urban problems. Jim Williams, associate director of the PUL, reflected the elasticity of many "militant" activists' political philosophies. Although he was a top administrator in the PUL, he was a former CORE organizer and strategist. Williams was also instrumental in establishing the Phoenix branch of the Opportunities of Industrialization Center (OIC) in 1967. Like the PUL, the OIC was a moderate grassroots organization that worked to address socioeconomic ills in the black community. OIC was supported primarily by rank-and-file blacks, whereas the PUL was maintained by the local black and white business establishment. Reflecting the contradictions inherent in his evolving political philosophy and professional activities, Williams was pivotal in integrating the board of the OIC with white people who recently had been bitterly opposed to CORE's agenda. Many members of the white power structure were "pleasantly surprised" by the action.[29]

The experiences and actions of activists like Ragsdale and Williams reflect larger questions that emerged during the later years of the civil rights movement: what constituted traditionalism and radicalism, and how should one differentiate between concession and compromise?

By 1967 historian Manning Marable argues, black radicalism, and Black Power in particular, had become the premier ideology among the majority of young African Americans. Black Power as a concept, however, was ambiguous. "Radical" activists created various definitions of Black Power, which often reflected the heterogeneity of the black community in general.[30] Stokely Carmichael and political scientist Charles V. Hamilton described Black Power as the ability of black people to "exercise control over our lives, politically, economically, and psychically." Radical CORE leader Robert Carson of Brooklyn, New York, believed that at its foundation, Black Power was a racialized socialist movement. He declared in 1968 that Black Power advocates did not "want anything to do with the white power structure as it is now. I believe that capitalism has to be destroyed if black people are to be free." Black Communists also described Black Power as a systematic critique of capitalism. Julius Lester of SNCC suggested that Black Power was a socialist movement and "another manifestation of what is transpiring in Latin America, Asia, and Africa. People are reclaiming their lives on those three continents and blacks in America are reclaiming theirs."[31]

Socialist thinker Harold Cruse, however, stated that the Black Power concept was not revolutionary or connected with Marxism. Cruse argued that "Black Power is nothing but the economic and political philosophy of Booker T. Washington given a 1960s' militant shot in the arm and brought up to date. The Black Power ideology is not at all revolutionary in terms of its economic and political ambitions; it is, in fact, a social reformist ideology. What does have a revolutionary implication about Black Power is the 'defensive violence' upheld and practiced by its ultra-extremist–nationalist–urban guerilla wing, which is revolutionary anarchist tendency." There was not, therefore, a single intelligible definition of black radicalism or Black Power. Marable believes that black radicalism and Black Power were eventually "transmitted to all strata of black society as a contradictory set of dogmas, platitudes, political beliefs, and cultural activities."[32]

Amid the emerging radicalism of the civil rights movement and the ongoing debate over the meaning of Black Power, the 1960s witnessed a revival of black communalism and pride. Despite Lincoln Ragsdale's conversion from outspoken civil rights leader to low-profile business boss, he continued to influence civil rights through financial support and inconspicuous political maneuvering. He continued to open his wallet and lend his expertise to the NAACP, PUL, and OIC. There is little evidence to suggest that Ragsdale treated more militant groups like CORE and SNCC with anything short of suspicion and antipathy. For their part, the NAACP, PUL, CORE, SNCC, and other predominantly African American organizations provided leadership, economic relief, legal assistance, and hope to African Americans.[33]

The militancy of the mid-to-late 1960s also ushered in a barrage of social services and cultural programming as well. The Black Panther Party's breakfast program in Oakland, California, is a perfect example. In Phoenix, the Broadway House apartments, supported by activists at the First Institutional Baptist Church and the Tanner Chapel Manor nursing home and sponsored by leaders at the Tanner Chapel AME Church, were created. Leaders such as Lincoln Ragsdale, George Brooks, and Olympic gold medalist Jessie Owens, who retired to Phoenix during the 1960s, supported new community medical centers. Joe Black, former Brooklyn Dodger and vice president of Greyhound Bus Lines, and other leading figures organized myriad youth programs for minorities in Phoenix, while Eugene Grigsby continued to teach African art at various institutions throughout the city. The spirited activism and renewed cultural pride that matured during this era helped reinvigorate the civil rights movement and give new meaning to black history.[34]

African American women continued to play a vital role in the socioeconomic advancement and stability of the black community. Eleanor Ragsdale remained active in various civil rights and benevolent associations. Arlena Seneca, an imposing and dynamic educator from the Phoenix Union High School District and former instructor at George Washington Carver High School, was recognized for her commitment to academic excellence and diversity. Vernell Coleman organized Juneteenth celebrations and Black History Month activities. Juneteenth, commonly referred to as "Emancipation Day" by many black people in the Southwest, is the annual holiday celebration that pays homage to the day in 1865 (June 19) when General Gordon Granger landed with the first Union soldiers at Galveston, Texas, and announced that all the African Americans held in bondage in the state had been liberated.[35] Although the Emancipation Proclamation, issued in September 1862 by President Abraham Lincoln, had become effective on January 1, 1863, most black people in the Southwest did not learn of the news until Granger arrived in Texas in June 1865. The Juneteenth celebration developed into a highly anticipated, well-attended event in Phoenix. Helen Mason, granddaughter of Phoenix's first black resident, Mary Green, who migrated to the city in 1868, worked diligently to make the Phoenix Black Theater Troupe a success. Middle-class and affluent black women like Eleanor Ragsdale promoted community projects, including educational opportunities for young black people. Through the local LINKS chapter, many of the city's leading black women also sponsored major social events, such as the annual debutante cotillion.[36]

Despite the durability and creativity that African Americans demonstrated during this tumultuous period, their problems in many ways worsened. The urban unrest of the late 1960s substantially limited the amount of support the federal government was able to give black people through Lyndon Johnson's Great Society agenda. His successful 1964 and 1965 legislation is legendary. The Economic Opportunity Act of 1964, for instance, gave rise to numerous programs: Head Start, for example, assisted preschool children; Upward Bound, to which Eleanor Ragsdale donated time and money, gave poor teenagers an opportunity to earn a college degree; and Volunteers in Service to America (VISTA) operated as a sort of domestic Peace Corps to assist the indigent and uneducated. Nevertheless, African Americans continued to lag behind their white counterparts in virtually every statistical category. This reality eventually prompted the imperious Martin Luther King Jr. to rethink the ways in which he should approach black advancement. Like the many proponents of Black Power, by 1968 King began to be more critical of America's economic system. It was not enough, he now reasoned, to attack discrimination. Socioeconomically oppressed people, he now argued, were compelled to demand an end to the systematic economic inequality that was their true enemy.[37]

King shifted his focus to poverty, workers' rights, and what he believed to be an unjustified war in Vietnam. In the process, he alienated white and black people who may have supported his stance on the most virulent forms of racism but were unwilling to question the foundation of American society: capitalism. The NAACP was particularly angry with his stance on Vietnam, as many of its members were middle class and loyal to Lyndon Johnson. In other words, most wealthy and middle-class white and black Americans could tolerate King's vision of a more equal society, but they were not willing to redistribute America's wealth on an equal basis to do so.[38] King's effort to construct a multicultural coalition that demanded civil rights, peace, and fundamental structural changes within America's capitalist system eventually led to his death. While in Memphis, Tennessee, in support of a garbage workers' strike, he was assassinated by James Earl Ray at the Lorraine Motel on April 4, 1968. King's death weakened the SCLC and other organizations that benefited greatly from his charismatic leadership. Immediately following King's murder, African Americans took to the streets again in a rash of violent riots from California to New York. Black communities in over 125 cities erupted, leaving 46 people dead, 35,000 injured, and 20,000 arrested. In the wake of these rebellions, Congress passed the Open Housing Act of 1968 largely as a conciliatory gesture. The act made it illegal for homeowners and realtors to discriminate on the basis of race, class, or sex.[39]

The passage of the 1964 Civil Rights Act and the 1965 Voting Rights Act were the high points of the civil rights movement. After 1965, the civil rights community split into many, sometimes warring factions: young and old; separatists and integrationists; socialists and capitalists; and cultural nationalists and multiracialists. Moreover, there were moderates whose political philosophies reflected elements of each concept. As in other urban areas, older African American leaders in Phoenix had a difficult time adjusting to the quickening pace and new militancy of the civil rights movement. Young activists, however, took the lead in protesting white supremacy and inequality. The most active group of young leaders in Phoenix belonged to CORE, but many also joined SNCC. Although their activist agenda and political ideology differed from those of older activists, young leaders in Phoenix continued to call upon leaders like Lincoln Ragsdale for moral, political, and financial support.[40]

As in other cities across the nation, in Phoenix, CORE and particularly SNCC continued to support separatism, while older groups such as the NAACP maintained their traditional interracial agenda. By 1968 the Black Panther Party was the most widely recognized and controversial black activist organization in America, but it failed to make inroads in Phoenix to the extent that CORE and SNCC did. Nationally, however, it continued to put forth its challenge to the existing capitalist, racial order. Internal conflicts involving sexism, violence, race, and questionable leadership, however, hurt the organization and divided the movement. The Johnson administration, however, crippled the movement. With the support of Johnson, the FBI targeted, harassed, and threatened civil rights organizations and leaders. It had constantly investigated and badgered civil rights leaders like Lincoln Ragsdale at the local level and Malcolm X and Martin Luther King Jr. at the national level. By 1970, during the presidency of Richard M. Nixon, the FBI conducted the covert Counter Intelligence Program (COINTELPRO), which succeeded in undermining and destroying Black Power groups such as the Black Panther Party and leaders such as Fred Hampton and Mark Clark.[41]

While some black leaders searched for new ways to move African Americans forward, others energized the reenfranchised black electorate to seek victories in electing candidates to political office. The rise in the number of black elected officials, in fact, stands as perhaps the most salient legacy of the civil rights movement. Although black people had been voting for one hundred years in the North, their influence was negligible. The emergence of the Black Power movement, however, and the power of the Voting Rights Act prompted black communities to demand representatives who reflected their population. Indeed, to many African Americans, including the Ragsdales, winning elected office was perhaps the most practical way that African Americans could develop and wield power in their communities and beyond. In Phoenix, a small number of blacks were elected to positions that previously had been unoccupied by African Americans. With the improvement in his business interests and a new mortuary at the base of South Mountain in Phoenix, Universal Sunset Chapel, Lincoln Ragsdale was in a strategic position to assist these new officials in their campaigns and professional aspirations.[42]

During the late 1960s and early 1970s, with Lincoln Ragsdale's support, William Bell became the city's first assistant city manager, attorney Hayzel B. Daniels was elected municipal judge, and Clovis Campbell Sr. continued to serve in the Arizona State Senate. Active in the Phoenix chapter of the NAACP, and with the assistance of leaders like Ragsdale throughout the 1970s, Campbell continued to protest discrimination and spoke out against injustice in his newspaper, the *Arizona Informant*. Campbell believed that notions of white supremacy among Phoenix's Euro-American population fueled the opposition to much of the progressive legislation and issues he championed. "I had quite a bit of legislation introduced that was considered quite a few years ahead of its time," Campbell recalled, "and so naturally, it didn't always get the approval of the people that it should have."[43]

The wall of political opposition that confronted Campbell and other black leaders and elected officials demonstrated that the early civil rights victories were the first in a long line of victories that needed to be won. Poor people, regardless of race, continued to suffer from unemployment, inadequate education, insufficient health care, and political marginalization. Each president between 1964 and 1980 tried to address these issues. Each had extremely limited success, and their efforts were met with tremendous white resistance. Problems remained in black communities throughout the nation, including Phoenix, but progress was made. National and local civil rights legislation, coupled with antipoverty programs, helped maintain black organizations like the NAACP, PUL, and OIC as vital forces in the black community.[44]

Lincoln and Eleanor Ragsdale played critical roles in producing some of the most progressive civil rights legislation, statues, and integrationist policies in Phoenix during the 1960s. These successes helped increase the representation of African Americans in Arizona's economic, political, and cultural mainstream. A number of black families joined the Ragsdales in previously all-white neighborhoods, and African Americans and issues that concerned them garnered much more attention. Stan Stovall, for example, was hired as a full-time broadcaster for Phoenix's ABC television affiliate, while Evelyn Thompson assumed comparable responsibilities for the city's CBS affiliate. During the early 1970s Lincoln and Eleanor Ragsdale served as mentors for black Phoenicians who continued to organize and work for racial equality and greater black political representation. In January 1972, for example, Lincoln Ragsdale protégés Pete Hillsman, chairman of the Black Political Action Association of Arizona, and Louis Montleih, housing director of the PUL, coordinated a Black Political Action Association voter drive. Their goal was to register all eligible black voters in Phoenix by June 30 of that year. They did not register all black Phoenicians by the target date, but they did record more African American voters in the Valley than at any other time in the city's history.[45]

On June 26, 1972, the Phoenix Federation of Colored Women (PFCW), part of the National Convention of Colored Women's Clubs (NCCWC), held its annual convention at the Valley Christian Center in

Phoenix. The PFCW's motto was "Rowing, Not Drifting" in the local and national movement to "uplift" women of color. The event's featured speakers included Charles Campbell, brother of Clovis Campbell Sr. The keynote speaker, Zenothia Wilburn, spoke of the need for black women to become more involved in politics and the community. Eleanor Ragsdale believed that these types of events were necessary in the overall effort to improve the status of African American women. She held regular events at her home in support of young black female members of Delta Sigma Theta sorority. At these fund-raisers and social events, which often resembled stately affairs, Eleanor would echo Wilburn's message to the PFCW. Eleanor advocated social, economic, and political awareness, and she urged these aspiring professionals and activists to get involved in their communities and to help less fortunate black women maximize their potential. She did this often, she maintained, "because I think life is for living, life is for action, and life is for doing and accomplishing."[46]

By the mid-1970s the Ragsdales were well positioned to provide a great deal of financial support to civil rights organizations, voluntary associations, educational groups, and churches. Since the couple reorganized their business in 1964, they had prospered and become one of the wealthiest black families in the American Southwest. Perhaps the most important factor in the Ragsdales' capacity to expand their mortuary business and wealth was Lincoln's ability to secure a lucrative contract with some of Arizona's largest indigenous groups. In 1974 he negotiated an unprecedented contract with Peter McDonald, a principal leader of the Navajo Nation, to prepare and transport the remains of Navajos who had perished in Phoenix's Indian Hospital to Navajo communities in northern Arizona. Ragsdale was also able to make similar arrangements with other indigenous peoples, including the Hopis and the Papagos. The Ragsdales were now servicing people of virtually every race and ethnicity in every corner of the state. They later expanded their life insurance enterprises to Louisiana, Alabama, and Texas, further increasing their fortune and catapulting them into millionaire status. Their financial success enabled them to live well beyond the capacity of most blacks and allowed them to travel extensively when they were not engaging in business and civil rights activities. After Eleanor recovered from a near fatal accident that almost claimed her left eye in 1972, for example, the couple traveled to Iran, Japan, China, and other subregions of the Middle East and

Asia. They took the time to "finally enjoy some of the fruits of their labor," but they never stopped counseling and supporting efforts to advance blacks in Phoenix.[47]

Eleanor and Lincoln Ragsdale were especially active in supporting black candidates for elected office in Phoenix. They channeled a great deal of money and devoted a fair amount of energy to aiding black Phoenicians' efforts to increase black voter turnout and black representation. Their efforts helped a few African Americans to secure and keep highly visible positions in public office. These politicians worked hard to advance agendas that benefited their black constituency and people of African descent at the state, national, and international levels. In 1971, for example, Clovis Campbell Sr. fought against corruption in the Arizona House of Representatives and the misappropriation of Arizona state income tax revenues. That same year Campbell had joined others in opposing state and national legislation that supported the ongoing trade with the South African apartheid regime. In 1972 Art Hamilton, a twenty-four-year-old deputy registrar from West Phoenix, worked tirelessly and registered over four hundred voters in a two-week period. His determination in the January 29 delegate election sought to improve African American voter turnout in predominantly black districts that had historically low voter participation. The efforts to register black voters in Phoenix were also driven by the questionable handling of voter registration records in previous years. Many black Phoenicians where unaware that they had been dropped from the registration rolls as of November 4, 1970. The Republican-controlled legislature had passed a law that struck all voters from the voter registration list. All citizens had to re-register to vote to be eligible for the 1972 presidential election. The *Arizona Informant* argued that "many political observers feel this law was [enacted] primarily to eliminate blacks, poor whites, and other ethnic minorities from participating in the forthcoming elections." Many black Phoenician leaders, including Eleanor and Lincoln Ragsdale, believed that a number of Republican officials assumed that voters in African American and other less affluent communities were less likely to re-register.[48]

The efforts of the Ragsdales and other leaders to register African Americans and get them to the polls did bear fruit. Twelve blacks won in the 1972 Democratic Party presidential preference election in Arizona. The winners included seven from the Phoenix metropolitan area: Clovis Campbell Sr., Leon Thompson, Ida Nobel, and Charles Campbell from District 28; Art Hamilton and Robert Louis from District 27; and Virgil Woods from District 29 in Chandler. In 1973 accountant Calvin Goode, who had served as chairman of LEAP, was elected to the Phoenix City Council from District 8. Calvin Goode and Art Hamilton, both of whom were influenced by the work of Lincoln and Eleanor Ragsdale, emerged as major leaders in their own right during the last decades of the twentieth century. Goode served eleven consecutive terms on the Phoenix City Council and was vice mayor in 1974 and 1984. A dynamic leader, he chaired numerous committees that worked to aid families, "at-risk" young people, and neighborhoods in his predominantly black and Mexican American district in central Phoenix. Goode, who purchased Eleanor and Lincoln Ragsdales' former home on Jefferson Street in 1953, committed himself to improving the lives of black Phoenicians and all of those he served in the epicenter of the city. He was particularly committed to the Booker T. Washington Child Development Center in downtown Phoenix and the Maricopa Association of Governments Coordinating Committee. Like his mentors, he was outspoken regarding issues of race, culture, and community. Goode argued that people of color should have unrestricted access to government and equal educational and employment opportunities.[49]

Art Hamilton rose to the position of House minority leader in the Arizona legislature. He fashioned a distinguished political career that included service as president of the National Conference of State Legislatures, vice chair of the Democratic Legislative Leaders Association, and member of the Joint Legislative Tax Committee and many other influential committees. He was recognized as a highly convincing and articulate spokesman for educational reform, economic diversification, and improvement in the quality of life of Arizona citizens, particularly African Americans. In addition to Goode and Hamilton, the efforts of Lincoln and Eleanor Ragsdale helped open doors for many black political leaders in the Greater Phoenix area and throughout the state of Arizona, including Benjamin Brooks, Herschella Horton, Sandra Kennedy, Coy Payne, and Morrison Warren. Many other council members, school board members, attorneys, and superior court judges throughout the state were directly or indirectly influenced by the leadership of the Ragsdales. Prominent black Phoenix attorney Judis Andrews credited Lincoln Ragsdale for helping to launch his legal and activist career. "Lincoln Ragsdale inspired me to further my education [and go to law school]. He was like a second father to me after the passing of my own father. My personal recollections of Lincoln and Eleanor Ragsdale are too numerous to recount, but suffice it to say, Eleanor was a distinguished civil rights pacesetter, and Lincoln was a giant in Phoenix, one of the true leaders of our time." [50]

The passage of significant civil rights legislation and ordinances, the official desegregation of the Phoenician workforce, the registration of a higher number of African Americans, and the election of more black officials helped improve the lives of many black Phoenicians. Many, however, were left behind in remaining pockets of poverty. The black community in Arizona during the 1970s continued to grow, and problems of racial discrimination became more subtle and difficult to ferret out. [51]

Nevertheless, the Ragsdales' direct and indirect leadership during the 1960s and early 1970s helped cultivate black benevolence and dignity and enhance African American political power. Lincoln Ragsdale and George Brooks led the NAACP, PUL, CORE, OIC, and many other black organizations and offered direction and inspiration as well as economic and legal assistance to black Phoenicians. These organizations provided social services and outlets for cultural expression. The Broadway House apartments, for example, administered by the First Institutional Baptist Church and the Tanner Chapel Manor nursing home, were established, and a neighborhood medical center was created with the support of local black leaders such as the Ragsdales and Jessie Owens. Joe Black, of the Brooklyn Dodgers, organized and administered many programs that targeted "at-risk" inner-city black young people. Celebrated artist Eugene Grigsby introduced positive images of people of African descent through his artworks and as an instructor at ASU. African American members of the Richard H. Hamilton American Legion Post 65 introduced many in the Valley to the patriotism and courage of African Americans who had served in the military. Victories in the area of civil rights ushered in a new appreciation of black history and life. [52]

Black women continued to work for the betterment of African Americans in Phoenix. Eleanor Ragsdale collaborated with local black churches and other mutual aid societies to cultivate faith and develop secular activities geared toward advancing the black community. She played a key role in creating and awarding scholarships to meritorious college students. Furthermore, she helped sponsor the highly anticipated annual debutante cotillion, hosted by her LINKS chapter. Indeed, Eleanor continued to promote community projects, particularly educational prospects through LINKS, throughout the 1970s.[53]

During the late 1960s and 1970s discrimination and racial inequality persisted in Phoenix, and the Ragsdales committed their financial resources and energies to the fight to eliminate them. According to a 1973 study of housing in Phoenix, for example, African Americans in Phoenix, like Mexican Americans, maintained a "disproportionate share of the overcrowded population as well as a disproportionate share of families with incomes under $7,000." Eleanor and Lincoln Ragsdale continued to be disturbed at the relatively low educational attainment and employment rates among black Phoenicians. They bemoaned the fact that a high number of African Americans and Mexican Americans lived in "dilapidated housing" concentrated south of Van Buren and north of Broadway between Twenty-seventh Avenue and Forty-eighth Street. Blacks were still among the poorest and most underrepresented citizens in Phoenix. Despite lingering racism and discrimination, Eleanor and Lincoln Ragsdale were able to help facilitate some social, economic, and political improvements following more militant protests by younger insurgents. Their successful efforts to create local statues and make use of national legislation to combat de facto segregation in employment, public accommodations, housing, and voting did not eradicate racial inequality, but their achievements did improve the lives of many African Americans in Phoenix, particularly middle-class African Americans, who were positioned to benefit from such legislation the most.[54]

The Ragsdales' leadership and civil rights victories in the Valley during the late 1960s and 1970s helped change the lives of black Phoenicians in particular and race relations in Phoenix in general. Militancy in Phoenix, African Americans' renewed interest in black culture and community, and the emphasis on political participation and representation, as they did elsewhere in the nation, continued the black freedom struggle that fought persistent housing segregation, rising unemployment, and recurring incidents of police brutality. One of the Ragsdales' most enduring legacies of the era was the extent to which they contributed to the growth in the number of black elected officials in Phoenix. The legislative victories that Eleanor and Lincoln helped secure during this period aided the cause of racial equality, but they also illuminated the need for more social, economic, and political changes if true racial parity was to be reached. Poor people, especially black people who are overrepresented among the indigent, needed improvements in education, housing, and health care. Presidents Johnson, Nixon, and Ford at the national level, and Clovis Campbell Sr., Charles Campbell, Calvin Goode, and Art Hamilton at the local level, attempted to address these needs. Their efforts bore conflicting results in the face of a disastrous war in Vietnam that drew attention and resources away from Johnson's civil rights agenda and War on Poverty. Johnson's more socially progressive Democratic Party was thrown into disarray as it fought over its official position on Vietnam. The mounting social problems at home, and the intense protests they spawned during this period, created a backlash to militancy of any kind, particularly black activism.[55]

During the 1980s socially conservative Republican politicians would exploit the political problems and blunders of more progressive Democrats and usher in a conservative era that would threaten to undercut much of the progress made in the area of civil rights over the previous thirty years. This resurgence of conservative leadership, which many proponents of civil rights would argue never diminished, and the scaling back of civil rights policies and programs were a call to arms for many civil rights leaders. The Ragsdales, Lincoln in particular, were among the activists who felt compelled to speak out against the attack on civil rights and the new face of discrimination. Resigned to lead primarily from behind the scenes between 1964 and 1980, Ragsdale resurfaced during America's "conservative revolution" to lend his experience and power to a movement that he believed was once again under attack.[56]

# Chapter 6

## Black and Chicano Leadership and the Struggle for Access and Opportunity

A true alliance is based upon some self-interest of each component group and a common interest into which they merge. For an alliance to have permanence and loyal commitment from its various elements, each of them must have a goal from which it benefits and none must have an outlook in basic conflict with the others.

Martin Luther King Jr., *Where Do We Go from Here?*

THROUGHOUT THE PEAK YEARS of the civil rights movement, African Americans such as Lincoln and Eleanor Ragsdale led the way in fighting racial discrimination and the oppression of minorities in Phoenix. Interracial alliances of civil rights activists existed, but as in other regions of the country, African Americans ultimately shouldered the responsibility of dramatizing their oppression. The most visible interracial coalitions in Phoenix were largely alliances between progressive black and white citizens. Indeed, despite the fact that Mexican Americans have always comprised the largest minority population in Phoenix and have also experienced the negative effects of white racism, Mexican Americans and African Americans have never been able to form a sustained partnership in their respective quests for racial equality. Between 1950 and 1968 only a small number of Mexican American leaders supported the efforts of people like the Ragsdales. In 1957, for example, the *Arizona Sun* reported that some Mexican American leaders convinced their supporters to avoid visible contributions to the efforts of local African American activists. They argued that "even though they sympathized with the plight of the blacks," they believed "that the black problem was a black problem." This editorial flies in the face of the popular assumption that racial minorities were somehow inherently suited for and willing to participate in cross-cultural collaboration with other racial minorities. During their crusade for justice, in fact, African American and Mexican American leaders in Phoenix came to understand that their shared racial subordination was not enough to unite them in a common struggle for freedom.[1]

Before 1968 other minorities largely left black Phoenicians to their own devices to make Phoenix a more open city. Collaboration between black and Chicano activists did not increase until the Chicano movement hit Phoenix in 1968. Even at that juncture, cooperation was usually limited to individual acts of solidarity. Although their collective oppression occasionally brought African American and Mexican American activists such as the Ragsdales and their protégés together in such cases, the exigencies of race, ethnicity, culture, and class ultimately undermined their ability to register a sustained, consolidated liberation movement on behalf of both groups. Few Mexican Americans participated in local sit-ins and marches headed by Eleanor and Lincoln Ragsdale, and even fewer spoke out in support of African Americans' calls for desegregation, access to public accommodations, and the end of racial discrimination in the workplace.[2]

The *Arizona Sun* argued that the fact that black and Mexican American activists did not unite was a result of the "divide and conquer" approach employed by powerful white Phoenicians. Some Euro-Americans in Phoenix met some of the socioeconomic demands of each group, but generally they played each group against each other, were antagonistic, and did not concede much. African Americans and Mexican Americans, therefore, fought for the few resources that were made available. Neither group was able to make considerable gains as a result. Thus the fact that African Americans and Mexican Americans were unable or unwilling to form a lasting coalition may be attributed, in part, to white subversion. Nevertheless, the two groups were responsible for their inability and unwillingness to collaborate. African Americans and Mexican Americans rarely attempted to forge lasting coalitions. This "lack of cooperation," posits Bradford Luckingham, "encouraged deterioration and distrust in the relationship between the two groups."[3]

The small number of Mexican Americans who demonstrated with and lent their support to leaders like the Ragsdales in the early 1960s formed lasting relationships with black Phoenicians. During the early part of the decade, however, the relationship between the two groups generally degenerated. This failure to find common ground would lead to poor communication and cooperation among the majority of the two groups for decades to come. As early as 1957 the *Arizona Sun* argued that African Americans and Mexican Americans "made a great mistake not to work together for the benefits of both."[4]

During the early 1960s the black liberation struggle was reaching its peak, while the Chicano movement had yet to emerge. African Americans, therefore, constituted the most vocal and organized group of oppressed minorities in the country who challenged white supremacy and inequality. Federal, state, and local government agencies in Phoenix and across the country responded to African American insurgency by creating programs to address the socioeconomic needs of black people. This allocation of resources for the advancement of black Phoenicians caused some Mexican Americans to question the fairness of such appropriations. For instance, in Phoenix's LEAP program, African Americans secured the majority of the leading positions. Mexican Americans, however, argued that they had many of "the same problems" and desired a more equitable distribution of assignments. This controversy only worsened a relationship marred by indifference and animosity, as the two groups became "rivals for goodies."[5]

Lincoln Ragsdale indicated that the inability of African Americans and Mexican Americans to cooperate carried over to other arenas as well. Although Ragsdale stated flatly in a 1990 interview that "Mexicans did not discriminate against us [African Americans]," he and other leaders stated otherwise at times. Ragsdale and his fellow activists also argued that many Mexican Americans considered themselves to be a kind of white ethnic group when black Phoenicians needed their allegiance but "Mexican" when African Americans had something they wanted. Some Mexican American businesses in the Valley had also refused to serve black people in Phoenix since the late nineteenth century and continued to do so during the 1960s. Ragsdale's brother-in-law, William Dickey, led a series of protests at El Rey Cafè. Following the protests, a number of black Phoenicians were so infuriated with the owner of the restaurant for refusing to accommodate black people that they threatened to "burn it down."[6]

Lincoln Ragsdale's conflicting recollections probably reflect his desire to be critical of African American and Mexican American relations during the 1960s while also casting the two groups in a favorable light. Lincoln and Eleanor devoted a great deal of time working to close the political gap between the two groups. They wanted to create a strong multiracial coalition of proponents of civil rights. Despite the reality of African American and Mexican American relations in Phoenix in the 1960s, Lincoln Ragsdale in particular probably believed it was in the best interest of both groups to market themselves as partners in a struggle against an oppressive white majority. On the other hand, Ragsdale may not have believed that there was anything contradictory about his statements. Ultimately, he characterized Mexican Americans' discriminatory actions as an unfortunate by-product of white supremacy and economics. He did not believe Chicanos possessed a profound racial resentment of African Americans, and he did not think that the tensions between blacks and Chicanos were analogous to those between blacks and whites. For example, when some restaurants owned by Mexican Americans primarily served Mexican Americans, Ragsdale suggested, African Americans were treated fairly. Nevertheless, when white Phoenicians chose to patronize the same businesses in large numbers, owners would adopt the prevailing racial mores and customs of their white clientele.[7]

The distinct relationship between African Americans and Chicanos in Phoenix has a long history. African Americans and Mexican Americans had already settled in the area when the city was founded. Unlike black Phoenicians, however, Americans of Mexican descent can trace their lineage in the Southwest to at least AD 300. Indigenous populations in the American Southwest and Mexico, through sexual liaisons with Spanish colonizers and Africans and cultural exchange, produced persons of Spanish-Indian descent and Indians who adopted the language, religion, and customs of the Spanish. By the late 1530s these people were referred to as *mestizos* in "New Spain." By the late nineteenth century *mestizos* constituted the majority population of what was by then the Mexican and the American southwestern populations. Mexican Americans in early Phoenix, therefore, were largely a *mestizo* people—acculturated Spanish-speaking Indians and persons with both Indian and Spanish ancestry. Since the late nineteenth century, Mexican Americans with *mestizo* roots have been instrumental in the development of Phoenix.[8]

During Phoenix's early years Mexican Americans performed much-needed agricultural work. They also participated in politics, and a number of them, unlike their black counterparts, won election to minor offices as early as the 1880s. There were 772 Mexican Americans in Phoenix in 1880 out of a total population of 1,708. As a result of their large numbers, their political participation and voting habits had to be taken into consideration. As more Euro-Americans moved to Phoenix, the percentage of Mexican Americans in the city declined. By the early twentieth century white boosters led an Americanization movement in Phoenix, and through persuasion, intimidation, and coercion, they worked vigorously to "Americanize" Mexican Americans. When "Americanization" failed, some white Phoenicians simply engineered the deportation of many Mexican Americans.[9]

As with African Americans, Mexican Americans were subjected to the racism of Phoenix's ruling white elite. Like black Phoenicians, Mexican American workers in Phoenix were exploited, underpaid, and restricted to the most menial labor. Unlike black people, however, Mexican Americans with fair skin and "European features" were often deemed white by the dominant society. This racial dynamic afforded some Mexican Americans more socioeconomic mobility than their black counterparts. The founders and early boosters of Phoenix were former southerners and embraced many of the antiblack attitudes that marked southern race relations. To them, blacks essentially were anathema. Mexican Americans, on the other hand, as early as the first decade of the twentieth century were looked upon as being inferior but more acceptable by virtue of their perceived European heritage. Some Mexican Americans considered themselves to be "ethnic," such as Italian Americans or Spanish Americans. This perspective angered and alienated many blacks, who considered Mexican Americans to be, like themselves, an oppressed racial minority. These differences created stress and caused conflict between the two groups throughout the twentieth century.[10]

Despite the fact that some Mexican Americans were deemed white and considered themselves to be white, most were subjected to the indignities of Jim Crow segregation in Phoenix. Most whites in the Valley discriminated against Mexican Americans and let it be known that they did not desire their presence in the city. White Phoenicians placed signs throughout the city that declared "No Mexicans Allowed" or "No Negroes, Mexicans or Dogs allowed." When Mexican Americans were permitted to enter certain establishments, they were limited to certain days. For example, local swimming pools hosted "Mexican Day." There were "Mexican nights" at the Riverside Ballroom, and the *Arizona Republic* sponsored a picnic for "Mexican kiddies." Like black Phoenicians, Mexican Americans in the city were segregated in schools, churches, hotels, theaters, and parks.[11]

Most Mexican Americans in Phoenix's neighborhoods lived apart from white Phoenicians by constraint and by choice. When Lincoln and Eleanor Ragsdale arrived in Phoenix in the late 1940s, Mexican Americans were still the "majority minority" in the city, with a population of over 9,740. Mexican Americans made up more than 15 percent of the Phoenix population. Like African Americans, the city's Mexican American lived primarily in poor neighborhoods in South Phoenix. Their communities were located in two central areas. The most impoverished neighborhoods were located between Sixteenth and Twenty-fourth streets, from Washington Street south to the Salt River. The second area could be found south of Washington Street between Second and Seventh avenues. Residents in both neighborhoods suffered from poor health and high death rates. Exclusion and inequity, coupled with inexpensive land and lodging, common language and cultural mores, bonds to family and friends, and the desire to maintain connections to their homeland and a link to American society brought more people of Mexican descent to Phoenix's barrios.[12]

Although they were discriminated against by Phoenix's white establishment, Mexican Americans, like black Phoenicians, created vibrant communities. Mexican American churches, schools, voluntary associations, and parks emerged to promote Mexican American advancement. As Bradford Luckingham has indicated, the Mexican American community also "cultivated a cultural identity and a cultural agenda. Most important was the family, the perspective bastion of Mexican culture." Mexican families and friends intermingled at birthday parties, dances, weddings, and funerals. There were Mexican American musical and theater performances. Spanish-language newspapers emerged, and by 1950 Phoenix hosted a Mexican American community as developed as that in any city in the Southwest.[13]

As Mexican Americans began to make inroads in employment, a small Mexican American middle class developed in Phoenix. By 1940 this group began to call for better opportunities for themselves in the Valley. These leaders laid the foundation for a more intense Mexican American freedom struggle that would commence in the years to come. As Mexican Americans became more active politically, moved up the socioeconomic ladder, and worked closer with the white establishment, many black leaders grew suspicious. They did not want the few resources that were available to minorities to be given disproportionately to Mexican Americans. They also knew that many Mexican Americans did not want to share some of the resources they had secured. For instance, in 1935 the Latin American Club of Arizona presented a resolution to the Phoenix City Council requesting the exclusion of black people from Southside Park in a predominantly Mexican American neighborhood. Mexican Americans, some black observers noted, viewed themselves as being superior to black people and were therefore their adversaries.[14]

African Americans were encouraged to adopt this competitive outlook by a racial order that often reserved its most disparaging attacks for people of African descent. As a result, leaders such as Eleanor Ragsdale and Madge Copeland have suggested the discrimination that Mexican Americans experienced, though capricious and damaging, was not as rigid as that experienced by blacks. There is evidence to support this observation. Mexican American leaders were able to overcome discrimination and segregation in some socioeconomic areas in Phoenix long before black people secured such freedoms. The segregation of Mexican Americans in places of public accommodation such as restaurants, schools, theaters, and swimming pools abated during the 1940s and 1950s. With the exception of schools, African Americans would not be able to access these venues until the 1960s. The fact that Mexican Americans in Phoenix, like Euro-Americans, would conspire to bar blacks from their neighborhoods reveals the extent to which both groups discriminated against African Americans. It appears that black Phoenicians rarely, if ever, undertook to systematically exclude anyone from black neighborhoods on the basis or race, class, sex, religion, or national origin.[15]

The ability of Mexican Americans to make some progress in the realms of finance and public accommodations at a time when black Phoenicians could not contributed to uneasy relations between the two groups. These advancements can be attributed to the efforts of both Mexican Americans and African Americans and to the social construction of race in America. "The conditions that led to the inequality of Mexican Americans," argues F. Arturo Rosales, "are steeped in a legacy of conquest and then labor exploitation." The oppressive treatment of African Americans, on the other hand, can be attributed to a more fixed construction of race. This construction places black people, by virtue of their dark skin and African origins, at the bottom of the racial hierarchy. Mexican Americans were "cast as undesirable because of their Indian features," Rosales posits, but they were not often perceived to be another species altogether. Discrimination against Mexican Americans, like that against white ethnic groups such as the Irish, had more to do with white American stereotypes that portrayed Mexicans and Mexican Americans as poor, culturally divergent, and idle. These dissimilar racial constructions greatly influenced the courses of the Mexican American and African American freedom struggles. The social construction of race as it pertained to Mexican Americans was more fluid. This more elastic construction of race caused many Mexican Americans to believe their problems were largely cultural and economic, not racial. African Americans, therefore, found it objectionable that Mexican Americans were a "race" when they benefited from race-conscious remedies to racial inequality but an "ethnic group" when they sought to set themselves above and apart from African Americans and other socially constructed racial minorities. Black people in the American context did not have escape clauses when it came to the "race problem." The "race problem," after all, can be viewed as a euphemism for the "black problem."[16]

In contrast, prior to the emergence of the Mexican American civil rights movement (*el movimiento*) in the 1960s, Mexican American leaders did not focus on white supremacy and racial injustice the way that African American leaders such as Lincoln and Eleanor Ragsdale did. Nevertheless, the persecution of black people by the white majority kept the black liberation struggle at the forefront of American political culture and eventually tapped into the frustration of oppressed Mexican Americans. The abuse of black people at the hands of Euro-Americans outraged younger, more militant Mexican American leaders. As Rosales observes, this outrage helped raise the race "consciousness that was necessary for Chicanos to take the first step into activism." One reason that Mexican American activism developed more slowly than black activism is that Mexican Americans enjoyed a kind of racialized "escape hatch."[17]

Mexican Americans who, because of their color or class, were not directly influenced by intense racial bigotry managed to disregard the condition of their more tyrannized black brothers and sisters. By the late 1960s, however, young individuals from the more oppressed Mexican classes in America began to identify with their Indian heritage and the salience of race. Although the concept of race is a social construction, it has had real, detrimental social, economic, and political effects on all Americans. As a result, young, more radical Mexican Americans during the late 1960s, like their black counterparts, realized that race could not be treated simply as a specious theoretical phenomenon but instead as a genuine verity that must be denounced to be truly rendered immaterial. By the late 1960s Mexican American activists began to call attention to the negative ways in which racism adversely affected them as an oppressed racial group. They initiated a grassroots quest for civil rights, which would evolve into the Chicano movement.[18]

While Mexican American and African American communities fought "for goodies" during the early 1960s, individual African American and Mexican American leaders began to collaborate in efforts to bring attention to the poor socioeconomic state of minorities in Phoenix. Both Mexican American and African American communities continued to suffer from economic and political isolation, inadequate housing, poor schools, and underemployment. Although African Americans in Phoenix had created a community of civil rights activists by 1960, they were unable to move through the Phoenix community with the same kind of fluidity that Mexican Americans could. Despite their being ahead of black Phoenicians in several categories, however, some studies indicated that Mexican Americans displayed a lesser achievement in areas such as education. Although they did not form a substantive coalition, individual Mexican American and African American leaders between 1960 and 1968 addressed problems that were common to both groups, such as voter participation and poverty.[19]

In the early 1960s Lincoln Ragsdale worked with members of the Mexican American Political Association (MAPA) and other activist organizations to promote increased voter registration and political activism. Ragsdale worked closely with Manuel Pena, a future Arizona legislator, in the ACT campaign of 1963. Pena, owner of the Pena Realty and Insurance Company, was born in the agricultural community of Cashion, Arizona, in 1924. From 1953 to 1956 Pena served as president of the Phoenix Community Service Organization, and from 1956 through 1960, along with Ragsdale, he was a member of the PUL. When Pena and Ragsdale helped launch the ACT campaign, they both were members of the GPCCU. The two men bemoaned the lack of minority representation on the Phoenix City Council. Pena worked with Ragsdale and other leaders to improve educational opportunities for minorities in Phoenix. He argued that the problems of Mexican Americans and other minorities "lie in education, and it is our great hope that as more and more youngsters and adults become educated they will be able to take their rightful place within the larger community."[20]

Eleanor Ragsdale collaborated with Grace Gill-Olivarez, a Mexican American radio broadcaster in Phoenix who spoke out against racial discrimination. Gill-Olivarez championed better educational opportunities and increased political participation for Mexican Americans and cited white fear as the cause of many of the problems of minorities. "That small but vociferous group of Anglos that dislike us undoubtedly base their dislike on fear. They fear us because they don't know us, and they don't know us because they haven't bothered to find out what we are really like. They judge the masses by a few individuals. And this sort of attitude, I think, is harmful to this nation, or should I say, 'our' nation, because, regardless of how anyone feels about us, we are American citizens." Eleanor Ragsdale helped Gill-Olivarez solicit funds to defray the costs for a number of Mexican American high school students to attend evening job-training workshops, and she also worked with administrators at ASU to establish financial aid programs for both incoming African American and Mexican American students.[21]

Pena's and Gill-Olivarez's efforts to improve educational opportunities for minorities opened the door for more militant Mexican American leaders to emerge in the late 1960s. Mexican American students at ASU followed the lead of California activists and brought the Chicano movement to the Valley. During the spring of 1968 students at ASU, led by Alfredo Gutierrez, who had visited Los Angeles and had been inspired by working with Cesar Chavez and the farm workers movement, extended an invitation to San Francisco leader Armando Valdez to speak on campus. Valdez's fiery oratory launched a wave of activism on the ASU campus and throughout the city. These young Chicano activists soon organized under the banner of the Mexican American Student Organization (MASO). Gutierrez and his supporters, which included radical white students from the Young Socialist Alliance (YSA) and Students for a Democratic Society (SDS), demonstrated against discriminatory practices targeted at Chicanos. Gutierrez, along with Joe "Eddy" Lopez, Rosie Lopez, Manuel Dominguez, and Gustavo Gutierrez, also helped establish organizations such as Chicanos por la Causa (CPLC) in Phoenix's barrios to combat racial discrimination.[22]

The kind of collaboration that occasionally occurred between Lincoln and Eleanor Ragsdale and local Mexican American leaders like Manuel Pena and Grace Gill-Olivarez would be rare by the 1970s. Although the Chicano movement was inspired by the black liberation struggle, the two movements never formed an alliance. Chicano activists, having a more sophisticated race consciousness than their predecessors, were not as prone to harbor the same antiblack feelings, however. They understood that the white supremacy that had terrorized and oppressed African Americans was in many ways the same white supremacy that had subjugated them. Nevertheless, Chicano activists in Phoenix were primarily interested in justice for their people, not integration with white or black Phoenicians. This approach, although it helped usher in positive change in the short term, would continue to undermine the ability of Mexican Americans and African Americans to work together effectively.[23]

Tensions between black and Chicano Phoenicians erupted during the fall of 1970, after competition over representation and resources at Phoenix Union High School reached a fever pitch. Alfredo Gutierrez, Joe "Eddy" Lopez, Manuel Dominquez, Earl Wilcox, several CPLC leaders, and the parents of a number of Mexican American students at the school argued that the high school did not responded appropriately to the needs of the expanding population of primarily black and Mexican American students. The school boasted few black and Mexican American teachers, and the school's predominantly white teachers and administrators were accused of running an institution that was "full of discrimination and exploitation." One observer noted that the school's leaders "have failed miserably to provide equality and equitable education" for people of color. The school's counselors were also known to lead Mexican American and African American students "toward manual rather than intellectual development, without consideration of the fact that such a choice produces and perpetuates economic-racial discrimination."[24]

The number of white students at Phoenix Union High School declined steadily following Phoenix's 1953 desegregation ruling. The landmark decision triggered white flight. By 1967 whites were abandoning the area and the school in large numbers. Between 1967 and 1970 the percentage of white students at Phoenix Union High School dropped from 35.1 percent to 19.3 percent. Many observers had begun to refer to the school as a "minorities" school. Although racial segregation in schools had been ruled illegal, the relative poor economic status and immobility of African Americans and Mexican Americans locked them into inner-city schools that were by now predominantly black and Chicano. Mexican Americans and African Americans had virtually no power, however, to shape the school's curriculum, hiring, structure, and administration. This segregated, unequal, and unstable environment exacerbated the already tense relationship between the Mexican American and African American students and their parents by forcing them to compete for inadequate resources. Fist fights and other violent confrontations between blacks and Chicanos occurred almost daily at the high school. Each side blamed the other for the altercations. Mexican American students claimed that they were routinely abused by black students. Chicano leaders "protested harassment of their children by black students and the school system's failure to cope with the high drop-out rate of Mexican American students." Chicano leaders held regular marches and demonstrations and demanded that the school's leaders move to correct these problems.[25]

On October 9, 1970, Chicano leaders initiated a boycott of Phoenix Union High School. The CPLC and the newly formed Parent-Student Boycott Committee (PSBC) demanded that "law and order on the campus be restored." The PSBC and CPLC also indicated that they would not end the boycott until the "unlawful activity by black students be addressed by authorities." The school's administrators, Chicano leaders complained, were scared to deal with black Phoenicians because of their fear of escalating the conflict. These events disturbed and saddened Lincoln and Eleanor Ragsdale. They had managed to help desegregate the city's schools, only to have whites flee these previously racially restricted institutions to leave black and Chicano students in what became poorly administered schools that discriminated against them and placed them in adversarial positions that were destined for trouble. The conflict between Chicano students and black students and the lack of security at Phoenix Union High School were major problems, but they were just two of many in the eyes of Chicano leaders. Protesters also desired a more demanding and culturally sensitive curriculum. The impasse was eventually resolved, and the high school's officials promised to hire more Latino employees and to implement programs that were more mindful of the instructional needs of Chicano students. Although officially settled, the crisis at Phoenix Union High School simply intensified alienation and anger between African Americans and Chicanos in Phoenix. The Ragsdales and their Mexican American counterparts had worked hard to form a substantive coalition, but the standoff at the high school seriously undermined their efforts.[26]

Like African Americans, greater numbers of individual Chicanos advanced as educational and employment opportunities developed in the wake of the civil rights movement. With the support of their individual constituencies, Chicano and black leaders made progress in the political arena. Black leader Calvin Goode and Rosendo Gutierrez, a Mexican American, won seats on the Phoenix City Council. Similarly, Art Hamilton and Alfredo Gutierrez were elected to the Arizona legislature. Gutierrez participated in a close, heated contest against incumbent and Lincoln Ragsdale understudy Clovis Campbell Sr. Both were running for seats from neighborhoods primarily composed of Mexican Americans and African Americans. Revealing the improved ability of Chicano activists to "get out the vote," Gutierrez won a tight election, where the greater numbers of Mexican Americans in the area proved to be the deciding factor. Campbell believed that the election "got down to who got out the more votes—Hispanics or blacks. He got out more Hispanic votes."[27]

During the 1970s and 1980s the percentage of Mexican Americans in Phoenix's population increased, and they remained the largest minority group in Phoenix through 1990. The increase in the Latino community greatly affected the African American community. Black neighborhoods hosted large influxes of Mexican Americans, which put pressure on local services that had previously been geared toward African Americans. One report observed that "African Americans complain that Hispanics are taking a bigger piece of that tiny slice of economic pie left for minorities. It's the same piece African Americans say they have fought for generations to get." Leaders of the city's Latino population answered by noting that African Americans "don't have an exclusive on the legacy of suffering, and that civil rights in this country, through programs like Affirmative Action, have favored African Americans." African Americans and Latinos, particularly Mexican Americans, continued to fight for insufficient resources, and as Latinos migrated to the Valley in much larger numbers than blacks, tensions remained. Moreover, the rising Latino and Chicano populations ushered in greater economic and political power that outpaced that of what continued to be a small black population. Many whites feared that this growing Latino population, coupled with the ongoing activism of an expanding black middle class, would pose a serious threat to the overall white socioeconomic and political order. Others cited historical precedent and argued that there remained those in the city "who would rather see" and work to make "the Hispanics and blacks divide and fight against themselves."[28]

Between 1970 and 1990 additional members of the Latino and black communities enjoyed the professional and financial success that the Ragsdales, Pena, and Gill-Olivarez did. Eventually, those who could afford to do so scattered throughout the city, leaving their African American and Mexican American communities. It was easier for middle-class Mexican Americans to move into predominantly white middle-class neighborhoods than it was for African Americans, however. The successes of the Chicano and civil rights movements, coupled with economic expansion, made it easier for Mexican Americans to benefit from new opportunities. Like African Americans, the majority of Mexican Americans and other Latinos continued to be mired in poverty.[29]

Despite the fact that most African Americans and Mexican Americans lived in poverty born of historic and lingering racial discrimination, each group continued to have a difficult time assisting one another. Coalition building was extremely challenging amid competition for resources and cultural distinction. The failure to find common ground was more than a minor concern, and by 1991 there were signs that both groups wanted to work harder to form a substantive alliance. Some Mexican American leaders voiced their concerns over the inability or unwillingness of both groups to work together. These leaders announced that "we've fought over limited resources, and we're tired of doing that. We want to unite for a greater share of the resources." Many people praised these ideals, but to create such a coalition proved to be quite complicated. The relationship between

Housing and income indicators in African American and Mexican
American high-concentration neighborhoods in Phoenix, 1970

| | Median value housing | Moderately crowded housing | Severely crowded housing | Families with public assistance income | Families with Social Security income |
|---|---|---|---|---|---|
| Phoenix | $18,582 | 7% | 2% | 3% | 20% |
| African American and Mexican American high-concentration neighborhoods | $8,991 | 12% | 9% | 16% | 21% |

| | Income <50% of poverty level | Income 50-100% of poverty level | Income 50-66% times of poverty level | Income >66% of poverty |
|---|---|---|---|---|
| Phoenix | 4% | 5% | 43% | 48% |
| African American and Mexican American high-concentration neighborhoods | 12% | 15% | 54% | 17% |

*Source:* John E. Crow, *Mexican Americans in Contemporary Arizona: A Social Demographic View* (San Francisco: R and E Research, 1975), 69; Bradford Luckingham, *Minorities in Phoenix: A Profile History of Mexican American, Chinese American, and African American Communities, 1860–1992* (Tucson: University of Arizona Press, 1994), 180.

Chicanos and black Phoenicians continued to be fragile, and both groups persisted in their bid for the status of most-favored minority.[30]

This competition to promote their unique cultures and shed light on their socioeconomic problems instigated bitter conflicts between the two groups in the last decade of the twentieth century. In September 1990, for example, African American parents called for the firing of Alexander Perez, the Mexican American superintendent of the predominantly Latino Roosevelt School District. The parents accused Perez of being "insensitive" to the needs of black students and African American personnel. Leaders of the African American Parents for Quality Education (AAPQE) also accused Perez of favoritism, charging him with hiring more Mexican Americans than African Americans. The controversy lingered for months, as African American leaders such as George Brooks and a number of Mexican American leaders participated in "educational politics."[31]

Some black and Chicano leaders denied that a racial conflict existed between the two groups, but the competition for jobs in the school district, the largest employer in South Phoenix, was formidable. The Chicano and black neighborhoods in South Phoenix suffered from economic isolation and deprivation and high unemployment. Jobs were precious, and each group wanted them.

Ultimately, the Roosevelt School District board, headed by Brooks, voted to buy out Perez's contract and initiate a search for a new superintendent. The three African American board members voted in favor of his departure, and the two Mexican American board members voted for his retention.[32]

Mexican Americans and African Americans have never been monolithic groups. Conflicts within the two communities, therefore, have also contributed to the inability of black and Chicano Phoenicians to form lasting alliances. Mexican Americans and African Americans found it difficult to agree among themselves, let alone with other racial minorities. Thus any attempt to form an alliance with another racial minority was bound to be fraught with complications. By the 1980s and 1990s African Americans were debating new strategies to obtain socioeconomic equality. A new cadre of black conservatives such as Ward Connerly, Ken Hamblin, Thomas Sowell, Shelby Steele, and Armstrong Williams emerged and stood in opposition to the traditional liberal politics of many African American activists. These new black conservatives, or "negrocons," as historian Robin D. G. Kelley has called them, placed much of the blame for the poor status of most African Americans during the 1980s and 1990s on "racial preferences" rather than racism. Black neoconservatives have argued that race-conscious remedies and civil rights legislation are virtually meaningless, as the socioeconomic woes of poor black people are the product of retrograde cultural practices, fragmented families, and black irresponsibility.[33] Despite the outward acceptance of such thinkers by the white conservative establishment, most African Americans have rejected the antiblack overtones embedded in their message. The political philosophies of these leaders are rooted in a capitalist ethos that privileges individual attainment, competition, and hubris.[34]

Likewise, by the 1980s and 1990s many people believed that Mexican Americans' individual aspirations for political power and enhanced material wealth wore away the "one-for-all" sense of unity that many had believed formed the foundation of Mexican American communities in the past. Mexican American leaders, it was argued, no longer saw themselves entirely as part of a suffering collective but, like so many of their white "me-generation contemporaries," began to "look out for *numero uno.*" Competing ambitions, although they no doubt existed in the past, had finally emerged from the realm of intraracial obscurity within the larger matrix of interracial race relations. During this period many Mexican American activists became part of Phoenix's establishment. Although they remained active, their politics now reflected their economic status. They became less involved in CPLC and similar groups. The Chicano leadership during this era, in many ways a product of the more activist 1960s and 1970s, one observer posited, may have been the "victim of its own earlier success."[35] Bradford Luckingham maintains that "the prevailing mood among the leaders appeared to be one of 'middle-class malaise,' with too few flashes of 'minority concern.' The 'good life' seemed to have carried them away from 'the struggle.' Hispanic leaders, it was said, were losing touch with the people they were supposed to be leading. Splits fragmented the Hispanic community and made it tougher to solve common problems."[36]

The conflicts that developed between individuals and groups within the African American and Mexican American communities in Phoenix demonstrated the heterogeneity of each group. Multiplicity permeated the lives of all African Americans and Mexican Americans in Phoenix. Despite the fact that the majority of their respective communities demonstrated solidarity in the face of sometimes overwhelming adversity, the 1980s and 1990s brought fragmentation and heightened ideological separatism to African American and Mexican American communities in Phoenix. Each group made progress, however, largely due to the efforts of leaders and activists such as Lincoln and Eleanor Ragsdale, Manuel Pena, Grace Gill-Olivarez, Alfredo Gutierrez, and Clovis Campbell Sr. Some African Americans and Mexican Americans, such as the Ragsdales and Pena, made more gains than others.[37]

By the 1950s and 1960s Mexican Americans began to see that the success of black civil rights leaders like Eleanor and Lincoln Ragsdale was secured by insisting that racism was responsible for many of the problems that both African Americans and Mexican Americans faced. The success of individuals such as Lincoln Ragsdale in integrating the armed forces, for instance, demonstrated that some victories could be won by appealing to the conscience of the white establishment. The efforts of Ragsdale and his contemporaries, posits Rosales, inspired Mexican Americans to forgo their claims of being "white Americans of ethnic descent—like Italian Americans or Polish Americans—and to start identifying with the course favored by blacks." Chicano activists also rejected the white ethnic identity because sometimes it "backfired." For example, "demands for a jury of peers," argued Rosales, "when the defendant was Mexican, were met with retorts that seating all-Anglo juries did not exclude the Mexican race since it was supposedly white."[38]

Mexican Americans were very impressed with the "success" of the black liberation struggle and by the late 1960s consciously or unconsciously emulated many of its strategies. Mexican Americans in Phoenix witnessed the victories black leaders like the Ragsdales were helping to win by employing boycotts, sit-ins, and political pressure and by directly charging white Phoenicians with racism. As Mexican American leaders such as Manuel Pena championed these methods, they opened the door for an entire generation of militant young Chicanos to become influential players in state and national politics by the 1990s. Lincoln and Eleanor Ragsdales' leadership in Phoenix, therefore, not only proved to be critical to the black freedom struggle in the city but also to the Chicano movement in the area as well.[39]

Although black and Chicano Phoenicians were unable to form a sustained alliance, Phoenix did benefit from the development of two racial liberation movements in the region. "In terms of strategy, tactics, and objectives," Quintard Taylor Jr. argues, "most western protests paralleled those waged east of the Mississippi River. However, many of these protests occurred in a milieu where African Americans were only one of a number of groups of color." As a result, Taylor maintains, "the region's multiracial population moved civil rights beyond 'black and white.'" Perhaps unwittingly, African Americans and Mexican Americans, and their respective liberation movements, forced the region's white population to address race in ways that other parts of the country had not.[40]

For example, the Ragsdales and leaders such as Alfredo Gutierrez and Joe "Eddy" Lopez pressed white city officials to address the many ills of black and Mexican American neighborhoods that suffered from racial discrimination and socioeconomic isolation. Both of these groups occupied various sections of central and South Phoenix, where de facto segregation limited their mobility and access to vital social and educational services. The Ragsdales and Gutierrez argued that the socioeconomic status of both African Americans and Mexican Americans was directly related to racial discrimination and the negative effects of white supremacy. The appeals of such leaders put forth penetrating calls for the end of white supremacist politics and racial discrimination in Phoenix. Together, these autonomous pleas constituted a collective outcry for racial equality. White Phoenicians were sometimes forced to listen and respond to these integrated demands, without acknowledging their bifurcated origins. By the 1970s the Ragsdales, along with Gutierrez and Lopez, continued to argue that racial inequality contributed to the creation and maintenance of segregated neighborhoods, housing, and schools. This spatial segregation, coupled with employment segregation, created a vicious cycle of poverty and hopelessness in African American and Mexican American neighborhoods.[41]

White flight to the suburbs, de facto segregation, high drop-out rates in inner-city schools, and government reductions in educational expenditures led to the closure of Phoenix Union High School in June 1982. The school's closing led to further dislocations in the school district. For instance, in 1987 the Phoenix Union High School District remained under federal court order to desegregate. Nevertheless, growing racial segregation patterns in housing in the predominantly African American and Mexican American neighborhoods that formed the district made it difficult to comply with the order. In response, the district created "magnet schools" to retain and recruit white students, and it revised enrollment requirements to thwart white flight. The success of these efforts was, at best, marginal. Given the socioeconomic status, high drop-out rates, and poor educational circumstances of most African Americans and Chicanos at the elementary and secondary levels in the Valley, few African Americans and Mexican Americans enrolled in ASU, the area's primary institution of higher learning. Moreover, many who did enroll dropped out. For example, in 1984 the *Arizona Republic* wrote that "only 2 to 3 percent of the more that 40,000 students at ASU are Hispanic and the percentage of faculty members is even smaller."[42] Critics such as Eleanor Ragsdale argued that "too few minority children receive the education they need to succeed in metropolitan Phoenix." Many of the university's recruiters bemoaned "the lack of qualified ethnic students available." Statistics revealed that the percentage of African Americans attending ASU was around half that of the black Phoenician population. Latino students at ASU represented just a third of the Latino population in the Greater Phoenix area.[43]

At least one ASU administrator argued that "attempts to increase the college enrollment and graduation rates need to begin in elementary school" and that "they need to consist of a combined effort by many community organizations, including business, churches and public schools." Many of the city's most active leaders, particularly Eleanor Ragsdale, argued that it was in the best interest of all Phoenicians to "provide opportunities for all children, regardless of race, to have a quality education." As late as 1990 Lincoln and Eleanor Ragsdale continued to criticize ASU for not being aggressive in its efforts to recruit and retain students, faculty, and administrators of color. The Ragsdales donated a great deal of money to ASU's Alumni Association and other organizations and programs that worked to increase the number of racial minorities who entered and graduated from the university. Lincoln Ragsdale's support of ASU in general was intense, and his devotion to diversifying the student population was profound. The Ragsdales' service and their ability to raise funds for various programs at the university led to Lincoln being elected president of the ASU Alumni Association. Despite the Ragsdales' efforts, the diversification of ASU was a slow process. Many Latino leaders throughout the city also lamented the low number of racial minorities among high-ranking ASU officials and the university's apparent unwillingness to address the issues promptly. In 1990, for example, Edward Valenzuela, leader of the Arizona Hispanic Community Forum, declared that "it is unacceptable for ASU officials to claim that there are 'no qualified' candidates. That ruse is old hat."[44]

Although African American and Mexican American leaders and activists such as the Ragsdales, Pena, and Gutierrez produced spirited and articulate calls for racial equality during the 1970s and 1980s, particularly in education, their autonomous yet ostensibly linked opposition to white supremacy was not enough to bring together a critical mass of African Americans and Chicanos to pose a formidable challenge to the status quo. Nonetheless, black Phoenicians, and the fight for racial equality in Phoenix, did benefit intellectually and strategically from the presence of two major racial liberation movements in the Valley. The Chicano population in Phoenix challenged the city's African Americans in ways that blacks in the East and South did not have to contemplate. The Chicano population in Phoenix, and throughout the West, "represented a paradox to black activists," Taylor writes. The presence of Mexican Americans in Phoenix "deflected prejudice from African Americans" at times, but "because they suffered less discrimination than blacks, most Chicanos remained silent on discrimination."[45] Like white Phoenicians, Mexican Americans also supported systematic campaigns to discriminate against black people. These facts inspired San Antonio NAACP leader Claude Black to state that "it's like having a brother violate [your] rights. You can hate the brother much more than you would the outsider because you expected more from the brother." The vital contributions of individual Chicano leaders to the civil rights movement, however, may have been the best that leaders like the Ragsdales could have expected. For African Americans and Chicanos, race, culture, and class were difficult to transcend, even in the face of an overwhelmingly oppressive white establishment.[46]

Despite the Ragsdales' efforts and the individual efforts of their Mexican American counterparts, by the end of the twentieth century the masses of African Americans and Mexican Americans continued to struggle, while leaders from both sides debated the degree to which each oppressed minority suffered the most. Under this competitive atmosphere, a sustained coalition of African American and Mexican American activists continued to be difficult to build. Nevertheless, hope for such an alliance remained. As long as each group experienced the negative effects of racial inequality, there existed a common ground upon which a union might be forged. History has demonstrated that such a union could not be based upon romanticized notions of the past and interracial solidarity but instead on practical prescriptions of cross-cultural collaboration that emphasized action and efficacy.[47]

Although the Ragsdales and their Mexican American collaborators made some inroads in interracial coalition building, African Americans and Mexican Americans found it very difficult to break out of the cycle of racial polarization and fragmentation. Many local observers assumed, incorrectly, that simply because the two groups chafed under the omnipresent corporeality of racial discrimination, they would be "natural" allies in the fight against white supremacy. A radical shift in the way both groups viewed their most fundamental relationship as human beings would have been required to overcome the racial divide that separated them. They would have had to, according to historian Richard W. Thomas, first "recognize the organic unity of the human race" and their shared experiences as peoples who suffered under the yoke of racial discrimination. This, Thomas maintains, "cannot occur

African American, Mexican American, and European
American population statistics: Phoenix, 1940–2000

| Year | African American population | African American percentage of population | Mexican American population | Mexican American percentage of population | Total Phoenix population |
|------|------|------|------|------|------|
| 1940 | 4,263 | 7 | 9,740 | 15 | 65,414 |
| 1950 | 5,217 | 5 | 16,000 | 15 | 106,818 |
| 1960 | 20,919 | 5 | 61,460 | 14 | 439,170 |
| 1970 | 27,896 | 5 | 81,239 | 14 | 584,303 |
| 1980 | 37,672 | 5 | 116,875 | 15 | 789,704 |
| 1990 | 51,053 | 5 | 176,139 | 18 | 983,403 |
| 2000 | 67,416 | 5 | 375,096 | 28 | 1,321,045 |

*Source:* U.S. Bureau of the Census, *Population of the United States,* 1940–2000. Between 1940 and 2000, Chinese Americans were perhaps third largest racial group in Phoenix. The Chinese population was recorded as being 431 in 1940, 448 in 1950, 1,092 in 1960, 1,483 in 1970, 3,493 in 1980, 4,254 in 1990, and 5,964 in 2000.

unless a person is deeply committed to a core set of values and principles" that include unqualified demands for the equal treatment of all persons before the law. If a critical mass of blacks and Chicanos, and any other group, would have been able to "reach this stage of commitment," argues Thomas, they would have be able to "break free of the cycle of racial polarization and fragmentation and move into a cycle of racial unity" based upon similarities rather than differences.[48]

Given the heterogeneity of the black and Chicano populations in Phoenix, it is not surprising that the two groups generally failed to "recognize the organic unity of the human race," overcome their differences, and build an alliance based upon similarities. Individual leaders such as Manuel Pena and Grace Gill-Olivarez, however, did support the local civil rights movement and leaders such as Lincoln and Eleanor Ragsdale. Pena, who was the lone Latino during the 1963–64 ACT campaign, aided the black freedom struggle and became one of a handful of Mexican Americans on the GPCCU. Rosendo Gutierrez, who served on the Phoenix City Council during the 1970s, advocated early childhood education for Mexican American and African American children and fought against racial discrimination in government and in the private sector. These Mexican Americans, like many white activists, truly identified with black calls for change and their indisputable critiques of the burdensome effects of racism and white supremacy. They also, however, believed that the success of the civil rights movement would lead to the eradication of discrimination against Mexican Americans as well. Although these individuals worked tirelessly in the interest of racial equality, Mexican Americans and African Americans largely fought racism and white supremacy on two fronts. A sustained African American and Mexican American coalition of civil rights activists and race workers would never emerge in the Valley.[49]

# Part Three

Moving Forward Counterclockwise

# Chapter 7

## The Struggle for Racial Equality in Phoenix, 1980–2000

> We leave a problem of racism for a period, but it returns. It always will. Race is a perpetual dilemma.
>
> Glover G. Hankins, *Crisis*, June 1986

BETWEEN 1946 AND 1980 the civil rights movement was very effective in breaking down legal and political barriers to African American socioeconomic equality. By the 1980s, however, black activists such as Lincoln and Eleanor Ragsdale realized that racial discrimination and the legacy of white supremacy continued to be crippling barriers between many African Americans and upward mobility. As the 1980s commenced, African Americans had reached an unprecedented period in their history. Due in large part to the successes of the civil rights movement, the largest black middle class in the nation's history had emerged. At the same time, however, millions of black people continued to live at or below the poverty line as a result of historic and persistent racial discrimination. Despite ongoing racial inequality in America, many conservative pundits cited the success of the black middle class and the notion of a "color blind" society as reasons to abandon race-conscious remedies to America's racial problems. Acting on these beliefs and others, conservative leaders ushered in an era of intense social and fiscal conservatism in America, the likes of which had not been seen in America since the 1950s. The impetus of this conservative renewal drew substantially from a broad-based negative reaction to civil rights agitation and African American advancement. These neoconservative forces sought to undermine the laws, court cases, and symbolic victories that leaders such as Lincoln and Eleanor Ragsdale had struggled to win. The Ragsdales believed that aspects of this neoconservative movement, especially its tendency to seek out and overturn race-conscious remedies to racial inequality and dismiss institutionalized symbols of racial solidarity, needed to be opposed. During the 1980s and 1990s the Ragsdales, particularly Lincoln, resurfaced as outspoken progressive leaders. Lincoln's goal was to work publicly again to help solve the problems of socioeconomic inequality and continual racial discrimination and disunity.[1]

Between 1946 and 1980 the civil rights movement, in addition to producing an impressive list of accomplishments, gave rise to intense divisions within the African American community. For generations, slavery, Jim Crow, and racial discrimination, and the arduous struggle to destroy them, had inspired black solidarity. Black people have never been a homogeneous group, but acute oppression compelled them to conceal many of their ideological differences. By 1980, however, African Americans began to disagree publicly on social, economic, and political issues more often. They no longer dissembled.[2] Conflicts between the expanding black middle class and dispossessed African Americans locked into decaying inner cities broadened. Disputes between the proponents of integration, assimilation, and black nationalism surged. Chief among the warring factions that emerged were black neoconservatives such as writers Thomas Sowell, Shelby Steele, Ward Connerly, and Armstrong Williams and the black liberal establishment, which included leaders such as civil rights activist Jessie Jackson, attorney Randall Robinson, historian Mary Francis Berry, and philosopher Cornel West. By the 1980s African Americans were embracing myriad strategies to obtain and maintain socioeconomic equality. Regardless of the various philosophies that were bandied about, however, at issue still were the progress and stability of the black community.[3]

By 1980 Lincoln and Eleanor Ragsdale had led a civil rights movement that had improved the lives of many African Americans in Phoenix and made the city a freer place in which to live. By this time the African American population in Phoenix was 37,672, or 5 percent of the total population. This was an increase of 9,776 since 1970. By 1990 the number of African Americans in the city reached 51,053. During this period many African Americans, a substantial percentage of whom were businesspeople, made their way into the middle class.

The more rewarding aspects of new awareness and sensitivity toward civil rights and racial equality enabled some African Americans to capitalize on new economic and political opportunities. Socioeconomic advancement for African Americans as a smaller racial group within the larger Phoenix population, however, continued to be sluggish.[4]

Progress was made in education and employment for individual African Americans, and changes in the composition of Phoenix's political structure yielded greater African American representation. For example, Phoenix switched to a district system of government in 1983. This allowed South and West Phoenix to elect more minorities to the Phoenix City Council. Calvin Goode, an African American, continued to represent District 8, while Mary Rose Garrido Wilcox, a Mexican American, was elected from District 7. Wilcox represented a district where Mexican Americans made up the majority of the residents, and Goode represented a district where African Americans and Mexican Americans together made up the voting majority. Progressive black leader Art Hamilton and Chicano leader Alfredo Gutierrez were elected to the Arizona legislature, where they represented districts comprised predominantly of African American and Mexican American voters.[5]

During the 1980s many African Americans who could afford it followed Lincoln Ragsdale to the suburbs. Indeed, by 1980 Lincoln Ragsdale had helped found the Southwest Savings and Loan Association and the Sun State Savings and Loan Association, expanding his fiscal connections and influence on Arizona's financial community. The Ragsdales had been among the richest black families in Phoenix for at least a decade, but by 1980 they were now among the wealthiest African American families in the Southwest. It came as no surprise, therefore, that when the Ragsdale family sold their home near the affluent "old-money" PalmCroft neighborhood in central Phoenix they purchased a new, palatial estate in the elite, predominantly white Phoenix suburb of Clearwater Hills in Paradise Valley in 1969. For most black Phoenicians, however, moving into wealthy white neighborhoods continued to be extremely difficult for economic and social reasons.[6] Although racism was "not as overt, not as blatant as it once was," declared Phoenix television reporter Evelyn Thompson, racial barriers still existed in Phoenix. "When I first came here in 1971," she maintained, "a real estate agent said to me, 'Blacks don't live north of Thomas Road. I'm not going to show you any apartments in that area because nobody will rent to you.'" Indeed, Phoenix's Equal Opportunity Department stated in 1987 that housing discrimination persisted in the Valley and continued to exacerbate segregated living patterns.[7]

Many black Phoenicians were disappointed when the Ragsdales moved to Paradise Valley. Persistent white antagonism and housing discrimination, the deterioration of black Phoenician neighborhoods, and the flight of successful black leaders from predominantly African American communities caused some black leaders to be critical of the Ragsdales' move. Moreover, between the mid-1960s and 1980 Lincoln Ragsdale had come to be regarded not as a progressive activist with a decidedly radical disposition but as a member of the establishment. Although his dedication to the betterment of African Americans never waned, his behind-the-scenes, work-within-the-system approach to black empowerment and the physical space between him and the majority of black Phoenicians began to conflict with the more nationalistic agenda of less conservative black leaders. Local leaders of the black liberation movement questioned Ragsdale's willingness to live in and publicly support the black community he had so willingly represented.[8]

The relatively small number of black Phoenicians who reached the middle and upper classes and moved to the city's suburbs, thanks to civil rights legislation and antipoverty programs, left less-fortunate African Americans behind in communities replete with economic and social problems. The departure of leading blacks such as Eleanor and Lincoln Ragsdale from the central city created a tremendous vacuum in the area of role models and mentors for would-be black professionals. In addition, their withdrawal, many observers argued, made the kind of race work the Ragsdales had engaged in difficult to maintain. Some observers celebrated the ascendancy of wealthy African Americans and cited their affluence as evidence of racial progress. Others argued that although many more blacks managed to reach middle-class status, blacks in general still lagged behind whites with regard to debt-to-income ratio, earnings, savings, home ownership, and overall wealth. The mobility of middle-class blacks, in and of itself, it was argued, did not signal a fundamental shift in the racial status quo or in the lives of most African Americans.

On the one hand, the growth of the black middle class reflected the success of the civil rights movement. On the other hand, the exodus of prosperous African Americans from black communities hastened the deterioration of black neighborhoods and undermined black electoral and economic autonomy. This dichotomy revealed the limitations of racial integration as a cure-all solution to racial inequality.[9]

Clovis Campbell Sr., former representative in the Arizona State Senate, African American newspaper publisher, community activist, and one-time Ragsdale protègè, believes that the Ragsdales' suburban emigration represented a destructive trend in post–civil rights African American history. Campbell has declared that "if you leave the neighborhood, you leave it for nothing but the hoods." Leaders such as Campbell have called attention to the fact that the movement of African American professionals from black urban communities to white suburban areas has lowered the number of black role models in the communities they have left behind, and "if [there's] one thing black young people need," Campbell maintains, "[it's] good images of their professional people. You've got a lot of people who want to teach and preach in South Phoenix, but they don't want to sleep in South Phoenix. They want to take all of the [black] resources out to Paradise Valley, Scottsdale, and Glendale. There's nothing wrong with [black professionals] moving [to the suburbs], that's great!" When these professionals do move to the suburbs, however, Campbell believes it would be appropriate for them to "go work there."[10] Campbell argues that the growing dispersal of affluent blacks to suburban communities has come at a high price:

> Many blacks, once they get appointed to their "antipoverty" jobs, have a tendency to become disinterested in "inner-city" problems. Sometimes they move so far from blacks that (believe it or not) the [the black-owned and -operated] *Arizona Informant* is their only way of knowing what is going on in the black community. So-called leaders were very articulate, and they convinced "the man" they were leaders and received insignificant appointments or small favors [in return]. Unfortunately these appointments helped the individual, while the black community remained the same, mired in poverty and underdeveloped.[11]

Activists such as Campbell also called for black professional leaders to return to active duty in the fight for black advancement during the 1980s. The decade witnessed a resurgence of white conservativism, attacks on gains made during the civil rights movement, and racialized violence. This resurgence prompted many local and national leaders to rededicate themselves to African American progress and racial healing. Lincoln Ragsdale stood tall throughout the fight for black freedom during the 1950s and 1960s, and many local activists were calling upon him to speak out again on behalf of the subordinated classes of racial minorities in Phoenix.[12] The Ragsdales were aware of the dilemma that their urban exodus created. The couple, therefore, worked to assist state and local agencies and organizations that sought to improve black neighborhoods by providing resources to stem the rising tide of poverty, crime, and increasing drug trafficking. By 1980 the Ragsdales had supported a black outreach program on East Broadway Road in South Phoenix that was administered by Gene Blue. The goal of the program was to address the growing problem of drug abuse in the area. Blue indicated that the program was "going to be an outreach and aftercare facility. We are interested in the total person and [we] will deal with his problems on an individual basis from detox right on through the long route to gainful employment." Residents in the South Phoenix neighborhood also initiated a volunteer program to prevent housing blight and improve school and park infrastructure. In addition, they worked to increase voter turnout in predominantly black electoral districts to mitigate the negative effects of the diffusion of the city's registered and active black voters.[13]

Despite the best efforts of the Ragsdales, social workers, mutual aid societies, and African American politicians, black communities still reeled in the face of de facto segregation, lingering racism, socioeconomic isolation, and "black flight." Black Phoenicians such as the Ragsdales were not immune to the kind of racial isolation and discrimination that African Americans in the inner city experienced. Both subtle and overt discrimination continued to saturate life in Phoenix and across the nation during the 1980s. "Racism is still a significant factor in the lives of blacks in Phoenix," noted one observer. "Discrimination and barriers are more subtle than they used to be, and the perception of them is defined by the individual's own attitudes and personal experiences, but it is still here."[14] Judis R. Andrews, local attorney and one-time Lincoln Ragsdale apprentice, believed that racism was still an issue in the 1980s and 1990s, and he argues that recent racial segregation is rooted primarily in economics. Segregation and discrimination have been curbed for the most part, he suggests, but "[racial] segregation remains along income and financial lines which impact all Americans inasmuch as we live in a fiscal country where the dollar remains king."[15]

By the time Lincoln Ragsdale neared the end of his life, in fact, he not only believed that integration was marginally successful in improving the socioeconomic status of most blacks and eradicating racial inequality, but he also thought that white people benefited more from racial integration. He argued that many black businesses, including his own, struggled at times after de jure segregation was destroyed. Many black businesses simply failed. Once blacks could access places of public accommodation and patronize any business they liked, he stated, "they did just that." Many African Americans, Lincoln Ragsdale Jr. maintains, took "their business and their dollars" to white businesses that would now serve them equally, while most whites refused to support black businesses. This scenario weakened the financial stability of black communities and, ostensibly, curbed the mobility of many blacks, while it pumped additional capital into white businesses and communities that already enjoyed more stable financial health.[16]

The adaptability and insidiousness of racial inequality continually tested the Ragsdales' resolve and sometimes placed a major burden on their marriage. As Lincoln Ragsdale became more aware of the limitations of racial integration and aggravated with the elasticity of white supremacy, he became increasingly affected. He often looked for outlets to release his frustration. Lincoln, for example, had always "enjoyed a good drink," but by the 1980s he began to consume alcoholic beverages often to relieve what Gwendolyn Ragsdale Madrid describes as the "unbelievable amount of stress that he endured." Ragsdale Madrid remembers her father coming home to their estate in Clearwater Hills one day and announcing to her that his physician had cautioned him to cut back on his drinking so as to avoid becoming a full-fledged "night-time alcoholic." Lincoln, who had always been known for his combativeness, also coped with his stress by lashing out at those closest to him. More often than not, the person closest to him was Eleanor. "Father would shout at mother regularly," Ragsdale Madrid recalls. "When he was extremely busy or on edge, father would become impatient and overwrought." Eleanor Ragsdale, who undoubtedly experienced high levels of stress as well, rarely if ever displayed the kind of volatility that was very much a part of Lincoln's personality. Ragsdale Madrid maintains that "mother managed the rigors of their emotionally demanding lives by shutting down. She simply never let anyone see her sweat." After Eleanor was hastened off of the telephone following one of Lincoln's tirades, Gwendolyn Ragsdale Madrid asked her mother: "How do you put up with father's emotional abuse?" Eleanor responded by saying, "Sweetheart, your father's words are like water rolling off a duck's back."[17]

During the spring of 1981 the Ragsdales faced a family crisis that exacerbated their emotional burdens. Rumors of Lincoln Ragsdale's infidelities had been bandied about since the 1960s, but by this time they had taken on mythical proportions. Various women across the Valley had sworn that they had extramarital affairs with the highly visible leader. This further tested the resilience and strength of both Lincoln and Eleanor Ragsdale. Unsubstantiated talk of Lincoln Ragsdale's affairs reached a fever pitch in 1981. During the spring of that year a woman who had escaped from a local mental institution stormed into Lincoln Ragsdale's Universal Memorial Center office, pulled out a gun, and fired eight shots at the unsuspecting Ragsdale. The first several shots missed him completely, allowing him to fall to the floor, where he lay motionless as the assailant fired five more shots at him. None of the shots hit him. Most were found lodged in his desk. Ragsdale pretended to be dead, and the attacker, believing that she had killed him, fled from the building. She was later apprehended as she wandered aimlessly down Jefferson Street in central Phoenix. She claimed that she was Ragsdale's mistress and that she wanted him dead for ending their long relationship.[18]

Gwendolyn Ragsdale Madrid observes that the Ragsdale family "never talked about the incident" after it happened and that Lincoln Ragsdale never admitted to having any extramarital affairs. "Father stated toward the end of his life that mother was the only woman he had ever loved," Ragsdale Madrid proclaimed. There is no evidence to confirm or refute allegations of Lincoln Ragsdale's infidelity. What is certain, however, is that by 1981 allegations of promiscuity, death threats, a murder attempt, the pressures of business, the resurgence of white resistance, and his renewed civil rights activity took a toll on Lincoln and Eleanor's emotional durability. Like most people, the Ragsdales, when faced with trying times and episodes of great sadness, became disheartened and sometimes detached. Despite personal anguish, however, they maintained their commitment to race work and social justice. As whites became increasingly antagonistic to civil

rights activity in Phoenix during the 1980s, for example, they continued to push for racial equality by working through the legislature, the
courts, and various interests in the private sector.[19]

During the 1980s Phoenix held on to its reputation as one of the
"whitest" cities in the United States. E. J. Montini, a local newspaper
editorialist, posited in 1987 that "Phoenix is, by far, the whitest big
city in America." He described the Valley of the Sun as "the polyester
suit of cities, the white bread, the fox trot, the Pat Boone of cities."
Many of Phoenix's white citizens failed to appreciate the truth or humor in Montini's message. One reader of Montini's article responded
by writing, "Wake up white man! You and the rag you work for
are what is [sic] wrong with America. You probably want to speak
Spanish too, you nigger-loving son of a bitch. Racism is alive and
well in Arizona as well as the entire country. Don't ever forget it."[20]
Judis Andrews cited the "whiteness" of Phoenix, its relatively small
black population, and the unwillingness of national African American leaders to bring their influence and visibility to Phoenix as the
main reasons racism continued to flourish in the city. "When people
have no power and cannot secure the help of their brothers and sisters throughout the country, then they suffer at the hands of those
in power. For years the leaders of the African [American] movement
wrote off this area as 'Goldwater Country' and did little or nothing to
secure the dream for this small minority of citizens. Those in power
yield to the 'squeaking wheel' philosophy."[21]

Phoenix emerged as a boomtown in the wake of World War II, and
its prosperity continued throughout the second half of the twentieth
century. Due to the requisite needs of white supremacy and racial
discrimination, black Phoenicians did not enjoy the level of upward
mobility that many of the city's whites did. As a result of Lincoln and
Eleanor Ragsdale's activism, and that of other activists, some African
Americans in the city were able to make substantive socioeconomic
gains, especially those who took advantage of new opportunities in
education, employment, and housing. Black Phoenicians had high expectations, however, and many believed that they had been left behind. One observer argued that "educational opportunities for blacks
in the Valley have improved considerably, but [blacks] still are not
proportionately represented in the professional, scientific and technological areas of advanced study." The one area that demonstrated the
most improvement was the Phoenix city government. Although most

blacks employed in city government held lower-level appointments, a few were able to secure high-ranking positions.[22]

Phoenix remained a racially segregated city, however, in the mid-1980s. The *Arizona Republic* reported in 1984 that "historically, the city of Phoenix has been a segregated city and census and other data show that it is becoming more so." Although many middle-class people of color owned attractive homes in South Phoenix, the predominantly black and Latino neighborhoods located between Van Buren Street, Broadway Road, Thirty-fifth Avenue, and Forty-eighth Street still lagged behind and were often home to the "majority of substandard housing units" in the city. Districts 7 and 8 continued to be primarily Mexican American and African American enclaves that possessed a disproportionate amount of the city's poor population. District 7 encompassed the majority of southwest Phoenix south of McDowell Road and west of Central Avenue, while District 8 covered southeast Phoenix south of McDowell Road and east of Central Avenue.[23]

Phoenix's small, fragmenting black population, the city's undisputed "whiteness," and antagonistic responses to race-conscious remedies to discrimination and black inequality limited and sometimes retarded black progress. These issues, in addition to the white conservative reaction to the civil rights establishment, nurtured racial inequality in Phoenix and kept it going. Following the election of Barry Goldwater admirer and conservative Ronald Reagan as president in 1980, the federal government rescinded its support for the extension of the civil rights superstructure. Moreover, it actively reduced programs for the indigent and mounted an aggressive attack on progressive strategies to correct past and present discrimination, such as affirmative action. Many powerful members of this "New Right" opposed many of the structural changes that had occurred in the United States since the 1960s, such as expanded equal rights for minorities and women, the Supreme Court's decision to ban mandatory prayer in schools, and the reconfiguration of voting districts to allow greater political participation and power to underrepresented racial minorities. Southerners who opposed the progressive changes created by the civil rights movement and white Northerners who condemned affirmative action, the busing of black students to predominantly white schools, and welfare programs identified with alleged black indolence and irresponsibility created the core of this new conservative alliance.[24]

The top priority of the New Right, it seemed, was to undermine progressive social welfare programs that targeted minorities and the poor. Between 1981 and 1993 Reagan and his conservative Republican heir, George H. W. Bush, substantially reduced federal aid to social welfare programs in American cities and simply dissolved others. Much of this aid, and the programs the funds supported, had stood between stability and abject poverty for millions of African Americans. The substantial reduction in federal aid to inner-city communities was reflected in the sharp decrease of city appropriations. As Darlene Clark Hine and others argue, "the percentage of city budgets derived from the federal government declined from 14.3 percent to 5 percent. As a consequence of these policies, inner-city neighborhoods, where 56 percent of poor residents were African American, became more unstable."[25] Reagan and his supporters championed what became known as the "trickle-down" philosophy. This economic "theory" held that if financial betterment of the nation's richest citizens continued, their good fortune would "trickle down" through the middle, working, and underprivileged classes. This did not happen. In fact, studies have shown that while America's wealthiest citizens became wealthier, the country's "truly disadvantaged" fell deeper into economic despair. The "trickle-down" theory, coupled with Reagan's laissez faire attitude toward civil rights and his hostility toward race-conscious remedies to black socioeconomic inequality, helped thwart some of the progress African Americans had made.[26]

By 1982, for example, the unemployment rate for black Americans had increased to 20 percent, which was twice the rate of unemployment of white Americans. Moreover, between 1980 and 1993 salaries for American chief executive officers (CEOs) skyrocketed by 514 percent, while the wages of American workers rose by 68 percent, which lagged well behind inflation. In 1992, argues Robin D. G. Kelley,

> the average CEO earned one hundred and fifty-seven times what the average factory worker earned. And as a result of changes in the tax laws, average workers are paying more to the government while CEOs and their companies are paying less. Corporate profits are reaching records highs, while "downsizing" and capital flight have left millions unem-

ployed. Between 1979 and 1992 the Fortune 500 companies' total labor force dropped from 16.2 million world-wide to 11.8. Yet, in 1993, these companies recorded profits of $62.6 billion.[27]

Racism, racial segregation, and racial inequality had always existed in Phoenix, and the apparent indifference of the New Right to the plight of black Phoenicians did very little to end this retrograde tradition. In Phoenix, the failure of "trickle-down" economics was clear. Throughout the de facto segregated black poor neighborhoods in Phoenix, high unemployment, poor educational opportunities, and substandard infrastructures were ubiquitous. The condition of black Phoenicians only worsened after World War II, when the economy became more technologically based and suburbanized. Moreover, acclaimed Harvard sociologist William Julius Wilson has argued that as neoconservatives dismantled Lyndon Johnson's Great Society agenda, cutting government and private support of local programs that once supplied job training, health care, and family planning, the inner city became home to concentrated poverty, health crises, unstable families, and gang violence. As jobs, better educational opportunities, and social support networks moved to the suburbs, socially and economically segregated and subordinated inner-city minorities became trapped in a vicious cycle of joblessness and hopelessness.[28]

Poor socioeconomic conditions wreaked havoc on the stability of black Phoenician families, particularly in the predominantly black and Chicano housing projects in South Phoenix. Hopelessness and the angst associated with it increased. A predominantly black neighborhood around Twenty-fourth Street and Broadway Road was characterized as "a war zone" where gangs ran amuck. The distribution and use of crack cocaine escalated to epidemic proportions, and drive-by shootings became commonplace. Some South Phoenix residents consumed with anxiety and frustration found it difficult to walk their neighborhood streets without trepidation and fear. Block Watch and other community-based support programs were created to combat the rising tide of urban decay during the 1980s, but the distressing conditions in black Phoenician communities were racial and economic and therefore required socially based, race- and class-conscious remedies to address them effectively.[29]

The social and economic problems that faced black Phoenicians, and all African Americans, during the 1980s were inextricably linked to the long-standing institutional and private exploitation and political control of people of African descent within a capitalist system based upon competition and the exploitation of marginalized individuals and groups. In short, the majority of black people during the 1980s were disproportionately mired in poverty and locked into besieged inner-city communities because of antiblack prejudice undergirded and nurtured by a European American–dominated capitalist regime, what Harold M. Baron has labeled "the web of urban racism." The individual and institutional manipulation of black people, Baron maintains, has undergone large-scale transformations throughout American history: from slavery to peonage and Jim Crow to the present web of urban racism.[30]

"For the present era," Baron argues, "it is within the institutional life of metropolitan America—North, West, and South—that the most characteristic structures of racial subjugation are found. Therefore American racism today cannot be understood apart from the operation of the major social systems within large cities." He maintains that within prominent institutional systems that function in urban areas, there has developed distinct black "subsectors" that operate on a subordinated basis, subject to the advantage, control, and priorities of the prevailing systems dominated by white people. White prejudice and the leading economic and social systems whites created have inspired and cultivated a "circular pattern of reinforcement between barriers that define the various black subsectors." If any one institution, the school system or the labor market, for example, would maintain its current activities outside the web of urban racism, its effectiveness in racial differentiation would significantly decline. "This is not to say that explicit racial barriers and discrimination no longer exist," notes Baron, but "it does say that once the fundamental institutional relationships have been established, overtly exclusionary barriers become less important for the overall oppressive functioning of the system of urban racism."[31]

What appears to be impartial institutions of large urban areas, such as corporations, financial establishments, real estate brokerage firms, schools, and universities, have been threaded into a web of urban racism that marginalizes and "entraps black people much as the spider's net holds flies—they can wiggle but they cannot move very far." The racial barriers created and maintained by each institution are meticulously pronounced and connected. One institution standing alone may not be the sole perpetrator of racial inequality, but the myriad threads of most institutions link together to form a formidable web. Here, however, Baron suggests, "the analogy breaks down." "In contrast to the spider's prey, the victim of urban racism has fed on stronger stuff and is on the threshold of tearing the web." The proliferation of racial controls through such a variety of institutions, coupled with differences in ideology, has made it very complicated to recognize the actual superstructure that "makes urban racism operational." [32]

To the majority of black people trapped in inner cities, it appears that "there is just a massive white sea that surrounds a black island." Indeed, the poorer and more isolated individuals are, the more likely they are to embrace this perception. White liberals, influential business and governmental administrators, and members of the black bourgeoisie are more likely to view the urban race problem as a plethora of issues directly related to the culture of inner-city black people. They tend to believe that the problems of beleaguered inner-city black residents are correctable via the allocation of resources through prevailing methods of business and social management and through the acceptance of a kind of white middle-class ethos. [33]

It was once fashionable, and remains so in some circles, to argue that the inner-city environment is antithetical to racism. Rural African American peasants, it was postulated, would simply require a generation or two to assimilate into the urban "melting pot." After all, Baron asks, "were they not just the newest immigrants—a kind of black Irish?" [34] Statistics and scholars such as Wilson and Kelley have demonstrated otherwise. The emigration of black people to urban areas has had little effect on the socioeconomic status of the masses of African Americans vis-à-vis white Americans in urban areas. The racial gap in social and economic advantage, though smaller between middle-class black people and their white counterparts, remained strikingly wide between the majority of African Americans in the inner cities and most white Americans even during the 1980s and 1990s, decades that witnessed unprecedented economic prosperity. Urban areas such as Phoenix, as Wilson and Kelley have shown, have their own mechanisms for locking in African Americans. A careful reading of the historical record will reveal that the functioning of the

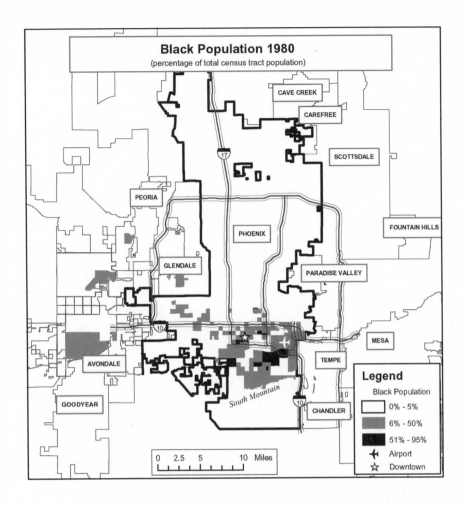

**Black Population 1980**
(percentage of total census tract population)

CAVE CREEK

CAREFREE

17

SCOTTSDALE

PEORIA

PHOENIX

FOUNTAIN HILLS

GLENDALE

PARADISE VALLEY

10

MESA

AVONDALE

TEMPE

GOODYEAR

*South Mountain*

10

CHANDLER

**Legend**

Black Population

☐ 0% - 5%

▨ 6% - 50%

■ 51% - 95%

✈ Airport

☆ Downtown

0   2.5   5        10   Miles

Distribution of black population in
Phoenix, 1980. *Source*: Remy Autz,
Geographic Information Services (GIS)
City of Phoenix.

urban superstructure still involves a perpetuation of racial prejudice and discrimination, segregation, subordination, and exploitation.[35]

Some black Phoenicians fared better than most. As in other major cities, for example, elite African American athletes lived a privileged life in the Valley of the Sun. For most African Americans who were upwardly mobile during the 1980s, progress was real. The gains that the Ragsdales and other activists helped secure in education, employment, and housing paved the way. Civil rights legislation, including affirmative action, also contributed to the advancement of a number of African Americans. Government agencies, African American voluntary associations, and local black churches continued to provide a number of programs that helped sustain the African American community. Leaders such as Lincoln and Eleanor Ragsdale continued to urge African Americans to address issues that were vital to the socioeconomic health of black Phoenicians. Clovis Campbell Sr. observed that "job discrimination is not as open as it used to be in the Phoenix area, but it is still here." Changes that did occur, he believed, did so not because of "any substantial change in the basic belief of white businessmen, but because of the efforts of such affirmative-action groups as the NAACP." Campbell posited that a great many problems in the realm of racial inequality could be blamed on Ronald Reagan. "Reagan," declared Campbell, "signaled to the business community that 'hey, you can go slow. You don't have to worry about it as long as I'm here.'" Campbell cited cutbacks in federal and local financial aid for social service programs and early childhood education as indirect attacks on African American advancement and racial equality. Junius Bowman, head of the PUL in 1985, noted that "a lot of programs that were begun during the Great Society have been cut back. There used to be a great and conscious promotion of economic development for blacks. Some of that is happening but not with such intensity as before."[36]

Although Lincoln and Eleanor Ragsdale were critical of Ronald Reagan's conservative stances on many social and political issues, such as his anti–affirmative action position and his dislike of federally funded welfare programs for the poor, they welcomed Reagan's support of racial minority entrepreneurs and small-business owners. They welcomed this support out of self-interest and because they believed that entrepreneurship provided the best hope for black progress. Lincoln and Eleanor Ragsdale's entrepreneurial status had given them

American and Mexican American demographic data, 1980

| | District 7 | District 8 | Phoenix Total |
|---|---|---|---|
| % minority | 50 | 58 | 22 |
| % female-headed families no husband present | 18 | 21 | 14 |
| % persons below poverty level | 21 | 27 | 11 |
| Median family income | $15,621 | $14,247 | $20,364 |
| Employment (persons 16 years and older) | | | |
|   % white-collar occupations | 17 | 20 | 28 |
|   % sales, clerical services | 56 | 58 | 57 |
|   % blue-collar occupations | 28 | 23 | 15 |
|   % of males in labor force | 79 | 75 | 83 |
|   % of females in labor force | 56 | 56 | 61 |
| Education (persons 25 years and older) | | | |
|   % high school graduates | 48 | 44 | 57 |
|   % of college graduates | 7 | 9 | 17 |
| Housing | | | |
|   % renter occupied | 40 | 46 | 36 |
|   % built since 1970 | 29 | 22 | 40 |
|   Median value, owner occupied | $39,278 | $34,608 | $56,291 |
|   Median rent, renter occupied | 165 | 157 | 245 |
|   % substandard dwelling | 56 | 77 | 31 |

Source: City of Phoenix Planning Department, *A Community Profile* (Phoenix: City of Phoenix Planning Department, 1985), 66–69; Bradford Luckingham, *Minorities in Phoenix: A Profile History of Mexican American, Chinese American, and African American Communities, 1860–1992* (Tucson: University of Arizona Press, 1994), 185.

flexibility and shelter against financial and personal attacks during the height of the civil rights movement. The couple believed that success in business could offer the same kind of flexibility and autonomy to most blacks if African American communities embraced entrepreneurship and if federal and state governments supported black businesses. Like the early-twentieth-century black leader Fannie Barrier Williams, Eleanor Ragsdale believed that if African Americans could "obtain and hold the confidence of the business world, [black people] would be in a position to conquer more prejudice than we have been able to estimate."[37]

Lincoln Ragsdale also believed, like black (fiscal) nationalist leaders such as Booker T. Washington, Marcus Garvey, Elijah Muhammad, and Malcolm X, that black self-determination and entrepreneurship held one of the keys to their advancement. He was pleased, therefore, when Senator Barry Goldwater recommended to Ronald Reagan in 1981 that he be made a member of the Advisory Committee on Small and Minority Businesses (ACSMB). The ACSMB, proposed in the Senate in part by Goldwater and passed by both houses of Congress, was charged with "conducting hearings and . . . [investigating] the economic conditions" of small businesses and those owned and operated by racial minorities and by women. Lincoln Ragsdale, appointed to the ACSMB along with eight other members, served for seven years. He attended over thirty-five hearings in major cities throughout the United States and Puerto Rico and also served as chair of the ACSMB Banking and Insurance Subcommittee. Ragsdale helped write rules and regulations for insurance companies and banks to participate in programs created by the Reagan administration to increase the number of minority-owned businesses. He distinguished himself on the ACSMB and endeared himself further to Goldwater and Reagan. Goldwater was so pleased with Ragsdale's efforts that he recommended him to Reagan as a possible nominee for an ambassadorship to South Africa in 1986. Ragsdale interviewed at the White House for the position and was offered the post. He declined the ambassadorship, however, "for personal reasons" and because he vehemently opposed the apartheid regime and "the racial situation in South Africa."[38]

Lincoln and Eleanor Ragsdale believed that Lincoln's work on the ACSMB held the potential to be a major contribution to black upward mobility. If they could encourage black people and the government to launch a major campaign to promote entrepreneurship among African Americans, the couple reasoned, black people's chances for serious socioeconomic advancement would increase. They estimated that successful black entrepreneurs would not only be able to funnel needed resources back into black communities as they had always done, but that it was far more likely, with hard work and dedication, that blacks would find more success in business than they would in sports or entertainment. The wealthiest and most mobile black Phoenicians at the time were professional athletes and entertainers who made Phoenix's suburbs their homes. These individuals and their families usually had a more positive view of race relations in Phoenix than did the general black population. By 1991, for instance, most black professional athletes in Phoenix believed that they could purchase a home and live in any neighborhood in the city. They thought that they could send their children to good schools, dine out, shop, and go about life's routines without incident. The lifestyles of professional athletes, regardless of their color, the Ragsdales believed, were atypical. Black professional athletes in particular were, and continue to be, racial anomalies with regard to wealth, status, and mobility in the American racial context. By this period, however, Lincoln and Eleanor Ragsdale, as wealthy and influential black Phoenicians, were also a statistical aberration. What this meant to the couple is unclear. It is apparent, however, that they recognized the persistence of racial inequality and discrimination, and they thought that entrepreneurship would provide more African Americans with opportunities for financial success than professional athletics and entertainment. During the early 1990s, as a man entering the winter of his life, Lincoln Ragsdale answered the calls of leaders like Clovis Campbell and responded to new attacks on black progress and persistent racial segregation by returning to the activism that defined his youth and by calling upon black people to open and support black businesses.[39]

Although the Ragsdale family was wealthy enough to buy into an expensive, predominantly white suburban neighborhood, and despite laws barring racial discrimination in places of public accommodation, Lincoln Ragsdale was denied membership in the lily-white Paradise Valley Country Club. Almost thirty years after national and state legislation rendered racial discrimination in places of public accommodation illegal, Phoenix's most prestigious country clubs remained all-white. Phoenix's country clubs routinely turned down the few African Americans who requested membership. For twenty years Ragsdale tried unsuccessfully to integrate the Paradise Valley Country Club. Ragsdale, who lived virtually across the street from the country club, said he asked two friends who were members to recommend him for membership. They declined, citing the probability of their being shunned by other white members if they were to support Ragsdale's candidacy. One of his "dear friends" said: "Lincoln, I would like to do it for you and I'm not a racist, but they would ostracize me and they wouldn't like it." The other stated: "I asked them and they said they didn't think the time was right to bring in the black guys." The two men informed him, under no uncertain terms, that "the club would not accept him because he is black."[40]

Lincoln Ragsdale's initial desire to be a member of the Paradise Valley Country Club was financially motivated. Joining the club, he reasoned, would allow him to make important business contacts and to socialize with prominent members of Phoenix's financial community. Although Ragsdale was a millionaire, his fortune was primarily secured through service to and interaction with minorities. Membership in the Paradise Valley Country Club would have opened doors, financial relationships, and markets that had previously been inaccessible to him. Members of the club conspired to keep Ragsdale from reaching a larger financial pool, which would have given him the opportunity to expand his fortune, influence, and ability to compete.[41]

When every one of his white neighbors in Clearwater Hills moved in, remembered Ragsdale, the country club would invite them over, "show them through the country club and let them see what the facilities are," and then ask them: "Are you interested?" If they were interested, "somebody in the club, a neighbor," he recalled, would initiate a petition for the their membership and "get two people to recommend them" for admission. Once they secured two recommendations, they were then admitted to the club, "assuming they wanted to pay the money." "They had different types of memberships," Ragsdale said, "one with golf, one without, one was social."[42] When one of Ragsdale's neighbors became president of the club, Lincoln asked him for a recommendation for admission. "I went to see him and said: 'Now that you're president, can you help me?' He and I had been friends for ten years, I watched him build his home up here in Clearwater and I knew the man; still lives here by the way. He said 'let me think about it.'" After three months passed, Ragsdale was finally given an answer. "Lincoln," the neighbor said, "they wouldn't take you. These people up here are not ready yet." In 1990, when Keven Willey, a reporter for the *Arizona Republic*, asked Leon Bentley, president of the Paradise Valley Country Club, to comment on the club's record of not admitting African Americans, he was told such information was "of no concern to you or anyone else."[43]

Joining Lincoln Ragsdale in his efforts to integrate the country club was wealthy black businessman Ray Johnson. Johnson obtained the necessary recommendations, submitted photographs of himself and his wife upon request, and visited the club with their sponsors. They were then told that the membership fee would be $80,000. Johnson replied, "Where do I send the check?" The membership committee rejected his petition promptly. "I was turned down and never given a reason why," Johnson recalled. "Nobody would talk about it." Undaunted in his efforts to desegregate the club, Lincoln Ragsdale took his case to the court of public opinion. Submitting to a series of interviews and public appearances, Ragsdale brought attention to the perpetuation of de facto racial segregation at the country club. Although he used his efforts to integrate the Paradise Valley Country Club as his primary example, he also voiced his displeasure with lingering racial segregation throughout Phoenix. [44]

Ragsdale's efforts were eventually brought to the attention of many of Arizona's top politicians. The local media approached former governor, millionaire, and member of the country club J. Fife Symington III about Ragsdale's ongoing ordeal with the club. Symington said that he was unaware of any discriminatory practices by the club and that he would work to change them if they existed. Symington stated that the club had no written rules banning black people and denied the accusation that the country club had a formal policy of discrimination, saying that "I know they have Hispanic members and many Jewish members." Symington spoke to Ragsdale and offered to sponsor his petition for membership to the club. Symington told reporters that he wished to "put the system to a test." [45]

John McCain, Arizona's Republican member of the U.S. Senate, indirectly challenged Symington to go a step further. "I strongly feel there should be black members at Paradise Valley Country Club," McCain declared, "and if they do not take steps to allow black members, I will return my membership." [46] Ragsdale ultimately declined Symington's offer, citing his desire to see a "more natural" process of inviting black people into the country club. He brought a substantial amount of attention to the fact that the club was racially segregated, and that had become his primary goal. Although he was still interested in becoming a member of the club, he had lost interest in the prospect after being the object of steadfast white resistance. "Don't get me wrong," Ragsdale noted, "I want to be a member, but I do not wish to be a token. I do not want to be used so they can say, 'Look, here's a black person.' What I'm saying is, let it be a very natural thing." [47]

Ragsdale, who had once entertained the idea of creating an exclusive club for black professionals, had no problem with private clubs setting up "some kind of criteria" for membership. After all, he declared, "this is America." The question Ragsdale asked, however, was "what kind of criteria are you going to have?" He did not object to the idea of racial- or gender-specific private organizations per se. He did, however, believe that there is a fine line between private groups that promote a specific form of solidarity and government-sanctioned and -supported groups that discriminate in an arbitrary and capricious manner. Country clubs and similar private institutions and groups that benefited from "the protection of the government through liquor licensing, police protection, fire protection," and tax relief were obligated to be as inclusive as possible. With regard to the Paradise Valley Country Club, Ragsdale argued that their golf greens were not being taxed and that this constituted government support of their institution, including its racially discriminatory practices. Since the club profited from governmental tax relief, Ragsdale reasoned, it had "no right to exclude people on the basis of race."[48]

The negative media publicity Ragsdale brought to Paradise Valley Country Club helped motivate the institution to open its doors to African Americans in 1992. Ragsdale did not renew his effort to join the club. As he saw it, his business and social ties were now well established. The primary reason he had wanted to join no longer existed. Some black nationalist leaders in Phoenix no doubt questioned the wisdom and motivation behind Ragsdale's crusade to be included in the elite white country club. It could be argued that Ragsdale's desire to become a member of the club demonstrated a yearning to assimilate further into what rhythm and blues performer George Clinton called the "Vanilla Suburbs." Some also believed that there were more critical issues that Ragsdale could have shed light on, such as police brutality and racial profiling. As they saw it, Ragsdale was simply a black millionaire trying desperately to be included in a club of white millionaires. All of the parties involved were privileged individuals, and as a result, Ragsdale's efforts did not always resonate with poor black inner-city residents. For her part, Eleanor Ragsdale did not put much stock in the relevance of calling attention to the Paradise Valley Country Club's segregationist practices, nor did she ever wish to be a member. When asked if she wanted to join the club, Eleanor remarked that "it didn't make a bit of difference to me." She supported Lincoln in his efforts, but she also believed that many blacks who became members of such exclusive clubs were often targets of "tokenism." She stated plainly that she "wouldn't want to be a part of that." She understood, however, that to Lincoln, the Paradise Valley Country Club's discriminatory practices were a product of naked racism, the same racism that locked poor black Phoenicians in decaying inner-city communities.[49]

While Lincoln Ragsdale was calling attention to persistent racial segregation in Phoenix during the late 1980s and early 1990s, he also spoke out against what he classified as the Phoenix Sky Harbor International Airport's racially unequal distribution of business leases. During the fall of 1990 the Phoenix Aviation Advisory Board recommended the city renegotiate leases with shops in Sky Harbor's terminals two and three. This action, Ragsdale and other minority leaders argued, would continue to prevent people of color from participating equally in airport businesses by bidding for space. Without a process of open bidding, the predominantly white-owned businesses at Sky Harbor would be given top priority through a private renegotiation process. Ragsdale, who served for seven years on the Phoenix Aviation Advisory Board, said that "minorities had been shut out of the process of running shops at Sky Harbor" by not being allowed to bid for space. Although federal law required minority participation of at least 10 percent in businesses at airports receiving federal funding, the law did not require that the city take bids for concessions at Sky Harbor.[50]

At issue were profitable contracts. The advisory board supported renegotiation because the airport and the city stood to benefit from higher revenues from established businesses; minority businesses supported bidding because they would be poised to reap substantial profits from newly secured contracts. The drive to win airport concession compacts was intense because stores in terminal two and three were likely to earn gross sales of around $12 million. Ragsdale led a charge of minority activists who protested what they said was a form of racial discrimination at Sky Harbor. The debate was heated, and Ragsdale proclaimed, "I haven't been in a fight like this since blacks went into the restaurants to eat."[51] Airport shop owners said that good business practice, and not discrimination, was at the heart of the proposal not to place the leases out to bid. "There are some things government can't do," said Phoenix city councilman Skip Rimza, "and negotiating in private contracts is one of them." Rimza and his supporters suggested that after the owners renegotiated their contracts, they would put forth a "good-faith" effort to hire minorities at airport concessions. Ragsdale wanted minorities to be prime contractors, not just subcontractors and employees. He also likened labor conditions for black airport workers to slavery and suggested that such conditions would improve if black people owned and operated airport concessions. "We don't need a job [at the airport]. In slavery we had a job." What black people needed, he argued, was "ownership."[52]

The intent of the bidding, Ragsdale reasoned, was for minorities "to have equity." "With renegotiation," he declared, "there is no equity." The Federal Aviation Administration's (FAA) civil rights division reviewed Sky Harbor's minority-hiring program in 1988 and "found it to be lacking in 'good faith' efforts to meet its hiring goals." Moreover, the FAA stated that the airport failed to hire a designated personnel officer to encourage minority businesses to apply for contracts. Ragsdale cited the FAA's evaluation throughout his public campaign for open bidding and balked at additional promises to put forth good-faith efforts to promote racial equality that were offered by white business owners and government leaders. He continued to fight through the fall of 1990. Ultimately, however, the advisory board voted to allow owners to renegotiate their contracts, much to the chagrin of Ragsdale and his supporters. The issue was far from resolved by 1991, however, and even at the time of Ragsdale death four years later, the topic remained a political and economic hot potato.[53]

For black Phoenicians who were upwardly mobile during the 1980s, progress continued to be made. Despite uphill battles with institutions like the Sky Harbor International Airport, gains were made in employment, housing, and education. Civil rights measures, including affirmative action, created many of these opportunities. The majority of black Phoenicians, however, remained mired in poverty. Social service programs and private black organizations worked diligently to improve conditions in the black community. Black churches such as First Institutional Baptist Church, which was led by the Reverend Warren H. Stewart Sr., also spearheaded movements to assist blacks in need.[54]

Black organizations and leaders like Lincoln Ragsdale, George Brooks, and Clovis Campbell called attention to the problems of African Americans in Phoenix. "I was the arrogant one," Ragsdale recalled, "Reverend Brooks was the one that would console and work with the people. My job was to go in and shake up the water, and his job was to come along and say he's [Ragsdale] a little too far out."[55] Ragsdale was shaking up the water in Phoenix again when he argued that job discrimination still existed in the city during the 1990s. Campbell maintained that "job discrimination is not as open as it used to be in the Phoenix area, but it is still here." The change that did occur, he suggested, was created by affirmative action and by civil rights groups like the NAACP, not because of "any substantial change in the basic belief of white businessmen."[56]

Like Clovis Campbell, many black leaders placed a great deal of the blame for the persistence of white racism and discrimination on Ronald Reagan and his fellow conservatives. They maintained that Reaganesque reductions in federal and state aid to the impoverished were extremely damaging. The Reagan-Bush years, argued Marvin Perry, leader of the Black Board of Directors Project in Phoenix, popularized a return to conservative politics, which promoted racial inequality and demonized civil rights. "Jim Crow is dead," he announced while talking about the birth of a new cynicism about civil rights during the Reagan-Bush years. "That is true. But James S. Crow, Esquire, his grandson, is alive and well."[57]

Neoconservative policies, white resistance to civil rights programs, and institutional racism led to a resurgence of racial antagonism during the 1990s at the national and local levels. In March 1991 members of the Los Angles police department removed motorist Rodney King from his vehicle by force, following a high-speed pursuit, and beat him repeatedly. The episode was captured on videotape and continually broadcast on television around the world. The incident placed the ongoing issue of police brutality of African Americans squarely at the forefront of American political and intellectual debates. A jury of eleven white Americans and one Hispanic American acquitted the four police officers charged in the beating of King. Following the verdict, South-central Los Angeles erupted in protest. Believing that the verdict demonstrated the perpetuation of American racial injustice, rioters looted and set buildings ablaze. Thousands of people were injured, four thousand were arrested, and upward of half a billion dollars worth of property was damaged or decimated.[58]

The Rodney King affair reverberated throughout black communities across the nation. In Phoenix, black activists like Lincoln Ragsdale cited local police brutality and the retreat from civil rights for thwarting the cultivation of constructive race relations. For instance, he and other black leaders characterized the "overwhelmingly" white Phoenix Police Department as being "insensitive to blacks." "Insensitive" may have been an understatement. For example, in March 1998 a jury awarded a $45 million judgment to the family of Edward Mallet, a twenty-five-year-old black man who died at the hands of Phoenix police officers in 1994. Mallet's family had filed the multimillion dollar lawsuit against the city for the actions of the Phoenix Police Department. Wrongly suspected of gang activity because of, among other things, his "physical appearance," Mallet, whose two legs had been amputated, was stopped, doused with pepper spray, and put in a neck hold by police officers. The neck hold administered by the police officers cut off Mallet's flow of oxygen and suffocated him to death. The police supported their actions by arguing that Mallet had resisted arrest. Despite the fact that Mallet's legs had been amputated, police officers claimed that he was a large man who displayed superior strength. His extraordinary strength, they argued, caused them to apply the life-ending neck hold. After appealing the jury's verdict, the city later settled, paying the family about $5 million.[59]

Racism and discrimination were reported in other sectors as well. The NAACP issued a report in September 1991 that highlighted "about 250 cases of discrimination each year in metropolitan Phoenix." The report underscored "a continuing cycle in the Valley of people being discriminated against in housing and jobs." Thirty years after Lincoln Ragsdale helped Phoenix desegregate its banks and major corporations, many black Phoenicians said that a "usually subtle, but occasionally overt racism still clouds their lives." "Black men and white men, Jews and Gentiles, Protestants and Catholics," Paul Brinkley-Rodgers of the *Arizona Republic* wrote in 1993, "they are not all, as [Martin Luther] King dreamed, free at last." "Advances have been made toward equal opportunities in employment," Brinkley-Rodgers observed, and "blacks no longer are denied voting rights. 'White only' signs are gone, but racist acts against African-Americans, two recent cross burnings at a black home in Phoenix, for example—are on the increase according to the U.S. Department of Justice."[60]

Dr. Duane Wooten, a Phoenician pediatrician, stated that when he enrolled in medical school at the University of Arizona, he was the first African American to do so in seven years. While he attended medical school, he recalled, the director of family practice, who was white, asked a class, "Why do you think there's so much black-on-black crime?" "A lot of students looked at me" in response, he said. "In the thirty years since he [Martin Luther King Jr.] made that speech, there's been so little change made in racism," Wooten believes. "Too many Caucasian-Americans feel themselves liberal and open-minded, but, at the same time, they feel superior in lifestyle. They feel they have an inherent right to protect their privilege, and it is so bad they don't even think about it."[61]

The general status of African Americans in Phoenix during the 1990s reflected a national trend. African Americans continued to be disproportionately locked out of the housing market and forced into low-cost, substandard accommodations. There were no black chief executive officers in the nation's top hundred corporations. Black unemployment stood at 13.8 percent in 1993, higher than in 1963 when it was 10.8 percent. Twenty-three percent of all black men age twenty to twenty-nine were in prison, on parole, or on probation in 1990, more than were in college. In 1992 the unemployment rate among black men aged twenty to twenty-four stood at 24.5 percent, compared with 10.4 percent for their white counterparts. Despite these startling statistics, however, black Phoenicians and African Americans throughout the country had made progress. Lincoln Ragsdale and Clovis Campbell remembered that during the 1960s, there were only two African American attorneys in Phoenix, Hayzel B. Daniels and Carl Stewart. In 1993 there were more than seventy. In 1965 there were only 280 black elected officials in America; in 1993 there were over 7,500. The Census Bureau reported median household income among African Americans at $4,325 in 1967; in 1991 it was $18,807. Forty-two percent of African Americans were living in poverty in 1966; in 1991 the figure was 32.7 percent.[62]

Lincoln and Eleanor Ragsdale believed that despite persistent racial adversity, African Americans had made substantial progress. When Democratic president Bill Clinton celebrated his forty-seventh birthday in 1993 at the Martha's Vineyard home of his black friend Vernon Jordan, the Ragsdales were pleased. "That means something," Eleanor Ragsdale said, "things are changing." Lincoln Ragsdale spoke with Jordan about the visit and shared his delight over the event. He and Jordan met and became friends while Jordan served as president of the NUL and board member of American Express in Phoenix. On the other hand, Ragsdale acknowledged that his dream of a better future was not shared by many young African Americans. "So many young black men look at life as having nothing for them," he stated.

> It's like "Nigger, you have your civil rights now, but there's no future for you." If I were seventeen or eighteen, sure, I'd know there were teenager jobs, but when I get to be twenty years,

who wants me? Some whites resent it if we get a job and if we succeed and get ahead. But this problem is an African American thing too. I'm 67, but when I go to the toilet, sometimes in my mind I see a "white only" sign there. I have a Ph.D., I have been with the U.S. president [Ronald Reagan], and I have even met the Queen of England, but sometimes I get screwed up because I remember how humiliating it was.[63]

At sixty-seven, Lincoln Ragsdale noted areas in which African American had made progress during the late 1980s and early 1990s, but he was also quick to point out how such progress was limited and often mitigated by social, economic, and political losses. For example, he argued, more African Americans entered ASU during this period, but their percentage of the overall student population remained under 3 percent. Moreover, the university employed only a handful of black faculty and administrators, and its curriculum and instruction reflected the overwhelmingly Eurocentric intellectual sensibility among ASU's leadership. Racial tensions and violence sparked by neo-Nazi and Ku Klux Klan activity on the campus triggered heated protests by black students and African Americans throughout the community. Indeed, as the reemergence of racial stereotyping and interracial conflict overtook some of the country's largest and most recognized colleges and universities at the time, ASU was unable to avoid the surge. Student leaders such as Jeremy Levitt and conscientious members of the Greater Phoenix community, including Phoenix Equal Opportunity director Carol Coles Henry, pressured ASU's administration to create a variety of programs to curb racism and promote racial tolerance on the campus. Organizations such as the African Consolidated Mentors for Enhancement (ACME), founded and directed by Levitt, and the Campus Environment Team (CET) took leading roles.[64]

Under Levitt's leadership, ACME helped promote racial understanding and black history, culture, and socioeconomic advancement. It achieved its goal by sponsoring educational and cultural programming through lectures and public events. A key component of ACME's efforts was an after-school program that endeavored to increase the self-esteem and academic performance of "at-risk" students in Phoenix's predominantly black and Hispanic Roosevelt School District. Leaders such as Levitt also pushed ASU to recruit and retain black faculty and to create courses and public programming that dealt with African American history, cultural awareness, and racial diversity. In response to this pressure, ASU's administration promised to hire more faculty of color and engage in substantive efforts to diversify the campus and recruit and retain black students, faculty, and administrators. By 2000 little progress had been made. African American students still constituted less than 3 percent of the university's student population, the number of ASU's black faculty continued to be small, black students and faculty remained isolated, and African Americans on the suburban campus were still exposed to occasional eruptions of white racism and hostility. Opposition to diversity initiatives and black studies lingered, and racial tensions endured.[65]

Although progress was made, maintaining it was often difficult for leaders such as Ragsdale. As Bradford Luckingham notes, "the population and the needs of the African American community were diverse. The gains made by middle-class African Americans increased the differences between them and the less fortunate classes, especially the so-called underclass left behind in the problem-plagued poorer neighborhoods." White Americans were not the only critics of poor African Americans and civil rights. By the 1980s African Americans who were "successful" often argued that poor inner-city black people were responsible for their own problems. Moreover, many of these members of the black bourgeoisie endeavored to dissociate themselves from what they perceived to be a fallen and corrupt black inner-city population. Among the class of well-to-do African Americans existed a growing circle of neoconservatives who were extremely critical of poor black inner-city residents and the progressive policies and programs that sought to help lift them out of poverty. This ever-expanding cadre of conservative black thinkers opposed the more liberal politics of many other African Americans. These two groups reflected the ideological diversity of and conflict within the black community. Each wanted to set the socioeconomic agenda for black America. Debates over the merits of their prescriptions for black progress became intense and acrimonious. As the two camps escalated their efforts to persuade and lead, it became increasingly difficult for African Americans to continue to mount a unified campaign for black socioeconomic advancement. The movement was weakened through fragmentation.[66]

Black neoconservatives such as Thomas Sowell, Shelby Steele, Alan Keyes, and Clarence Thomas have suggested that many of the problems of poor urban black people are caused by flawed cultural traits and the American welfare system. For instance, Sowell believes that African Americans in the inner city often suffer from sloth and indecency, which perpetuates their poverty and socioeconomic isolation. Rather than expand social programs to help impoverished black people, Sowell would like to see affirmative action and welfare programs terminated because he believes they undermine middle-class values of hard work and frugality. These conservative leaders suggest that racism as it was known in the 1950s and 1960s no longer existed in the 1980s and 1990s. As a result, they have argued, the problems of masses of African Americans during the Reagan-Bush years were not rooted in government policy or corporate capitalism. Rather, their problems stemmed from black folk themselves—their delinquent youth, welfare mothers, and deadbeat dads.[67]

These neoconservative thinkers generally defined government assistance of any kind as the antithesis of personal responsibility, unless, as Robin D. G. Kelley argues, "one is talking about government subsidies to industry or tax breaks for the wealthy." Their arguments, many liberal black leaders suggest, reveal neoconservatives' questionable faith in the free market to inspire and promote equality. These conservative supporters of black capitalism, black liberals posit, believe profits obtained from black businesses will "trickle down to impoverished black people without any system to redistribute wealth. They take for granted that the 'free market' actually operates free of racism and that the playing field is even, which is why they have called for 'color blind' social policies completely rejecting any race-based entitlements or special privileges." Black and white conservatives are lauding the virtues of the free market, Kelly suggests, when they really should be calling for a free and fair market.[68]

Liberal black leaders such as Jessie Jackson attempted to counter the effects of the new conservatism and its loyal black supporters. In 1983 Jackson and his People United to Serve Humanity (PUSH) spearheaded a campaign to inspire black progressive political activism. In November of that year Jackson announced his candidacy for the Democratic nomination for president. Throughout his campaign, he appealed to the traditional black liberal establishment, working-class white Americans, Latinos, feminists, and young people. This alliance became known as the Rainbow Coalition. Building upon a long liberal tradition, his platform included, among other things, increasing employment opportunities. Jackson visited Phoenix often during his campaign, and during his stops he and Lincoln Ragsdale became friends and comrades in the struggle for racial equality. Jackson garnered nearly one-fourth of the votes cast in the Democratic primaries and caucuses, and he secured one-eighth of the delegates to the convention. Ultimately, Walter Mondale won the Democratic Party's presidential nomination. Mondale, in turn, lost to incumbent Ronald Reagan by a wide margin. Reagan logged a landslide victory, winning 59 percent of the popular vote.[69]

Jackson's influence and his liberal response to the new conservatism and its black supporters reflected the expanding ideological and political heterogeneity within the black community. The public solidarity African Americans demonstrated during the 1950s and 1960s appeared to be a thing of the past. Some observers wondered if African Americans would ever enjoy the kind of unity they forged during the height of the civil rights movement. The deepening conflict between liberal and conservative African Americans was not the only problem. Much of the ideological dislocation rested in the fact that a great many "successful" black leaders, liberal and conservative, no longer had substantive connections to the truly disadvantaged in the black community. Some observers wondered if the black community would ever be able to produce a unified movement on behalf of African American advancement again. In Phoenix, for example, one black observer indicated that "recently a group of successful blacks were called together with the intent of alleviating the many severe problems of youth in the black community. Several good suggestions were offered. Unfortunately, 90 percent of those at the meeting did not live within the area where so-called black problems exist, and did not seem to understand problems in the black community."[70]

During the 1980s poverty in South Phoenix rose sharply among African Americans and Chicanos. White Phoenicians, however, saw their poverty rates decline. By 1990 in Phoenix, 47 percent of African American children, 39 percent of Hispanic children, and 17 percent of Anglo children under age five lived in poverty. The reality and negative effects of poverty throughout communities of color in Phoenix during this period were profound. Most white Phoenicians, however, were either unwilling or unable to see such poverty. Moreover, people of color who enjoyed middle-class status were also prone to underestimate the intensity, despair, and hopelessness in the city's Latino and African American neighborhoods. Class divisions appeared to be contributing to socioeconomic despair in black inner-city neighbor-hoods.[71]

Although class conflict contributed to the segmentation of the black community, some common "affronts and setbacks" united it. During the early 1990s Arizona was cast into the national spotlight when America was introduced to the state's highly controversial and contested fight over the passage of a paid Martin Luther King Jr. Day state holiday. This battle reenergized the black freedom struggle in Phoenix, bringing African Americans of all persuasions to the state's capitol to demand symbolic recognition of the relevance of King's message and the importance of racial equality. This drama included leaders such as Clovis Campbell Sr., Rev. Warren Stewart, and Lincoln Ragsdale, as well as Governors Bruce Babbitt and Evan Mecham. Many grassroots activist and average Arizonans also joined the battle, as the "King Day fiasco" captured the hearts and minds of the entire nation.[72]

Clovis Campbell Sr. introduced the first bill for a paid Martin Luther King Jr. Day state holiday in 1969. Campbell's bill met with strong resistance in the Arizona legislature. For years he was pitted against "very strong, right-wing conservatives who don't believe that any contribution of black folks should be recognized." They routinely rejected the bill. During the early 1970s, however, the Martin Luther King Jr. Striving Committee (MLKSC), a group of black ministers and other community leaders, including Lincoln and Eleanor Ragsdale and George Brooks, organized to pressure the legislature to create a paid Martin Luther King Day state holiday. The committee drew up petitions and solicited signatures throughout the city. They also received letters of support from King's widow, Coretta Scott King, and volunteer help from the Phoenix College Afro-American Club.[73]

Arizona representative Art Hamilton joined Campbell's and MLKSC's efforts when he introduced additional legislation to create a paid state holiday "honoring the life and philosophies of Martin Luther King, Jr." The Arizona legislature, as it had done in the past, rejected his efforts. In 1986 Rev. Stewart, leader of Phoenix's First Institutional Baptist Church, invited then-governor Bruce Babbitt to the congregation to comment on the significance of creating a "King Day" in Arizona. Babbitt, who supported a paid state holiday honoring the slain civil rights leader, announced to the gathering that he intended to issue an executive order that would create a paid Martin Luther King Day state holiday in Arizona. Stewart recalled that no one present at the service "had any knowledge that he really meant that." As promised, however, Babbitt created the holiday by executive order shortly after appearing at the church.[74]

The newly adopted holiday was short-lived. Governor Evan Mecham, Babbitt's successor, argued that Babbitt exceeded his power in creating the holiday. Mecham nullified the order, substituting it with an unpaid holiday that was to be observed on the third Sunday in January. Stewart, the Ragsdales, and other activists believed that Mecham thought that King did not deserve a holiday. Stewart organized a meeting with Mecham and the MLKSC at the First New Life Baptist Church. The local media sent a large delegation to the meeting, for which Stewart was the moderator. The debate was intense, and Mecham indicated that he had no intention of altering his views. Many in attendance argued that Mecham's position was inspired by racist views and that he possessed no substantive concern for their opinions. Following the event, which accomplished virtually nothing, Stewart organized a group of black ministers who called themselves Arizonans for a Martin Luther King Holiday (AMLKH). He quickly became the leading spokesman for the King Day cause. The AMLKH began lobbying the legislature vigorously. According to Stewart, however, the legislature "wouldn't accept reason," and Mecham "wouldn't listen to us, he was set." Mecham placed himself on the front lines of the debate with his bullish persona, intemperate disposition, and inflammatory comments. Historian Peter Iverson noted that "through one comment after another that a great many people considered insensitive or incompetent at best, and ignorant and racist at worst, ranging from use of the word pickaninnies to a comment about the shape of Asian eyes, Mecham quickly became a political pariah" and the arch enemy of proponents of a Martin Luther King Jr. Day holiday.[75]

Many Arizona residents, particularly African Americans, were furious with Mecham's words and actions. Lincoln and Eleanor Ragsdale, Brooks, and Stewart led a march of ten thousand supporters to the state capitol. Stewart called for public acknowledgment of King's vision of an America free of racial inequality. He believed that America had become a different country than it was prior to the civil rights movement because of King and his vision, and he urged everyone to remember King's contributions. Stewart proclaimed that King deserved to be recognized with a paid holiday in Arizona, and he vowed to fight for the holiday as long as he lived in the state. The Ragsdales,

Stewart, and most Arizona residents believed that it might take a lifetime to create such a holiday, as the state legislature continued to reject legislation that would do so. Each year, however, civil rights activists marched to the state capitol to protest the absence of a paid King holiday.[76]

In 1989 the Arizona legislature approved a Martin Luther King Day state holiday. It did not want to increase the number of paid state holidays, however, so it moved Columbus Day to a Sunday. Italian Americans were extremely vocal in expressing their displeasure at the change. The legislature responded by restoring Columbus Day as a paid holiday while retaining the King holiday. In a 1990 referendum, however, the King holiday was defeated by less than 1 percent of the vote. This pleased Mecham and his supporters immensely, but it angered African Americans and their supporters. Lincoln Ragsdale voiced his displeasure with the holiday's rejection and helped lead the way in labeling Arizona as a racist state. Individuals and organizations throughout the nation boycotted Arizona because of its handling of the issue. The National Football League (NFL) removed its 1993 Super Bowl from Phoenix because of the controversial proposition. Arizona lost hundreds of millions of dollars in tourism and convention revenues as a result.[77]

Lincoln Ragsdale, other black leaders, and many white Arizonans wanted a paid King holiday and continued to work to obtain it. Proponents believed they lost the election because of questionable ballots and what was perceived to be the intrusion of the NFL. Voters had two ballot propositions on the King holiday during the 1990 election. One established a paid King holiday, and another exchanged a King holiday for Columbus Day. Exit polls demonstrated that each proposition failed because the "yes" vote split, while the "no" vote did not. Polls also indicated that many people voted "no" because they were offended by threats from the NFL, and some critics bemoaned the added expense of creating another paid holiday. Arizona's influential white conservative rural voters largely opposed a King holiday, and questions about King's character constituted another reason why people voted against the measures.[78]

Despite ongoing opposition, Lincoln Ragsdale and other local leaders continued to apply pressure on elected officials and private interests to support a paid King holiday in Phoenix. In 1991, after twenty-one years of maneuvering on the part of Campbell, Hamilton, and

Lincoln Ragsdale, Phoenix joined many other cities, states, and the federal government in creating a paid King holiday. During that same year, however, Arizona was the only state in the union that did not boast some kind of King holiday. Another King holiday proposal was placed on the November 1992 ballot. It advocated Martin Luther King Jr.–Civil Rights Day on the third Monday of January, corresponding with the federal commemoration of the legacy of King. It also proposed to combine the Washington and Lincoln state holidays in February into a single holiday, corresponding to the nation's President's Day holiday. It guaranteed that the number of paid state holidays remained the same. Ragsdale and others looked forward to the proposal passing, which it did in November 1992. Proponents of the measure had utilized a brochure with endorsements by Barry Goldwater and Ronald Reagan. In the brochure, Goldwater, in a statement that endorsed King's nonviolence and victories for civil and human rights, proclaimed that "I feel [the law] is right for Arizona and right for America." The holiday received 62 percent approval, with only the Phoenix suburb of Mesa and some rural areas of the state rejecting the statue. Citizens of Mesa proved to be particularly hostile to the idea of a paid King holiday. When volunteers such as Mary Boozer attempted to solicit the support of Mesa residents for such a holiday, the majority declined. Many responded by saying "he was Communist," while one resident proclaimed that "I'm not interested in that nigger." Others spewed even more vulgar racial epitaphs. Barry Goldwater, while addressing a class at ASU in 1995, indicated that Mesa voters had been primarily responsible for delaying the passage of the holiday. In the minds of many black Phoenicians, including Lincoln Ragsdale, Warren Stewart, Richard Harris, and George Brooks, however, Mesa and Arizona at large were simply "backward." Stewart stated emphatically that Arizona had demonstrated more interest in "taking better care of cattle" than many of its people, especially African Americans.[79]

The King Day conflict revealed many of the problems black Phoenicians, and African Americans in general, faced during this era. Socioeconomic problems continued to challenge younger leaders such as Stewart and older activists such as the Ragsdales well into the 1990s. The Ragsdales and other leaders remained hopeful that black Phoenicians, and all black people, would continue to build upon their past successes. The symbolic victory of the King holiday appeared to be a step in the right direction. If the measure had been rejected again, however, activists would have continued to fight. In January 1991, for example, as legendary civil rights activist Rosa Parks looked on, Phoenix mayor Paul Johnson, a supporter of a King Day state holiday, proclaimed that he hoped Arizona would "get its King holiday in 1992, but if we don't we'll be back in 1994. If we don't get it then, we'll be back in 1996, and every time, our resolve will get stronger." Another observer noted that "we are not giving up until we celebrate in this state of ours a paid Martin Luther King, Jr. holiday." Art Hamilton echoed these remarks when he declared that, "if necessary, we will be back, and we will be back, and we will be back until we accomplish our goal." [80]

After celebrating one last victory in helping to create a holiday honoring a man who had inspired them to be the one of the influential couples in Phoenix and in the history of the civil rights movement, Lincoln and Eleanor Ragsdale pondered their legacy and shared their hopes for the future. Paul Johnson stated that "creating the holiday was an important symbol, but now we need to move from symbol to substance." Lincoln and Eleanor Ragsdale agreed. They argued that in order to usher in "substantive" change, Arizona and its capital city would have to emerge as places in which every person, regardless of race, had equal rights and access to opportunities to succeed. The King Day struggle proved to be the Ragsdales' last major completed piece of race work. Lincoln Ragsdale was sixty-seven years old in 1992 and had devoted a tremendous amount of energy to the black liberation struggle. For the first time in the controversial and fiery civil rights and business leader's life, he began to "mellow." "Twenty years ago I was very bitter, I wanted to blame more people," he stated. "I'm in my sixties now, and I don't have that fight like I used to. I'm looking for peace. I'm looking for solace. I'm looking for something other than fighting battles." [81]

Eleanor Ragsdale was pleased with the victories she helped secure in many of the civil rights battles and was encouraged that Arizona finally passed a paid Martin Luther King Jr. state holiday. Nevertheless, she was still troubled about the economic status of poor and working-class black people. "What good is a Martin Luther King Day if you're unemployed?" she asked. When you are unemployed she declared, "every day is a holiday." Lincoln Ragsdale believed that discrimination against black people in the labor market was subtle and perhaps the most damaging. "It's not overt anymore," he argued. "Employers don't put up signs anymore that say: 'No coloreds allowed, no need to apply.' They just take your application and file it." In battling discrimination, Lincoln Ragsdale believed that black people have three choices: "You will either accept [it], rebel, or excel."[82]

By the 1990s, thanks to efforts of activists such as the Ragsdales, many black Phoenicians found and enjoyed a level of comfort that few blacks enjoyed a generation earlier. Cody Williams, son of real estate developer and civil rights activist Travis Williams and CEO of the Greater Phoenix Black Chamber of Commerce, argued that the civil rights movement and the King holiday victory in Arizona opened the door for more affluent blacks to migrate to the state. This migration, in turn, raised the median incomes of all blacks in the city. Some observers argued that "they wouldn't have come if the state had the stigma of not having a paid holiday." Art Hamilton believed that by 2000, "ten years removed from the controversy of establishing a paid King holiday in Arizona, it [was] clear that this recognition has improved the general sense of well-being of African Americans in our state." Not all blacks fared well between 1990 and 2000, however. When compared with other racial groups, black Phoenicians were more likely to live in poverty, die younger, go to prison more often, and have children before they reached adulthood. While the black Phoenician population grew by 44 percent between 1990 and 2000, huge population gains by Latinos and whites left the African American population at just 3 percent of the city's overall population. Nevertheless, many black Phoenicians believe that the black freedom struggle and the legacy of Lincoln and Eleanor Ragsdale have made Phoenix a better place to live. The Ragsdales' activities and the black freedom struggle in Phoenix have "made a significant difference in the external and internal perception of the state, economically, socially, and philosophically," argued Gene Blue, CEO of the OIC.[83]

Between 1990 and 2000 the median household income for African Americans in Phoenix rose 65 percent, from $20,564 to $33,922, giving them the twelfth highest median income for blacks in the nation. This represented a faster rate of growth than for whites in the city, who saw a 47 percent increase, from $29,958 to $44,148. Relatively speaking, "the quality of life has become very good here," one observer noted. The black indigence rate fell nearly 8 percent between 1990 and 2000, but many black leaders stressed the fact that nearly

20 percent of the city's black population were still mired in poverty. The black unemployment rate in Phoenix continued to be among the highest in the nation, and blacks throughout Arizona remained underrepresented in the state legislature. Of the ninety legislators in the Arizona House of Representatives and Senate in 2000, only one, Democratic representative Leah Landrum Taylor, was African American. "It blows peoples minds," she stated at the time, "when I tell them I am the only African American" in the legislature. "People around here joke sometimes and say, 'Here is the African American caucus,' and that would be me." Landrum Taylor believes that the number of black legislators, which was always small, fell during this period because black leaders were not doing a good job of "identifying potential candidates." In addition, African American electoral power was adversely affected in several traditional black voting strongholds, such as Districts 7 and 8, by influxes of Latino residents and by the movement of a large number of blacks to the city's suburbs.[84]

Home ownership, a benchmark for measuring economic success and upward mobility, remained stagnant for black Phoenicians during the 1990s. Only 45 percent owned their own homes, the lowest rate for all racial groups. About 73 percent of whites, 55 percent of Latinos, and 61 percent of indigenous peoples owned their own homes during this period. Affluent blacks who made gains as a result of the black freedom struggle continued to move to the suburbs of Chandler, Goodyear, Mesa, Peoria, Scottsdale, Tempe, and others in significant numbers. Phil Westbrooks, a black member of the Chandler City Council who grew up in a segregated Valley community, noted that most black suburbanites are "educated professionals who can live anywhere we want," an opportunity that "our parents did not have."[85] Eleanor Ragsdale, who substantially reduced her civil rights activities during the 1990s, believed that the passing of the paid King holiday and the increased mobility of blacks reflected "marvelous and positive attitude changes" in Phoenix and across the nation. "I'm wondering," however, she said, "whether the battle is ever won when you're talking about one human being's acceptance of another." Eleanor Ragsdale acknowledged that blacks in Phoenix had made substantial gains during her lifetime, but she also noted that African Americans still found themselves at or near the bottom of every major statistical measure of political, economic, and educational attainment. She declared that "far more work needs to be done."[86]

While denouncing racial segregation at the Paradise Valley Country Club, fighting racial discrimination at Sky Harbor, and lobbying the Arizona legislature for a Martin Luther King Day holiday, Lincoln Ragsdale continued to fight, despite his deteriorating health. Indeed, as he fought for the King Day holiday, he also fought the cancer that was claiming his life. None of this, however, stopped him from speaking out on the status of African Americans. He believed at the end of his life that African Americans should dedicate themselves to excellence, particularly in the realm of business. African Americans, he argued, were "not economically oriented." According to Ragsdale, African Americans' best hope for overcoming the effects of racism lay in their ability to improve their understanding of economics. He also called upon black people to rededicate themselves to diligence and hard work. In 1993 he stated: "I battle racism every day. I do it through excellence. I do it through hard work." Only by embracing these habits did he believe that black people would blaze new trails for themselves and their children.[87]

As hard as he worked, Lincoln Ragsdale could not have accomplished what he did without Eleanor's help. "She's been my friend, she's been my companion, she's been my wife, the mother of our children," he remarked. He also credited Eleanor with challenging him to be undaunted in all of his efforts. "She had more guts about these things than I have even had," he maintained. Lincoln Ragsdale was undaunted until the day his body could no longer fight the cancer that overcame it. He died on June 9, 1995, at sixty-nine years of age, leaving a legacy of leadership and activism. The lists of those who attended his funeral reflected the deep impact he had on business and civil rights.[88]

Eleanor Dickey Ragsdale died three years later at seventy-two years of age. She, too, was eulogized and remembered by family members and many local leaders. The Universal Memorial Center and the Universal Memorial Sunset Chapel continue to serve the Phoenix community. Two of their children, Lincoln Jr. and Emily, both of whom are fourth-generation morticians and business leaders, are guiding their family's enterprises into the twenty-first century. During the 1980s Lincoln and Eleanor Ragsdale recognized that even after nearly thirty years of civil rights activism, racism and socioeconomic inequality continued to be serious problems for the masses of African Americans. Despite the neoconservative forces that sought to undermine the laws,

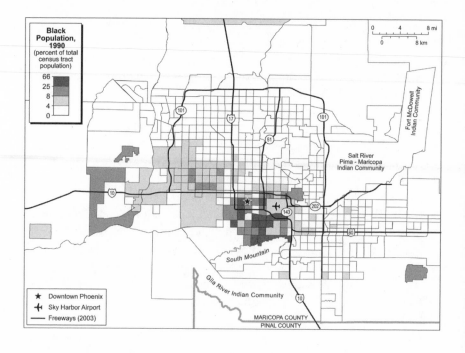

Distribution of black population in Phoenix,
1990. Source: Barbara Trapido-Lurie and
Patricia Gober, Department of Geography, at
Arizona State University, Tempe.

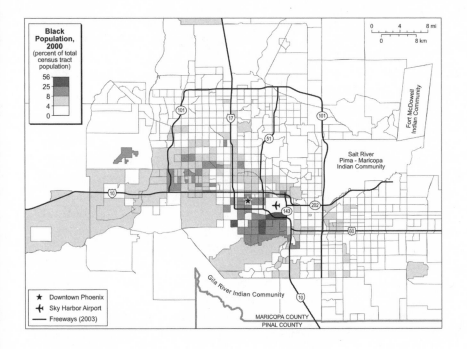

Distribution of black population
in Phoenix, 2000. Source: Barbara
Trapido-Lurie and Patricia Gober,
Department of Geography, Arizona
State University, Tempe.

court cases, and symbolic victories that the couple had helped secure between 1950 and 1980, the Ragsdales fought to create more opportunities and symbolic victories for African Americans. Lincoln Ragsdale in particular resurfaced during the conservative Reagan-Bush years as an outspoken proponent of black socioeconomic progress. He ended his life in Phoenix in the same way it began, working to help reverse the negative effects of racism and black socioeconomic isolation. Even with the many setbacks and persistent problems in employment, education, health care, housing, and police brutality, he, with the help of Eleanor, recorded a significant list of victories. Lincoln and Eleanor Ragsdale, despite personal limitations and losses, accomplished much. Although Phoenix and many other urban centers still suffer from racial inequality, the contributions of such leaders have helped many African Americans enjoy freedoms and a standard of living unparalleled in American history. The Ragsdales' experiences and legacies place them among the most compelling black leaders and activists in American civil rights history.

When asked, however, to reflect upon their contribution to the black freedom struggle and their work on behalf of racial equality, Eleanor Ragsdale spoke for the couple. "I would have liked that we would not have had to do that at all," she said. "I would have liked to have thought that because we were born in America, and we were trying to be upright citizens, that we should not have had to go through that kind of struggle. But certainly I would not have changed the fact that we were involved in it. I think that was very important at the time. You have to live in the time in which you were born, and you have to deal with the challenges you meet at the time you are alive. And then you look back, and you have to be proud that you could be a part of it, and that you had enough strength, courage, and faith to have done it." [89]

# Conclusion

*Racial Uplift in Phoenix*

A diamond is the result of extreme pressure. Less pressure is crystal, less than that is coal, less than that is fossilized leaves or plain dirt. Pressure can change you into something quite precious, quite wonderful, quite beautiful and extremely hard.

Maya Angelou, *USA Today*, March 5, 1985

ON APRIL 8, 1990, Lincoln Johnson Ragsdale Sr. reflected upon what he believed was a rewarding career. The entrepreneur, civil rights activist, World War II veteran and Tuskegee Airman, and philanthropist, thankful and resolute, declared that "Phoenix has been wonderful." During his tenure as a leader in Phoenix, however, circumstances were not always "wonderful." What Ragsdale might have been referring to were the victories black Phoenicians secured against a system that oppressed them. The city, like the rest of the nation, played host to social and economic inequality cultivated and sustained by white supremacy. Lincoln Ragsdale, along with his wife, Eleanor, fought to eradicate this inequality. Although the Ragsdales and other activists encountered many obstacles during the black liberation struggle, Lincoln Ragsdale believed that "the good thing [was] that through it all," African Americans "have been able to overcome." Even though the degree to which the Ragsdales and their fellow activists were "successful" is debatable, Lincoln Ragsdale believed that their work "speaks for itself."[1]

The Ragsdales occupy an important place in Phoenix's history and the history of the civil rights movement. Together, they resisted social, economic, and political subjugation for more than half a century. Between 1946 and 2000, like black leaders and activists in other cities throughout the United States, the couple was instrumental in helping African Americans overcome many inequalities prescribed by a white-dominated power structure. The black freedom struggle that they helped to lead was lengthy, the progress they helped bring about was often slow, and the unfettered fairness and justice they sought proved to be elusive. The movement in which they were involved was intricate and demanding, but it yielded significant advancements that prompted its leaders and participants to look to the future with hope and anticipation for the realization of racial parity.[2]

The Ragsdales were raised in the black professional tradition. Despite being reared in different regions of the country, their shared experience as heirs to a legacy of black professional leadership paved the way for their future role as influential civil rights leaders. As heirs of the black professional tradition, leadership and community service were a part of their heritage. Their familial backgrounds inspired Lincoln and Eleanor Ragsdale to accomplish much personally, while also motivating them to work for the advancement of the African American community. To prepare them to be "race workers," their families educated them in the demands of professional work and racial uplift. The Ragsdales learned that black professional people were often called upon to be leaders in their fields and in the black freedom struggle.[3]

By the late 1940s Lincoln and Eleanor Ragsdale had left their homes in Oklahoma and Pennsylvania, respectively, to follow career paths in the military and teaching. Eventually, their interests brought them together in a small desert community named Phoenix. Although it was billed as a bastion of freedom and opportunity, the city was greatly influenced by white supremacy. There were few opportunities for black people and other people of color. Lincoln and Eleanor were surprised and disappointed with the socioeconomic status of the African American community when they relocated to the city. They found out quickly that the black Phoenician community was similar to the ones they left behind—racially segregated and, in Lincoln's case, impoverished and terrorized. By the late 1940s the Ragsdales had settled in Phoenix, and they began to use their skills and commitment to "racial uplift" to combat racial inequality in the city. Their efforts quickly began to change Phoenix forever.[4]

The Ragsdales began their careers in Phoenix on the heels of World

War II, an event that had a profound impact on African Americans throughout the nation. World War II hastened the end or curtailment of racial discrimination in some areas, particularly in the Pacific Northwest, while others remained virtually unchanged. White supremacy continued to rule in Phoenix, even as wartime migration brought more African Americans, including the Ragsdales, to the city. An outgrowth of this migration was the rise of more vocal black leaders like the Ragsdales. Having served as a Tuskegee Airman during World War II, Lincoln Ragsdale had recently developed the confidence and determination to demand personal and cultural freedom and justice.

Like most blacks who served in the military during World War II, Lincoln Ragsdale emerged from the war with a renewed determination to secure more socioeconomic opportunities and liberty for black people. He soon became an outspoken leader. Having fought a war to defeat fascism and racism abroad, he believed it was time for blacks to be treated equally as American citizens. "Tuskegee changed my life," Ragsdale declared. "I had been told all my life that I was insignificant, I was black, I was dumb, I couldn't do it. At Tuskegee, they told me I could do it, and they treated me with respect. Of all the experiences I've ever had, of all the accolades, being an officer and a pilot in the forties during war time, and the prestige that went with it, changed my whole life. It made me feel as though I could do anything." He, with the Eleanor's help and the confidence he cultivated at Tuskegee, undertook to improve race relations and the lives of black Phoenicians. The leaders were successful, but the struggle was grueling.[5]

Aided by the GI Bill and other postwar grants, some African Americans were able to improve their lives. For their part, the Ragsdales helped infuse the black Phoenician community with a tempered optimism and a resolution to build upon the advances black people made during World War II. Their heads for business and desire to work on behalf of the African American community following World War II made them two of the most compelling leaders in the American West. Between 1947 and 1954 the Ragsdales helped push Phoenix into an era of aggressive progressivism that emphasized elevated national and international awareness of racial equality. During these years their activism reached its peak with the defeat of residential segregation and de jure school segregation in Phoenix. The leaders participated in, and led, traditional civil rights organizations, such as the local branch of the NAACP, the GPCCU, and the PUL. They called for positive change and accelerated the drive for racial justice. White resistance, however, made it difficult for the Ragsdales and other activists to destroy white supremacy in Phoenix.[6]

Many whites, despite their exposure to the horrors of nazism and the most virulent manifestations of white supremacy during World War II, the work of respected scholars who refuted the idea of race and racial superiority, and the advocacy of leaders such as the Ragsdales, were steadfast in their belief in black inferiority. The increased number of blacks in urban centers such as Phoenix due to wartime and postwar migration exacerbated existing interracial tensions and conflict. As a result, socioeconomic progress and racial justice for black Phoenicians continued to be elusive during the postwar years. Restrictive covenants, for example, barred black Phoenicians from purchasing homes wherever they wished. While most whites began to move to suburban areas, most blacks became trapped in a decaying and socially, economically, and politically isolated inner city. Many black Phoenicians aspired to move into suburban neighborhoods but were barred from doing so. As one observer noted, "Negro buyers, regardless of affluence, education, or credit rating, would be refused and discouraged if they should attempt to purchase a home in the new developments which cater to the white market."[7]

During the 1950s, despite continuing racial discrimination, Eleanor and Lincoln Ragsdale and other activists were able to help usher in reforms following more aggressive protests. The Ragsdales had a notion of freedom and justice that was reflected in their unyielding desire to question the ruling white Phoenix establishment. Their diligent race work infused the Phoenician movement with creativity, tenacity, and craftiness that could not be found in Phoenix before their arrival. Retired colonel Lloyd McKeethen, a longtime friend of Lincoln's and fellow war veteran, remembered the Ragsdales as people who always had goals and high personal standards. Lincoln, in particular, he recalled, "really had some vision, had some goal that was probably in his mind all of the time, not that he always talked about it, but Lincoln was a thinker."[8]

Although white supremacy had a long history in Phoenix, the city's racial customs were more fluid and less brutal than those in southern cities. The Ragsdales exploited this fluidity to systematically undermine the white power structure in the Valley. Eleanor Ragsdale's ingenuity and courage, for example, were instrumental in desegregating Phoenix's Encanto District, the city's wealthiest and most racially exclusive white neighborhood, in 1953. The couple's business acumen, organizational prowess, and leadership qualities helped facilitate the desegregation of Phoenix schools prior to the landmark *Brown v. Board of Education* decision of 1954. Between 1954 and 1967, despite ongoing racial prejudice and discrimination, black progress corresponded to increasing militancy. The civil rights movement quickened during this period, producing the most intense and effective civil rights activity in American history. From the *Brown* decision to the Montgomery bus boycott to the passage of the Civil Rights and Voting Rights acts, activists such as the Ragsdales changed the ways in which race and democracy were perceived. They helped achieve victories against segregated schools and discrimination in employment, housing, places of public accommodation, and voter registration in Phoenix.[9]

Although most white Phoenicians vigorously resisted changes in the racial status quo, the Ragsdales continued to fight. They led black Phoenicians to multiple victories against racism and inequality. Like black people across the nation, they were met with defiance and aggression by staunch white counteraction. They responded by embracing their supporters and cultivating effective interracial coalitions of civil rights activists. In Phoenix and elsewhere, national and local civil rights legislation created more socioeconomic opportunities for African Americans, particularly upwardly mobile blacks who were best prepared to benefit from these advances. For many blacks, the struggle continued. As one study indicated, "both blacks and [Hispanics] have a disproportionate share of the overcrowded population as well as a disproportionate share of families with incomes under $7,000." The Ragsdales and activists such as Manuel Pena and Alfredo Gutierrez bemoaned the poor educational opportunities and living conditions among blacks and Chicanos in Phoenix.[10]

Despite their shared status as racial minorities who reeled under an oppressive white power structure, racial minorities, particularly African Americans and Mexican Americans, rarely formed substantive coalitions to oppose white supremacy and racial discrimination. The Ragsdales and other black activists led the way in protesting white supremacy and racial discrimination in Phoenix. They did, however, work tirelessly to form activist partnerships with Mexican American leaders such as Manuel Pena and Grace Gill-Olivarez, believing that such partnerships would move their respective communities closer to forging lasting activist and entrepreneurial relationships that would advance both communities. Bonds between African Americans and other minority activists existed in Phoenix, as in other areas of the nation, but black Phoenicians ultimately bore the responsibility of calling attention to their own oppression. The most visible interracial alliances in Phoenix were primarily coalitions among liberal black and white citizens. Although Mexican Americans have always been the city's largest minority population and have always been subjected to white racism, oppression, and exploitation, most Mexican Americans and African Americans never developed a sustained union throughout their crusades for equality. Lincoln Ragsdale and his Mexican American counterparts came to understand that their mutual subordination was insufficient to bridge many of the cultural and political barriers standing between the two groups.[11]

The Chicano movement, which made its way to Phoenix in 1968, helped bring about an increase in cooperation between African American and Chicano activists. Still, collaboration was primarily limited to individual efforts to build coalitions. Although the negative effects of white supremacy and racial discrimination periodically brought African American and Mexican American activists together, the demands of race, ethnicity, culture, and class usually impaired their capacity to record a sustained, combined liberation movement. Despite the fact that African American and Chicano Phoenicians were unable to form a lasting coalition, Phoenix did benefit from the development of the two racial liberation movements. Since the black liberation struggle in Phoenix unfolded in an environment where blacks were simply one of several racial minorities, Phoenix's multiracial population pushed the issue of civil rights and social justice beyond black and white. The black freedom struggle and the Chicano movement forced the city's ruling whites to deal with race and democracy in ways that whites in other regions of the country did not.[12]

The presence of Mexican Americans in Phoenix occasionally ameliorated the effects of "Negrophobia" by diverting intolerance from blacks. Nevertheless, inasmuch as Mexican Americans endured discrimination that was at once similar to and yet different than that faced by most black people, many Mexican Americans chose not to speak out in opposition to racial discrimination against black Phoenicians. Like white Phoenicians, some Mexican Americans also discriminated against African Americans. Black Phoenicians, who were not immune to racial chauvinism, often failed to acknowledge the degree to which Mexican Americans suffered under the yoke of white supremacy. This fact did nothing to advance the relationship between the two groups. The occasional contributions of individual Chicano leaders to the civil rights movement and the infrequent investment of some black leaders in the Chicano movement were perhaps the most that leaders like the Ragsdales could have hoped for. For both groups, race, culture, and class were ultimately too difficult to overcome, even though each group was discriminated against by an oppressive white Phoenician majority. Despite the Ragsdales' efforts and the individual efforts of Mexican Americans such as Pena, Gill-Olivarez, and Gutierrez, most members of each group continued to struggle, while leaders from both camps jockeyed for the status of champion of the most deserving minority. It was no surprise, then, that a viable alliance of blacks and Chicanos remained elusive.[13]

As the black and Mexican American middle classes grew during the 1970s, 1980s, and 1990s, each group made progress, especially with regard to employment opportunities and residential mobility. As Bradford Luckingham has indicated, however, "historically, the failure of minority groups to unite in the struggle to conquer common problems, and their traditional tendency to dislike each other and to see each other as rivals, proved debilitating." Growing Latino immigration greatly affected the African American community. Previously all-black neighborhoods were quickly transformed into areas with substantial Latino, particularly Mexican American, populations. This change led to disputes over meager resources and representation between the two groups throughout the remainder of the twentieth century.[14]

Although the Ragsdales and other black activists had to "go it alone" throughout the peak years of the civil rights movement in Phoenix, they were able to win some of the most groundbreaking civil rights battles in Arizona history and benefit from trail-blazing national civil rights victories. Between 1964 and 1980, in fact, a new era of black activism emerged. Although the enactment of a statewide public accommodations law and the national 1964 Civil Rights Act and the 1965 Voting Rights Act were major victories for proponents of civil rights, these laws did not end racial discrimination in Arizona.

Many white Phoenicians reacted to such legislation by circumventing their directives, ignoring them altogether, or creating legal and extralegal barriers to thwart African American progress. A number of whites who opposed progressive legislation forged campaigns that protested or abolished such decrees in many states. Many civil rights activists argued that these barriers needed new, more radical strategies and organizations to overcome them. As whites paraded their disapproval of racial reform, young black activists called for more radical ways of securing black liberation. The new black activism that emerged offered a critique of the link between white supremacy, capitalism, and racism. By 1964 more militant activist organizations, such as the local chapters of the SNCC and CORE, decried the poverty and discrimination in South Phoenix.[15]

Unlike the NAACP, for which Lincoln Ragsdale served as vice president, CORE was decentralized and more democratic. The aggressiveness of CORE and SNCC appealed to young activists in Phoenix who believed that the NAACP was too conservative. SNCC, in particular, attracted activists who supported black nationalism and rejected integration. Lincoln Ragsdale, who described himself as "a radical for love and integration," balked at cultural nationalism and supported multiculturalism. Although he advocated black economic nationalism, his social integrationist philosophy was often at odds with the more vocal and militant leaders and organizations of the late 1960s and early 1970s. By the early 1970s the Ragsdales were looked upon by younger, more militant activists as people whose goals and concerns operated in conflict with those of poor and working-class blacks.[16]

As acrimonious as the critiques of Lincoln Ragsdale's social, economic, and political philosophy may have been at the time, they did highlight the volatile and vexing question of class and economics in the black freedom struggle. Ragsdale succeeded in bringing attention to the problems associated with racial discrimination in Phoenix and American society, but he failed to sufficiently understand or address the interconnectedness of race, class, and gender. Had Lincoln Ragsdale not accumulated an impressive list of concessions from Phoenix's white power structure, tensions that simmered between his inner circle of conservative leaders and working-class militants may have exploded into full-fledged intraracial class conflict. Lincoln Ragsdale never paid any substantive attention to sexism, particularly as it related to black women. Eleanor Ragsdale, however, took it upon herself to use their resources to aid black women in their unique struggle. Due to the paucity of sources, it is not possible to analyze many of the nuances of their relationship and their individual views on feminism and women's rights. Nevertheless, it is safe to say that Lincoln was quite comfortable with Eleanor interacting and administering to the needs and desires of black women in Phoenix, even though he appeared to be quite unable or unwilling to do so himself.[17]

Class divisions had always existed among African Americans in Phoenix and in other parts of the country, as they did among all Americans. These divisions reached new heights, however, during the 1980s and 1990s. Throughout urban America at this time, the growing number of affluent blacks became more diffused, while the so-called black underclass also expanded but became more concentrated in inner cities. These circumstances prompted some observers to proclaim that "class had become more important than race in determining black life-chances."[18] On the other hand, there were blacks, such as the Ragsdales, who amassed large sums of money while also working to uplift African Americans who remained marginalized and mired in poverty. For example, Eleanor Ragsdale, through the Black Women's Task Force established in Phoenix in 1983, helped indigent black Phoenicians lift themselves out of poverty through work opportunities and job training.[19]

Between 1950 and 1980 Eleanor and Lincoln Ragsdale had led a civil rights movement in Phoenix that was effective in tearing down many barriers to black equality. By the 1980s, however, they came to understand that racism was still a major obstacle standing between most African Americans and socioeconomic equality. As the nation hosted the largest black middle class in its history, its poor and working-class black citizens were locked into decaying inner cities marked by poverty, inferior educational facilities, poor health care, and violence. A troubling imbalance emerged among upwardly mobile beneficiaries of the civil rights movement and those who were left behind. Race, it appeared, still mattered, and class did as well.[20]

Historical and ongoing racial discrimination generated and nurtured poverty and hopelessness among black people, especially those sequestered in decaying urban areas. Despite persistent racial inequality, many conservative leaders pointed to the "success" of the black bourgeoisie and unfunctional concepts of "color blindness" as a basis to destroy race-conscious antidotes to America's racial inequality.

Crusading on behalf of these ideals, conservative scholars, lawmakers, activists, and politicians propelled America into a new conservative era in the nation's history, one in which individualism and personal responsibility were touted as panaceas for every socioeconomic problem. Black progress and progressive activism helped inspire this conservative rebirth among whites, while the problems of poor blacks helped inspire a conservative renaissance among middle-class African Americans. The forces of this neoconservative movement worked to reverse the legal, political, economic, and symbolic victories that leaders like the Ragsdales had fought to win. Lincoln Ragsdale in particular saw a need to oppose this brand of conservativism. During the 1980s and 1990s he resurfaced as an outspoken proponent of racial tolerance and justice.[21]

The civil rights movement between 1946 and 1980 was able to illuminate the retrograde nature of American race relations, the plight of African Americans, and the need for systemic solutions to the "race problem." It also helped unmask and intensify divisions within black communities. Black people no longer had slavery and Jim Crow to contend with or the struggle to destroy these institutions and systems to unite them. By 1980 black people began to disagree more often on fundamental social, economic, and political issues. Conflicts between the expanding number of affluent black people like the Ragsdales and impoverished African Americans seemingly trapped in distressed inner cities widened. Arguments between integrationists and black nationalists intensified. As always, the ultimate issue was what was in the best interest of black people, in spite of the many theories that each faction put forth.[22]

Although the Ragsdales and other activists welcomed progress and the growth of the black middle class during the 1980s and 1990s, problems remained. Blacks who were able to access the middle class reflected the ability of some African Americans to free themselves from the "web of urban racism" in Phoenix and across the nation. For most, employment, housing, and educational opportunities were scarce. Similitude with white Americans appeared to be obtainable for middle-class blacks but improbable for the majority of African Americans isolated in inner cities. Many unskilled Americans, including white people and minorities, also found advancement elusive during the recession that marked the late 1980s and early 1990s. Blacks, who were often disproportionately represented among the "truly disadvantaged," were especially vulnerable to the economic downturn.[23]

Lincoln Ragsdale and other observers argued that jobs and higher salaries would suspend the deterioration of poor black communities. Urban areas definitely needed employment opportunities, as the "deindustrialization of America" and the movement of corporations to suburban areas devastated inner cities and the economic viability of black communities. Black Phoenicians and other minorities remained in the interior of the city. The Ragsdales' "successful" emigration to Clearwater Hills was a rising trend, but it remained atypical. In 1980 just 21 percent of black households and 31 percent of Chicano households in the Phoenix metropolitan area resided beyond the bounds of the central city of Phoenix. Forty-nine percent of white Phoenicians called the suburbs home.[24]

The Ragsdales believed that the most pressing problems facing African Americans by this time were the lack of quality educational opportunities and economic depression. The local and national labor markets were virtually closed to many young, uneducated blacks, while the number of African American families headed by single women remained disproportionately high. The percentage of such families in black communities increased faster than that in white communities. Often accountable for the well-being of small children and unable to secure or maintain employment, black women were routinely overrepresented among those who depended upon public aid for subsistence. Moreover, low educational attainment and lower wage levels, engendered in part by the history and life of racial and gender discrimination, put black women at a greater disadvantage in virtually every walk of life. Like other women of color, they suffered from the triple burden of racial, gender, and economic oppression.[25]

The Ragsdales believed that increased job opportunities, higher wages, and entrepreneurship held the key to reversing these tendencies. They argued that more jobs and opportunities for blacks to start their own businesses had to be created in the inner city. Deindustrialization and technological changes, coupled with the legacy of white supremacy in America, made this necessary. Manufacturers, offices, and services relocated to the suburbs, along with a great deal of social, economic, and political capital. Despite the hard work in which most blacks and other people of color engaged, they argued, these groups continued to suffer tremendously because of this trend.[26]

Nevertheless, by 1995 in Phoenix, Lincoln and Eleanor Ragsdale had led a black liberation movement that had improved the lives of many African Americans and made the city more tolerant and inclusive. They were content, having reemerged during the 1980s and early 1990s, to lead progressive activists, business leaders, and politicians to more victories in the name of freedom, equality, and democracy. As late as 1993 they had helped call attention to persistent de facto segregation in Phoenix, were instrumental in creating more opportunities for minorities to own their own businesses, and had played a critical role in establishing a paid Martin Luther King Jr. holiday in the state of Arizona. For his part, Lincoln Ragsdale displayed a righteous indignation and anger about racial discrimination, and he relished his role as an agitator. "I was very controversial. I was a radical," he proclaimed.[27]

Many people prefer to remember the young Lincoln Ragsdale of the 1950s and early 1960s, when he was "truly radical." "I like to hear about the Lincoln who came here forty years ago or more, because that's the radical Lincoln," Warren Stewart remarked. "That's not the Mercedes driving, you know, suave, debonair Lincoln. That's the guy who used to cause trouble on behalf of civil rights and equal rights. I like to hear him talk about when they boycotted, or sat-in at the Woolworth's department store that didn't serve blacks at that time because of their color; about how he led the civil rights movement in Arizona." Many people did not appreciate some of the things Lincoln Ragsdale did or said. "He was a splash of water in the face of the status quo," wrote the *Arizona Republic* in 1995. "He made sure people knew when things were wrong, and he was there to help make things right."[28]

As Lincoln aged and the civil rights movement evolved, he was perceived less as a radical or militant activist and was regarded as an wealthy elder statesmen of the civil rights movement who championed antiquated notions of racial integration. Many people labeled Lincoln and Eleanor Ragsdale as "sell-outs" because of the less confrontational and less "radical" positions they took as they aged. Many more labeled Lincoln a "capitalist Uncle Tom" for his devotion to entrepreneurship, the pursuit of riches, and an extravagant lifestyle. It is too simplistic, however, to label the Ragsdales "sell-outs" or to say that they embodied the Washingtonian model of entrepreneurship. Like Booker T. Washington, the Ragsdales believed in capitalism, self-help, and black entrepreneurship. Unlike Washington, however, they believed in racial integration, political agitation, and direct and affirmative action. Their beliefs and actions made them proponents of Washingtonian racial uplift as much as they made them proponents of W. E. B. DuBois's brand of race work. Placing them into a dichotomous Washington versus DuBois model would be unwise. In reality, the teachings and beliefs of both Washington and DuBois were reflected in the Ragsdales' words and actions. As he grew older, however, Lincoln Ragsdale behaved more like Washington and less like DuBois.

Lincoln was not completely out of step with younger, more black nationalist voices by 1990. By then he admitted that his generation of activists overestimated the efficacy of racial integration. As he and other black activists saw it, the only people who truly benefited from integration were white Americans. According to Lincoln Ragsdale Jr., his father came to "believe that black people were not ready for integration" during the 1950s, 1960s, and 1970s. When American society began to desegregate, "black people who had black businesses lost out. They lost their market." Blacks began to patronize white-owned businesses, but "white people did not come to the black entrepreneur. The black entrepreneur, the black businessman who had his cleaning business, restaurants and clubs," was forced out of business as his black customers "ventured off into other areas" and patronized white businesses.[29]

Desegregation, Lincoln Ragsdale believed, virtually destroyed the economic base of black communities, and it also severely damaged black social and cultural networks. The institutions and groups that bound black people together and sustained them through generations of white supremacy—the black church, blacks schools, and black social and political organizations—have suffered dislocation and fragmentation. Despite his inability to acclimate himself to an activist environment during the 1970s, 1980s, and 1990s that popularized black nationalism and embraced quasi-socialist solutions to inequality, Lincoln Ragsdale clearly understood the extent to which his generation of activists had underestimated the insidiousness of racism and socioeconomic inequality. Toward the end of his life he, like many black nationalists and more militant black leaders of the 1960s and 1970s, believed that "economics was the new way of segregating people." By then he thought that for African Americans to advance, they would have to combat racism and economic oppression simultaneously. The civil rights movement created many opportunities for black people, he mused, but opportunity in a capitalist system means very little without money.[30]

By 1989 Lincoln Ragsdale had taken stock of the work he and Eleanor had accomplished. Although he acknowledged that they had helped usher in racial progress in the social arena, he believed that they had failed to win the economic battle, which he believed to be the most important battle of all. In his dissertation, "Minority Entrepreneurship," he wrote:

> During a later phase in my life there were significant changes in the American scene with respect to the attitude of the majority of society toward the [racial] minorities. A greater portion of this change was in the social area. Little, if anything, transpired in the lives of the minorities, as their poverty and deprivation continues. Their communities look exactly the same, despite these social changes. This causes one to seek some other answers to the problems of the minorities. Obviously, political and social advances are not enough. As one ponders over this situation, it becomes evident that in order to take full advantage of one's citizenship in the United States, one must develop economically. It matters not what privileges are available; one cannot partake of them unless one is financially able to do so. It is relatively simply to open the way and then price the way beyond someone's means.[31]

Lincoln and Eleanor Ragsdale believed in civil rights and social integration, but by the end of their lives they firmly believed that entrepreneurship and financial power, secured through calculated black economic nationalism and facilitated by interracial business channels, would lead to the ultimate liberation of black people within America's capitalist system. Neither Lincoln nor Eleanor Ragsdale ever indicated that they thought that transforming America into a more socialist state was the answer to the "race problem" in the United States. They did not concern themselves with socialist prescriptions for racial change, nor did they acknowledge the inextricably linked nature of capitalism, exploitation, and the commodification and differentiation of labor along race, class, gender, and ethnic lines. Simply put, black people needed both social and economic capital to subsidize their overall advancement, and Lincoln and Eleanor Ragsdale believed that entrepreneurship and success in business were the answer in post–civil rights America.

Although Eleanor Ragsdale did not entertain socialist prescriptions for remedying black suffering, she did promote more gendered and female-centered prescriptions for fighting racial oppression. She worked constantly with traditional civil rights groups and activist women's organizations to combat racial and gender inequality. Lincoln Ragsdale, it seems, did not concern himself much with gender equality. He did, however, work closely with Eleanor in their businesses and in the overall effort to attack white supremacy. He either failed to see or chose not to acknowledge the unique challenges faced by black women in a society that was both racist and sexist. Although Lincoln has been credited with being the architect of the Ragsdales' legacy of entrepreneurship and activism, Eleanor's role in the family's ascendancy was critical. Her leadership, cunning, diligence, and influence on Lincoln and his ability to tap into specific resources in the black community cannot be overstated. Together, Lincoln and Eleanor Ragsdale, through their activism and interracial networks, formed a formidable tandem in shaping a meaningful struggle for black freedom that was both consistent with the national civil rights movement and noticeably different.[32]

Even after Lincoln's death, Eleanor continued to work on behalf of their family interests and on behalf of racial inclusion. Her activities during the height of the civil rights movement are as noteworthy as those of her more celebrated husband. As hard working as Lincoln was, he could not have accomplished what he did without the benefit of Eleanor's intellectual acumen, hard work, and moral support.[33] It was Eleanor's relentless drive and "sincere love for mankind" that inspired her to be an agent for racial tolerance and equality. She believed that "if you have enough love, and enough faith in yourself and mankind, that you can make a difference. Everyday that you wake up you make a decision whether you're going to be happy that day. You make a decision whether you're going to influence someone's life for good. You make a decision whether you're going to be positive, and joyful, and enthusiastic, despite it all." Being positive and hopeful is what drove Eleanor Ragsdale, in addition to her belief in the universal human right to freedom and prosperity. To "love your neighbor and be a force for good is a decision and a discipline," she proclaimed. "I think that's what life is all about."[34]

The contribution of the Ragsdales to the black freedom struggle in Phoenix rivals most of the more privileged histories of black professional activism and race work in American history. The Ragsdales gave new meaning to black entrepreneurship in Phoenix, as achievement became their trademark through myriad business endeavors. The couple was often willing to step to the fore and lead when it would have been much easier to stay in the shadows.[35] The direct-action efforts of western black civil rights activists such as the Ragsdales, however, did not eliminate racial inequality. During the 1990s the progress and prosperity of the black middle class increased the differences between it and less-fortunate blacks who remained lost in an arresting maze of urban poverty and immobility. Class divisions, geographical separation, and lingering racial discrimination made it increasingly difficult to maintain cohesion and unity within black communities. Black Phoenicians unified behind important issues such as the Martin Luther King Jr. Day holiday in Arizona, but they continued to be fragmented during less embattled times as a cornucopia of individuals and groups advanced their own ideas and programs.[36]

Despite obstacles and setbacks, the Ragsdales and their fellow activists helped destroy generations of barriers to equal opportunity and racial equality. The progress that they helped usher in was always achieved amid omnipresent racial discrimination and systematic oppression. A combination of Euro-American social Darwinism, Protestant ethics, capitalist exploitation, and western "frontier conditions," in conflict with a steady influx of black immigrants, made Phoenix a place ripe for disharmony and racial discord. As the lives and legacy of the Ragsdales reveal, the area of the United States east of the Mississippi River had no monopoly on white supremacy.[37] Although the racial etiquette in the West was generally less rigid, white westerners systematically denied black people equal opportunity to access the primary means of production and distribution. Despite these adversities, Lincoln and Eleanor Ragsdale resisted subjugation and helped shape African American designs on racial equality and black autonomy into a dynamic movement to secure peace and prosperity in Phoenix. Lincoln and Eleanor Ragsdale, particularly during the 1950s and 1960s, led African Americans in an intense local battle that had national implications. Their efforts yielded greater educational, occupational, and entrepreneurial opportunities for African Americans and, ostensibly, all Americans. Whenever they discovered a case of racial discrimination and intolerance, they gave their energies and lent their name, resources, and political power to individuals and organizations that opposed it. Lincoln and Eleanor Ragsdale helped the city of Phoenix, like the legendary bird that reemerged from its own ashes, rise anew from the remnants of its segregated and white supremacist past.[38]

## African American Population in the Phoenix Metropolitan Area and Selected Suburbs, 2000

| City | Population | Percentage of population | Total population |
|------|-----------|--------------------------|------------------|
| Phoenix | 67,416 | 5.0 | 1,321,045 |
| Glendale | 10,270 | 5.0 | 218,812 |
| Mesa | 9,977 | 3.0 | 396,375 |
| Chandler | 6,151 | 3.0 | 176,581 |
| Tempe | 5,801 | 4.0 | 158,625 |
| Peoria | 3,012 | 3.0 | 108,364 |
| Scottsdale | 2,501 | 1.0 | 202,705 |
| Avondale | 1,866 | 5.0 | 35,883 |
| Goodyear | 983 | 5.0 | 18,911 |
| Paradise Valley | 100 | 0.07 | 13,664 |

*Source:* U.S. Bureau of the Census, *Population of the United States,* 2000.

## Regional Racial Distribution in
## Selected Arizona Cities, 2000

| Race | U.S. | Phoenix | Tucson | Flagstaff | Yuma | Prescott |
|---|---|---|---|---|---|---|
| | | | Percentage of Population | | | |
| African American | 12 | 5 | 4 | 2 | 3 | 1 |
| Mexican American | 7 | 28 | 30 | 13 | 39 | 6 |
| White (Non-Hispanic) | 69 | 56 | 54 | 70 | 48 | 88 |
| Asian/Pacific Islander | 4 | 2 | 2 | 1 | 2 | 1 |
| Native American | 1 | 2 | 2 | 9 | 2 | 1 |
| Other races | 0 | 0 | 0 | 0 | 0 | 0 |
| Two or more races | 2 | 2 | 2 | 2 | 2 | 0 |

*Source:* U.S. Bureau of the Census, *Population of the United States*, 2000.

## Selected American Western Cities with Black Populations Exceeding Fifty Thousand as of 2000

| City | Black population | Total population | Black percentage of total population |
|------|------------------|------------------|--------------------------------------|
| Phoenix | 67,416 | 1,321,045 | 5 |
| Dallas | 306,122 | 1,188,204 | 25 |
| Denver | 60,579 | 554,636 | 11 |
| Houston | 493,149 | 1,954,848 | 25 |
| Los Angeles | 411,089 | 3,694,834 | 11 |
| Oakland | 141,294 | 399,477 | 35 |
| Oklahoma City | 76,478 | 505,963 | 15 |
| San Antonio | 75,804 | 1,144,554 | 7 |
| San Diego | 94,539 | 1,223,341 | 8 |
| Seattle | 46,716 | 563,375 | 8 |

*Source:* U.S. Bureau of the Census, *Population of the United States*, 2000.

## APPENDIX D

# Ragsdale Businesses and Financial Enterprises

Ragsdale Mortuary (1947)

Ragsdale Realty and Insurance Agency (1950)

International Investment Company (1952)

International Construction Company (1953)

Valley Life and Casualty Insurance (1955)

Century Skyroom Restaurant and Jazz Club (1963)

Universal Memorial Center (1964)

Universal Ambulance, Inc. (1965)

Universal Sunset Chapel (1967)

David's Flowers (1971)

Valley Life and Casualty Insurance of Louisiana (1980)

Valley Life Insurance Company of Alabama (1980)

Valley Life and Casualty Insurance Company of Texas (1983)

Source: Universal Memorial Center, *A Celebration and Worship Service Honoring the Life of Dr. Lincoln Johnson Ragsdale, Sr.* (Phoenix: Universal Memorial Center, 1995).

# Professional Organizations and Boards for which Lincoln Ragsdale Served

Arizona Club Board of Trustees

Arizona Historical Foundation

Arizona State University Alumni Association, President

Downtown Young Men's Christian Association (YMCA) Board of Directors

Kiwanis Club of Phoenix

Municipal Aeronautics Advisory Board, Chairman

National Conference of Christians and Jews

National Urban League Board of Trustees

Olta Sigma Alha, Honor Society

Phoenix Chamber of Commerce

Phoenix Press Club, Associate Member

Phoenix Urban League

Planned Parenthood Advisory Board

Rust College Board of Trustees (North Carolina)

Sigma Pi Phi (Boule) Fraternity, Inc.

Sun State Savings and Loan

Union Graduate School Board of Trustees (Ohio)

University Club Board of Trustees

Source: Universal Memorial Center, *A Celebration and Worship Service Honoring the Life of Dr. Lincoln Johnson Ragsdale, Sr.* (Phoenix: Universal Memorial Center, 1995).

APPENDIX F

## Professional Organizations and Boards for which Eleanor Ragsdale Served

Arizona Coordinating Committee for International Women's Year

Arizona Historical Foundation

Black Women's Task Force and the University Club of Phoenix

Coalition '76 (group concerned with the passage of ERA)

Delta Sigma Theta Sorority, Golden Life Member. President
of Phoenix Metropolitan Chapter, Alumni Chapter of Phoenix,
Far West Region; National Committees: Constitution and By-Laws

First Institutional Baptist Church

Greater Phoenix Urban League

KAET Channel 8 (PBS), Community Advisory Board

Knights and Daughters of Tabor #6

NAACP

National Smart Set, Scottsdale Chapter

Phoenix Chapter of Links, Inc.

Planned Parenthood of Central and Northern Arizona Advisory Board

UJIMA House

United Negro College Fund, Phoenix

Young Women's Christian Association (YWCA)

Source: Universal Memorial Center, *A Celebration and Worship Service Honoring the Life of Mrs. Eleanor Dickey Ragsdale* (Phoenix: Universal Memorial Center, 1995).

APPENDIX G

## Lincoln Ragsdale's Honors and Distinctions

Arizona Civil Liberties Union Pioneer of Racial Justice Award
  (posthumous award, May 18, 2001)
Arizona State University Outstanding Alumnus Awards, School of
  Liberal Arts and School of Business Administration
Black Lawyers Association Community Service Award (Phoenix)
Booker T. Washington Award, National Outstanding Business Man
City of Phoenix Human Rights Award for Twenty-five Years of
  Community Service
First in class and cadet captain of the Cadet Corps 45-H, Tuskegee, Alabama
Hall of Fame, Arizona State University College of Business Administration
National Business League, Washington DC, Entrepreneurship Award
National Outstanding Business Man, Washington DC
Outstanding Business Man, First Institutional Baptist Church, Phoenix
U.S. Small Business Administration Award
Young Men's Christian Association, Leadership Development Center
  Community Service Award

Source: Universal Memorial Center, *A Celebration and Worship Service Honoring the Life of Dr. Lincoln Johnson Ragsdale, Sr.* (Phoenix: Universal Memorial Center, 1995).

# NOTES

### INTRODUCTION

1. *Arizona Republic*, June 17, 1995, May, 14, 1998; *Arizona Informant*, June 17, 1995; Leon Sullivan, *Moving Mountains: The Principles and Purposes of Leon Sullivan* (Valley Forge PA: Judson Press, 1998), ix–xvi, 1–57, 96–112; Universal Memorial Center, *A Celebration and Worship Service Honoring the Life of Dr. Lincoln Johnson Ragsdale, Sr.* (Phoenix: Universal Memorial Center, 1995), 6. Presidential Medal of Freedom recipient Leon Sullivan authored several books on race relations, self-help, and humanitarianism. In 1970 Sullivan was elected to the board of directors of the General Motors Corporation, where he served for more than twenty years. In 1977 he developed the Sullivan Principles, a code of conduct for human rights and equal opportunity for companies operating in South Africa. The Sullivan Principles are acknowledged to have been one of the most effective efforts to end discrimination against blacks in the workplace in South Africa and to have contributed to the dismantling of apartheid. To further expand human rights and economic development to all communities, Rev. Sullivan created the Global Sullivan Principles of Social Responsibility in 1997. His principles and activism led to the formation of organizations that have trained millions of people, from all races, for jobs in the United States and around the world.

2. *Arizona Republic*, June 11, 1995; Lincoln Ragsdale Sr., "Minority Entrepreneurship: Profiling an African American Entrepreneur" (Ph.D. diss., Union Graduate School, 1989), 80. For the purpose of this study, I define "racism" as the active and sometimes coordinated socioeconomic exploitation of socially constructed racial groups (often but not exclusively minority populations) and the political and cultural preeminence of capital's interests over said racial groups. Furthermore, I define "white supremacy" as the preservation of economic, political, and social privilege and power for white people in an effort to systematically exclude nonwhites from equal access to the production and distribution of material and ethereal resources, political authority, and formal and informal circles of social and economic privilege. In so defining these terms, I follow the work of George M. Fredrickson, *Racism: A Short History* (Princeton NJ: Princeton University Press, 2003); Fredrickson, *White Supremacy: A Comparative Study in American and South African History* (New York: Oxford University Press, 1982); Thomas Guglielmo, *White on Arrival: Italians, Race, Color, and Power in Chicago, 1890–1945* (New York: Oxford University Press, 2003); David Ignatiev, *How the Irish Became*

*White* (New York: Routledge, 1995); Robin D. G. Kelley, *Freedom Dreams: The Black Radical Imagination* (Boston: Beacon, 2002); Kelley, *Hammer and Hoe: Alabama Communists during the Great Depression* (Chapel Hill: University of North Carolina Press, 1990); Manning Marable, *How Capitalism Underdeveloped Black America: Problems in Race, Political Economy, and Society* (Cambridge MA: South End Press, 2000); France Widdance Twine, *Racism in a Racial Democracy: The Maintenance of White Supremacy in Brazil* (New Haven CT: Rutgers University Press, 1997); Malcolm X, *The End of White Supremacy: Four Speeches by Malcolm X* (New York: Arcade, 1989); and Malcolm X, *The Autobiography of Malcolm X*, with the assistance of Alex Haley (New York: Ballantine Books, 1964).

3. Universal Memorial Center, *A Celebration and Worship Service Honoring the Life of Mrs. Eleanor Dickey Ragsdale* (Phoenix: Universal Memorial Center, 1998), 3–14, 19; Lincoln Ragsdale Sr. and Eleanor Ragsdale, interview by Dean E. Smith, April 4 and November 3, 1990, Phoenix, transcripts, Arizona Collections, Arizona State University, Tempe (hereafter cited as TS, ACASU); Eleanor Ragsdale, interview by Mary Melcher, June 16, 1991, Phoenix, tape recording, Arizona Historical Society, Central Arizona Division, Tempe (hereafter cited as TP, AHSCAD).

4. Darlene Clark Hine, *Speak Truth to Power: The Black Professional Class in United States History* (New York: Carlson, 1996), xvii; Lincoln Ragsdale Sr. and Eleanor Ragsdale, interview; Eleanor Ragsdale, interview, June 16, 1991; Universal, *Mrs. Eleanor Dickey Ragsdale*, 3–14.

5. Universal, *Mrs. Eleanor Dickey Ragsdale*, 3–14; Lincoln Ragsdale Sr. and Eleanor Ragsdale, interview; Eleanor Ragsdale, interview, June 16, 1991.

6. Universal, *Dr. Lincoln Johnson Ragsdale, Sr.*, 3; Eleanor Ragsdale, interview, June 16, 1991; Universal, *Mrs. Eleanor Dickey Ragsdale*, 3–14; Lincoln Ragsdale Sr. and Eleanor Ragsdale, interview.

7. Vincent Harding, Robin D. G. Kelley, and Earl Lewis, "We Changed the World, 1945–1970," in *To Make Our World Anew: A History of African Americans*, ed. Robin D. G. Kelley and Earl Lewis, 445–542 (New York: Oxford University Press 2000).

8. Quintard Taylor Jr. *In Search of the Racial Frontier: African Americans in the American West, 1528–1990* (New York: W. W. Norton, 1998), 179–280; William Mahoney, interview by Mary Melcher, February 16, 1990, tape recording, Arizona Historical Foundation, Arizona State University, Tempe (hereafter cited as TP, AHFASU); Mary Melcher, "Blacks and Whites Together: Interracial Leadership in the Phoenix Civil Rights Movement," *Journal of Arizona History* 32 (Summer 1991): 292.

9. John Barber quoted in Richard E. Harris, *The First 100 Years: A History of Arizona's Blacks* (Apache Junction AZ: Relmo Press, 1983), 124–25; Melcher, "Blacks and Whites Together," 198.

10. Universal, *Dr. Lincoln Johnson Ragsdale, Sr.*, 3; Universal, *Mrs. Eleanor Dickey Ragsdale*, 3–14; Lincoln Ragsdale Sr. and Eleanor Ragsdale, interview; Mahoney, interview. For more on the concept of "race work," see Paula Giddings, *When and Where I Enter: The Impact of Black Women on Race and Sex in America* (New York: William and Morrow, 1984); Darlene Clark Hine, Wilma King, and Linda Reed, eds., *We Specialize in the Wholly Impossible: A Reader in Black Women's History* (Brooklyn NY: Carlson, 1995); Stephanie Shaw, *What a Woman Ought to Be and to Do: Black Professional Women Workers during the Jim Crow Era* (Chicago: University of Chicago Press, 1996); Wil Haygood, *King of the Cats: The Life and Times of Adam Clayton Powell, Jr.* (New York: Houghton Mifflin, 1992).

11. Universal, *Dr. Lincoln Johnson Ragsdale, Sr.*, 3. My approach to this study is influenced by theoretical frameworks put forth in the following works: Taylor Branch, *Parting the Waters: America in the King Years, 1954–1963* (New York: Simon and Schuster, 1989), xii; Branch, *Pillar of Fire: America in the King Years, 1963–1965* (New York: Simon and Schuster, 1997), xiv; Albert S. Broussard, *African-American Odyssey: The Stewarts, 1853–1963* (Lawrence: University of Kansas Press, 1998), 1; David Levering Lewis, *W. E. B. DuBois: Biography of a Race, 1868–1919* (New York: Henry Holt, 1993), 4–10; Lewis, *W. E. B. DuBois: The Fight for Equality and the American Century*, vol. 2, *1919–1963* (New York: Henry Holt, 2000), 1.

12. Books that identify the American West as a place, not a process, include: Patricia Nelson Limerick, *The Legacy of Conquest: The Unbroken Past of the American West* (New York: W. W. Norton, 1987); Clyde A. Milner II, ed., *A New Significance: Re-envisioning the History of the American West* (New York: Oxford University Press, 1996); Peggy Pascoe, *Relations of Rescue: The Search for Female Moral Authority in the American West, 1874–1939* (New York: Oxford University Press, 1990); Vicki L. Ruiz, *Cannery Women, Cannery Lives: Mexican Women, Unionization, and the California Food Processing Industry, 1930–1950* (Albuquerque: University of New Mexico Press, 1987); Taylor, *In Search of the Racial Frontier*; Richard White, *"It's Your Misfortune and None of My Own": A New History of the American West* (Norman: University of Oklahoma Press, 1991).

13. Lori K. Baker, "Lincoln Ragsdale: The Man Who Refused to Be Invisible," *Phoenix Magazine*, January 1993, 97–99.

14. Herbert L. Ely, interview by author, July 17, 2000, Phoenix, tape recording and transcript, Arizona Collection, Arizona State University, Tempe (hereafter cited as TP and TS, ACASU); George B. Brooks, interview by News Channel 3, KTVK, February 16, 1995, in NewsChannel 3, KTVK, "A Tribute to Lincoln Ragsdale," presented at the Phoenix Urban League Whitney M. Young Jr. Awards Dinner, Phoenix, February 16, 1995.

15. Andrew M. Manis, *"A Fire You Can't Put Out": The Civil Rights Life of Birmingham's Reverend Fred Shuttlesworth* (Tuscaloosa: University of Alabama Press, 1999), xi; Peter Novick, *That Noble Dream: The "Objectivity Question" and the American Historical Profession* (Cambridge: Cambridge University Press, 1988), 1; Universal, *Dr. Lincoln Johnson Ragsdale, Sr.*, 3; Universal, *Mrs. Eleanor Dickey Ragsdale*, 3–14; Lincoln Ragsdale Sr. and Eleanor Ragsdale, interview; Eleanor Ragsdale, interview, June 16, 1991; Gwendolyn Ragsdale Madrid, telephone interview by author, August 11, 2003, transcript in author's possession.

16. Wesley Johnson Jr., "Directing Elites: Catalysts for Social Change," in *Phoenix in the Twentieth Century: Essays in Community History*, ed. Wesley Johnson Jr., 31 (Norman: University of Oklahoma Press, 1993). I have chosen to use the terms "Mexican American" and "Chicano" in this study. The term "Mexican American" will be used when referring to persons of Mexican descent in the United States prior to 1960. The term "Chicano" will be used when referencing people of Mexican descent after 1960. Between 1960 and 1970, Mexican American activists engaged in massive resistance to socioeconomic subjugation and waged a heated struggle for equal rights. This effort gave rise to myriad Mexican American civil and human rights organizations and labor organizations. The movement escalated and eventually erupted into a national crusade for "first-class citizenship" and cultural renewal. During this cultural renaissance, many Mexican Americans adopted the name Chicanos, a name that had been used for some time to ridicule them. They gave new meaning to the label, employed it as a call to arms, and ascribed to its use an oppositional consciousness, affirmation, and dignity.

17. There is a growing body of literature that underscores the critical role local leaders played in the national civil rights movement. This book has been influenced by the following work: Glenn T. Eskew, *But for Birmingham: The Local and National Movements in the Civil Rights Struggle* (Chapel Hill: University of North Carolina Press, 1997); Chana Kai Lee, *For Freedom's Sake: The Life of Fanny Lou Hamer* (Urbana: University of Illinois Press, 1999); John Lewis, *Walking with the Wind: A Memoir of the Movement* (New York: Harcourt Brace, 1999); Manis, *"Fire You Can't Put Out"*; Jo Ann Ginson Robinson, *The Montgomery Bus Boycott and the Women Who Started It: The Memoir of Jo Ann Gibson Robinson* (Knoxville: University of Tennessee Press, 1987).

18. See Broussard, *African-American Odyssey*; Taylor, *In Search of the Racial Frontier*; White, *"It's Your Misfortune."*

19. Frederick Jackson Turner, "The Significance of the Frontier in American History," American Historical Association, *Annual Report for the Year 1893* (1894), 3.

20. See Allan G. Bogue, *Frederick Jackson Turner: Strange Roads Going Down* (Norman: University of Oklahoma Press, 1998); Taylor, *In Search of the Racial Frontier*, 19.

21. See Grechen Cassel Eick, *Dissent in Wichita: The Civil Rights Movement in the Midwest, 1954–1972* (Urbana: University of Illinois Press, 2001); Geta LeSeur, *Not All Okies Are White: The Lives of Black Cotton Pickers in Arizona* (Columbia: University of Missouri Press, 2000); Shirley A. Moore, *To Place Our Deeds: The African American Community in Richmond, California, 1910–1963* (Berkeley: University of California Press, 1999); Gretchen Lemke-Santangelo, *Abiding Courage: African American Migrant Women and the East Bay Community* (Chapel Hill: University of North Carolina Press, 1996); Douglas Henry Daniels et al., eds., *Peoples of Color in the American West* (Lexington MA: D. C. Heath, 1994); Quintard Taylor Jr., *The Forging of a Black Community: Seattle's Central District from 1870 through the Civil Rights Era* (Seattle: University of Washington Press, 1994); Taylor, *In Search of the Racial Frontier*; Albert S. Broussard, *Black San Francisco: The Struggle for Racial Equality in the West, 1900–1954* (Lawrence: University Press of Kansas, 1993); Broussard, *African-American Odyssey*; William Loren Katz, *The Black West: A Documentary and Pictorial History of the African American Role in the Westward Expansion of the United States* (New York: Touchstone, 1987).

22. Taylor, *In Search of the Racial Frontier*, 17–23, 27; Walter Prescott Webb, "The American West: Perpetual Mirage," *Harper's Magazine*, May 1957, 30; David J. Weber, "The Spanish-Mexican Rim," in *The Oxford Dictionary of the American West*, ed. Clyde A. Milner II, Carol A. O'Connor, and Martha A. Sandweiss, 48 (New York: Oxford University Press, 1994). I define "the West" as the area of the United States west of the 98th meridian, or, roughly, the Mississippi River. On the exploits of Nat Love, see Nat Love, *The Life and Adventures of Nat Love* (Lincoln: University of Nebraska Press, 1995).

23. The phrase "struggle for racial equality" is borrowed from Broussard, *Black San Francisco*; Taylor, *In Search of the Racial Frontier*, 21.

24. On the multiple dimensions of the racial frontier, see Arnoldo De Leon, *Racial Frontiers: Africans, Chinese, and Mexicans in Western America, 1848–1890* (Albuquerque: University of New Mexico Press, 2002); Bradford Luckingham, *Minorities in Phoenix: A Profile History of Mexican American, Chinese American, and African American Communities, 1860–1992* (Tucson: University of Arizona Press, 1994); Luckingham, *The Urban Southwest: A Profile History of Albuquerque, El Paso, Phoenix and Tucson* (El Paso: Texas Western Press, 1982); Lawrence A. Cardoso, *Mexican America Emigration to the United States, 1897–1931* (Tucson: University of Arizona Press, 1980).

25. Taylor, *In Search of the Racial Frontier*, 27–102; Luckingham, *Minorities in Phoenix*, 3–4.

26. Lawrence B. De Graaf, "Significant Steps on an Arduous Path: The Impact of World War II on Discrimination against African Americans in the West," *Journal of the West* 35, no. 1 (January 1996): 1; Luckingham, *Minorities in Phoenix*, 157–71; Universal, *Dr. Lincoln Johnson Ragsdale, Sr.*, 3; Lincoln Ragsdale Sr., interview by Mary Melcher, April 8, 1990, TP, AHFASU. See also Michael L. Cooper, *The Double V. Campaign: African Americans and World War II* (New York: NAL, 1997); Universal, *Mrs. Eleanor Dickey Ragsdale*, 14; Eleanor Ragsdale, interview by Mary Melcher, Spring 1990, TP, AHFASU; Eleanor Ragsdale, interview, June 16, 1991.

27. Universal, *Mrs. Eleanor Dickey Ragsdale*, 14; Eleanor Ragsdale, interview, Spring 1990; Eleanor Ragsdale, interview, June 16, 1991.

28. Lincoln Ragsdale Sr., interview; Eleanor Ragsdale, interview, Spring 1990; Ragsdale, "Minority Entrepreneurship," 80. See also Matt McCoy, "The Desert Metropolis: Image Building and the Growth of Phoenix, 1940–1965" (Ph.D. diss., Arizona State University, 2000); U.S. Bureau of the Census, *Population of the United States*, 1940; Universal, *Dr. Lincoln Johnson Ragsdale, Sr.*, 3; Lincoln Ragsdale Sr., interview; Universal, *Mrs. Eleanor Dickey Ragsdale*, 14; Eleanor Ragsdale, interview, Spring 1990.

29. John Barber quoted in Harris, *First 100 Years*, 124–25; Melcher, "Blacks and Whites Together," 198; Universal, *Mrs. Eleanor Dickey Ragsdale*, 14; Eleanor Ragsdale, interview, Spring 1990; Eleanor Ragsdale, interview, June 16, 1991; Laurence B. de Graaf, "Race, Sex and Region: Black Women in the American West, 1850–1920," *Pacific Historical Review* 49 (May 1980): 285–314; Alwyn Barr, "Blacks in Southwestern Cities," *Red River Valley Historical Review* 6 (Spring 1981): 5–7; Robert Nimmons, "Arizona's Forgotten Past: The Negro in Arizona, 1539–1965" (master's thesis, Northern Arizona University, 1971), 92–93; *Arizona Republican*, June 4–6, 1915, March 3, April 19, 24, 1916; *Phoenix Independent*, July 20, 1922; *Phoenix Tribune*, July 22, 29, August 14, October 14, 1922; Sue Wilson Abbey, "The Ku Klux Klan in Arizona, 1921–1925," *Journal of Arizona History* 14 (Spring 1973): 10–30. See also LeSeur, *Not All Okies Are White*; Luckingham, *Urban Southwest*.

30. See Michael J. Kotlanger, "Phoenix, Arizona, 1920–1940" (Ph.D. diss., Arizona State University, 1983); Nimmons, "Arizona's Forgotten Past," 92–93; *Arizona Republican*, June 4–6, 1915, March 3, April 19, 24, 1916; *Phoenix Independent*, July 20, 1922; *Phoenix Tribune*, July 22, 29, August 14, October 14, 1922.

31. Bradford Luckingham, *Phoenix: The History of a Southwestern Metropolis* (Tucson: University of Arizona Press, 1995), 8, 15.

32. L. Jeffrey Cook, "Patterns of Desert Urbanization: The Evolution of

Metropolitan Phoenix," in *Urban Planning for Arid Zones: American Experiences and Directions*, ed. Gideon Golaney, 205–8 (New York: Praeger, 1978); Geoffrey Padraic Mawn, "Phoenix, Arizona: Central City of the Southwest, 1870–1920" (Ph.D. diss., Arizona State University, 1979), 2–3; Michael H. Bartlett, Thomas M. Kolaz, and David A. Gregory, *Archaeology in the City: A Hohokam Village in Phoenix, Arizona* (Tucson: University of Arizona Press, 1986), 17–34; Luckingham, *Phoenix*, 8, 15.

33. Luckingham, *Phoenix*, 8, 15; Cook, "Patterns of Desert Urbanization," 205–8; Mawn, "Phoenix," 2–3; Bartlett, Kolaz, and Gregory, *Archaeology in the City*, 17–34.

34. Arizona Territorial Legislature, Comp. Laws, 1877, C. 30, Sec. 3; *Arizona Reports: Reports of Cases Argued and Determined in the Supreme Court of the Territory of Arizona, to April 16, 1893*, vol. 5; *Arizona Republican*, April 4, 7, 10, 1912; Melcher, "Blacks and Whites Together," 196; Harris, *First 100 Years*, 53–57; Bradford Luckingham, Barbara Luckingham, and Lori Parks, eds., *Discovering Greater Phoenix: An Illustrated History* (Phoenix: Heritage Media, 1998), 58.

35. Melcher, "Blacks and Whites Together," 196; Harris, *First 100 Years*, 53–57; Luckingham, Luckingham, and Parks, *Discovering Greater Phoenix*, 58.

36. Federal manuscript census schedules, 1940, 1950, 1960, Government Documents, Hayden Library, Arizona State University; *Arizona Republic*, November 27–28, 30, 1942, February 26, 1943; *Arizona Sun*, February 1, 8, 16, 23, 1951; Taylor, *In Search of the Racial Frontier*, 270–71; Luckingham, *Minorities in Phoenix*, 156–57; Thomas E. Sheridan, *Arizona: A History* (Tucson: University of Arizona Press, 1995), 273–74; Universal, *Dr. Lincoln Johnson Ragsdale, Sr.*, 4.

37. Hayzel Burton Daniels, "A Black Magistrate's Struggle," in *Arizona Memories*, ed. Anne Hodges Morgan and Rennard Strickland, 337–38 (Tucson: University of Arizona Press, 1984); Melcher, "Blacks and Whites Together," 201; Luckingham, *Minorities in Phoenix*, 161–62; Greater Phoenix Council for Civic Unity [GPCCU], ed., *To Secure These Rights* (Phoenix: Phoenix Sun, 1961), 6; Keith Jerome Crudup, "African Americans in Arizona: A Twentieth-Century History" (Ph.D. diss., Arizona State University, 1998), 327–86; Philip R. VanderMeer, *Phoenix Rising: Making of a Desert Metropolis, 1940–2000* (Carlsbad CA: Heritage Media, 2002), 43–73.

38. *Arizona Republic*, September 27, October 27, 1965, July 18, 26, 31, 1967, August 24, 1969; Melcher, "Blacks and Whites Together," 201; Luckingham, *Minorities in Phoenix*, 161–62; GPCCU, *To Secure These Rights* 6.

39. *Arizona Gazette*, May 24, 1919; Luckingham, *Phoenix*, 98. See also Jackie Thul, "Blacks in Arizona from Early Settlement to 1990: A Historic

Context Study," prepared for the Arizona State Historic Preservation Office. Arizona Collection of the Hayden Library, Arizona State University, Tempe.

40. Luckingham, *Phoenix*, 98; Ernestine Jenkins and Darlene Clark Hine, eds., *A Question of Manhood: A Reader in U.S. Black Men's History and Masculinity*, vol. 2, *The 19th Century: From Emancipation to Jim Crow* (Bloomington: Indiana University Press, 2001), xi–xvii; Glenda Elizabeth Gilmore, *Gender and Jim Crow: Women and the Politics of White Supremacy in North Carolina, 1896–1920* (Chapel Hill: University of North Carolina Press, 1996), 61–90; *Arizona Sun*, February 1, July 19, 1962.

41. Darlene Clark Hine, "Which Way Is Freedom? Black Power and the Rise of Black Elected Officials," an address given at Michigan State University, East Lansing, November 13, 1997. See also Lee, *For Freedom's Sake*; Deborah Grey White, *Too Heavy a Load: Black Women in Defense of Themselves, 1894–1994* (New York: W. W. Norton, 1998); Darlene Clark Hine and Kathleen Thompson, *A Shining Thread of Hope: The History of Black Women in America* (New York: Broadway Books, 1998); Vicki L. Crawford et al., eds., *Women in the Civil Rights Movement: Trailblazers and Torchbearers, 1941–1965* (Bloomington: Indiana University Press, 1993); Darlene Clark Hine, Elsa Barkley Brown, and Rosalyn Terborg-Penn, eds., *Black Women in America: An Historical Encyclopedia*, vols. A–L and M–Z (Bloomington: Indiana University Press, 1993); and Robinson, *Montgomery Bus Boycott*.

42. Eleanor Ragsdale, interview, Spring 1990; Eleanor Ragsdale, interview, June 11, 1991.

43. *Arizona Republic*, September 27, October 27, 1965, July 18, 26, 31, 1967, August 24, 1969; Branch, *Pillar of Fire*, 553–613; Manning Marable, *Race, Reform, and Rebellion: The Second Reconstruction in Black America, 1945–1990* (Jackson: University Press of Mississippi, 1991), 86–113.

44. Lincoln Ragsdale Sr., interview.

45. Universal, *Dr. Lincoln Johnson Ragsdale, Sr.*, 4.

46. Lincoln Ragsdale Sr. and Eleanor Ragsdale, interview.

47. For an illuminating report on race relations and the socioeconomic status of African Americans by the mid-1990s, see Andrew Hacker, *Two Nations: Black and White, Separate, Hostile, Unequal* (New York: Ballantine Books, 1995).

48. Lincoln Ragsdale Sr., interview; Eleanor Ragsdale, interview, Spring 1990; Lincoln Ragsdale Sr. and Eleanor Ragsdale, interview.

49. Lincoln Ragsdale Sr., interview; Eleanor Ragsdale, interview, Spring 1990; Lincoln Ragsdale Sr. and Eleanor Ragsdale, interview.

50. Ragsdale, "Minority Entrepreneurship," 80.

51. Luckingham, *Minorities in Phoenix*, 205–7; Melcher, "Blacks and Whites Together," 206.

52. Universal, *Dr. Lincoln Johnson Ragsdale, Sr.*, 4.

1. On black professionals and black professionalism, see Carter G. Woodson, *The Negro Professional Man in the Community* (New York: Negro University, 1934); James Summerville, *Educating Black Doctors: A History of Meharry Medical College* (Birmingham: University of Alabama Press, 1983); Genna Rae McNeil, *Groundwork: Charles Hamilton Houston and the Struggle for Civil Rights* (Philadelphia: University of Pennsylvania Press, 1983); Darlene Clark Hine, *Black Women in White: Racial Conflict and Cooperation in the Nursing Profession, 1890–1950* (Bloomington: Indiana University Press, 1989); Willard B. Gatewood, *Aristocrats of Color: The Black Elite, 1880–1920* (Bloomington: Indiana University Press, 1990); Shaw, *What a Women Ought to Be.*

2. Hine, *Speak Truth to Power,* xvii.

3. For illuminating analyses of Reconstruction, see Eric Foner, *Reconstruction: America's Unfinished Revolution, 1863–1877* (New York: Harper and Row, 1988); James C. Mohr, *Radical Republicans in the North: State Politics during Reconstruction* (Baltimore: Johns Hopkins University Press, 1976); W. E. B. DuBois, *Black Reconstruction in America, 1860–1880* (New York: Simon and Schuster, 1935); Maldwyn A. Jones, *The Limits of Liberty: American History, 1607–1992* (New York: Oxford University Press, 1995).

4. Foner, *Reconstruction,* xix–xxvii.

5. Foner, *Reconstruction,* 602–12.

6. See Allen W. Trelease, *White Terror: The Ku Klux Klan Conspiracy and Southern Reconstruction* (Baton Rouge: Louisiana State University Press, 1995), xi–xiv. The terms "Klansman" and "Klansmen" are narrow and limiting because white women, although they were not formally admitted to the Klan prior to the 1920s, did support and participate informally in Klan activities. During the "second rising" of the Klan in the second decade of the twentieth century, women became formal members and played a critical role in the organization's day-to-day activities. For an engrossing history of women in the "New Klan," see Kathleen M. Blee, *Women of the Klan: Racism and Gender in the 1920s* (Berkeley: University of California Press, 1991).

7. Hine, *Speak Truth to Power,* xviii. See also Howard N. Rabinowitz, *Race Relations in the Urban South, 1865–1890* (Athens: University of Georgia Press, 1996); C. Vann Woodward, *Reunion and Reaction: The Compromise of 1877 and the End of Reconstruction* (New York: Oxford University Press, 1951); Rayford Logan, *The Negro in American Life and Thought: The Nadir, 1877–1901* (New York: Dial Press, 1954).

8. Hine, *Speak Truth to Power,* xviii.

9. Lincoln Ragsdale Sr., interview; Eleanor Ragsdale, interview, Spring 1990; Lincoln Ragsdale Sr. and Eleanor Ragsdale, interview; Universal Me-

morial Center, *Ragsdale Family History in Funeral Service* (Phoenix: Universal Memorial Center, 1999), 1.

10. U.S. Bureau of the Census, *Population of the United States*, 1920; Universal, *Ragsdale Family History*, 1.

11. Leon F. Litwack, *Trouble in Mind: Black Southerners in the Era of Jim Crow* (New York: Alfred A. Knopf, 1998), 175, 314; Litwack, *Been in the Storm So Long: The Aftermath of Slavery* (New York: Vintage, 1980), xi–xviii, 160. See also Edward L. Ayers, *The Promise of the New Southerners in the Age of Jim Crow* New York: Oxford University Press, 1992); C. Vann Woodward, *The Strange Career of Jim Crow* (New York: Oxford University Press, 1955).

12. Litwack, *Trouble in Mind*, 175, 314; Litwack, *Been in the Storm*, xi–xviii, 160.

13. Nell Irvin Painter, *Exodusters: Black Migration to Kansas after Reconstruction* (New York: W. W. Norton, 1976), 146–59; *Salt River Herald*, May 11, 1878; *Arizona Republican*, July 21, November 27, 1889; "History of Blacks in Phoenix Notes," Geoffrey P. Mawn Files, Arizona Historical Foundation, Hayden Library, Arizona State University; Harris, *First 100 Years*, 1; Kotlanger, "Phoenix, Arizona," 444; federal manuscript census schedule, Oklahoma Territory, 1880.

14. Roscoe Dungee quoted in *Oklahoma City Black Dispatch*, April 23, 1931.

15. Jimmie Lewis Franklin, *Journey toward Hope: A History of African Americans in Oklahoma* (Norman: University of Oklahoma Press, 1982), 23.

16. Thomas Edwards, referenced in Franklin, *Journey toward Hope*, 24–25.

17. *Oklahoma City Oklahoma News*, November 3, 1936; *Tulsa Eagle*, September 12, 1968.

18. Universal, *Ragsdale Family History*, 1.

19. Baker, "Lincoln Ragsdale," 96.

20. Lincoln Ragsdale Sr., interview.

21. Oklahoma Legislature, *Session Laws of Oklahoma, 1907–1908* (Oklahoma City: Oklahoma State Capitol, Department of Manuscripts and Archives), 201–4.

22. Oklahoma Legislature, *Session Laws of Oklahoma*, 553–57.

23. "Political Activities of the Negro Before Statehood." Oklahoma WPA Records, Oklahoma Historical Society, Oklahoma City.

24. Franklin, *Journey toward Hope*, 59.

25. Franklin, *Journey toward Hope*, 59.

26. Michael A. Plater, *African American Entrepreneurship in Richmond, 1890–1940: The Story of R. C. Scott* (New York: Garland, 1996), 41–81; Woodson, *Negro Professional*, 1–44; Gatewood, *Aristocrats of Color*, 4–26.

27. W. E. B. DuBois, *The Philadelphia Negro: A Social Study* (Philadelphia: Publications of the University of Pennsylvania, 1899), 118.

28. Booker T. Washington, *The Negro in Business* (Boston: Hertel, Jenkins, 1907), 94.

29. Plater, *African American Entrepreneurship*, 41–81; Jessica Mitford, *The American Way of Death* (New York: Simon and Schuster, 1963), 222–41; Vanderlyn R. Pine, *Caretaker of the Dead: The American Funeral Director* (New York: Irvington, 1975), 25–41.

30. Plater, *African American Entrepreneurship*, xvii–xviii, xx, 164.

31. Plater, *African American Entrepreneurship*, xvii–xviii, xx, 164.

32. Plater, *African American Entrepreneurship*, 162–65.

33. Joseph E. Holloway, *Africanisms in American Culture* (Bloomington: Indiana University Press, 1990), 81–91. On African cultural retentions in the United States, see E. Franklin Frazier, *The Negro Family in the United States* (Chicago: University of Chicago Press, 1939); Melville Herskovits, *The Myth of the Negro Past* (New York: Harper and Brothers, 1941); Eugene D. Genovese, *Roll, Jordan, Roll: The World the Slaves Made* (New York: Vintage Books, 1974); Peter Wood, *Black Majority: Negroes in Colonial South Carolina from 1670 through the Stono Rebellion* (New York: Alfred A. Knopf, 1974); Herbert Gutman, *The Black Family in Slavery and Freedom, 1750–1925* (New York: Pantheon Books, 1976); Lawrence Levine, *Black Culture Black Consciousness* (New York: Oxford University Press, 1977); David R. Rodiger, "And Die in Dixie: Funerals, Death and Heaven in the Slave Community," *Massachusetts Review* 22 (1981), 163–68; Charles Joyner, *Down by the River Side* (Urbana: University of Illinois Press, 1984); Daniel C. Littlefield, *Rice and Slaves: Ethnicity and the Slave Trade in Colonial South Carolina* (Urbana: University of Illinois Press, 1991); Gwendolyn Midlo Hall, *Africans in Colonial Louisiana: The Development of Afro-Creole Culture in the Eighteenth Century* (Baton Rouge: Louisiana State University Press, 1992); Philip D. Morgan, *Slave Counterpoint: Black Culture in the Eighteenth-Century Chesapeake and Lowcountry* (Chapel Hill: University of North Carolina Press, 1998); Robert Crafton Sr., *An Autobiography Dictated to Anthony J. Binga, Sr.* (Richmond VA: n.p., 1953–57), 18.

34. Plater, *African American Entrepreneurship*, xvii–xviii, xx, 162–65.

35. Plater, *African American Entrepreneurship*, xvii–xviii, xx, 162–65.

36. Crafton, *Autobiography*, 18.

37. Plater, *African American Entrepreneurship*, xx, xvii–xviii, 162–65; Scott, *Autobiography*, 18.

38. James S. Hirsch, *Riot and Remembrance: The Tulsa Race War and Its Legacy* (New York: Houghton Mifflin, 2002), 6–7, 50–73. See also Blee, *Women of the Klan*; James N. Upton, *Urban Riots in the Twentieth Century: A Social History* (New York: Wyndham Press, 1989).

39. Wyn Craig Wade, *The Fiery Cross: The Ku Klux Klan in America* (New York: Oxford University Press, 1998), 60–89.

40. Hirsch, *Riot and Remembrance*, 6–7, 50–73; *Tulsa Tribune*, May 30, 1921. On African American men and the rape myth, see Ida B. Wells-Barnett, *Crusade for Justice: The Autobiography of Ida B. Wells*, ed. Alfreda M. Duster (Chicago: University of Chicago Press, 1970); Linda O. McMurry, *To Keep the Waters Troubled: The Life of Ida B. Wells* (New York: Oxford University Press, 2000).

41. Hirsch, *Riot and Remembrance*, 99–113; Hartwell Ragsdale Jr., interview by author, June 6, 2002, San Diego CA, TP and TS, ACASU; Hartwell Ragsdale III, interview by author, June 6, 2002, San Diego CA, TP and TS, ACASU; Lincoln Ragsdale Jr., interview by author, June 6, 2002, San Diego CA, TP and TS, ACASU.

42. Hirsch, *Riot and Remembrance*, 93; Darlene Clark Hine, William C. Hine, and Stanley Harrold, *The African American Odyssey*, 2nd ed. (Upper Saddle River NJ: Prentice Hall, 2003), 387; Hartwell Ragsdale Jr., interview; Hartwell Ragsdale III, interview; Lincoln Ragsdale Jr., interview, June 6, 2002.

43. Hirsch, *Riot and Remembrance*, 93; Hartwell Ragsdale Jr., interview; Hartwell Ragsdale III, interview; Lincoln Ragsdale Jr., interview, June 6, 2002. Most of the accounting books, official papers, and advertisements of all of the Ragsdale mortuaries, which document the history of the business and their holdings up to 1921, were consumed in the fires that destroyed the Tulsa mortuary. Hartwell had recently transferred these files to Tulsa in an effort to centralize the businesses archives. The destruction of these archives has made it difficult to reconstruct the early history of the Ragsdale mortuaries. Oral testimony, however, has provided for the limited yet illuminating reconstruction of the Ragsdales' business endeavors.

44. Universal, *Ragsdale Family History*, 1; Lincoln Ragsdale, Enlisted Record of and Report of Separation: Honorable Discharge WD, AGO Form 53–55, U.S. Army Air Corps, November 19, 1945, Washington DC.

45. Lincoln Ragsdale Sr. and Eleanor Ragsdale, interview.

46. Lincoln Ragsdale Sr., interview. In this interview, Ragsdale states that Onlia Ragsdale "was president of the Colored Women's Federated Association." I have been unable to locate a record of an organization by this name. I suspect that Lincoln did not remember the exact name of the association. It is much more likely that the organization his mother presided over was the Oklahoma Federation of Colored Women's Clubs. It is perhaps more plausible that she led or participated in an Oklahoma-based chapter of National Association of Colored Women.

47. Elaine M. Smith, "Mary McLeod Bethune," in Hine, Brown, and Terborg-Penn, *Black Women in America*, 117; White, *Too Heavy*, 21–55;

Stephanie F. Shaw, "Black Club Women and the Creation of the National Association of Colored Women," in Hine, King, and Reed, *We Specialize in the Wholly Impossible*, 441; Hine and Thompson, *Shining Thread*, 180–81; Rosalyn Terborg-Penn, *African American Women in the Struggle for the Vote, 1850–1920* (Bloomington: Indiana University Press, 1998), 90–106.

48. Wanda A. Hendricks, *Gender, Race, and Politics in the Midwest: Black Club Women in Illinois* (Bloomington: Indiana University Press, 1998), xii.

49. Lincoln Ragsdale Sr., interview.

50. Lincoln Ragsdale Sr., interview.

51. Ragsdale, "Minority Entrepreneurship," 72.

52. Lincoln Ragsdale Sr., interview; Ragsdale, "Minority Entrepreneurship," 72.

53. Ragsdale, "Minority Entrepreneurship," 72.

54. Ragsdale, "Minority Entrepreneurship," 72.

55. Lincoln Ragsdale Sr. and Eleanor Ragsdale, interview.

56. Baker, "Lincoln Ragsdale," 96; Franklin, *Journey toward Hope*, 149–184.

57. Franklin, *Journey toward Hope*, 149–84.

58. Lincoln Ragsdale Sr. and Eleanor Ragsdale, interview.

59. Lincoln Ragsdale Sr. and Eleanor Ragsdale, interview.

60. Lincoln Ragsdale Sr. and Eleanor Ragsdale, interview.

61. Hartwell Ragsdale Jr., interview; Hartwell Ragsdale III, interview; Lincoln Ragsdale Jr., interview, June 6, 2002.

62. John J. Parker quoted in Hine, Hine, and Harrold, *African American Odyssey*, 387; Darlene Clark Hine, *Hine Sight: Black Women and the Re-Construction of American History* (New York: Carlson, 1994), 129–45. Paul K. Conklin, *The New Deal* (Wheeling IL: Harlon Davidson, 1992), provides a wonderful overview of the New Deal era. The most detailed and revealing study of Elijah Muhammad is Andrew Claude Clegg, *An Original Man: The Life and Times of Elijah Muhammad* (New York: St. Martin's, 1997), and the most helpful study of Mary McLeod Bethune is Audrey Thomas McCluskey and Elaine M. Smith, eds., *Mary McLeod Bethune* (Bloomington: Indiana University Press, 2002).

63. Lawrence P. Scott and William W. Womack, *Double V: The Civil Rights Struggle of the Tuskegee Airmen* (East Lansing: Michigan State University Press, 1998), i; Lincoln Ragsdale Sr. and Eleanor Ragsdale, interview.

64. Scott and Womack, *Double V*, i; Lincoln Ragsdale Sr. and Eleanor Ragsdale, interview.

65. Lincoln Ragsdale Sr. and Eleanor Ragsdale, interview.

66. Lincoln J. Ragsdale, interview by NewsChannel 3, KTVK, February 16, 1995, "A Tribute to Lincoln Ragsdale"; Lincoln Ragsdale Sr. and Eleanor Ragsdale, interview.

67. Lincoln Ragsdale Sr. and Eleanor Ragsdale, interview.

68. Lincoln Ragsdale Sr. and Eleanor Ragsdale, interview.

69. Lincoln Ragsdale Sr. and Eleanor Ragsdale, interview.

70. Lincoln Ragsdale Sr. and Eleanor Ragsdale, interview.

71. Eleanor Ragsdale, interview, Spring 1990; Lincoln Ragsdale Sr. and Eleanor Ragsdale, interview; Universal, *Mrs. Eleanor Dickey Ragsdale*, 14; Samuel Chapman Armstrong quoted in Donal F. Lindsey, *Indians at Hampton Institute, 1877–1923* (Urbana: University of Illinois Press, 1995), 9.

72. Eleanor Ragsdale, interview, Spring 1990.

73. Eleanor Ragsdale, interview, Spring 1990; Lincoln Ragsdale Sr. and Eleanor Ragsdale, interview; Universal, *Mrs. Eleanor Dickey Ragsdale*, 14–15.

74. Eleanor Ragsdale, interview, Spring 1990; Lincoln Ragsdale Sr. and Eleanor Ragsdale, interview; Lincoln Ragsdale Sr., interview; Hartwell Ragsdale Jr., interview; Hartwell Ragsdale III, interview; Lincoln Ragsdale Jr., interview, June 6, 2002; Universal, *Mrs. Eleanor Dickey Ragsdale*, 14–15.

75. Lincoln Ragsdale Sr. and Eleanor Ragsdale, interview.

76. Universal, *Mrs. Eleanor Dickey Ragsdale*, 14; Lincoln Ragsdale Sr. and Eleanor Ragsdale, interview.

77. Shaw, *What a Woman Ought to Be*, 4, 5, 10.

78. Shaw, *What a Woman Ought to Be*, 10.

79. Universal, *Mrs. Eleanor Dickey Ragsdale*, 14; Lincoln Ragsdale Sr. and Eleanor Ragsdale, interview; Eleanor Ragsdale, interview, Spring 1990.

80. Eleanor Ragsdale, interview, Spring 1990.

81. Eleanor Ragsdale, interview, Spring 1990.

82. Eleanor Ragsdale, interview, Spring 1990.

83. Eleanor Ragsdale, interview, Spring 1990.

84. Eleanor Ragsdale, interview, Spring 1990; Universal, *Mrs. Eleanor Dickey Ragsdale*, 14.

85. Eleanor Ragsdale, interview, Spring 1990.

86. For a thorough examination of African American attitudes regarding education, see James D. Anderson, *The Education of Blacks in the South, 1860–1935* (Chapel Hill: University of North Carolina Press, 1988).

87. Shaw, *What a Woman Out to Be*, 13–67.

88. Giddings, *When and Where I Enter*, 9, 101, 103–4, 330; Evelyn Brooks Higginbotham, *Righteous Discontent: The Women's Movement in the Black Baptist Church, 1880–1920* (Cambridge: Harvard University Press, 1993), 2; Shaw, *What a Woman Ought to Be*, 13–67; Hine, *Shining Thread*, 5, 205–8; Hine, *Black Women in White*, 25, 203–8; Hendricks, *Gender, Race, and Politics*, 44; White, *Too Heavy*, 11–18; Cheyney University of Pennsylvania, *Cheyney University of Pennsylvania Undergraduate Catalog, 1999–2002* (Cheyney: Cheyney University of Pennsylvania, 2000), 4–5.

89. Eleanor Ragsdale, interview, Spring 1990.

90. Eleanor Ragsdale, interview, Spring 1990; Cheyney University, *Cheyney University of Pennsylvania*, 4–5.

91. Cheyney University, *Cheyney University of Pennsylvania*, 5; Eleanor Ragsdale, interview, Spring 1990.

92. Lincoln Ragsdale Sr. and Eleanor Ragsdale, interview; Luckingham, *Minorities in Phoenix*, 134; Luckingham, *Phoenix*, 53–65; Thul, *Blacks in Arizona*, 22–24.

93. Eleanor Ragsdale, interview, Spring 1990.

94. Lincoln Ragsdale Sr. and Eleanor Ragsdale, interview; Eleanor Ragsdale, interview, Spring 1990.

95. Eleanor Ragsdale, interview, Spring 1990.

96. Dean E. Smith quoted in Lincoln Ragsdale Sr. and Eleanor Ragsdale, interview; Eleanor Ragsdale, interview, Spring 1990.

97. Lincoln Ragsdale Sr. and Eleanor Ragsdale, interview; Eleanor Ragsdale, interview, Spring 1990.

98. Eleanor Ragsdale, interview, Spring 1990.

99. Lincoln Ragsdale Sr. and Eleanor Ragsdale, interview.

100. Lincoln Ragsdale Sr. and Eleanor Ragsdale, interview.

101 Eleanor Ragsdale, interview, Spring 1990.

102. Eleanor Ragsdale, interview, Spring 1990.

103. Harris, *First 100 Years*, 53–57, 124–25.

104. Madge Johnson Copeland, interview by Maria Hernandez, Summer 1981, Phoenix, TP and TS, ACASU.

105. Copeland, interview.

106. John Barber quoted in Harris, *First 100 Years*, 124–25; Alton Thomas, "Minority Housing in Phoenix," in GPCCU, *To Secure These Rights*, 9; Shirley J. Roberts, "Minority Group Poverty in Phoenix: A Socio-Economic Survey," *Journal of Arizona History* 14 (Winter 1973): 357–58; Kotlanger, "Phoenix, Arizona," 447–48; Mattie Hackett, "A Survey of Living Conditions of Girls in the Negro Schools of Phoenix, Arizona" (master's thesis, Arizona State University, 1939), 17, 43; *Arizona Republic*, November 13, 1937, August 21, October 9, 1938; Works Progress Administration, Division of Professional Service Projects, *Narrative Report on Arizona Works Progress Administration*, ed. W. J. Jamisson, State Administrator (Washington DC: Government Printing Office, 1939), 1–132. Of all the aid programs in Arizona and Phoenix, the Public Works Administration (PWA) was the most hostile to black people. Only a small number of African Americans were ever hired by the PWA, and those who were could only count on menial tasks and employment as janitors. There were no black camps in this program because only twenty or thirty African Americans ever worked on PWA projects, but when black laborers were employed, all camps were carefully segregated. African Americans lived

in the most decrepit facilities, were fed unhealthy food, posted the highest disease and death rates, and received the most meager wages. By 1935 the Works Progress Administration (WPA) emerged as the most successful relief agency in Phoenix. Unlike the majority of other agencies, the WPA elected to appoint several black Phoenicians as local project supervisors. The WPA, however, was not devoid of racial discrimination. The selection of black supervisors belied the racial hierarchy in the agency, as all programs were strictly segregated.

107. On African Americans, the New Deal era, and the early civil rights movement, see Howard Sitkoff, *A New Deal for Blacks: The Emergence of Civil Rights as a National Issue*, vol. 1, *Depression Decade* (New York: Oxford University Press, 1978); Patricia Sullivan, *Days of Hope: Race and Democracy in the New Deal Era* (Chapel Hill: University of North Carolina Press, 1996); Christopher R. Reed, *The Chicago NAACP and the Rise of Black Professional Leadership, 1910–1966* (Bloomington: Indiana University Press, 1997); Mark V. Tushnet, *The NAACP's Legal Strategy against Segregated Education, 1925–1950* (Chapel Hill: University of North Carolina Press, 1987); Darlene Clark Hine, *Black Victory: The Rise and Fall of the White Primary in Texas*, 2nd ed. (Columbia: University of Missouri Press, 2003); and Hine, *Hine Sight.*

108. See Kelley, *Hammer and Hoe*; Dan T. Carter, *Scottsboro: A Tragedy of the American South* (Baton Rouge: Louisiana State University Press, 1990). Arguably the most repugnant example of white supremacy and racism and prejudice during this period was "The Tuskegee Study of Untreated Syphilis in the Male Negro," otherwise known as "The Tuskegee Experiment." See James H. Jones, *Bad Blood: The Tuskegee Syphilis Experiment* (New York: Free Press, 1987).

109. John Barber quoted in Harris, *First 100 Years*, 124–25.

110. Roberts, "Minority Group Poverty," 348–49.

## 2. TUSKEGEE, WORLD WAR II, AND THE NEW BLACK ACTIVISM

1. On the connection between African Americans' battle for freedom and democracy in the United States and Africans' fight against colonialism, see Robin D. G. Kelley, *Race Rebels: Culture, Politics, and the Black Working Class* (New York: Free Press, 1994), 123–59.

2. Kelley, *Race Rebels*, 161–82; Howard Sitkoff, "Racial Militancy and Interracial Violence in the Second World War," *Journal of American History* 58, no. 3 (1971): 663–83; Lincoln Ragsdale Sr. and Eleanor Ragsdale, interview; Herb Whitney quoted in "Shooting Down Racism: Civic Leader Recalls Battle to Win Dignity," *Arizona Republic*, ca. 1985. This article was obtained from the personal papers of Lincoln Ragsdale Sr. It was in poor condition and listed no publication date. A copy of the piece is currently in my possession.

3. Lincoln Ragsdale Sr. and Eleanor Ragsdale, interview.

4. Lincoln Ragsdale Sr. and Eleanor Ragsdale, interview.

5. Ragsdale, Honorable Discharge; Lincoln Ragsdale Sr. and Eleanor Ragsdale, interview.

6. Lincoln Ragsdale Sr. and Eleanor Ragsdale, interview; Scott and Womack, *Double V*, 84.

7. Lincoln Ragsdale Sr. and Eleanor Ragsdale, interview.

8. Lincoln Ragsdale Sr. and Eleanor Ragsdale, interview.

9. Lincoln Ragsdale Sr. and Eleanor Ragsdale, interview.

10. Lincoln Ragsdale Sr. and Eleanor Ragsdale interview; John Morton Blum, *V Was for Victory: Politics and American Culture during World War II* (New York: Harcourt Brace Jovanovich, 1996), 182–220; Sitkoff, "Racial Militancy," 664–69; John Hope Franklin and Alfred A. Moss, *From Slavery to Freedom: A History of African Americans*, 8th ed. (New York: Alfred A. Knopf, 2000), 445.

11. Lincoln Ragsdale Sr. and Eleanor Ragsdale, interview.

12. Lincoln Ragsdale Sr. and Eleanor Ragsdale, interview.

13. Lincoln Ragsdale Sr. and Eleanor Ragsdale, interview; Scott and Womack, *Double V*, 84. Many former Tuskegee cadets and black World War II military personnel have testified to how difficult it was not only to become an officer during this period but also simply to survive as enlisted personnel. For a wider discussion of this history, see Benjamin O. Davis Jr. *American: An Autobiography* (Washington DC: Smithsonian Institution Press, 1991); Charles W. Dryden, *A-Train: Memoirs of a Tuskegee Airman* (Tuscaloosa: University of Alabama Press, 1997).

14. Lincoln Ragsdale Sr. and Eleanor Ragsdale, interview.

15. Lincoln Ragsdale Sr. and Eleanor Ragsdale, interview.

16. Robert A. Rose, *Lonely Eagles: The Story of the American Black Air Force in World War II* (Los Angeles: Tuskegee Airmen, Inc., Los Angeles Chapter, 1976), 14–15; Ulysses G. Lee, *The Employment of Negro Troops* (Washington DC: Center of Military History, 1990), 118; Davis, *American*, 63.

17. Scott and Womack, *Double V*, 84.

18. Scott and Womack, *Double V*, 159.

19. Scott and Womack, *Double V*, 159.

20. Whitney, "Shooting Down Racism," 1; Lincoln Ragsdale Sr. and Eleanor Ragsdale, interview; Lincoln Ragsdale Sr., interview. See also Richard Dalfiume, *Desegregation of the U.S. Armed Forces: Fighting on Two Fronts 1939–1953* (Columbia: University of Missouri Press, 1969); Mary Penick Motley, *The Invisible Soldier: The Experience of the Black Soldier, World War II* (Detroit: Wayne State University Press, 1975); Alan M. Osur, *Blacks in the Army Air Forces during World War II: The Problem of Race Relations*

(Washington DC: Office of Air Force History, 1977); Lou Potter, *Fighting on Two Fronts in World War II* (New York: Harcourt Brace Jovanovich, 1992); Dryden, *A-Train.*

21. *Arizona Republic*, November 27–28, 30, 1942, February 26, 1943; *Arizona Sun*, February 1, 8, 16, 23, 1951; Luckingham, *Phoenix*, 136–46; Luckingham, *Minorities in Phoenix*, 156–58.

22. Dempsey Travis quoted in Hine, Hine, and Harold, *African-American Odyssey*, 476.

23. Franklin and Moss, *From Slavery to Freedom*, 445.

24. Lincoln Ragsdale Sr., interview; De Graaf, "Significant Steps," 25.

25. "Doris Miller: First U.S. Hero of World War II," *Ebony*, December 1969, 132–38.

26. *Arizona Republic*, January 15, 22, June 7, 24, August 11, 16, 1941; Edward H. Peplow Jr., "The Thunderbirds," *Phoenix Magazine*, May 1976, 36–39; Susan M. Smith, "Litchfield Park and Vicinity" (master's thesis, University of Arizona, 1948), 94–101.

27. Taylor, *In Search of the Racial Frontier*, 257.

28. Luckingham, *Phoenix*, 137–39.

29. On the participation of African American women in defense industries during World War II, see Gretchen Lemke-Santangelo, *Abiding Courage: African American Migrant Women and the East Bay Community* (Chapel Hill: University of North Carolina Press, 1996).

30. De Graaf, "Significant Steps," 25–26.

31. De Graaf, "Significant Steps," 25–26.

32. De Graaf, "Significant Steps," 25–26.

33. Benjamin Quarles, "A. Philip Randolph: Labor Leader at Large," in *Black Leaders of the Twentieth Century*, ed. John Hope Franklin and August Meier, 139–64 (Urbana: University of Illinois Press, 1982). See also Paula F. Pfeffer, *A. Philip Randolph: Pioneer of the Civil Rights Movement* (Baton Rouge: Louisiana State University Press, 1990).

34. Sitkoff, "Racial Militancy," 667–69; De Graaf, "Significant Steps," 25–26; Quarles, "A. Philip Randolph," 156–58.

35. *Pittsburgh Courier*, January 31, April 11, 1942.

36. *Pittsburgh Courier*, January 31, April 11, 1942.

37. *Pittsburgh Courier*, January 31, April 11, 1942.

38. On the importance of Robert Vann, his call for the "Double V," and black militancy during the World War II era, see Andrew Buni, *Robert Vann of the Pittsburgh Courier* (Pittsburgh: University of Pittsburgh Press, 1974); Walter White, *A Man Called White: The Autobiography of Walter White* (Athens: University of Georgia Press, 1995).

39. Quarles, "A. Philip Randolph," 139–64; Haygood, *King of the Cats,*

3–39; White, *Man Called White*, 294–328; Buni, *Robert Vann*, 4–29; Hine, *Black Women in White*, 162–86.

40. Sitkoff, "Racial Militancy," 667–69; De Graaf, "Significant Steps," 25–26.

41. U.S. Navy, "Commanding Officer Praises Negro Personnel Who Served at Port Chicago after Explosion Monday Night, 20 July 1944," Navy Department Press Releases, July 16–31, 1944, folder, Box 55, World War II Command File, Operational Archives Branch, U.S. Naval Historical Center, Washington DC; *Chicago Defender*, July 21, 1944; *New York Times*, December 24, 1999. See also Robert Loring Allen, *The Port Chicago Mutiny* (New York: Harper and Row, 1993). For additional examples of similar incidents involving racial violence during World War II, see Ulysses G. Lee, *United States Army in World War II, Special Studies: The Employment of Negro Troops* (Washington DC: Office of the Chief of Military History, 1966).

42. VanderMeer, *Phoenix Rising*, 19.

43. *Arizona Republic*, November 27–28, 30, 1942.

44. *Arizona Republic*, November 27–28, 30, 1942, February 26, 1943.

45. *Arizona Republic*, November 27–28, 30, 1942, February 26, 1943, December 3, 1978; *Arizona Sun*, February 1, 8, 16, 23, 1951.

46. *Arizona Republic*, December 3, 1978; *Arizona Sun*, February 1, 8, 16, 23, 1951; Taylor, *In Search of the Racial Frontier*, 270–71; Luckingham, *Minorities in Phoenix*, 156–57; Sheridan, *Arizona*, 273–74.

47. Taylor, *In Search of the Racial Frontier*, 270–71; Luckingham, *Minorities in Phoenix*, 156–57; Sheridan, *Arizona*, 273–74.

48. Whitney, "Shooting Down Racism," 1; Baker, "Lincoln Ragsdale," 96–97.

49. Baker, "Lincoln Ragsdale," 96–97.

50. Baker, "Lincoln Ragsdale," 96–97.

51. Lincoln Ragsdale Sr. and Eleanor Ragsdale, interview; Lincoln Ragsdale Sr., interview; Baker, "Lincoln Ragsdale," 96–97.

52. Lincoln Ragsdale Sr. and Eleanor Ragsdale, interview; Lincoln Ragsdale Sr., interview; Whitney, "Shooting Down Racism," 1; Baker, "Lincoln Ragsdale," 96–97.

53. Matthew C. Whitaker, " 'Creative Conflict': Lincoln and Eleanor Ragsdale, Collaboration, and Community Activism in Phoenix, 1953–1965," *Western Historical Quarterly* 34, no. 2 (2003): 168; Baker, "Lincoln Ragsdale," 96–97.

54. Robert Franklin Jefferson, "Making the Men of the 93rd: African American Servicemen in the Years of the Great Depression and the Second World War, 1935–1947" (Ph.D. diss., University of Michigan, 1995), 231–32, 234, 243.

55. Baker, "Lincoln Ragsdale," 96–97; Lincoln Ragsdale Sr. and Eleanor Ragsdale, interview; Lincoln Ragsdale Sr., interview.

56. Lincoln Ragsdale Sr. and Eleanor Ragsdale, interview; Baker, "Lincoln Ragsdale," 96–97.

57. Lincoln Ragsdale Sr. and Eleanor Ragsdale, interview.

58. Lincoln Ragsdale Sr. and Eleanor Ragsdale, interview.

59. Whitney, "Shooting Down Racism," 2.

60. Whitney, "Shooting Down Racism," 2.

61. Lincoln Ragsdale Jr., interview by author, April 6, 2000, Phoenix, TP and TS, ACASU; Lincoln Ragsdale Jr., interview, June 6, 2002.

62. Whitney, "Shooting Down Racism," 2.

63. Whitney, "Shooting Down Racism," 2.

64. Quarles, "A. Philip Randolph," 139–64; Hine, *Black Women in White*, 162–86.

65. De Graaf, "Significant Steps," 26–29.

66. U.S. Bureau of the Census, *Population of the United States*, 1940; U.S. Bureau of the Census, *Population of the United States*, 1950.

67. Taylor, *In Search of the Racial Frontier*, 256–57.

68. Broussard, *Black San Francisco*, 206–8; Taylor, *Forging of a Black Community*, 175.

69. *Portland Oregonian*, June 16, 1947.

70. Luckingham, *Minorities in Phoenix*, 133–34.

71. Taylor, *In Search of the Racial Frontier*, 256; De Graaf, "Significant Steps," 29; Kelley, *Race Rebels*, 161–81.

72. De Graaf, "Significant Steps," 29; Taylor, *In Search of the Racial Frontier*, 269.

73. *Arizona Sun*, May 9, October 3, 1947.

74. De Graaf, "Significant Steps," 29.

75. De Graaf, "Significant Steps," 29.

76. See Hine, *Black Victory*.

77. De Graaf, "Significant Steps," 32; GPCCU, *To Secure These Rights*, 6.

78. Scott and Womack, *Double V*, 288–89; Quarles, "A. Philip Randolph," 139–64; Haygood, *King of the Cats*, 3–39; White, *Man Called White*, 294–328; Buni, *Robert Vann*, 4–29; Hine, *Black Women in White*, 162–86.

79. Quarles, "A. Philip Randolph," 139–64.

80. Scott and Womack, *Double V*, 271.

81. White, *Man Called White*, 322–23.

82. Luckingham, *Minorities in Phoenix*, 156–57.

83. Blum, *V Was for Victory*, 182–220; Sitkoff, "Racial Militancy," 664–69.

84. Arnold Rampersad, *Jackie Robinson: A Biography* (New York: Alfred A. Knopf, 1997), 83–187.

85. Robert Garland Landolt, *The Mexican-America Workers of San Antonio, Texas* (New York: Arno, 1976), 268.

86. Daniels, "Black Magistrate's Struggle," 336.

87. Whitney, "Shooting Down Racism," 1; Lincoln Ragsdale Sr. and Eleanor Ragsdale, interview; Lincoln Ragsdale Sr., interview; Universal, *Dr. Lincoln Johnson Ragsdale, Sr.*, 4; Ely, interview; George Brooks, interview by author, April 6, 2000, Phoenix, TP and TS, ACASU; George Brooks, interview by Mary Melcher, January 31, 1990, Phoenix, TP, AHSCAD.

88. Whitney, "Shooting Down Racism," 1; Lincoln Ragsdale Sr. and Eleanor Ragsdale, interview; Lincoln Ragsdale Sr., interview; Universal, *Dr. Lincoln Johnson Ragsdale, Sr.*, 4.

## 3. MOBILIZATION, AGITATION, AND PROTEST

1. Lincoln Ragsdale Sr. and Eleanor Ragsdale, interview.

2. Universal, *Mrs. Eleanor Dickey Ragsdale*, 14.

3. Emmett McLoughlin, *People's Padre* (Boston: Beacon, 1954), 101–12; Luckingham, *Phoenix*, 66, 173–76; *Arizona Sun*, February 5, May 17, June 2, July 5, November 22, 1946, February 2, 1947; Lincoln Ragsdale Sr., interview; Lincoln Ragsdale Sr. and Eleanor Ragsdale, interview.

4. *Arizona Sun*, February 5, May 17, June 2, July 5, November 22, 1946, February 2, 1947.

5. *Arizona Sun*, May 17, 1946.

6. *Arizona Sun*, July 5, 1946.

7. *Arizona Sun*, July 5, 1946.

8. *Arizona Sun*, November 22, 1946, February 2, 1947.

9. *Arizona Republic*, November 27–28, 30, 1942; *Arizona Sun*, February 1, 8, 16, 23, 1951; Luckingham, *Minorities in Phoenix*, 157; Luckingham, *Phoenix*, 143–44; Lincoln Ragsdale Sr., interview.

10. Luckingham, *Minorities in Phoenix*, 158–59.

11. *Arizona Sun*, May 17, September 13, October 17, 20, 1946, February 2, 21, March 2, June 20, October 24, 1947, April 2, August 27, September 24, November 5, 1948, February 20, April 15, 1949, September 19, 1952; *Arizona Republic*, January 20, 1946; Hackett, "Survey of Living Conditions," 43–50.

12. Irene McClellan King, interview by Maria Hernandez, Summer 1981, Phoenix, TP, ACASU; Mahoney, interview; Lincoln Ragsdale Sr., interview; Lincoln Ragsdale Sr. and Eleanor Ragsdale, interview; Harris, *First 100 Years*, 69–74, 81–98, 138–41.

13. Quoted in Luckingham, *Minorities in Phoenix*, 160.

14. Melcher, "Blacks and Whites Together," 198; Mahoney, interview; Thomasena Grigsby, interview by Mary Melcher, February 7, 1990, Phoenix,

TP, AHFASU; J. Eugene Grigsby Jr., interview by Mary Melcher, February 12, 1990, Phoenix, TP, AHFASU.

15. GPCCU, *To Secure These Rights*, 6, 9–13, 17–46; Melcher, "Blacks and Whites Together," 195–216.

16. Daniels, "Black Magistrate's Struggle," 337–38; Melcher, "Blacks and Whites Together," 201; Luckingham, *Minorities in Phoenix*, 161–62; Mahoney, interview; Thomasena Grigsby, interview.

17. Baker, "Lincoln Ragsdale," 97; Ely, interview.

18. Ely, interview.

19. Ragsdale, "Minority Entrepreneurship," 74–75.

20. Ragsdale, "Minority Entrepreneurship," 74–75; Lincoln Ragsdale Sr., interview; Hartwell Ragsdale Jr., interview; Lincoln Ragsdale Jr., interview, April 6, 2000; *Arizona Sun*, October 10, 1947.

21. Lincoln Ragsdale Jr., interview, April 6, 2000.

22. Lincoln Ragsdale Jr., interview, April 6, 2000; U.S. Bureau of the Census, *Population of the United States*, 1950; Plater, *African American Entrepreneurship*, 162–65.

23. Lincoln Ragsdale quoted in Baker, "Lincoln Ragsdale," 97; Lincoln Ragsdale Jr., interview, April 6, 2000; William Dickey, interview by author, April 6, 2000, Phoenix, TS, ACASU.

24. Lincoln Ragsdale quoted in Baker, "Lincoln Ragsdale," 97.

25. Baker, "Lincoln Ragsdale," 97; *Arizona Sun*, October 10, 1947; Lincoln Ragsdale Sr., interview; Hartwell Ragsdale Jr., interview; Lincoln Ragsdale Jr., interview, April 6, 2000.

26. *Arizona Sun*, January 7, 1948; Eleanor Ragsdale, interview, Spring 1990.

27. *Arizona Sun*, January 7, 1948.

28. *Arizona Sun*, October 10, 1947, July 2, 1948; Universal, *Dr. Lincoln Johnson Ragsdale, Sr.*, 3; Ragsdale, "Minority Entrepreneurship," 75.

29. *Arizona Sun*, October 10, 1947, July 2, 1948; Universal, *Dr. Lincoln Johnson Ragsdale, Sr.*, 3.

30. Universal, *Mrs. Eleanor Dickey Ragsdale*, 15.

31. Universal, *Mrs. Eleanor Dickey Ragsdale*, 15.

32. Lincoln Ragsdale Jr., interview, April 6, 2000; Lincoln Ragsdale Sr. and Eleanor Ragsdale, interview; Hartwell Ragsdale Jr., interview; Dickey, interview; Lincoln Ragsdale Sr., interview.

33. Lincoln Ragsdale Sr., interview; *Arizona Sun*, July 2, 1948; Lincoln Ragsdale Jr., interview, April 6, 2000.

34. Lincoln Ragsdale Jr., interview, April 6, 2000.

35. Lincoln Ragsdale Jr., interview, April 6, 2000; Holloway, *Africanisms in American Culture*, 81–91; Plater, *African American Entrepreneurship*, 162–

65; Dickey, interview; Brooks, interview by author; Brooks, interview by Melcher; Melcher, "Blacks and Whites Together," 195–216.

36. Lincoln Ragsdale Jr., interview, April 6, 2000; Universal, *Mrs. Eleanor Dickey Ragsdale*, 15; Eleanor Ragsdale, interview, Spring 1990; Emily Ragsdale, interview by author, April 6, 2000, Phoenix, TP and TS, ACASU; Dickey, interview.

37. Eleanor Ragsdale, interview, Spring 1990.

38. Eleanor Ragsdale, interview, Spring 1990.

39. Luckingham, *Phoenix*, 98. See also White, *Too Heavy*.

40. Lincoln Ragsdale Sr. and Eleanor Ragsdale, interview.

41. Lincoln Ragsdale Sr., interview; Lincoln Ragsdale Sr. and Eleanor Ragsdale, interview; Emily Ragsdale, interview; Dickey, interview; Baker, "Lincoln Ragsdale," 97; Whitney, "Shooting Down Racism," 1; Kotlanger, "Phoenix, Arizona," 445–46.

42. Ely, interview.

43. Luckingham, *Phoenix*, 3, 51, 90–92, 132; Ely, interview; U.S. Department of the Interior, National Park Service in Cooperation with the Phoenix Historic Preservation Commission, Encanto-PalmCroft Historic District Publication (National Register of Historic Places Inventory-Nomination Form, Continuation Sheet 81, Item Number 8), 3. This National Register document provides a detailed history of the development of both the PalmCroft and Encanto subdivisions. It highlights the history behind the architecture, community planning, and landscape of one of Phoenix's oldest subdivisions. It also contains photographs of the original PalmCroft area, residential maps, and a residential legend.

44. U.S. Department of the Interior, Encanto-PalmCroft, 3, 9; Luckingham, *Phoenix*, 91.

45. Phoenix Real Estate Board Charter quoted in Kotlanger, "Phoenix, Arizona," 445–46; Lincoln Ragsdale Sr., interview; Luckingham, *Minorities in Phoenix*, 164–65; Melcher, "Blacks and Whites Together," 203; Baker, "Lincoln Ragsdale," 97–98; Lincoln Ragsdale Sr. and Eleanor Ragsdale, interview; Emily Ragsdale, interview.

46. *Arizona Republican*, March 15, 1929; *Phoenix Independent*, July 20, 1922.

47. Nimmons, "Arizona's Forgotten Past," 101.

48. *Arizona Republican*, February 25, March 4, 7, 19, 1912.

49. Thul, *Blacks in Arizona*, 12; Frank Shirley quoted in Luckingham, *Minorities in Phoenix*, 133–34; Mawn, "Blacks in Phoenix," 347–48; Kotlanger, "Phoenix, Arizona," 445–46.

50. Thul, *Blacks in Arizona*, 12; J. R. Feagin, *Discrimination American Style: Institutional Racism and Sexism* (Englewood Cliffs NJ: Prentice Hall, 1978), 87–90; Copeland, interview.

51. *Arizona Republican*, January 21, May 26, 1920, September 29, 1921, November 19, 1922; *Arizona Republic*, July 14, 1935; Kotlanger, "Phoenix, Arizona," 446; Eleanor Ragsdale, interview, Spring 1990.

52. Lincoln Ragsdale Sr., interview; Luckingham, *Minorities in Phoenix*, 164–65; Melcher, "Blacks and Whites Together," 203; Baker, "Lincoln Ragsdale," 97–98; Lincoln Ragsdale Sr. and Eleanor Ragsdale, interview; Emily Ragsdale, interview.

53. Lincoln Ragsdale Sr., interview; Luckingham, *Minorities in Phoenix*, 164–65; Melcher, "Blacks and Whites Together," 203; Baker, "Lincoln Ragsdale," 97–98; Lincoln Ragsdale Sr. and Eleanor Ragsdale, interview; Emily Ragsdale, interview.

54. Lincoln Ragsdale Sr., interview; Luckingham, *Minorities in Phoenix*, 164–65; Melcher, "Blacks and Whites Together," 203; Baker, "Lincoln Ragsdale," 97–98.

55. Baker, "Lincoln Ragsdale," 97–98; Lincoln Ragsdale Sr. and Eleanor Ragsdale, interview; Emily Ragsdale, interview; Dickey, interview; Kelley, *Race Rebels*, 8–9. Kelley emphasizes the black working class, but I believe his analysis can be applied in this case.

56. Baker, "Lincoln Ragsdale," 97–98; Lincoln Ragsdale Sr. and Eleanor Ragsdale, interview.

57. Baker, "Lincoln Ragsdale," 97–98; Lincoln Ragsdale Sr. and Eleanor Ragsdale, interview.

58. Howard Sitkoff, *The Struggle for Black Equality, 1954–1980* (New York: Farrar, Straus and Giroux, 1981), 90

59. Sitkoff, *Struggle for Black Equality*, 90; Anne Standley, "The Role of Black Women in the Civil Rights Movement," in Crawford et al., *Women in the Civil Rights Movement*, 183–84; Baker, "Lincoln Ragsdale," 97–98; Lincoln Ragsdale Sr. and Eleanor Ragsdale, interview; Emily Ragsdale, interview; Dickey, interview; Eleanor Ragsdale, interview, Spring 1990.

60. Abbey, "Ku Klux Klan in Arizona," 10–30; *Arizona Republican*, June 4–6, 1915.

61. Kibbey quoted in John S. Goff and Mary E. Gill, "Joseph H. Kibbey and School Segregation in Arizona," *Journal of Arizona History* 21 (Winter 1980): 411–22.

62. Moeur quoted in Kotlanger, "Phoenix, Arizona," 296–99; Goff and Gill, "Joseph H. Kibbey," 411–22; Morris J. Richards, *The Birth of Arizona: The Baby State* (Phoenix: Arizona State Department of Education, 1940), 16–24.

63. Crump quoted in Luckingham, *Minorities in Phoenix*, 134; *Arizona Republican*, March 31, 1910, January 3, March 12, 1911; Goff and Gill, "Joseph H. Kibbey," 411–22.

64. Crump quoted in Luckingham, *Minorities in Phoenix*, 134.

65. Booker T. Washington, *Up from Slavery* (New York: Double Day, 1901), 162; *Arizona Republican*, September 23–24, October 19, 1911; Booker T. Washington, "The Race Problem in Arizona," *Phoenix Independent*, October 1911, 909–13.

66. Kotlanger, "Phoenix, Arizona," 455; Luckingham, *Minorities in Phoenix*, 134; Harris, *First 100 Years*, 65; *Arizona Democrat*, April 29, 1912. For more on W. E. B. DuBois and Booker T. Washington and their views with regard to racial and gender equality, "the franchise," and black political philosophy, see Manning Marable, *W. E. B. DuBois: Black Radical Democrat* (New York: Macmillan, 1987); Louis Harlan, *Booker T. Washington: The Wizard of Tuskegee, 1901–1915* (New York: Oxford University Press, 1983).

67. Kotlanger, "Phoenix, Arizona," 455; Luckingham, *Minorities in Phoenix*, 134; Harris, *First 100 Years*, 65.

68. Donald R. Van Petten, *The Constitution and Government of Arizona* (Phoenix: Jahn and Tyler, 1952), 141; Harris, *First 100 Years*, 63–67.

69. W. A. Robinson quoted in Harris, *First 100 Years*, 63–67.

70. W. A. Robinson quoted in Harris, *First 100 Years*, 63–67; W. A. Robinson, "The Progress of Integration in the Public Schools," *Journal of Negro Education* 25 (Fall 1956): 371–79, Harris, *First 100 Years*, 69–74, 81–98, 138–41; Lincoln Ragsdale Sr. and Eleanor Ragsdale, interview.

71. King, interview; *Arizona Sun*, September 13, 1946. See also Mary Logan Rothschild and Pamela Claire Hronek, *Doing What the Day Brought: An Oral History of Arizona Women* (Tucson: University of Arizona Press, 1992).

72. *Arizona Sun*, March 21, 1947.

73. *Arizona Sun*, October 8, 15, 1948; Martin Bauml Duberman, *Paul Robeson* (New York: Alfred A. Knopf, 1988), 19–68, 215–16, 383–465.

74. Duberman, *Paul Robeson*, 19–68, 215–16, 383–465; Baker, "Lincoln Ragsdale," 97.

75. *Arizona Sun*, October 26, 1951.

76. Harris, *First 100 Years*, 87; Lincoln Ragsdale Sr. and Eleanor Ragsdale, interview; Peter Iverson, *Barry Goldwater: Native Arizonan* (Norman: University of Oklahoma Press, 1997), 68–78.

77. Lincoln Ragsdale Sr. and Eleanor Ragsdale, interview.

78. Lincoln Ragsdale Sr. and Eleanor Ragsdale, interview; Iverson, *Barry Goldwater*, 68–78, 121–22; Crudup, "African Americans in Arizona," 57.

79. *Arizona Sun*, April 20, October 26, 1951, December 1, 1960; Daniels, "Black Magistrate's Struggle," 335–38; Melcher, "Blacks and Whites Together," 195–216; Luckingham, *Minorities in Phoenix*, 161–62; Mahoney, interview; Lincoln Ragsdale Sr. and Eleanor Ragsdale, interview; GPCCU, *To Secure These Rights*, 9–13, 17–46; Harris, *First 100 Years*, 69–74, 81–98, 138–41.

80. *Arizona Sun*, February 13, 1953, December 1, 1960; Daniels, "Black Magistrate's Struggle," 335–38; Melcher, "Blacks and Whites Together," 195–216; Luckingham, *Minorities in Phoenix*, 161–62; Mahoney, interview; Lincoln Ragsdale Sr. and Eleanor Ragsdale, interview; Lincoln Ragsdale Sr., interview; GPCCU, *To Secure These Rights*, 9–13, 17–46; Harris, *First 100 Years*, 69–74, 81–98, 138–41. On the NAACP's methods for opposing school segregation, see Tushnet, NAACP's *Legal Strategy*; Reed, *Chicago NAACP*.

81. Fred Struckmeyer quoted in *Arizona Sun*, February 13, 1953; Daniels, "Black Magistrate's Struggle," 335–38; Luckingham, *Minorities in Phoenix*, 161–62; Lincoln Ragsdale Sr. and Eleanor Ragsdale, interview.

82. Luckingham, *Minorities in Phoenix*, 161–62; Lincoln Ragsdale Sr. and Eleanor Ragsdale, interview; Mahoney, interview. On the significance of the *Brown v. Board of Education* decision at the national level, see Richard Kluger, *Simple Justice: The History of Brown v. Board of Education and Black America's Struggle for Equality* (New York: Vintage Books, 1975).

83. *Arizona Sun*, February 13, 1953; Luckingham, *Minorities in Phoenix*, 162; Baker, "Lincoln Ragsdale," 97.

84. Robinson, "Progress of Integration," 371.

85. Lincoln Ragsdale Sr. and Eleanor Ragsdale, interview.

86. W. A. Robinson, Testimony on School Desegregation in Phoenix, *Hearings before the United States Commission on Civil Rights, Phoenix, Arizona, February 3, 1962* (Washington DC: Government Printing Office, 1962), 17–18 (hereafter cited as *Hearings*).

87. Robinson, Testimony on School Desegregation, 17–18.

88. Quoted in Baker, "Lincoln Ragsdale," 98.

89. Lincoln Ragsdale Sr. and Eleanor Ragsdale, interview; Eleanor Ragsdale quoted in Baker, "Lincoln Ragsdale," 98; Eleanor Ragsdale, interview, Spring 1990; Emily Ragsdale, interview.

90. Lincoln Ragsdale Jr., interview, April 6, 2000.

91. *Arizona Republic*, September 19, 23, 26, 1952; Hayzel B. Daniels, interview by Richard Harris, spring 1983, Tucson, transcript, Arizona Historical Society, Southern Arizona Division, Tucson.

92. Thomasena Grigsby, interview; J. Eugene Grigsby Jr., interview.

93. Thomasena Grigsby quoted in *Chicago Defender*, January 19, 1952.

94. Thomasena Grigsby quoted in *Chicago Defender*, January 19, 1952; *Arizona Sun*, September 13, 1946; Thomasena Grigsby, interview; J. Eugene Grigsby Jr., interview; *Arizona Sun* September 13, 1946; Lincoln Ragsdale Sr., Testimony on the Negro in Phoenix, *Hearings*, 16–26. For more on Eugene Grigsby's views on racial segregation, see *Hearings*, 16–26, 34–68, 101–39.

95. Lincoln Ragsdale Sr., interview.

96. Mahoney, interview; Thomasena Grigsby, interview; J. Eugene Grigsby Jr., interview.

97. *Arizona Gleam*, December 15, 1929; Copeland, interview.

98. Copeland, interview.

99. Copeland, interview.

100. Copeland, interview; Eleanor Ragsdale, interview, Spring 1990; Lincoln Ragsdale Sr. and Eleanor Ragsdale, interview.

101. Copeland, interview; Mahoney, interview; Thomasena Grigsby, interview; J. Eugene Grigsby Jr., interview; Lincoln Ragsdale Sr., interview; Lincoln Ragsdale Sr. and Eleanor Ragsdale, interview.

102. The phrase "shooting down racism" is taken from Whitney, "Shooting Down Racism."

### 4. RESISTANCE AND INTERRACIAL DISSENT

1. See Marable, *Race, Reform, and Rebellion*; Daniels, "Black Magistrate's Struggle," 337–38; Melcher, "Blacks and Whites Together," 201; Luckingham, *Minorities in Phoenix*, 161–62; GPCCU, *To Secure These Rights*, 6; Steven F. Lawson and Charles Payne, *Debating the Civil Rights Movement, 1945–1968* (New York: Rowman and Littlefield, 1998), 12.

2. Kenneth O'Reilly, *Nixon's Piano: Presidents and Racial Politics from Washington to Clinton* (New York: Free Press, 1995), 170; Lawson and Payne, *Debating the Civil Rights Movement*, 12.

3. O'Reilly, *Nixon's Piano*, 170; *Arizona Sun*, May 19, 1960. On the lynching of Emmett Till, see Christopher Metress, ed., *The Lynching of Emmett Till: A Documentary Narrative* (Charlottesville: University Press of Virginia, 2002); Stephen J. Whitfield, *A Death in the Delta: The Story of Emmett Till* (Baltimore: Johns Hopkins University Press, 1991).

4. Harris, *First 100 Years*, 96; Crudup, "African Americans in Arizona," 347.

5. The PUL statistics were reported in *Hearings*, 16–26, 34–68, 101–39; Harris, *First 100 Years*, 69–74, 81–98, 138–41.

6. *Phoenix Gazette*, December 1, 1960; local observer quoted in Luckingham, *Minorities in Phoenix*, 166; federal manuscript census schedule, 1940, 1950, 1960.

7. Ragsdale, Testimony on the Negro in Phoenix, 16–26, 34–68, 101–39; Harris, *First 100 Years*, 69–74, 81–98, 138–41.

8. Clyde Webb quoted in Luckingham, *Minorities in Phoenix*, 166.

9. Luckingham, *Minorities in Phoenix*, 166.

10. *Arizona Sun*, July 14, 1960, June 29, 1961.

11. *Arizona Sun*, June 29, 1961.

12. *Arizona Sun*, August 25, 1960.

13. Baker, "Lincoln Ragsdale," 98; Clayborne Carson, *In Struggle: SNCC and the Black Awakening of the 1960s* (Cambridge: Harvard University Press,

1995), 9–18. Gretchen Cassel Eick, in *Dissent in Wichita*, has demonstrated with detail, perspective, and clarity that the first major sit-ins were not in Greensboro, North Carolina, but in Wichita, Kansas, during the summer of 1958.

14. Brooks, interview by author.

15. Brooks, interview by author.

16. Brooks, interview by author.

17. *Arizona Sun*, April 15, 1960.

18. *Arizona Republic*, February 28, 1993.

19. Brooks, interview by author.

20. Brooks, interview by author.

21. Baker, "Lincoln Ragsdale," 98; George Brooks and Lincoln Ragsdale interview quoted in *Arizona Republic*, February 28, 1993; Luckingham, *Minorities in Phoenix*, 166; Melcher, "Blacks and Whites Together," 204–5; Brooks, interview by author; Brooks, interview by Melcher.

22. Baker, "Lincoln Ragsdale," 98; *Arizona Republic*, February 28, 1993; Luckingham, *Minorities in Phoenix*, 166; Melcher, "Blacks and Whites Together," 204–5; Brooks, interview by author; Brooks, interview by Melcher.

23. *Hearings*, 16–26; Matthew C. Whitaker, "Michigan Committee on Civil Rights," in *Organizing Black America: An Encyclopedia of African American Associations*, ed. Nina Mjagkij, 331–32 (New York: Garland, 2000).

24. George B. Brooks, Testimony on the Negro in Phoenix, *Hearings*, 16–26, 34–68, 101–39.

25. KSC Management Corporation, the Phoenix Urban League, and the United States Commission on Civil Rights, *The Search: Hearings before the United States Commission on Civil Rights, Phoenix, Arizona, February 3, 1962* (Phoenix: AirLab Times, 1962) (video recording of the hearing before the U.S. Commission on Civil Rights, copy in author's possession); Brooks, Testimony on the Negro in Phoenix, 16–26, 34–68, 101–39.

26. KSC Management et al., *Search*; Ragsdale, Testimony on the Negro in Phoenix, 16–26, 58.

27. Ragsdale, Testimony on the Negro in Phoenix, 16–26.

28. Ragsdale, Testimony on the Negro in Phoenix, 16–26; KSC Management et al., *Search*; Herbert L. Ely, Testimony on the Negro in Phoenix, *Hearings*, 48.

29. Lincoln Ragsdale Sr., interview.

30. Brooks, interview by Melcher.

31. *Arizona Sun*, April 6, 1961; Travis Williams, interview by author, April 6, 2000, Phoenix, TP and TS, ACASU.

32. Maricopa County Welfare Department memo quoted in *Arizona Sun*, April 19, 1962; Melcher, "Blacks and Whites Together," 206.

33. Brooks, interview by Melcher; Harris, *First 100 Years*, 69–74; Melcher, "Blacks and Whites Together," 195, 206–16; Luckingham, *Minorities in Phoenix*, 167.

34. Lincoln Ragsdale quoted in Baker, "Lincoln Ragsdale," 98; Clovis Campbell Sr., interview by author, August 6, 1996, Phoenix, tape recording in author's possession.

35. Campbell, interview by author; Clovis Campbell Sr., interview by Mary Melcher, June 1, 2001, Phoenix, TP, AHSCAD; Clovis Campbell Sr., *I Refused to Leave the "Hood"* (Phoenix: Clovis C. Campbell Sr. 2002), 1–99.

36. Campbell, interview by author; Campbell, *I Refused to Leave*, 1–99.

37. Eleanor Ragsdale and an unnamed NAACP spokesperson quoted in *Arizona Sun*, February 1, 1962.

38. Della Marie Wright, "What Was the Wool Worth?" in *Living the Dream in Arizona: The Legacy of Martin Luther King, Jr.*, ed. Gretchen M. Bataille et al., 47 (Tempe: ACASU, 1992); Eleanor Ragsdale, interview, Spring 1990.

39. Lincoln Ragsdale Sr. and Eleanor Ragsdale, interview.

40. Luckingham, *Minorities in Phoenix*, 177; Dickey, interview: Crudup, "African Americans in Arizona," 361.

41. Francisco A. Rosales, *Chicano!: The History of the Mexican American Civil Rights Movement* (Houston: Art Pùblico Press, 1996), 1–52; *Prescott Weekly Arizona Minor*, May 13, 1871, April 13, 1872; *Phoenix Herald*, August 17, 1883; *Phoenix Daily Herald*, May 8, 1896; *Territorial Expositor*, June 25, 1880; federal manuscript census schedule, *Arizona Territory*, 1870, 1880; Nimmons, "Arizona's Forgotten Past," 92–93; federal manuscript census schedule, 1940; Luckingham, *Phoenix*, 2–39.

42. Rosales, *Chicano!* 1–52.

43. Lincoln Ragsdale Sr. and Eleanor Ragsdale, interview; Luckingham, *Minorities in Phoenix*, 167. According to the U.S. Bureau of the Census, *Population of the United States*, 1960, there were 356,791 whites, 61,460 Mexican Americans, and 20,919 African Americans in Phoenix.

44. Lincoln Ragsdale Sr. and Eleanor Ragsdale, interview; Luckingham, *Minorities in Phoenix*, 167.

45. *Arizona Sun*, February 1, July 19, 1962.

46. Lincoln Ragsdale quoted in Baker, "Lincoln Ragsdale," 98.

47. Jenkins and Hine, *Question of Manhood*, xi–xvii; Gilmore, *Gender and Jim Crow*, 61–90; *Arizona Sun*, July 19, 1962; Baker, "Lincoln Ragsdale," 98.

48. Lincoln Ragsdale Sr. and Eleanor Ragsdale, interview; Lincoln Ragsdale Sr., interview; Eleanor Ragsdale, interview, Spring 1990; Lincoln Ragsdale Jr., interview, April 6, 2000; Ragsdale, "Minority Entrepreneurship," 71–90.

49. *Arizona Sun*, March 1, 8, 1962; Ely, interview.

50. *Arizona Sun*, March 1, 8, 1962; Manis, *"Fire You Can't Put Out"*, 253–99.

51. Melcher, "Blacks and Whites Together," 207; Brooks, interview by Melcher; J. Eugene Grigsby Jr., interview; Thomasena Grigsby, interview; Taylor, *In Search of the Racial Frontier*, 278–99; City of Phoenix Human Rights Commission, *First Annual Report, 1963–1964* (Phoenix: City of Phoenix, 1964), 2–6; Martin Luther King Jr. *The Autobiography of Martin Luther King, Jr.* (New York: Warner Books, 1998), 223–27.

52. Fran Waldman, interview by Mary Melcher, January 31, 1990, Phoenix, TP, AHFASU; Brooks, interview by Melcher; Thomasena Grigsby, interview; J. Eugene Grigsby Jr., interview; Melcher, "Blacks and Whites Together," 207; Taylor, *In Search of the Racial Frontier*, 278–99; Stephen F. Lawson, *Running for Freedom: Civil Rights and Black Politics in America since 1941*, 2nd ed. (New York: McGraw Hill, 1997), 78.

53. *Arizona Sun*, May 17, 1946, November 14, 1947; City of Phoenix Human Rights Commission, *Report*, 2–6; *Arizona Republic* editorial quoted in *Arizona Sun*, December 7, 1956; *Arizona Republic* editorial quoted in *Arizona Sun*, April 6, 1961; Luckingham, *Minorities in Phoenix*, 167.

54. Dan Smoot quoted in *Arizona Sun*, March 9, 1961.

55. Eleanor Ragsdale, interview, Spring 1990; Lincoln Ragsdale Sr. and Eleanor Ragsdale, interview.

56. *Arizona Sun*, July 12, 1962; Dickey, interview.

57. Dickey, interview.

58. Dickey, interview.

59. Dickey, interview; Eleanor Ragsdale, interview, Spring 1990; Lincoln Ragsdale Sr. and Eleanor Ragsdale, interview.

60. Dickey, interview.

61. *Arizona Sun*, February 1, 1962.

62. Lincoln Ragsdale quoted in Crudup, "African Americans in Arizona," 363; Ely, interview; August Meier and Elliot Rudwick, *ptpt pt CORE: A Study in the Civil Rights Movement, 1942–1968* (Urbana: University of Illinois Press, 1975), 1–36; Lincoln Ragsdale Sr. and Eleanor Ragsdale, interview.

63. Crudup, "African Americans in Arizona," 363; Ely, interview; Lincoln Ragsdale Sr. and Eleanor Ragsdale, interview.

64. Lincoln Ragsdale quoted in Crudup, "African Americans in Arizona," 363.

65. Crudup, "African Americans in Arizona," 363; Ely, interview; Lincoln Ragsdale Sr. and Eleanor Ragsdale, interview; Harris, *First 100 Years*, 95–115.

66. Waldman, interview; Harris, *First 100 Years*, 95–115; *Arizona Republic*, April 5, 1964.

67. Waldman, interview; Harris, *First 100 Years*, 95–115.

68. Richard Newhall, "The Negro in Phoenix," *Phoenix Point West,* September 1965, 15–18.

69. Luckingham, *Minorities in Phoenix,* 174; Dickey, interview; Lincoln Ragsdale Sr. and Eleanor Ragsdale, interview.

70. Melcher, "Blacks and Whites Together," 209; Action Citizens Committee Paid Political Advertisement, "ACT Slate Takes Lead in Election Campaign" (Phoenix: Action Citizens Committee, 1963); Luckingham, *Phoenix,* 150–53; Ely, interview; Lincoln Ragsdale Sr. and Eleanor Ragsdale, interview.

71. *Arizona Republic,* February 28, 1993; Luckingham, *Phoenix,* 179; Melcher, "Blacks and Whites Together," 209; Ely, interview.

72. Ely, interview; Waldman, interview; Luckingham, *Minorities in Phoenix,* 168; Eleanor Ragsdale, interview, Spring 1990; Lincoln Ragsdale Sr., interview.

73. Luckingham, *Minorities in Phoenix,* 169; Action Citizens Committee Paid Political Advertisement, "Pena Supports Opportunity for Underprivileged Youth" (Phoenix: Action Citizens Committee, 1963); GPCCU, *To Secure These Rights,* 16; *Hearings,* 100–139.

74. Calvin Goode, interview by author, July 31, 2002, Phoenix, TP and TS, ACASU.

75. Brooks, interview by Melcher; Brooks, interview by author; Copeland, interview.

76. Brooks, interview by Melcher; Brooks, interview by author; Lincoln Ragsdale Sr., interview; Ragsdale, Testimony on the Negro in Phoenix, 16–26.

77. *Hearings,* 100–139.

78. *Arizona Republic,* June 4, 1964; *Arizona Sun,* March 1, 8, 1962; Ely, interview.

79. Baker, "Lincoln Ragsdale," 99; Lincoln Ragsdale Sr. and Eleanor Ragsdale, interview; Emily Ragsdale, interview.

80. Baker, "Lincoln Ragsdale," 99; Robert D. Loevy, *To End All Segregation: The Politics and Passage of the Civil Rights Act of 1964* (Landham MD: University Press of America, 1990), 1–35; Branch, *Pillar of Fire,* 606–12.

81. *Arizona Republic,* June 4, 1964; Baker, "Lincoln Ragsdale," 99.

82. Luckingham, *Minorities in Phoenix,* 205–7; Melcher, "Blacks and Whites Together," 206.

83. Luckingham, *Minorities in Phoenix,* 205–7.

84. Jenkins and Hine, *Question of Manhood,* xi–xvii; Gilmore, *Gender and Jim Crow,* 61–90; *Arizona Sun,* July 19, 1962; Baker, "Lincoln Ragsdale," 98; Brooks, interview by Melcher; Brooks, interview by author; Lincoln Ragsdale Sr., interview.

85. Luckingham, *Minorities in Phoenix,* 167; Melcher, "Blacks and Whites Together," 206.

1. Terry H. Anderson, *The Sixties*, 2nd ed. (New York: Pearson Longmann, 2004), 45–208; William L. Van Deburg, *New Day in Babylon: The Black Power Movement and American Culture, 1965–1975* (Chicago: University of Chicago Press, 1992), 29–62, 248–308; Lawson and Payne, *Debating the Civil Rights Movement*, 3–44; Iverson, *Barry Goldwater*, 68–78, 121–22.

2. Melcher, "Blacks and Whites Together," 211; Van Deburg, *New Day in Babylon*, 29–62, 248–308; Lawson and Payne, *Debating the Civil Rights Movement*, 3–44. On the history of SNCC, see Carson, *In Struggle*; Barbara Ransby, *Ella Baker and the Black Freedom Movement: A Radical Democratic Vision* (Chapel Hill: University of North Carolina Press, 2003).

3. Anderson, *Sixties*, 74–102; Lawson and Payne, *Debating the Civil Rights Movement*, 3–44.

4. There is a large body of literature on the emergence, evolution, and legacy of the Black Power movement. Some of the most interesting and analytical works include Stokely Carmichael and Charles V. Hamilton, *Black Power: The Politics of Liberation in America* (New York: Vintage, 1967); Carson, *In Struggle*; Steve Clark, ed., *The Final Speeches of Malcolm X: February 1965* (New York: Pathfinder, 1992); Van Deburg, *New Day in Babylon*; Theodore Cross, *The Black Power Imperative: Racial Inequality and the Politics of Nonviolence* (New York: Faulkner Books, 1984); Philip S. Foner, ed., *The Black Panthers Speak* (Philadelphia: Lippincott, 1970); Robert L. Allen, *Black Awakening in Capitalist America* (Trenton: Africa World Press, 1990); Malcolm X, *Autobiography*.

Established in April 1964, the MFDP was organized to challenge Mississippi's Democratic Party, which had denied African Americans access to the ballot and the electoral process. While it boasted an interracial membership, the MFDP was primarily driven by disenfranchised blacks. The MFDP organized thousands of Mississippians and worked unsuccessfully to unseat the state Democratic Party's delegates at the 1964 national convention. During the convention, MFDP delegate Fannie Lou Hamer addressed the credentials committee in front of a national television audience about the injustices resulting from white supremacy and black disenfranchisement in Mississippi. President Johnson undercut Hamer's message by having the television coverage of her address cut to make way for what he described as an emergency speech of his own. After a long and intense debate over a possible compromise, Democratic Party leaders offered the MFDP delegation two seats at large but with no power to vote on any issue. The MFDP refused this offer.

5. Lawson and Payne, *Debating the Civil Rights Movement*, 34–35; Marable, *Race, Reform, and Rebellion*, 86–113; Lawson, *Running for Freedom*, 113–27; Branch, *Pillar of Fire*, 571–613; Paul K. Conkin, *Big Daddy*

*from the Pedernales: Lyndon Baines Johnson* (Boston: Twayne, 1986), 208–42. See also Robert Dalleck, *Flawed Giant: Lyndon B. Johnson and His Times, 1961–1973* (New York: Oxford University Press, 1998).

6. Lincoln Ragsdale Sr. and Eleanor Ragsdale, interview; Newhall, "Negro in Phoenix," 15–18; Douglas S. Massey and Nancy S. Denton, *American Apartheid: Segregation and the Making of the Underclass* (Cambridge: Harvard University Press, 1993), 1–16.

7. Jerry Cohen and William S. Murphy, *Burn Baby, Burn! The Los Angeles Race Riot, August 1965* (New York: E. P. Dutton, 1966), 1–10; Emily Ragsdale, interview.

8. *Arizona Republic*, September 27, October 27, 1965, July 18, 26, 31, 1967, August 24, 1969; Brooks, interview by Melcher; Brooks, interview by author.

9. *Arizona Republic*, September 27, October 27, 1965, July 18, 26, 31, 1967, August 24, 1969; Brooks, interview by Melcher.

10. *Arizona Republic*, September 27, October 27, 1965, July 18, 26, 31, 1967, August 24, 1969; Brooks, interview by Melcher; Brooks, interview by author.

11. *Arizona Republic*, October 27, 1965, July 18, 26–31, 1967; City of Phoenix, *Chronological History of LEAP* (Phoenix: City of Phoenix, 1967), 1–16; Luckingham, *Phoenix*, 213–14; VanderMeer, *Phoenix Rising*, 60.

12. *Arizona Republic*, October 27, 1965.

13. Quoted in Luckingham, *Phoenix*, 213–14; quoted in City of Phoenix, *Chronological History*, 1–16.

14. Quoted in John Preston, "Look Who's Fighting 'Police Harassment, AP" *Arizona*, May 3, 1970, 7–9.

15. A number of books chronicle the rash of race riots that erupted in the United States during the tumultuous 1960s. Some of the more fascinating include Thomas J. Sugrue, *The Origins of the Urban Crisis: Race and Inequality in Postwar Detroit* (Princeton NJ: Princeton University Press, 1996); Upton, *Urban Riots*; Robert H. Connery, ed., *Urban Riots: Violence and Social Change* (New York: W. W. Norton, 1969).

16. *Phoenix Evening Telegram*, March 31, 1964.

17. Harris, *First 100 Years*, 100; Malcolm X, *Autobiography*, 289; Claude Andrew Clegg III, *An Original Man: The Life and Times of Elijah Muhammad* (New York: St. Martin's, 1997), 176.

18. Long and Ragsdale quoted in Harris, *First 100 Years*; *Arizona Republic*, May 20, 1964; Malcolm X, *Autobiography*, 371–89.

19. *Arizona Republic*, February 28, 1993; Emily Ragsdale, interview by NewsChannel 3, KTVK, February 16, 1995, "A Tribute to Lincoln Ragsdale."

20. *Arizona Republic*, May 20, 1964; Ragsdale quoted in *Arizona Republic*, February 28, 1993.

21. Ragsdale quoted in *Arizona Republic*, February 28, 1993, June 11, 1995.

22. The Webber family mortuary on East Jefferson Street in downtown Phoenix was the only other black-owned mortuary in the city at the time. Many elected to patronize the Ragsdales' mortuary complex over Webber's because of its larger size, ability to host diverse community events, elegant facilities, and efficient management.

23. Eleanor Ragsdale, interview, Spring 1990; Lincoln Ragsdale quoted in *Arizona Republic*, February 28, 1993.

24. Eleanor Ragsdale, interview, Spring 1990; Lincoln Ragsdale Sr. and Eleanor Ragsdale, interview; Lincoln Ragsdale Sr., interview; Lincoln Ragsdale Jr., interview, April 6, 2000; Universal, *Ragsdale Family History*, 2.

25. Lincoln Ragsdale quoted in *Arizona Republic*, February 28, 1993; Eleanor Ragsdale, interview, Spring 1990.

26. Lincoln Ragsdale Jr. interview, April 6, 2000; Universal, *Ragsdale Family History*, 2.

27. Lincoln Ragsdale Sr. and Eleanor Ragsdale, interview; Lincoln Ragsdale Sr., interview; Lincoln Ragsdale Jr. interview, April 6, 2000; Universal, *Ragsdale Family History*, 2; Eleanor Ragsdale, interview, Spring 1990.

28. Harris, *First 100 Years*, 102; Phoenix Urban League, *A Brief History of the Urban League in Phoenix* (Phoenix: Phoenix Urban League, 1981), 10–11.

29. Harris, *First 100 Years*, 102–3.

30. Marable, *Race, Reform, and Rebellion*, 96–97.

31. Carmichael and Hamilton, *Black Power*, vi, vii; Meir and Rudwick, *CORE*, 423.

32. Harold Cruse, *Rebellion or Revolution?* (New York: William and Morrow, 1968), 201; Marable, *Race, Reform, and Rebellion*, 99.

33. Luckingham, *Minorities in Phoenix*, 177.

34. *Arizona Sun*, May 9, 1957; *Arizona Informant*, December 4, 1974, July 30, 1975; *Arizona Republic*, July 16–17, 1967, April 28, 1986; Harris, *First 100 Years*, 102–38; Melcher, "Blacks and Whites Together," 195–216; Phoenix Urban League, *Brief History*, 10–11.

35. Lincoln Ragsdale Sr. and Eleanor Ragsdale, interview; *Arizona Informant*, December 4, 1974, July 30, 1975; *Arizona Republic*, July 16–17, 1967, April 28, 1986; Harris, *First 100 Years*, 102–38; Nelson L. Haggerson, *Oh Yes I Can! A Biography of Arlena E. Seneca* (Tempe AZ: Nornel, 1994), 20–55.

36. *Arizona Informant*, December 4, 1974, July 30, 1975; *Arizona Republic*, July 16–17, 1967, April 28, 1986; Eleanor Ragsdale, interview, Spring 1990.

37. Branch, *Pillar of Fire*, 30, 31, 291, 311, 556; King, *Autobiography*, 346–66.

38. Branch, *Pillar of Fire*, 556; King, *Autobiography*, 346–66.

39. Branch, *Pillar of Fire*, 556; King, *Autobiography*, 346–66; Marable, *Race, Reform, and Rebellion*, 105.

40. Harris, *First 100 Years*, 94–114; Marable, *Race, Reform, and Rebellion*, 105; Luckingham, *Phoenix*, 213.

41. There is a significant amount of information on individual and organized efforts to undermine and eliminate groups advocating Black Power. This information can be found in books and anthologies such as Lawson, *Running for Freedom*, 133–34; Kenneth O'Reilly, *Racial Matters: The* FBI's *Secret File on Black America, 1960–1972* (New York: Free Press, 1991), 1–28; Clayborne Carson, *Malcolm X: The* FBI *File* (Berkeley CA: Carroll and Gaff, 1991), 45–46. See also Angela Y. Davis, ed., *If They Come in the Morning* (New York: Bantam, 1975); Foner, *Black Panthers Speak*; Caroline Ross and Ken Lawrence, *J. Edgar Hoover's Detention Plan: The Politics of Repression in the United States, 1939–1976* (Jackson MS: Anti-Repression Resource Team, 1978); Thomas Wagstaff, ed., *Black Power* (Beverly Hills CA: Glencoe, 1969).

42. Harris, *First 100 Years*, 103.

43. Harris, *First 100 Years*, 103; Campbell, interview by Melcher; Campbell, interview by author.

44. Conkin, *Big Daddy*, 208–42; Lawson and Payne, *Debating the Civil Rights Movement*, 34–35.

45. *Arizona Informant*, December 29, 1971.

46. *Arizona Informant*, July 1, 1971; Eleanor Ragsdale, interview, Spring 1990.

47. Ragsdale Madrid, interview, August 11, 2003; Gwendolyn Ragsdale Madrid, telephone interview by author, September 16, 2003, transcript in author's possession; Lincoln Ragsdale Sr. and Eleanor Ragsdale, interview; Brooks, interview by author; Emily Ragsdale, interview; Eleanor Ragsdale, interview, Spring 1990.

48. Calvin Goode, interview; Georgie Goode, interview by author, July 31, 2002, Phoenix, TS, ACASU; Campbell, interview by Melcher; Campbell, interview by author; Crudup, "African Americans in Arizona," 377.

49. Calvin Goode, interview; Georgie Goode, interview; Campbell, interview by Melcher; Campbell, interview by author; Crudup, "African Americans in Arizona," 377.

50. Crudup, "African Americans in Arizona," 377; Judis R. Andrews Sr., questionnaire to author, April 18, 2000, Phoenix, in author's possession.

51. Luckingham, *Minorities in Phoenix*, 175–79; Crudup, "African Americans in Arizona," 377; Martin Carnoy, *Faded Dreams: The Politics and Eco-*

*nomics of Race in America* (Cambridge: Cambridge University Press, 1994), 1–47.

52. *Arizona Informant*, July 1975; *Arizona Republic*, July 16–17, 1967; Harris, *First 100 Years*, 102–38; Melcher, "Blacks and Whites Together," 195–216; J. Eugene Grigsby Jr., interview; James J. Franklin, Betty L. Mc-Cummings, and Eileen A. Tynan, *Minorities in the Sunbelt* (New Brunswick NJ: Rutgers University Center for Urban Policy Research, 1984), 135–39; Luckingham, *Minorities in Phoenix*, 174.

53. *Arizona Informant*, July 1975; Harris, *First 100 Years*; Haggerson, *Oh Yes I Can!* 1–38; Eleanor Ragsdale, interview, Spring 1990; Luckingham, *Minorities in Phoenix*, 174.

54. City of Phoenix Commission on Housing, *Housing in Phoenix* (Phoenix: City of Phoenix, 1973), 70–74, 110–57; Eleanor Ragsdale, interview, Spring 1990; Lincoln Ragsdale Sr. and Eleanor Ragsdale, interview.

55. Lincoln Ragsdale Sr. and Eleanor Ragsdale, interview; Brooks, interview by author; Emily Ragsdale, interview; Eleanor Ragsdale, interview, Spring 1990; Campbell, interview by author; Andrews, questionnaire; Ely, interview; Dickey, interview.

56. Luckingham, *Minorities in Phoenix*, 178. See also Robert Dallek, *Ronald Reagan: The Politics of Symbolism* (Cambridge: Harvard University Press, 1984); Carnoy, *Faded Dreams*, 1–47.

6. BLACK AND CHICANO LEADERSHIP

1. *Arizona Informant*, December 4, 1974, July 30, 1975; *Arizona Republic*, July 17, 1967; Harris, *First 100 Years*, 102–38; City of Phoenix, *Chronological History*, 1–16.

2. *Arizona Sun*, May 9, 1957; Carl E. Craig, interview, 1978, Phoenix, Phoenix History Project, TP, PHPAHS.

3. *Arizona Sun*, May 9, 1957; Craig, interview; GPCCU, *To Secure These Rights*, 16; Luckingham, *Minorities in Phoenix*, 177.

4. *Arizona Sun*, May 9, 1957.

5. *Arizona Informant*, December 4, 1974, July 30, 1975; *Arizona Republic*, July 17, 1967; Harris, *First 100 Years*, 102–38; City of Phoenix, *Chronological History*, 1–16.

6. Lincoln Ragsdale Sr. and Eleanor Ragsdale, interview; Lincoln Ragsdale Sr., interview; *Arizona Sun*, May 9, 1957; Luckingham, *Minorities in Phoenix*, 167.

7. Lincoln Ragsdale Sr. and Eleanor Ragsdale, interview; Dickey, interview; Luckingham, *Minorities in Phoenix*, 167.

8. Rosales, *Chicano!* 1–52; R. Douglass Cope, *The Limits of Racial Domination: Plebeian Society in Colonial Mexico City, 1600–1720* (Madison: Uni-

versity of Wisconsin Press, 1994), 66; Luckingham, *Phoenix*, 2–39. On the roots of Mexican American history in the Southwest, see also Thomas E. Skidmore and Peter H. Smith, *Modern Latin America*, 3rd ed. (New York: Oxford University Press, 1992); John Charles Chasteen and Joseph S. Tulchin, eds., *Problems in Modern Latin American History: A Reader* (Wilmington DE: SR Books, 1994). For concise histories of Mexican American history and the Chicano movement, see Rodolfo Acuna, *Occupied America: A History of Chicanos* (New York: Addison Wesley Longman, 1999); Juan Gomez-Quinones, *Chicano Politics: Reality and Promise, 1940–1990* (Albuquerque: University of New Mexico Press, 1990); Vicki L. Ruiz, *From Out of the Shadows: Mexican Women in Twentieth-Century America* (New York: Oxford University Press, 1999).

9. *Weekly Arizona Minor*, May 13, 1871, April 13, 1872; *Phoenix Herald*, August 17, 1883; *Phoenix Daily Herald*, May 8, 1896; *Territorial Expositor*, June 25, 1880; federal manuscript census schedule, Arizona Territory, 1870, 1880.

10. Nimmons, "Arizona's Forgotten Past," 92–93; U.S. Bureau of the Census, *Population of the United States*, 1940. See also Kotlanger, "Phoenix, Arizona."

11. *Arizona Republic*, August 4, 1935; Roberts, "Minority Group Poverty," 358–59; Kotlanger, "Phoenix, Arizona," 403–6. See also Gordon Connell-Smith, *The Inter-American System* (New York: Oxford University Press, 1962); Federico G. Gill, *Latin American–United States Relations* (New York: Harcourt Brace Jovanovich, 1971).

12. *Arizona Republic*, August 4, 1935; Roberts, "Minority Group Poverty," 358–59; Kotlanger, "Phoenix, Arizona," 403–6.

13. Luckingham, *Phoenix*, 95–96; Kotlanger, "Phoenix, Arizona," 443. See also Luckingham, *Urban Southwest*.

14. *Arizona Republic*, June 20, 1934, August 15, 1935, July 23, 1936, September 16, 1938, August 1, 1940; *Phoenix Gazette*, July 20, 1940.

15. GPCCU, *To Secure These Rights*, 14–16, 62–65; Eleanor Ragsdale, interview, Spring 1990; Lincoln Ragsdale Sr. and Eleanor Ragsdale, interview.

16. Rosales, *Chicano!* xxi. For a fascinating discussion of the treatment of Irish immigrants by Anglo Americans and how Irish Americans became "American," in part, by accepting the prevailing racial stereotypes about black people and their alleged inferiority, see David Ignatiev, *How the Irish Became White* (New York: Routledge, 1995). Ignatiev posits that the Irish were initially discriminated against in the United States by Anglo Americans and that they "became white" by embracing racism, a concept that Ignatiev describes as uniquely American. Ignatiev illuminates the cause of racial conflict between Irish Americans and African Americans and draws a powerful connection between Irish "success" in nineteenth-century American society

and their embrace of white supremacy. For an equally captivating history, see Thomas A. Guglielmo, *White on Arrival: Italians, Race, Color, and Power in Chicago, 1890–1945* (New York: Oxford University Press, 2003). Guglielmo argues that while many Italian immigrants suffered from racial prejudice and discrimination in America, Italian immigrants, unlike the Irish, were viewed as white on arrival in the "corridors of American power." By identifying instances of discrimination against Italians based upon the socioeconomic benefits they collected from their recognition as whites, Guglielmo "counters the claims of many ethnic Americans that hard work alone enabled their extraordinary success, especially when compared to non-white groups," particularly African Americans, "whose upward mobility languished." Guglielmo, *White on Arrival*, 3–4.

17. Rosales, *Chicano!* xxii.

18. Rosales, *Chicano!* xxii; Acuna, *Occupied America*, 328–85; Ruiz, *Out of the Shadows*, 99–126.

19. *Arizona Sun*, May 9, 1957; Luckingham, *Minorities in Phoenix*, 57, 177; Rosales, *Chicano!* xxii; Acuna, *Occupied America*, 328–85; Ruiz, *Out of the Shadows*, 99–126.

20. Action Citizens Committee, "Pena Supports Opportunity for Underprivileged Youth"; GPCCU, *To Secure These Rights*, 16; Manuel Pena, Testimony on Migrants in Phoenix, *Hearings*, 74–75.

21. Grace Gill-Olivarez, Testimony on Mexican Americans in Phoenix, *Hearings*, 89.

22. *New Times*, June 11, 1986; Patricia A. Adank, "Chicano Activism in Maricopa County—Two Incidents in Retrospective," in *An Awakened Minority: The Mexican Americans*, ed. Manuel P. Servin, 246–65 (Beverly Hills CA: Sage, 1974).

23. *New Times*, June 11, 1986; Adank, "Chicano Activism," 246–65.

24. *Arizona Republic*, October 9, December 2, 1970; *Phoenix Gazette*, October 7, December 3, 1970, January 13, 16, February 2, 1971; Yvonne Garrett, "Chicano Politics in the Phoenix Metropolitan Area," 1–17, typescript, Chicano Collection, Hayden Library, Arizona State University, Tempe.

25. *Arizona Republic*, October 9, December 2, 1970; *Phoenix Gazette*, October 7, December 3, 1970, January 13, 16, February 2, 1971; Garrett, "Chicano Politics," 1–17.

26. Quoted in Luckingham, *Minorities in Phoenix*, 61; Lincoln Ragsdale Sr. and Eleanor Ragsdale, interview; Dickey, interview.

27. *New Times*, June 11, 1986; Adank, "Chicano Activism," 246–65; Luckingham, *Minorities in Phoenix*, 60.

28. Quoted in *Phoenix Gazette*, March 21, 1993.

29. *Arizona Republic*, December 13, 1981; U.S. Bureau of the Census, *Population of the United States*, 1970, 1980, 1990.

30. *El Sol*, January 18, February 1, April 12, July 5, 12, August 2, 16, 30, 1991. The newspaper *El Sol*, one of Phoenix's oldest and most widely read periodicals, focuses on the experiences of the city's Latino residents.

31. *Arizona Informant*, September 19, October 8, 1990, April 3, 10, June 5, August 7, November 28, December 25, 1991.

32. *Arizona Informant*, October 8, 1990, April 3, 10, June 5, August 7, November 28, December 25, 1991.

33. Ward Connerly, *Creating Equal: My Fight against Race Preferences* (San Francisco: Encounter Books, 2000), 22–86; Ken Hamblin, *Pick a Better Country* (New York: Touchstone, 1997), 13–32, 139–56; Thomas Sowell, *Race and Culture: A World View* (New York: Basic Books, 1995), 81–186; Shelby Steele, *Content of Our Character: A New Vision of Race in America* (New York: Perennial Press, 1998), 1–20, 111–48; Armstrong Williams, *Letters to a Young Victim: Hope and Healing in America's Inner Cities* (New York: Free Press, 1996), 1–65.

34. Robin D. G. Kelley, *Yo' Mama's Disfunktional!: Fighting the Culture Wars in Urban America* (Boston: Beacon, 1997), 89; Marable, *Race, Reform, and Rebellion*, 201–2.

35. *El Sol*, January 18, February 1, April 12, July 5, 12, August 2, 16, 30, 1991; *Phoenix Gazette*, May 4, 1983, June 14, 1984, January 21, 1985, November 7, 1986, January 1–2, February 3, March 9, 26, 1987, May 3, 10, June 2, 15, 1990, February 28, March 29, April 1, 22, September 13, 30, November 11, 1991; *Arizona Republic*, December 20, 1983, May 17, 1986, January 4, 17, 25, March 27, April 12, 1987, August 30, 1990, January 17, September, 25, 1991; January 27, 1992; *New Times*, January 30, February 5, May 4, 1985, May 21, 1986.

36. Luckingham, *Minorities in Phoenix*, 72.

37. Lincoln Ragsdale Sr. and Eleanor Ragsdale, interview; Lincoln Ragsdale Sr., interview; Garrett, "Chicano Politics," 1–17; Eleanor Ragsdale, interview, Spring 1990; Campbell, interview by author; Andrews, questionnaire; Ely, interview; Dickey, interview.

38. Rosales, *Chicano!* 108.

39. Action Citizens Committee, "Pena Supports Opportunity for Underprivileged Youth"; GPCCU, *To Secure These Rights*, 16; Pena, Testimony on Migrants in Phoenix, 74–75; Lincoln Ragsdale Sr. and Eleanor Ragsdale, interview; Lincoln Ragsdale Sr., interview.

40. Taylor, *In Search of the Racial Frontier*, 292–93.

41. *El Sol*, January 18, February 1, April 12, July 5, 12, August 2, 16, 30, 1991; Barry Edward Lamb, "The Making of a Chicano Civil Rights Activist: Ralph Estrada of Arizona" (master's thesis, Arizona State University, 1988), 122–60; Lincoln Ragsdale Sr. and Eleanor Ragsdale, interview; Garrett, "Chicano Politics," 1–17; Campbell, interview by author; Kris Aron, "Chicanos

por la Causa: Developing Leadership for the Future," *Phoenix*, December 1984, 101–2, 130–35; Joe Alvarado, interview, 1977, Phoenix, Phoenix History Project, TP, AHSCAD; Val Cordova, interview, 1977, Phoenix, Phoenix History Project, TP, AHSCAD; Charles Lama Jr., interview, 1977, Phoenix, Phoenix History Project, TP, AHSCAD.

42. *Arizona Republic*, April 29, 1984.

43. John E. Crow, *Mexican Americans in Contemporary Arizona: A Social Demographic View* (San Francisco: R and E Research, 1975), 78–79, 83–84.

44. ASU official quoted in *New Times*, January 6, 1987; Lincoln Ragsdale Sr. and Eleanor Ragsdale, interview; Universal, *Dr. Lincoln Johnson Ragsdale, Sr.*, 3; Edward Valenzuela quoted in Crow, *Mexican Americans*, 78–79, 83–84.

45. Taylor, *In Search of the Racial Frontier*, 292–93.

46. Robert Alan Goldberg, "Racial Change on the Southern Periphery: The Case of San Antonio, Texas, 1960–1965," *Journal of Southern History* 49, no. 3 (1983): 362, 370.

47. Action Citizens Committee, "Pena Supports Opportunity for Underprivileged Youth"; GPCCU, *To Secure These Rights*, 16; Pena, Testimony on Migrants in Phoenix, 74–75; Lincoln Ragsdale Sr. and Eleanor Ragsdale, interview; Lincoln Ragsdale Sr., interview; Taylor, *In Search of the Racial Frontier*, 292–93; Goldberg, "Racial Change," 362, 370.

48. Richard W. Thomas, *Understanding Interracial Unity: A Study of U.S. Race Relations* (London: Sage, 1996), 201.

49. *New Times*, June 11, 1986; Adank, "Chicano Activism," 246–65; Luckingham, *Minorities in Phoenix*, 60; Action Citizens Committee, "Pena Supports Opportunity for Underprivileged Youth"; GPCCU, *To Secure These Rights*, 16; Pena, Testimony on Migrants in Phoenix, 74–75; Lincoln Ragsdale Sr. and Eleanor Ragsdale, interview; Lincoln Ragsdale Sr., interview.

## 7. THE STRUGGLE FOR RACIAL EQUALITY IN PHOENIX

1. Kelley, *Yo' Mama's Disfunktional!* 1–89; Steele, *Content of Our Character*, 1–20, 111–48; Cornel West, *Race Matters* (New York: Vintage, 1994), 71–90; Michael Eric Dyson, *Race Rules: Navigating the Color Line* (New York: Vintage Books, 1997), 150–95; Lincoln Ragsdale Sr. and Eleanor Ragsdale, interview; Lincoln Ragsdale Sr., interview; Luckingham, *Minorities in Phoenix*, 173–90; Crudup, "African Americans in Arizona," 327–86; VanderMeer, *Phoenix Rising*, 43–73.

2. Kelley, *Yo' Mama's Disfunktional!* 1–89; Steele, *Content of Our Character*, 1–20, 111–48; West, *Race Matters*, 71–90; Dyson, *Race Rules*, 150–95; Connerly, *Creating Equal*, 22–86; Hamblin, *Pick a Better Country*, 13–32, 139–56; Sowell, *Race and Culture*, 81–186.

3. Lincoln Ragsdale Sr. and Eleanor Ragsdale, interview; Lincoln Ragsdale Sr., interview. For additional examples of black neoconservative political philosophies, see Carnoy, *Faded Dreams*; Thomas Sowell, *Preferential Politics: An International Perspective* (New York: William Morrow, 1990); Joseph Perkins, ed., *A Conservative Agenda for Black Americans* (Washington DC: Heritage Foundation, 1987). For examples of traditional black liberal political philosophies, see Eddie Stone, *Jessie Jackson: An Intimate Portrait* (Los Angeles: Holloway House, 1981); Randall Robinson, *The Debt: What America Owes to Blacks* (New York: Dutton, 2000); Mary Francis Berry, *Black Resistance, White Law: A History of Constitutional Racism in America* (New York: Viking Penguin, 1995); Cornel West, *The Cornel West Reader* (New York: Basic Civitas Books, 1999).

4. U.S. Bureau of the Census, *Population of the United States*, 1980, 1990. See also Data Network for Human Services, *Demographic Trends in Maricopa County: Cities, Towns and Places, 1880–1990* (Phoenix: Data Network for Human Services, 1992).

5. *Arizona Republic*, March 1, 1984, June 16, 1985; *Phoenix Gazette*, January 19, 1983, March 9, 1984, March 16, 1986, April 6, 1987; *New Times*, December 31, 1986; Franklin, McCummings, and Tynan, *Minorities in the Sunbelt*, 62–81, 135–39.

6. Universal, *Dr. Lincoln Johnson Ragsdale, Sr.*, 3; Lincoln Ragsdale Sr. and Eleanor Ragsdale, interview; Lincoln Ragsdale Sr., interview; Ely, interview.

7. Boye De Mente, "Living Black in Phoenix," *Phoenix*, September 1982, 102–5, 125–26.

8. Lincoln Ragsdale Sr. and Eleanor Ragsdale, interview; Lincoln Ragsdale Sr., interview; Lincoln Ragsdale Jr., interview, April 6, 2000; Luckingham, *Minorities in Phoenix*, 184.

9. Campbell, interview by author; Massey and Denton, *American Apartheid*, 1–83; William Julius Wilson, *When Work Disappears: The World of the New Urban Poor* (New York: Alfred A. Knopf, 1996), 1–50.

10. Campbell, interview by author.

11. *Arizona Informant*, February 9, 1972.

12. *Arizona Informant*, February 9, 1972.

13. Lincoln Ragsdale Sr. and Eleanor Ragsdale, interview; Lincoln Ragsdale Sr., interview; Lincoln Ragsdale Jr., interview, April 6, 2000; Gene Blue quoted in *Arizona Informant*, February 9, 1972.

14. De Mente, "Living Black in Phoenix," 102–5, 125–26.

15. Andrews, questionnaire.

16. Lincoln Ragsdale Sr. and Eleanor Ragsdale, interview; Lincoln Ragsdale Sr., interview; Lincoln Ragsdale Jr., interview, April 6, 2000.

17. Ragsdale Madrid, interview, August 11, 2003; Ragsdale Madrid, interview, September 16, 2003.

18. Lincoln Ragsdale Jr., interview, April 6, 2000; Ragsdale Madrid, interview, August 11, 2003; Ragsdale Madrid, interview, September 16, 2003.

19. Lincoln Ragsdale Jr., interview, April 6, 2000; Ragsdale Madrid, interview, August 11, 2003.

20. *Phoenix Gazette*, March 24, June 17, 1987, July 17, 1989; *Arizona Republic*, March 24, May 31, June 12, 1987.

21. Andrews, questionnaire.

22. Quoted in Luckingham, *Minorities in Phoenix*, 183.

23. Quoted in *Arizona Republic*, September 19, 1984; *Arizona Republic*, February 22, 27, 1985, March 23, May 31, June 12, 1987, May 5, 1988, April 30, June 12, August 20, 1989, January 13, April 2, 1990, August 8, October 27, December 10–13, 19–20, 29, 1991, June 13, 1992.

24. Samuel Myers, *Civil Rights and Race Relations in the Post Reagan-Bush Era* (New York: Praeger, 1997), 1–28, 217–25.

25. Myers, *Civil Rights*, 217–25.

26. William Julius Wilson, *The Truly Disadvantaged: The Inner City, the Underclass, and Public Policy* (Chicago: University of Chicago Press, 1987), 220–29; Myers, *Civil Rights*, 1–28, 217–25.

27. Kelley, *Yo' Mama's Disfunktional!* 7–8.

28. Wilson, *When Work Disappears*, 3–50.

29. *Arizona Informant*, August 20, October 8, 1980, February 27, May 1, 1985; *Phoenix Gazette*, March 30–31, 1983, April 1, June 15, July 3, 1984, March 13, 1986, March 24, June 17, 1987, July 17, 1989, March 16, June 28, August 3, 8, November 30, 1990, December 25, 1991; *Arizona Republic*, September 19, 1984, February 22, 27, 1985, March 24, May 31, June 12, 1987, May 5, 1988, April 30, June 12, August 20, 1989, January 13, April 2, 1990, August 8, October 27, December 10–13, 19–20, 29, 1991, June 13, 1992; *New Times*, December 19, 1984, February 13, April 24, 1991.

30. Harold M. Baron, "The Web of Urban Racism," in *Institutional Racism in America*, ed. Louis Knowles and Kenneth Prewitt, 134–35 (New York: Prentice Hall, 1969). Despite the fact that Baron made this argument in 1969, it is was still applicable in 1980, 1990, and 2000.

31. Baron, "Web of Urban Racism," 144.

32. Baron, "Web of Urban Racism," 144–45.

33. Baron, "Web of Urban Racism," 145.

34. Baron, "Web of Urban Racism," 145.

35. Wilson, *When Work Disappears*, 3–50; Kelley, *Yo' Mama's Disfunktional!* 1–13.

36. Clovis Campbell Sr. quoted in *Arizona Informant*, August 20, October 8, 1980; Junius Bowman quoted in *Arizona Informant*, February 27, May 1, 1985.

37. Ragsdale, "Minority Entrepreneurship," 80; Fannie Barrier Williams,

speech given to the National Negro Business League, Tuskegee, Alabama, 1903, transcript, Washington Collection, Tuskegee University, Tuskegee; Lincoln Ragsdale Sr. and Eleanor Ragsdale, interview.

38. Washington, *Up from Slavery*, 159–73; Edmund David Cronon, *Moses: The Story of Marcus Garvey and the Universal Negro Improvement Association* (Madison: University of Wisconsin Press, 1969), 39–72; Clegg, *Original Man*, 235–65; Malcolm X, *Autobiography*, 215–39; Ragsdale, "Minority Entrepreneurship," 80.

39. *Arizona Informant*, August 20, October 8, 1980, February 27, May 1, 1985; *Phoenix Gazette*, March 30–31, 1983, April 1, June 15, July 3, 1984, March 13, 1986, March 24, June 17, 1987, July 17, 1989, March 16, June 28, August 3, 8, November 30, 1990, December 25, 1991; *Arizona Republic*, September 19, 1984, February 22, 27, 1985, March 24, May 31, June 12, 1987, May 5, 1988, April 30, June 12, August 20, 1989, January 13, April 2, 1990, August 8, October 27, December 10–13, 19–20, 29, 1991, June 13, 1992; *New Times*, December 19, 1984, February 13, April 24, 1991; Ragsdale, "Minority Entrepreneurship," 80.

40. Lincoln Ragsdale Sr. and Eleanor Ragsdale, interview; Baker, "Lincoln Ragsdale," 99; *Arizona Republic*, August 2–3, 1990.

41. Lincoln Ragsdale Sr. and Eleanor Ragsdale, interview; Baker, "Lincoln Ragsdale," 99. For an illuminating discussion of predominantly white social clubs and the extent to which they have served as hubs of white power and privilege, see Lawrence Otis Graham, *A Member of the Club: Reflections on Life in a Racially Polarized World* (New York: Perennial Press, 1996).

42. Lincoln Ragsdale Sr. and Eleanor Ragsdale, interview.

43. Lincoln Ragsdale Sr. and Eleanor Ragsdale, interview; Keven Willey quoted in *Arizona Republic*, August 2, 1990.

44. Quoted in Luckingham, *Minorities in Phoenix*, 184–85.

45. *Arizona Republic*, August 2, 1990.

46. *Arizona Republic*, August 2, 1990.

47. *Arizona Republic*, August 2, 1990.

48. Lincoln Ragsdale Sr. and Eleanor Ragsdale, interview.

49. Baker, "Lincoln Ragsdale," 99; *Arizona Republic*, August 2–3, 1990; Lincoln Ragsdale Sr. and Eleanor Ragsdale, interview; Parliament, "Chocolate City," on *Parliament: Tear the Roof Off, 1974–1980*, sound recording on CD, New York: Polygram Records, 1993, original recording on LP, Polygram Records, 1975; Eleanor Ragsdale, interview, Spring 1990.

50. Ragsdale quoted in *Arizona Republic*, August 31, 1990. Estimates for concession contracts in fiscal year 1991 were based upon the total airport business gross earnings of fiscal year 1990. During that year the concession grossed $12 million.

51. *Arizona Republic*, September 22, 1990.

52. Skip Rimza and Lincoln Ragsdale quoted in *Arizona Republic*, September 22, 1990.

53. Lincoln Ragsdale quoted in *Arizona Republic*, September 22, 1990.

54. Luckingham, *Minorities in Phoenix*, 186. See also June Mays, Sylvia Anderson, and Terri Dunlap, eds. *Greater Shiloh Missionary Baptist Church: From Then until Now, 73rd Anniversary Celebration* (Phoenix: Greater Shiloh Missionary Baptist Church, 1997).

55. Lincoln Ragsdale, interview, "A Tribute to Lincoln Ragsdale."

56. *Arizona Informant*, August 20, October 8, 1980, February 27, May 1, 1985.

57. *Arizona Informant*, August 20, October 8, 1980, February 27, May 1, 1985; *Arizona Republic*, August 28, 1993.

58. Jewelle Taylor Gibbs, *Race and Justice: Rodney King and O. J. Simpson in a House Divided* (Indianapolis IN: Jossey-Bass, 1996), 1–96.

59. *Arizona Republic*, March 19, 1999.

60. *Arizona Republic*, September 13, 1991, August 28, 1993.

61. *Arizona Republic*, August 28, 1993.

62. *Arizona Republic*, August 28, 1993; Lincoln Ragsdale Sr. and Eleanor Ragsdale, interview; Campbell, interview by author; U.S. Bureau of the Census, *Population of the United States*, 1970.

63. Lincoln Ragsdale quoted in *Arizona Republic*, August 28, 1993, June 11, 1995; Lincoln Ragsdale Sr. and Eleanor Ragsdale, interview.

64. Jeremy I. Levitt, letter to author, February 4, 2001; Luckingham, *Minorities in Phoenix*, 181–82.

65. Levitt, letter; Joseph Stoker, "Are Blacks Losing Hard-Won Ground?" *Phoenix*, May 1985, 24.

66. Luckingham, *Minorities in Phoenix*, 187.

67. Kelley, *Yo' Mama's Disfunktional!* 7–8, 91; Sowell, *Race and Culture*, 81–186.

68. Kelley, *Yo' Mama's Disfunktional!* 91; West, *Race Matters*, 73–90.

69. Harris, *First 100 Years*, 114–15.

70. Quoted in Luckingham, *Minorities in Phoenix*, 187.

71. *Arizona Republic*, January 1, 1993.

72. *Arizona Informant*, January 1985, April 11, July 25, October 3, November 14, 21, 1990, January 16, August 21, 1991.

73. *Arizona Informant*, February 16, 1972.

74. Warren Stewart quoted in Crudup, "African Americans in Arizona," 379; *Arizona Informant*, January 1985, April 11, July 25, October 3, November 14, 21, 1990, January 16, August 21, 1991; *Arizona Republic*, May 10, 1986, March 23, April 4, May 28, 1987, September 26, December 22, 1989.

75. Warren Stewart quoted in Crudup, "African Americans in Arizona," 380; Iverson, *Barry Goldwater*, 231.

76. *Arizona Informant*, January 1985, April 11, July 25, October 3, November 14, 21, 1990, January 16, August 21, 1991; *Arizona Republic*, May 10, 1986, March 23, April 4, May 28, 1987, September 26, December 22, 1989.

77. *Arizona Republic*, November 8, 15, 1990, January 22, May 15, September 13, November 3, 1991, January 17–21, 1992, January 1, 1993; *Phoenix Gazette*, March 30, May 17, 1990, February 5, 7, May 15, August 8–15, 19, December 2, 1991, June 6, 1992.

78. *Arizona Republic*, November 8, 15, 1990, January 22, May 15, September 13, November 3, 1991, January 17–21, 1992, January 1, 1993; *Phoenix Gazette*, March 30, May 17, 1990, February 5, 7, May 15, August 8–15, 19, December 2, 1991, June 6, 1992; *New Times*, May 25, November 14, 1990, February 27, April 24, 30, 1991, November 4, 1992.

79. *Arizona Republic*, November 8, 15, 1990, January 22, May 15, September 13, November 3, 1991, January 17–21, 1992, January 1, 1993; *Phoenix Gazette*, March 30, May 17, 1990, February 5, 7, May 15, August 8–15, 19, December 2, 1991, June 6, 1992.

80. Paul Johnson quoted in *Arizona Informant*, January 16, 1991; Art Hamilton and Henry Barnwell quoted in *Arizona Informant*, August 21, 1991.

81. Paul Johnson quoted in *Arizona Republic*, January 1, 1993; Lincoln Ragsdale quoted in Baker, "Lincoln Ragsdale," 99.

82. Eleanor Ragsdale quoted in Baker, "Lincoln Ragsdale," 99; Lincoln Ragsdale quoted in Baker, "Lincoln Ragsdale," 99.

83. Cody Williams quoted in *Arizona Republic*, January 20, 2003; Cody Williams, interview by author, August 20, 2002, Phoenix, TP, TS, ACASU.

84. U.S. Bureau of the Census, *Population of the United States*, 2000; Leah Landrum Taylor quoted in *Arizona Republic*, January 20, 2003.

85. U.S. Bureau of the Census, *Population of the United States*, 2000.

86. Eleanor Ragsdale quoted in Baker, "Lincoln Ragsdale," 99.

87. Lincoln Ragsdale quoted in Baker, "Lincoln Ragsdale," 99.

88. Lincoln Ragsdale quoted in Baker, "Lincoln Ragsdale," 99.

89. Eleanor Ragsdale, interview by NewsChannel 3, KTVK, February 16, 1995, "A Tribute to Lincoln Ragsdale."

CONCLUSION

1. Lincoln Ragsdale quoted in Luckingham, *Phoenix*, 69; Universal, *Dr. Lincoln Johnson Ragsdale, Sr.*, 3–5; Eleanor Ragsdale, interview, "A Tribute to Lincoln Ragsdale"; Lincoln Ragsdale Sr. and Eleanor Ragsdale, interview; Lincoln Ragsdale Sr., interview.

2. Baker, "Lincoln Ragsdale," 97–99. See also Woodson, *Negro Profes-*

*sional Man*; Summerville, *Educating Black Doctors*; McNeil, *Groundwork*; Hine, *Black Women in White*; Gatewood, *Aristocrats of Color*; Shaw, *What a Women Ought to Be*.

3. Baker, "Lincoln Ragsdale," 97–99. See also Woodson, *Negro Professional Man*; Summerville, *Educating Black Doctors*; McNeil, *Groundwork*; Hine, *Black Women in White*; Gatewood, *Aristocrats of Color*; Shaw, *What a Women Ought to Be*.

4. Universal, *Dr. Lincoln Johnson Ragsdale, Sr.*, 3–5; Eleanor Ragsdale, interview, "A Tribute to Lincoln Ragsdale"; Lincoln Ragsdale Sr. and Eleanor Ragsdale, interview; Lincoln Ragsdale Sr., interview.

5. Lincoln Ragsdale Sr., interview; Eleanor Ragsdale, interview, "A Tribute to Lincoln Ragsdale".

6. Baker, "Lincoln Ragsdale," 97–99; *Arizona Republic*, September 29, 2002; Whitaker, " 'Creative Conflict,' " 165–68; Universal, *Dr. Lincoln Johnson Ragsdale, Sr.*, 3–5; Eleanor Ragsdale, interview, "A Tribute to Lincoln Ragsdale"; Lincoln Ragsdale Sr. and Eleanor Ragsdale, interview; Lincoln Ragsdale Sr., interview.

7. Quoted in Joe T. Darden, "Choosing Neighbors and Neighborhoods: The Role of Race in Housing Preference," in *Divided Neighborhoods: Changing Patterns of Racial Segregation*, ed. Gary A. Tobin, 15–42 (Beverly Hills CA: Sage, 1987). On black migration before and after World War II, see Nicholas Lemann, *The Promised Land: The Great Black Migration and How It Changed America* (New York: Random House, 1991).

8. Lloyd McKeethen, interview by NewsChannel 3, KTVK, February 16, 1995, "A Tribute to Lincoln Ragsdale."

9. Baker, "Lincoln Ragsdale," 97–99; *Arizona Republic*, September 29, 2002; Whitaker, " 'Creative Conflict,' " 165–68; Universal, *Dr. Lincoln Johnson Ragsdale, Sr.*, 3–5; Eleanor Ragsdale, interview, "A Tribute to Lincoln Ragsdale"; Lincoln Ragsdale Sr. and Eleanor Ragsdale, interview; Lincoln Ragsdale Sr., interview.

10. Whitaker, " 'Creative Conflict,' " 165–68; Universal, *Dr. Lincoln Johnson Ragsdale, Sr.*, 3–5; Eleanor Ragsdale, interview, "A Tribute to Lincoln Ragsdale"; Lincoln Ragsdale Sr. and Eleanor Ragsdale, interview; Lincoln Ragsdale Sr., interview.

11. *Arizona Sun*, May 9, 1957.

12. Rosales, *Chicano!* xxi–xxiii; *New Times*, June 11, 1986; Adank, "Chicano Activism," 246–65.

13. Rosales, *Chicano!* xxi–xxiii; *New Times*, June 17, 1986; Adank, "Chicano Activism," 246–66.

14. Quoted in City of Phoenix Commission on Housing, *Housing in Phoenix*, 70–74; Luckingham, *Minorities in Phoenix*, 230.

15. Melcher, "Blacks and Whites Together," 211; Hine, Hine, and Harold, *African American Odyssey*, 563–64.

16. *Arizona Republic*, June 12, 1995.

17. Standley, "Role of Black Women," 183–84; Baker, "Lincoln Ragsdale," 97–98; Lincoln Ragsdale Sr. and Eleanor Ragsdale, interview; Emily Ragsdale, interview; Dickey, interview.

18. Quoted in the *Phoenix Gazette*, March 21, 1993. See also Wilson, *Truly Disadvantaged*; Andrew Hacker, *Money: Who Has How Much and Why* (New York: Simon and Schuster, 1998); Hacker, *Two Nations*.

19. Lynette Myles Gibbs quoted in *Phoenix Gazette*, February 11, 1993.

20. Lincoln Ragsdale Sr. and Eleanor Ragsdale, interview; West, *Race Matters*, 35–49.

21. West, *Race Matters*, 35–49; Hine, Hine, and Harold, *African American Odyssey*, 563–64.

22. West, *Race Matters*, 35–49.

23. Baron, "Web of Urban Racism," 134–35; Wilson, *Truly Disadvantaged*.

24. Leonard Gordon and Albert J. Mayer, "Housing Segregation and Housing Conditions for Hispanics in Phoenix and Other Southwestern Cities," in *Urban Housing Segregation of Minorities in Western Europe and the United States*, ed. in Elizabeth D. Huttman, 285–300 (Durham NC: Duke University Press, 1991); Nicolas Lemann, "Healing the Ghettos: A Vision of the Possible in Race Relations," *Atlantic*, March 1991, 22–24; Hacker, *Two Nations*; William Julius Wilson, *The Declining Significance of Race: Blacks and Changing American Institutions* (Chicago: University of Chicago Press, 1978); Alphonse Pickney, *The Myth of Black Progress* (Cambridge: Harvard University Press, 1984).

25. Whitaker, " 'Creative Conflict,' " 165–68; Universal, *Dr. Lincoln Johnson Ragsdale, Sr.*, 3–5; Eleanor Ragsdale, interview, "A Tribute to Lincoln Ragsdale"; Lincoln Ragsdale Sr. and Eleanor Ragsdale, interview; Lincoln Ragsdale Sr., interview; Luckingham, *Minorities in Phoenix*, 207.

26. Whitaker, " 'Creative Conflict,' " 165–68; Universal, *Dr. Lincoln Johnson Ragsdale, Sr.*, 3–5; Eleanor Ragsdale, interview, "A Tribute to Lincoln Ragsdale"; Lincoln Ragsdale Sr. and Eleanor Ragsdale, interview; Lincoln Ragsdale Sr., interview; *Phoenix Gazette*, February 11, 1993.

27. *Phoenix Gazette*, February 11, 1993.

28. Warren H. Stewart, interview by NewsChannel 3, KTVK, February 16, 1995, "A Tribute to Lincoln Ragsdale"; *Arizona Republic*, June 12, 1995.

29. Lincoln Ragsdale Jr., interview, April 6, 2000.

30. Lincoln Ragsdale Sr., interview.

31. Ragsdale, "Minority Entrepreneurship," 71–72.

32. Eleanor Ragsdale, interview, "A Tribute to Lincoln Ragsdale"; Lincoln

Ragsdale Sr. and Eleanor Ragsdale, interview; Jenkins and Hine, *Question of Manhood*, xi–xvii; Gilmore, *Gender and Jim Crow*, 61–90; *Arizona Sun*, July 19, 1962; Baker, "Lincoln Ragsdale," 98; Brooks, interview by Melcher; Brooks, interview by author; Lincoln Ragsdale Sr., interview.

33. Universal, *Dr. Lincoln Johnson Ragsdale, Sr.*, 3–5; Universal, *Mrs. Eleanor Dickey Ragsdale*, 14–17.

34. Eleanor Ragsdale, interview, Spring 1990.

35. Universal, *Dr. Lincoln Johnson Ragsdale, Sr.*, 4–5; Universal, *Mrs. Eleanor Dickey Ragsdale*, 16–17.

36. Universal, *Dr. Lincoln Johnson Ragsdale, Sr.*, 3–5; Eleanor Ragsdale, interview, "A Tribute to Lincoln Ragsdale"; Lincoln Ragsdale Sr. and Eleanor Ragsdale, interview; Lincoln Ragsdale Sr., interview; Universal, *Mrs. Eleanor Dickey Ragsdale*, 16–17; Luckingham, *Minorities in Phoenix*, 208.

37. Taylor, *In Search of the Racial Frontier*, 17–23; Broussard, *Black San Francisco*, 1–7; De Graaf, "Significant Steps," 1; Luckingham, *Minorities in Phoenix*, 157–71; Universal, *Dr. Lincoln Johnson Ragsdale, Sr.*, 5.

38. Taylor, *In Search of the Racial Frontier*, 17–23; De Graaf, "Significant Steps," 1; Luckingham, *Minorities in Phoenix*, 157–71; Universal, *Dr. Lincoln Johnson Ragsdale, Sr.*, 5.

# BIBLIOGRAPHY

Primary Sources
Archives and Manuscript Collections
Proceedings, Statutes, and Reports
Letters, Interviews, and Questionnaires
Secondary Sources

PRIMARY SOURCES

### Archives and Manuscript Collections

Arizona Collection, Hayden Library, Arizona State University, Tempe
Arizona Historical Foundation, Hayden Library, Arizona State University, Tempe
Arizona Historical Society and Museum at Papago Park, Central Arizona Division, Tempe
Chicana/o Collection, Hayden Library, Arizona State University, Tempe
Department of Manuscripts and Archives, Arizona State Capitol, Phoenix
Department of Manuscripts and Archives, Oklahoma State Capitol, Oklahoma City
George Washington Carver Museum and Cultural Center, Phoenix
Library of Michigan, Lansing
National Archives, Washington DC
Phoenix Museum of History, Phoenix
Southwest Collections, Hayden Library, Arizona State University, Tempe
The Washington Collection, Tuskegee University, Tuskegee, Alabama

### Proceedings, Statues, and Reports

*Arizona Reports: Reports of Cases Argued and Determined in the Supreme Court of the Territory of Arizona, to April 16, 1893*, vol. 5. Phoenix: Arizona State Capitol, Department of Manuscripts and Archives.

Arizona Territorial Legislature, Comp. Laws, 1865, C. 30: Arizona Territorial Legislature Comp. Laws, 1877, C. 30, Sec. 3. Phoenix: Arizona State Capitol, Department of Manuscripts and Archives.

Bennet, Mary. "Recording the History of Phoenix Memorial Hospital." Arizona Collection of the Hayden Library, Arizona State University, Tempe.

City of Phoenix. *Chronological History of* LEAP. Phoenix: City of Phoenix, 1967.

City of Phoenix Commission on Housing, *Housing in Phoenix*. Phoenix: City of Phoenix, 1973.

City of Phoenix Human Rights Commission, *First Annual Report, 1963–1964*. Phoenix: City of Phoenix, 1964.

City of Phoenix Planning Department. *A Community Profile*. Phoenix: City of Phoenix Planning Department, 1985.

Data Network for Human Services. *Demographic Trends in Maricopa County: Cities, Towns and Places, 1880–1990*. Phoenix: Data Network for Human Services, 1992.

Garrett, Yvonne Garrett, "Chicano Politics in the Phoenix Metropolitan Area." Typescript. Chicano Collection, Hayden Library, Arizona State University, Tempe.

Green, George M., ed. *Arizona Black Leadership Journal: Motivating and Leading a New Generation*. Tempe: Omega Psi Phi Fraternity, Inc., 1991. Arizona Historical Foundation, Hayden Library, Arizona State University.

*Hearings before the United States Commission on Civil Rights, Phoenix, Arizona, February 3, 1962*. Washington DC: Government Printing Office, 1962.

"History of Blacks in Phoenix Notes." Geoffrey P. Mawn Files, Arizona Historical Foundation, Hayden Library, Arizona State University, Tempe.

Lee, Ulysses G. *The Employment of Negro Troops*. Washington DC: Government Printing Office, 1966.

Oklahoma Legislature. *Session Laws of Oklahoma, 1907–1908*. Oklahoma City: Oklahoma State Capitol, Department of Manuscripts and Archives.

"Political Activities of the Negro Before Statehood." Oklahoma WPA Records, Oklahoma Historical Society, Oklahoma City.

Ragsdale, Lincoln, Sr. Enlisted Record of and Report of Separation: Honorable Discharge WD, AGO Form 53–55, U.S. Army Air Corps, November 19, 1945, Washington DC.

Thul, Jackie. "Blacks in Arizona from Early Settlement to 1990: A Historic Context Study." Prepared for the Arizona State Historic Preservation Office, 1993. Arizona Collection of the Hayden Library, Arizona State University, Tempe.

U.S. Bureau of the Census, *Population of the United States*, 1920, 1940, 1950, 1960, 1970, 1980, 1990, 2000.

U.S. Department of the Interior, National Park Service in Cooperation with the Phoenix Historic Preservation Commission. *Encanto-Palm-*

*Croft Historic District Publication.* National Register of Historic Places Inventory-Nomination Form, Continuation Sheet 81, Item Number 8.

U.S. Navy. "Commanding Officer Praises Negro Personnel Who Served at Port Chicago after Explosion Monday Night, 20 July 1944." Navy Department Press Releases, July 16–31, 1944, folder, Box 55, World War II Command File, Operational Archives Branch, U.S. Naval Historical Center, Washington DC.

Works Progress Administration, Division of Professional Service Projects. *Narrative Report on Arizona Works Progress Administration*, ed. W. J. Jamisson, State Administrator. Washington DC: Government Printing Office, 1939.

### Letters, Interviews, and Questionnaires

Alvarado, Joe. Interview, 1977, Phoenix. Tape recording. Phoenix History Project, Arizona Historical Society, Central Arizona Division, Tempe.

Andrews, Judis R., Sr. Questionnaire to author, April 18, 2000, Phoenix. In author's possession.

Barber, John. Interview by Maria Hernandez, Summer 1981, Phoenix. Tape recording. Arizona Collection, Hayden Library, Arizona State University, Tempe.

Brooks, George B. Interview by author, April 6, 2000, Phoenix. Transcript. Arizona Collection, Hayden Library, Arizona State University, Tempe.

———. Interview by Mary Melcher, January 31, 1990, Phoenix. Tape recording. Oral History Collection, Arizona Historical Society, Central Arizona Division, Tempe.

Campbell, Clovis, Sr. Interview by author, August 6, 1996, Phoenix. Tape recording in author's possession.

———. Interview by Dallas Teat, March 2004, Phoenix. Video. George Washington Carver Museum and Cultural Center, Phoenix.

———. Interview by Mary Melcher, June 1, 2001, Phoenix. Tape recording. Oral History Collection, Arizona Historical Society, Central Arizona Division, Tempe.

Copeland, Madge Johnson. Interview by Maria Hernandez, Summer 1981, Phoenix. Tape recording and transcript. Arizona Collection, Hayden Library, Arizona State University, Tempe.

Corbin, William. Interview by author, March 23, 2004, Phoenix. Video. George Washington Carver Museum and Cultural Center, Phoenix.

Cordova, Val. Interview, 1977, Phoenix. Tape recording. Phoenix History Project, Arizona Historical Society, Central Arizona Division, Tempe.

Craig, Carl E. Interview, 1978, Phoenix. Tape recording. Phoenix History Project, Arizona Historical Society, Central Arizona Division, Tempe.

Crump, Princess. Interview by author, July 2002, Phoenix. Tape recording and transcript. Arizona Collection, Hayden Library, Arizona State
University, Tempe.

Daniels, Hayzel B. Interview by Richard Harris, Spring 1983, Tucson.
Transcript. Arizona Historical Society, Southern Arizona Division, Tucson.

Dickey, William D. Interview by author, April 6, 2000, Phoenix. Transcript. Arizona Collection, Hayden Library, Arizona State University,
Tempe.

Ely, Herbert L. Interview by author, July 17, 2000, Phoenix. Transcript.
Arizona Collection, Hayden Library, Arizona State University, Tempe.
————. Interview by Dallas Teat, March 11, 2004. Video. George Wash-
ington Carver Museum and Cultural Center, Phoenix.

Finn, Ruth. Interview by Dallas Teat, February 2004, Phoenix. Video.
George Washington Carver Museum and Cultural Center, Phoenix.

Flores, Raymond. Interview by author, March 2004, Phoenix. Video.
George Washington Carver Museum and Cultural Center, Phoenix.

Garcia, Pete. Interview, 1978. Tape recording. Phoenix History Project,
Arizona Historical Society, Central Arizona Division, Tempe.

Goode, Calvin. Interview by author, July 31, 2002, Phoenix. Transcript.
Arizona Collection, Hayden Library, Arizona State University, Tempe.

Goode, Georgie. Interview by author, July 31, 2002, Phoenix. Transcript.
Arizona Collection, Hayden Library, Arizona State University, Tempe.

Grigsby, J. Eugene, Jr. Interview by author, March 2004, Phoenix. Video.
George Washington Carver Museum and Cultural Center, Phoenix.
————. Interview by Mary Melcher, February 12, 1990, Phoenix. Tape
recording. Arizona Historical Foundation, Hayden Library, Arizona
State University, Tempe.

Grigsby, Thomasena. Interview by Mary Melcher, February 7, 1990,
Phoenix. Tape recording. Arizona Historical Foundation, Hayden Library, Arizona State University, Tempe.

Johnson, Michael. Interview by author, August 2002, Phoenix. Tape
recording and transcript. Arizona Collection, Hayden Library, Arizona
State University, Tempe.

King, Ed, Rev. Interview by Thomas Summerhill and author, November
1999, East Lansing MI. Tape recording. Vincent Voice Library, Michigan State University, East Lansing.

King, Irene McClellan. Interview by Maria Hernandez, Summer 1981,
Phoenix. Tape recording. Arizona Collection, Hayden Library, Arizona
State University, Tempe.

Lama, Charles, Jr. Interview, 1977, Phoenix. Tape recording. Phoenix

History Project, Arizona Historical Society, Central Arizona Division, Tempe.

Levitt, Jeremy I. Letter to author, February 4, 2001.

Mahoney, William. Interview by Mary Melcher, February 16, 1990, Phoenix. Tape recording. Arizona Historical Foundation, Hayden Library at Arizona State University, Tempe.

Orduna, Edward F. Interview, 1977. Tape recording. Phoenix History Project, Arizona Historical Society, Central Arizona Division, Tempe.

Ragsdale, Eleanor. Interview by Mary Melcher, June 16, 1991, Phoenix. Tape recording. Arizona Historical Society, Central Arizona Division, Tempe.

———. Interview by Mary Melcher, Spring 1990, Phoenix. Tape recording. Arizona Historical Society, Central Arizona Division, Tempe.

Ragsdale, Emily. Interview by author, April 6, 2000, Phoenix. Tape recording and transcript. Arizona Collection, Hayden Library, Arizona State University, Tempe.

Ragsdale, Hartwell, Jr. Interview by author, June 6, 2002, San Diego CA. Tape recording and transcript. Arizona Collection, Hayden Library, Arizona State University, Tempe.

Ragsdale, Hartwell, III. Interview by author, June 6, 2002, San Diego CA. Tape recording and transcript. Arizona Collection, Hayden Library, Arizona State University, Tempe.

Ragsdale, Lincoln, Jr. Interview by author, April 6, 2000, Phoenix. Tape recording and transcript. Arizona Collection, Hayden Library, Arizona State University, Tempe.

———. Interview by author, June 6, 2002, San Diego CA. Tape recording and transcript. Arizona Collection, Hayden Library, Arizona State University, Tempe.

———. Telephone interview by author, July 2003. Transcript in author's possession.

Ragsdale, Lincoln, Sr. Interview by Mary Melcher, April 8, 1990, Phoenix. Tape recording. Arizona Historical Foundation, Hayden Library, Arizona State University, Tempe.

———. Letter to Lincoln Ragsdale Jr., ca. 1991. In author's possession.

Ragsdale, Lincoln, Sr., and Eleanor Ragsdale. Interview by Dean E. Smith, April 4 and November 3, 1990, Phoenix. Transcript. Arizona Collection, Hayden Library, Arizona State University, Tempe.

Ragsdale Madrid, Gwendolyn. Questionnaire to author, August 15, 2003, Phoenix. Arizona Collection, Hayden Library, Arizona State University, Tempe.

———. Telephone interview by author, August 11, 2003. Transcript in author's possession.

———. Telephone interview by author, September 16, 2003. Transcript in author's possession.

Waldman, Frances. Interview by Mary Melcher, January 31, 1990, Phoenix. Tape recording. Arizona Historical Foundation, Hayden Library, Arizona State University, Tempe.

Warren, Morrison. Interview, 1978. Tape recording. Arizona Collection, Hayden Library, Arizona State University, Tempe.

Williams, Cody. Interview by author, August 20, 2002, Phoenix. Tape recording and transcript. Arizona Collection, Hayden Library, Arizona State University, Tempe.

Williams, Travis. Interview by author, April 6, 2000, Phoenix. Tape recording and transcript. Arizona Collection, Hayden Library, Arizona State University, Tempe.

SECONDARY SOURCES

Abajian, James. *Black Contributions to the American West.* Boston: G. K. Hall, 1974.

Abbey, Sue Wilson. "The Ku Klux Klan in Arizona, 1921–1925." *Journal of Arizona History* 14 (Spring 1973): 10–30.

Abbot, Carl. *The Metropolitan Frontier: Cities in the Modern American West.* Tucson: University of Arizona Press, 1995.

Acuna, Rodolfo. *Occupied America: A History of Chicanos.* New York: Addison Wesley Longman, 1999.

Allen, Barbara, and William Lynwood Montell. *Using Oral Sources in Local Historical Research.* Nashville: American Association for State and Local History, 1981.

Allen, Robert L. *Black Awakening in Capitalist America.* Trenton NJ: Africa World Press, 1990.

———. *The Port Chicago Mutiny.* New York: Harper Trade, 1993.

American Broadcasting Company. *Amazing Grace: The Life of Martin Luther King, Jr. Like It Is.* New York: American Broadcasting Company, McGraw Hill Films, 1978.

Anderson, James D. *The Education of Blacks in the South, 1860–1935.* Chapel Hill: University of North Carolina Press, 1988.

Anderson, Karen. "Work, Gender, and Power in the American West." *Pacific Historical Review* 61 (1992): 481–99.

Anderson, Terry H. *The Sixties,* 2nd ed. New York: Pearson Longmann, 2004.

Armitage, Susan, Susan Banfield, Theresa Smart, and Jacobus Smart. "Black Women and Their Communities in Colorado." *Frontiers* 2 (1977): 45–51.

Armitage, Susan, and Elizabeth Jameson, eds. *The Women's West*. Norman: University of Oklahoma Press, 1987.

Aron, Kris. "Chicanos por la Causa: Developing Leadership for the Future." *Phoenix*, December 1984, 101–35.

Atkinson, Paul. *Horizon: "Civil Rights."* Phoenix: Public Broadcasting System, KAET-TV Channel 8, January 17, 2000.

Auerbach, Jerold. *Unequal Justice: Lawyers and Social Change in Modern America*. New York: Oxford University Press, 1976.

Baker, Lori K. "Lincoln Ragsdale: The Man Who Refused to Be Invisible." *Phoenix Magazine*, January 1993, 97–99.

Bakken, Gordon Morris, and Brenda Farrington, eds. *The Gendered West*. New York: Garland, 2001.

Balkin, Jack M., ed. *What Brown v. Board of Education Should Have Said: The Nation's Top Legal Experts Rewrite America's Landmark Civil Rights Decision*. New York: New York University Press, 2002.

Bartlett, Michael H., Thomas M. Kolaz,, and David A. Gregory. *Archaeology in the City: A Hohokam Village in Phoenix, Arizona*. Tucson: University of Arizona Press, 1986.

Bataille, Gretchen M., ed. *Living the Dream in Arizona: The Legacy of Martin Luther King, Jr*. Tempe: Arizona Collections, Arizona State University, 1992.

Bennet, Leorone, Jr. *Before the Mayflower: A History of Black America*. Chicago: Johnson, 2003.

Berstein, Michael H. "Geographical Perspectives on Skid Row in Phoenix, Arizona." Master's thesis, Arizona State University, 1971.

Berry, Mary Francis. *Black Resistance, White Law: A History of Constitutional Racism in America*. New York: Viking Penguin, 1995.

Billington, Monroe Lee, and Roger D. Hardaway, eds. *African Americans on the Western Frontier*. Niwot: University of Colorado Press, 1998.

Blackwelder, Julia Kirk. *Women of the Depression: Caste and Culture in San Antonio, 1929–1039*. College Station: Texas A&M University Press, 1984.

Blee, Kathleen M. *Women of the Klan: Racism and Gender in the 1920s*. Berkeley: University of California Press, 1991.

Blum, John Morton. *V Was for Victory: Politics and American Culture during World War II*. New York: Harcourt Brace Jovanovich, 1996.

Bogue, Allan G. *Frederick Jackson Turner: Strange Roads Going Down*. Norman: University of Oklahoma Press, 1998.

Bramlett, Sharon. *Profile and Status of African American Women in Arizona: A Background Report to the 1994 Arizona Black Town Hall*. Tempe: College of Public Programs, Arizona State University, 1994.

Branch, Taylor. *Parting the Waters: America in the King Years, 1954–1963*. New York: Simon and Schuster, 1989.

———. *Pillar of Fire: America in the King Years, 1963–1965*. New York: Simon and Schuster, 1997.

Broussard, Albert S. *African-American Odyssey: The Stewarts, 1853–1963*. Lawrence: University of Press of Kansas, 1998.

———. *Black San Francisco: The Struggle for Racial Equality in the West, 1900–1954*. Lawrence: University Press of Kansas, 1993.

———. "Carlotta Stewart Lai: A Black Teacher in the Territory of Hawaii." *Hawaiian Journal of History* 24 (1990): 129–54.

Brown, Elaine. *A Taste of Power: A Black Woman's Story*. New York: Pantheon Books, 1992.

Brown, Malcolm, and Orin Cassmore. *Migratory Cotton Pickers in Arizona*. Washington DC: Government Printing Office, 1939.

Buni, Andrew. *Robert Vann of the Pittsburgh Courier*. Pittsburgh: University of Pittsburgh Press, 1974.

Campbell, Clovis C., Sr. *I Refused to Leave the "Hood."* Phoenix: Clovis C. Campbell Sr., 2003.

Carmichael, Stokely, and Charles V. Hamilton. *Black Power: The Politics of Liberation in America*. New York: Vintage, 1967.

Carnoy, Martin. *Faded Dreams: The Politics and Economics of Race in America*. Cambridge: Cambridge University Press, 1994.

Carroll, John M., ed. *The Black Military Experience in the American West*. New York: Liveright, 1974.

Carson, Clayborne. *In Struggle: SNCC and the Black Awakening of the 1960s*. Cambridge: Harvard University Press, 1995.

———. *Malcolm X: The FBI File*. Berkeley CA: Carroll and Gaff, 1991.

Casteneda, Antonia I. "Women of Color and the Rewriting of Western History: The Discourse, Politics, and Decolonization of History." *Pacific Historical Review* 61 (1992): 501–33.

Chafe, William H. *Civilities and Civil Rights: Greensboro, North Carolina and the Black Struggle for Equality*. New York: Oxford University Press, 1980.

Chanin, Abraham S. "McNary—A Transplanted Town." *Arizona Highways*, August 1990, 30–35.

———. *This Land, These Voices: A Different View of Arizona History in the Words of Those Who Lived It*. Flagstaff: Northland Press, 1977.

Chasteen, John Charles, and Joseph S. Tulchin, eds. *Problems in Modern Latin American History: A Reader*. Wilmington DE: SR Books, 1994.

Cheyney University of Pennsylvania. *Cheyney University of Pennsylvania Undergraduate Catalog, 1999–2002*. Cheyney: Cheyney University of Pennsylvania, 2000.

Clark, Steve, ed. *The Final Speeches of Malcolm X: February 1965*. New York: Pathfinder, 1992.

Cleaver, Eldridge. *Soul on Ice*. New York: Dell, 1968.

Clegg, Claude Andrew, III. *An Original Man: The Life and Times of Elijah Muhammad*. New York: St. Martin's, 1997.

Cohen, Jerry, and William S. Murphy. *Burn Baby, Burn! The Los Angeles Race Riot, August 1965*. New York: E. P. Dutton, 1966.

Collins, Karen Sikes. *Index to Arizona: The Journal of Arizona History, 1960–1964*. Tucson: Arizona Pioneers Historical Society, 1970.

Conkin, Paul K. *Big Daddy from the Pedernales: Lyndon Baines Johnson*. Boston: Twayne, 1986.

Connell-Smith, Gordon. *The Inter-American System*. New York: Oxford University Press, 1962.

Connerly, Ward. *Creating Equal: My Fight against Race Preferences*. San Francisco: Encounter Books, 2000.

Connery, Robert H., ed. *Urban Riots: Violence and Social Change*. New York: W. W. Norton, 1969.

Cooper, Michael L. *The Double V. Campaign: African Americans and World War II*. New York: NAL, 1997.

Cop, Thomas C. *Blacks in Topeka, Kansas, 1865–1915*. Baton Rouge: Louisiana State University Press, 1982.

Cope, R. Douglass. *The Limits of Racial Domination: Plebeian Society in Colonial Mexico City, 1600–1720*. Madison: University of Wisconsin Press, 1994.

Corley, Julie A. "Conflict and Community: St. Mary's Parish, Phoenix, Arizona." Master's thesis, Arizona State University, 1991.

Crafton, Robert, Sr. *An Autobiography Dictated to Anthony J. Binga, Sr.* Richmond VA: n.p., 1957.

Crawford, Vicki L., Jacqueline Anne Rouse, Barbara Woods, and Marymal Dryden. *Women in the Civil Rights Movement: Trailblazers and Torchbearers, 1941–1965*. Bloomington: Indiana University, Press, 1993.

Cronon, Edmund David. *Moses: The Story of Marcus Garvey and the Universal Negro Improvement Association*. Madison: University of Wisconsin Press, 1969.

Cronon, William, Jay Gitlin, George A. Miles, George Jay, and Miles Jay, eds. *Under an Open Sky: Rethinking America's Western Past*. New York: W. W. Norton, 1992.

Cross, Theodore. *The Black Power Imperative: Racial Inequality and the Politics of Nonviolence*. New York: Faulkner Books, 1984.

Crow, John E. *Discrimination, Poverty, and the Negro: Arizona in the National Context*. Tucson: University of Arizona Press, 1968.

———. *Mexican Americans in Contemporary Arizona: A Social Demographic View*. San Francisco: R and E Research, 1975.

Crudup, Keith Jerome. "African Americans in Arizona: A Twentieth-Century History." Ph.D. diss., Arizona State University, 1998.

Cruse, Harold. *Rebellion or Revolution?* New York: William and Morrow, 1968.

Dalfiume, Richard. *Desegregation of the U.S. Armed Forces: Fighting on Two Fronts 1939–1953*. Columbia: University of Missouri Press, 1969.

Dalleck, Robert. *Flawed Giant: Lyndon B. Johnson and His Times, 1961–1973*. New York: Oxford University Press, 1998.

———. *Ronald Reagan: The Politics of Symbolism*. Cambridge: Harvard University Press, 1984.

Daniels, Douglas Henry. *Pioneer Urbanites: A Social and Cultural History of Black San Francisco*. Philadelphia: Temple University Press, 1980.

Daniels, Douglas Henry, Sucheng Chan, Mario T. Garcia, and Terry P. Wilson, eds. *Peoples of Color in the American West*. Lexington MA: D. C. Heath, 1994.

Davis, Angela Y., ed. *If They Come in the Morning*. New York: Bantam, 1975.

Davis, Benjamin O., Jr. *American: An Autobiography*. Washington DC: Smithsonian Institution Press, 1991.

Dean, David R. "Rising from the Ashes: Phoenix and the Cold War, 1946–1963." Master's thesis, Arizona State University, 2001.

De Graaf, Lawrence B. "The City of Black Angles: The Emergence of the Los Angeles Ghetto, 1890–1930." *Pacific Historical Review* 39 (1970): 323–70.

———. "Race, Sex and Region: Black Women in the American West, 1850–1920." *Pacific Historical Review* 49 (1980): 285–313.

———. "Recognition, Racism, and Reflections on the Writing of Western Black History." *Pacific Historical Review* 44 (1975): 22–51.

———. "Significant Steps on an Arduous Path: The Impact of World War II on Discrimination against African Americans in the West." *Journal of the West* 35, no. 1 (1996): 24–33.

De Mente, Boye. "Living Black in Phoenix." *Phoenix*, September 1982, 102–26.

Dryden, Charles W. *A-Train: Memoirs of a Tuskegee Airman*. Tuscaloosa: University of Alabama Press, 1997.

Duberman, Martin Bauml. *Paul Robeson*. New York: Alfred A. Knopf, 1988.

DuBois, W. E. B. *Black Reconstruction in America, 1860–1880*. New York: Simon and Schuster, 1935.

———. *The Negro Common School*. Atlanta: Atlanta University Press, 1901.

———. *The Philadelphia Negro: A Social Study*. Philadelphia: Publications of the University of Pennsylvania, 1899.

———. *The Souls of Black Folk*. New York: Alfred A. Knopf, 1903.

Dunlaney, Marvin. *Black Presence in Dallas: A History of Black Political Activism in Dallas from 1936–1986*. Dallas: Museum of African American Life and Culture, 1987.

Dunne, John Gregory. "The Ugly Mood of Watts: Militant Leaders in Los Angeles' Negro Ghetto Are Trying to Win Power by Threatening Whites with Violence-and Behind Their Threats Lies Hatred." *Saturday Evening Post* July 16, 1966, 85–86.

Dyson, Michael Eric. *Race Rules: Navigating the Color Line*. New York: Vintage Books, 1997.

Eagles, Charles, ed. *The Civil Rights Movement in America*. Jackson: University of Mississippi Press, 1986.

Edley, Christopher. *Not All Black and White: Affirmative Action and American Values*. New York: Farrar, Straus and Giroux, 1998.

Eick, Gretchen Cassel. *Dissent in Wichita: The Civil Rights Movement in the Midwest, 1954–1972*. Urbana: University of Illinois Press, 2001.

Eskew, Glenn T. *But for Birmingham: The Local and National Movements in the Civil Rights Struggle*. Chapel Hill: University of North Carolina Press, 1997.

Fairclough, Adam. *Race and Democracy: The Civil Rights Struggle in Louisiana, 1915–1972*. Athens: University of Georgia Press, 1999.

Feagin, J. R. *Discrimination American Style: Institutional Racism and Sexism*. Englewood Cliffs NJ: Prentice Hall, 1978.

Foner, Eric. *Reconstruction: America's Unfinished Revolution, 1863–1877*. New York: Harper and Row, 1988.

Foner, Philip S., ed. *The Black Panthers Speak*. Philadelphia: J. B. Lippincott, 1970.

Franklin, J. James, Betty L. McCummings, and Eileen A. Tynan. *Minorities in the Sunbelt*. New Brunswick NJ: Rutgers University Center for Urban Policy Research, 1984.

Franklin, Jimmie Lewis. *Journey toward Hope: A History of Blacks in Oklahoma*. Norman: University of Oklahoma Press, 1982.

Franklin, John Hope, and John Whittington Franklin. *The Autobiography of Buck Colbert Franklin*. Baton Rouge: Louisiana State University Press, 1997.

Franklin, John Hope, and August Meier, eds. *Black Leaders of the Twentieth Century*. Urbana: University of Illinois Press, 1982.

Franklin, John Hope, and Alfred A. Moss. *From Slavery to Freedom: A*

History of African Americans, 8th ed. New York: Alfred A. Knopf, 2000.

Franklin, Robert Jefferson. "Making the Men of the 93rd: African American Servicemen in the Years of the Great Depression and the Second World War, 1935–1947." Ph.D. diss., University of Michigan, 1995.

Frazier, E. Franklin. The Negro Family in the United States. Chicago: University of Chicago Press, 1939.

Fredrickson, George M. Racism: A Short History. Princeton NJ: Princeton University Press, 2003.

———. White Supremacy: A Comparative Study in American and South African History. New York: Oxford University Press, 1982.

Gates, Henry Louis, Jr. The Two Nations of Black America. New York: Public Broadcasting System, February 3, 1998.

Gatewood, Willard B. Aristocrats of Color: The Black Elite, 1880–1920. Bloomington: Indiana University Press, 1990.

Gibbs, Jewelle Taylor. Race and Justice: Rodney King and O. J. Simpson in a House Divided. Indianapolis: Jossey-Bass, 1996.

Giddings, Paula. When and Where I Enter: The Impact of Black Women on Race and Sex in America. New York: William and Morrow, 1984.

Gill, Federico G. Latin American–United States Relations. New York: Harcourt Brace Jovanovich, 1971.

Gilmore, Glenda Elizabeth. Gender and Jim Crow: Women and the Politics of White Supremacy in North Carolina, 1896–1920. Chapel Hill: University of North Carolina Press, 1996.

Goff, John S., and Mary E. Gill. "Joseph H. Kibbey and School Segregation in Arizona." Journal of Arizona History 21 (Winter 1980): 411–22.

Golaney, Gideon, ed. Urban Planning for Arid Zones: American Experiences and Directions. New York: Praeger, 1978.

Goldberg, Robert Alan. "Racial Change on the Southern Periphery: The Case of San Antonio, Texas, 1960–1965." Journal of Southern History 49, no. 3 (1983): 349–74.

Goldfield, David R. Black, White, and Southern: Race Relations and Southern Culture, 1940 to the Present. Baton Rouge: Louisiana State University Press, 1990.

Gomez-Quinones, Juan. Chicano Politics: Reality and Promise, 1940–1990. Albuquerque: University of New Mexico Press, 1990.

Goodall, Leonard E. Urban Politics in the Southwest. Tempe: Arizona State University, 1967.

Graham, Lawrence Otis. A Member of the Club: Reflections on Life in a Racially Polarized World. New York: Perennial Press, 1996.

Grant, Joanne. *Ella Baker: Freedom Bound*. New York: John Wiley, Sons, 1998.

Greater Phoenix Council for Civic Unity, ed. *To Secure These Rights*. Phoenix: Phoenix Sun Publishing, 1961.

Grigsby, Eugene, Jr. *Art and Ethnics: Background for Teaching in a Pluralistic Society*. Dubuque IA: Wm. C. Brown, 1977.

———. *The Eye of Shamba: The Art of Eugene Grigsby, Jr.* Phoenix: Phoenix Art Museum, 2001.

Guglielmo, Thomas. *White on Arrival: Italians, Race, Color, and Power in Chicago, 1890–1945*. New York: Oxford University Press, 2003.

Guinier, Lani, and Gerald Torres. *The Miner's Canary: Enlisting Race, Resisting Power, Transforming Democracy*. Cambridge: Harvard University Press, 2003.

Gutman, Herbert. *The Black Family in Slavery and Freedom, 1750–1925*. New York: Pantheon Books, 1976.

Hacker, Andrew. *Money: Who Has How Much and Why*. New York: Simon and Schuster, 1998.

———. *Two Nations: Black and White, Separate, Hostile, Unequal*. New York: Ballantine Books, 1995.

Hackett, Mattie. "A Survey of Living Conditions of Girls in the Negro Schools of Phoenix, Arizona." Master's thesis, Arizona State University, 1939.

Haggerson, Nelson L. *Oh Yes I Can! A Biography of Arlena E. Seneca*. Tempe AZ: Nornel Associates, 1994.

Hait, Pam. "South Phoenix." *Phoenix*, August 1974, 54, 119.

Hamblin, Ken. *Pick a Better Country*. New York: Touchstone, 1997.

Hampton, Henry, Judith Vecchione, and Jon Else. *Eyes on the Prize: America's Civil Rights Years*. Boston: Blackside, 1987.

Harlan, Louis R. *Booker T. Washington: The Wizard of Tuskegee, 1901–1915*. New York: Oxford University Press, 1983.

Harris, Richard E. "First Families." *Black Heritage in Arizona* 1 (1976): 1–5.

———. *The First 100 Years: A History of Arizona's Blacks*. Apache Junction AZ: Relmo, 1983.

Harris, William. *The Harder We Run: Black Workers since the Civil War*. New York: Oxford University Press, 1982.

Hay, Vicki. "Calvin C. Goode: South Phoenix Survivor." *Phoenix* April 1984, 57–58.

Haygood, Wil. *King of the Cats: The Life and Times of Adam Clayton Powell, Jr.* New York: Houghton Mifflin, 1992.

Hendricks, Wanda A. *Gender, Race, and Politics in the Midwest: Black Club Women in Illinois*. Bloomington: Indiana University Press, 1998.

Herskovits, Melville. *The Myth of the Negro Past.* New York: Harper and
Brothers, 1941.

Hill, Mozell C. "The All-Negro Communities of Oklahoma: The Natural
History of a Social Movement." *Journal of Negro History* 31, no. 3
(1946): 254–68.

Hine, Darlene Clark. *Black Victory: The Rise and Fall of the White Primary in Texas,* 2nd ed. Columbia: University of Missouri Press, 2003.

———. *Black Women in White: Racial Conflict and Cooperation in the
Nursing Profession, 1890–1950.* Bloomington: Indiana University Press,
1989.

———. *Hine Sight: Black Women and the Re-Construction of American
History.* New York: Carlson, 1994.

———. "Rape and the Inner Lives of Black Women in the Middle West:
Preliminary Thoughts on the Culture of Dissemblance." *Signs* 14
(1989): 912–20.

———. *Speak Truth to Power: The Black Professional Class in United
States History.* New York: Carlson, 1996.

———. " 'Which Way is Freedom?': Black Power and the Rise of Black
Elected Officials." Lecture, November 13, 1997, Michigan State University, East Lansing.

———, ed. *The State of Afro-American History: Past, Present, and Future.* Baton Rouge: Louisiana State University Press, 1986.

Hine, Darlene Clark, Elsa Barkley Brown, and Rosalyn Terborg-Penn, eds.
*Black Women in America: An Historical Encyclopedia.* Vols. A–L and
M–Z. Bloomington: Indiana University Press, 1993.

Hine, Darlene Clark, Clayborne Carson, David Garrow, Vincent Hard-
ing, and Gerald Gill, eds. *The Eye's on the Prize Civil Rights Reader:
Documents, Speeches, and Firsthand Accounts from the Black Freedom
Struggle.* New York: Viking Penguin, 1991.

Hine, Darlene Clark, William C. Hine, and Stanley Harrold. *The African
American Odyssey.* Upper Saddle River NJ: Prentice Hall, 2003.

Hine, Darlene Clark, and Ernestine Jenkins, eds. *A Question of Manhood:
A Reader in U.S. Black Men's History and Masculinity.* Vol. 1, *Manhood Rights: The Construction of Black Male History and Manhood,
1750–1870.* Bloomington: Indiana University Press, 1999.

Hine, Darlene Clark, Wilma King, and Linda Reed, eds. *We Specialize in
the Wholly Impossible: A Reader in Black Women's History.* Brooklyn
NY: Carlson, 1995.

Hine, Darlene Clark, and Kathleen Thompson. *A Shining Thread of
Hope: The History of Black Women in America.* New York: Broadway
Books, 1998.

Higginbotham, Evelyn Brooks. *Righteous Discontent: The Women's*

*Movement in the Black Baptist Church, 1880–1920.* Cambridge: Harvard University Press, 1993.

Hill, Lance. *The Deacons for Defense: Armed Resistance and the Civil Rights Movement.* Chapel Hill: University of North Carolina Press, 2004.

Hirsh, James S. *Riot and Remembrance: The Tulsa Race War and Its Legacy.* New York: Houghton Mifflin, 2002.

Holloway, Karla F. C. *Passed On: African American Mourning Stories: A Memorial.* Durham NC: Duke University Press, 2002.

Holloway, Joseph E. *Africanisms in American Culture.* Bloomington: Indiana University Press, 1990.

hooks, bell. *Ain't I a Woman: Black Women and Feminism.* Cambridge MA: South End Press, 1981.

———. *Where We Stand: Class Matters.* New York: Taylor and Francis, 2000.

Horton, Arthur G. *An Economic, Political and Social Survey of Phoenix and the Valley of the Sun.* Tempe AZ: Southside Progress, 1941.

Hudson, Lynn M. "A New Look, or 'I'm Not Mammy to Everybody in California': Mary Ellen Pleasant, a Black Entrepreneur." *Journal of the West* 32 (1993): 35–40.

Hull, Gloria T., Patricia Bell Scott, and Barbara Smith, eds. *All the Women Are White, All the Blacks Are Men, but Some of Us Are Brave: Black Women's Studies.* Old Westbury NY: Feminist Press, 1982.

Huttman, Elizabeth D., ed. *Urban Housing Segregation of Minorities in Western Europe and the United States.* Durham NC: Duke University Press, 1991.

Ignatiev, David. *How the Irish Became White.* New York: Routledge, 1995.

Iverson, Peter. *Barry Goldwater: Native Arizonan.* Norman: University of Oklahoma Press, 1997.

Jackson, T. C. "Negro Education in Arizona." Master's thesis, University of Arizona, 1941.

James, Franklin J., Eileen A. Tynan, and Betty L. McCummings, eds. *Minorities in the Sunbelt.* New Brunswick NJ: Rutgers University Press, 1984.

Jameson, Elizabeth, and Susan Armitage, eds. *Writing the Range: Race, Class, and Culture in the Women's West.* Norman: University of Oklahoma Press, 1997.

Jefferson, Robert Franklin, "Making the Men of the 93rd: African American Servicemen in the Years of the Great Depression and the Second World War, 1935–1947." Ph.D. diss., University of Michigan, 1995.

Jenkins, Ernestine, and Darlene Clark Hine, eds. *A Question of Manhood:*

*A Reader in U.S. Black Men's History and Masculinity*. Vol. 2, *The 19th Century: From Emancipation to Jim Crow*. Bloomington: Indiana University Press, 2001.

Johnson, G. Wesley, Jr., *Phoenix, Valley of the Sun*. Tulsa OK: Continental Heritage Press, 1982.

———, ed. *Phoenix in the Twentieth Century: Essays in Community History*. Norman: University of Oklahoma Press, 1993.

Jones, Jacqueline. *Labor of Love, Labor of Sorrow: Black Women, Work, and the Family from Slavery to the Present*. New York: Basic Books, 1985.

Jones, James H. *Bad Blood: The Tuskegee Syphilis Experiment*. New York: Free Press, 1981.

Jones, Maldwyn A. *The Limits of Liberty: American History, 1607–1992*. New York: Oxford University Press, 1995.

Joyce, Davis D., ed. *"An Oklahoma I Had Never Seen Before": Alternative Views of Oklahoma History*. Norman: University of Oklahoma Press, 1994.

Katz, William Loren. *The Black West: A Documentary and Pictorial History of the African American Role in the Westward Expansion of the United States*. New York: Touchstone, 1987.

Kelley, Robin D. G. *Freedom Dreams: The Black Radical Imagination*. Boston: Beacon, 2002.

———. *Hammer and Hoe: Alabama Communists during the Great Depression*. Chapel Hill: University of North Carolina Press, 1990.

———. *Race Rebels: Culture, Politics, and the Black Working Class*. New York: Free Press, 1994.

———. *Yo' Mama's Disfunktional!: Fighting the Culture Wars in Urban America*. Boston: Beacon Press, 1997.

Kelley, Robin D. G., and Earl Lewis, eds. *To Make Our World Anew: A History of African Americans*. New York: Oxford University Press, 2000.

King, Martin Luther, Jr. *The Autobiography of Martin Luther King, Jr.* New York: Warner Books, 1998.

Kluger, Richard. *Simple Justice: The History of Brown v. Board of Education and Black America's Struggle for Equality*. New York: Vintage Books, 1975.

Knowles, Louis, and Kenneth Prewitt, eds. *Institutional Racism in America*. New York: Prentice Hall, 1969.

Konig, Michael. "Toward Metropolitan Status: Charter Government and the Rise of Phoenix, Arizona, 1945–1960." Ph.D. diss., Arizona State University, 1983.

Kotlanger, Michael J. "Phoenix, Arizona, 1920–1940." Ph.D. diss., Arizona State University, 1983.

Kozol, Jonathan. *Amazing Grace: The Lives of Children and the Conscience of a Nation.* New York: HarperPerennial, 1995.

———. *Savage Inequalities: Children in America's Schools.* New York: HarperCollins, 1992.

KSC Management Corporation, the Phoenix Urban League, and the United States Commission on Civil Rights. *The Search: Hearings before the United States Commission on Civil Rights, Phoenix, Arizona, February 3, 1962.* Phoenix: AirLab Times, 1962.

Lamb, Barry Edward. "The Making of a Chicano Civil Rights Activist: Ralph Estrada of Arizona." Master's thesis, Arizona State University, 1988.

Landry, Bart. *The New Black Middle-Class.* Berkeley: University of California Press, 1987.

Lapp, Rudolph. *Afro-Americans in California.* New Haven CT: Yale University Press, 1977.

Landolt, Robert Garland. *The Mexican-America Workers of San Antonio, Texas.* New York: Arno, 1976.

Lawson, Steven F. *Running for Freedom: Civil Rights and Black Politics in America since 1941,* 2nd ed. New York: McGraw Hill, 1997.

Lawson, Steven F., and Charles Payne. *Debating the Civil Rights Movement, 1945–1968.* New York: Rowman and Littlefield, 1998.

Leckie, William H. *Buffalo Soldiers: A Narrative of the Negro Cavalry in the West.* Norman: University of Oklahoma Press, 1967.

Lee, Chana Kai. *For Freedom's Sake: The Life of Fanny Lou Hamer.* Urbana: University of Illinois Press, 1999.

Lee, Ulysses G. *United States Army in World War II, Special Studies: The Employment of Negro Troops.* Washington DC: Office of the Chief of Military History, 1966.

Leiker, James N. *Racial Borders: Black Soldiers along the Rio Grande.* College Station: Texas A&M University Press, 2002.

Lemann, Nicholas. *The Promised Land: The Great Black Migration and How It Changed America.* New York: Random House, 1991.

Lemke-Santangelo, Gretchen. *Abiding Courage: African American Migrant Women and the East Bay Community.* Chapel Hill: University of North Carolina Press, 1996.

LeSeur, Geta. *Not All Okies Are White: The Lives of Black Cotton Pickers in Arizona.* Columbia: University of Missouri Press, 2000.

Levine, Lawrence. *Black Culture Black Consciousness.* New York: Oxford University Press, 1977.

Lewis, David Levering. *W. E. B. DuBois: Biography of a Race, 1868–1919.* New York: Henry Holt, 1993.

———. *W. E. B. DuBois: The Fight for Equality and the American Century.* Vol. 2, *1919–1963.* New York: Henry Holt, 2000.

Lewis, John. *Walking with the Wind: A Memoir of the Movement.* New York: Harcourt Brace, 1999.

Limerick, Patricia Nelson. *The Legacy of Conquest: The Unbroken Past of the American West.* New York: W. W. Norton, 1987.

Lindsey, Donal F. *Indians at Hampton Institute, 1877–1923.* Urbana: University of Illinois Press, 1995.

Litwack, Leon F. *Been in the Storm So Long: The Aftermath of Slavery.* New York: Vintage, 1980.

———. *Trouble in Mind: Black Southerners in the Era of Jim Crow.* New York: Alfred A. Knopf, 1998.

Loevy, Robert D. *To End All Segregation: The Politics of the Passage of the Civil Rights Act of 1964.* Lanham MD: University Press of America, 1990.

Logan, Rayford. *The Negro in American Life and Thought: The Nadir, 1877–1901.* New York: Dial Press, 1954.

Love, Nat. *The Life and Adventures of Nat Love.* Lincoln: University of Nebraska Press, 1995.

Luckingham, Bradford. *Minorities in Phoenix: A Profile History of Mexican American, Chinese American, and African American Communities, 1860–1992.* Tucson: University of Arizona Press, 1994.

———. *Phoenix: The History of a Southwestern Metropolis.* Tucson: University of Arizona Press, 1989.

———. *The Urban Southwest: A Profile History of Albuquerque, El Paso, Phoenix and Tucson.* El Paso: Texas Western Press, 1982.

Luckingham, Bradford, Barbara Luckingham, and Lori Parks, eds. *Discovering Greater Phoenix: An Illustrated History.* Phoenix: Heritage Media, 1998.

Luey, Beth, and Noel J. Stowe, eds. *Arizona at Seventy-Five: The Next Twenty-five Years.* Tucson: University of Arizona Press, 1987.

Manis, Andrew M. *"A Fire You Can't Put Out": The Civil Rights Life of Birmingham's Reverend Fred Shuttlesworth.* Tuscaloosa: University of Alabama Press, 1999.

Marable, Manning. *How Capitalism Underdeveloped Black America: Problems in Race, Political Economy, and Society.* Cambridge MA: South End Press, 2000.

———. *Race, Reform, and Rebellion: The Second Reconstruction in Black America, 1945–1990.* Oxford: University Press of Mississippi, 1991.

———. *W. E. B. DuBois: Black Radical Democrat*. New York: Macmillan, 1987.

Massey, Douglas S., and Nancy A. Denton. *American Apartheid: Segregation and the Making of the Underclass*. Cambridge: Harvard University Press, 1993.

Mawn, Geoffrey Padraic. "Phoenix, Arizona: Central City of the Southwest, 1870–1920." Ph.D. diss., Arizona State University, 1979.

Mays, June, Sylvia Anderson, and Terri Dunlap, eds. *Greater Shiloh Missionary Baptist Church: From Then until Now, 73rd Anniversary Celebration*. Phoenix: Greater Shiloh Missionary Baptist Church, 1997.

McCoy, Matt. "The Desert Metropolis: Image Building and the Growth of Phoenix, 1940–1965." Ph.D. diss., Arizona State University, 2000.

McCune, William. *Almost Free: A History of Arizona Blacks*. William McCune Productions for Television, Phoenix, 1990.

McLoughlin, Emmett. *People's Padre*. Boston: Beacon, 1954.

McMurry, Linda O. *To Keep the Waters Troubled: The Life of Ida B. Wells*. New York: Oxford University Press, 1998.

McNeil, Genna Rael. *Groundwork: Charles Hamilton Houston and the Struggle for Civil Rights*. Philadelphia: University of Pennsylvania Press, 1983.

Meier, August, and Elliot Rudwick. CORE: *A Study in the Civil Rights Movement, 1942–1968*. Urbana: University of Illinois Press, 1975.

Melcher, Mary. "Blacks and Whites Together: Interracial Leadership in the Phoenix Civil Rights Movement." *Journal of Arizona History* 32 (Summer 1991): 195–216.

———. "Madge Copeland and Placida Garcia Smith: Community Organizers, Phoenix, Arizona, 1930–1960." Manuscript, Women's Studies, Arizona State University, Tempe, 1987.

Mellinger, Phillip. "Discrimination and Statehood in Oklahoma." *Chronicles of Oklahoma* 49 (1971): 340–78.

Metress, Christopher, ed. *The Lynching of Emmett Till: A Documentary Narrative*. Charlottesville: University of Virginia Press, 2002.

Miller, Joseph. *The Arizona Story*. New York: Hastings House, 1952.

Milner, Clyde A., II. *A New Significance: Re-envisioning the History of the American West*. New York: Oxford University Press, 1996.

———, ed. *Major Problems in the History of the American West*. Lexington MA: D. C. Heath, 1989.

Milner, Clyde A., II, Carol A. O'Connor, and Martha A. Sandweiss, eds. *The Oxford Dictionary of the American West*. New York: Oxford University Press, 1994.

Mitford, Jessica. *The American Way of Death*. New York: Simon and Schuster, 1963.

———. *The American Way of Death Revisited*. New York: Alfred A. Knopf, 1998.

Mjagkij, Nina, ed. *Organizing Black America: An Encyclopedia of African American Associations*. New York: Garland, 2000.

Mohr, James C. *Radical Republicans in the North: State Politics during Reconstruction*. Baltimore: Johns Hopkins University Press, 1976.

Moore, Joan W. "Residential Segregation in the Urban Southwest; A Comparative Study." Los Angeles: Division of Research, Graduate School of Business Administration, University of California, 1966.

Moore, Shirley A. *To Place Our Deeds: The African American Community in Richmond, California, 1910–1963*. Berkeley: University of California Press, 1999.

Morgan, Anne Hodges, and Rennard Strickland, eds. *Arizona Memories*. Tucson: University of Arizona Press, 1984.

Motley, Mary Penick. *The Invisible Soldier: The Experience of the Black Soldier, World War II*. Detroit: Wayne State University Press, 1975.

Myers, David G. *Social Psychology*, 5th ed. New York: McGraw-Hill, 1996.

Myers, Samuel. *Civil Rights and Race Relations in the Post Reagan-Bush Era*. New York: Praeger, 1997.

Myrdal, Gunnar. *An American Dilemma*. New York: Harper and Row, 1962.

Nash, Gerald D. *The American West Transformed: The Impact of the Second World War*. Bloomington: Indiana University Press, 1985.

National Urban League. *Economic and Cultural Progress of the Negro: Phoenix, Arizona*. New York: Urban League, 1965.

Newhall, Richard, "The Negro in Phoenix," *Phoenix Point West*, September 1965, 15–18.

NewsChannel 13, KTVK. "A Tribute to Lincoln Ragsdale." Presented at the Phoenix Urban League Whitney M. Young Jr. Awards Dinner, February 16, 1995.

Newton, Huey P. *Revolutionary Suicide*. New York: Harcourt Brace Jovanovich, 1973.

Niebur, Jay Edward. "The Social and Economic Effect of the Great Depression on Phoenix, Arizona, 1929–1934." Master's thesis, Arizona State University, 1967.

Nimmons, Robert. "Arizona's Forgotten Past: The Negro in Arizona, 1539–1965." Master's thesis, Northern Arizona University, 1971.

Noble, Daniel E. "Motorola Expands in Phoenix." *Arizona Business and Economic Review* 3 (June 1954): 1–2.

Novick, Peter. *That Noble Dream : The "Objectivity Question" and the*

*American Historical Profession*. Cambridge: Cambridge University Press, 1988.

Oliver, Melvin L., and Thomas M. Shapiro. *Black Wealth, White Wealth: New Perspectives on Racial Inequality*. New York: Routledge, 1997.

O'Reilly, Kenneth. *Nixon's Piano: Presidents and Racial Politics from Washington to Clinton*. New York: Free Press, 1995.

———. *Racial Matters: The FBI's Secret File on Black America, 1960–1972*. New York: Free Press, 1991.

Osur, Alan M. *Blacks in the Army Air Forces during World War II: The Problem of Race Relations*. Washington DC: Office of Air Force History, 1977.

Painter, Nell Irvin. *Exodusters: Black Migration to Kansas after Reconstruction*. New York: W. W. Norton, 1976.

Parliament. "Chocolate City." On *Parliament: Tear the Roof Off, 1974–1980*. Sound recording on CD. New York: Polygram Records, 1993. Original recording on LP, Polygram Records, 1975.

Pascoe, Peggy. *Relations of Rescue: The Search for Female Moral Authority in the American West, 1874–1939*. New York: Oxford University Press, 1990.

Payne, Charles. *I've Got the Light of Freedom: The Organizing Tradition and the Mississippi Freedom Struggle*. Berkeley: University of California Press, 1996.

Peplow, Edward H., Jr. "You'll Like Living in Phoenix." *Arizona Highways*, April 1957, 14–35.

Perkins, Joseph, ed. *A Conservative Agenda for Black Americans*. Washington DC: Heritage Foundation, 1987.

Pfeffer, Paula F. *A. Philip Randolph: Pioneer of the Civil Rights Movement*. Baton Rouge: Louisiana State University Press, 1990.

Phoenix Urban League. *A Brief History of the Urban League in Phoenix*. Phoenix: Phoenix Urban League, 1981.

Pickney, Alphonse. *The Myth of Black Progress*. Cambridge: Harvard University Press, 1984.

Pine, Vanderlyn R. *Caretaker of the Dead: The American Funeral Director*. New York: Irvington, 1975.

Plater, Michael A. *African American Entrepreneurship in Richmond, 1890–1940: The Story of R. C. Scott*. New York: Garland, 1996.

Porter, Kenneth Wiggins. *The Negro on the America Frontier*. New York: Arno, 1970.

Potter, Lou Potter. *Fighting on Two Fronts in World War II*. New York: Harcourt Brace Jovanovich, 1992.

Powell, Lawrence C. *Arizona: A Bicentennial History*. New York: W. W. Norton, 1972.

Preisler, Dennis. "Phoenix during the 1940's: Decade of Change." Master's thesis, Arizona State University, 1992.

Rabinowitz, Howard. *Race, Ethnicity, and Urbanization*. Columbia: University of Missouri Press, 1994.

———. *Race Relations in the Urban South, 1865–1890*. Athens: University of Georgia Press, 1996.

Ragsdale, Lincoln, Sr. "Minority Entrepreneurship: Profiling an African American Entrepreneur." Ph.D. diss., Union Graduate School, 1989.

Rampersad, Arnold. *Jackie Robinson: A Biography*. New York: Alfred A. Knopf, 1997.

Ransby, Barbara. *Ella Baker and the Black Freedom Movement: A Radical Democratic Vision*. Chapel Hill: University of North Carolina Press, 2003.

Reed, Christopher R. *The Chicago NAACP and the Rise of Black Professional Leadership, 1910–1966*. Bloomington: Indiana University Press, 1997.

Richards, Morris J. *The Birth of Arizona: The Baby State*. Phoenix: Arizona State Department of Education, 1940.

Riley, Carroll L. "Blacks in the Early Southwest." *Ethnohistory* 19 (1972): 247–60.

Riley, Glenda. "American Daughters: Black Women in the West." *Montana: The Magazine of Western History* 38 (1988): 14–27.

Roberts, Darryl. *Profits of Death: An Insider Exposes the Death Care Industries*. Chandler AZ: Five Star Publications, 1997.

Roberts, Shirley J. "Minority Group Poverty in Phoenix: A Socio-Economic Survey." *Journal of Arizona History* 14 (Winter 1973): 347–62.

Robinson, Jo Ann Gibson. *The Montgomery Bus Boycott and the Women Who Started It: The Memoir of Jo Ann Gibson Robinson*. Knoxville: University of Tennessee Press, 1987.

Robinson, Randall. *The Debt: What America Owes to Blacks*. New York: Dutton, 2000.

———. *The Reckoning: What Blacks Owe to Each Other*. New York: Dutton, 2002.

Robinson, W. A. "The Progress of Integration in the Public Schools." *Journal of Negro Education* 25 (Fall 1956): 371–79.

Rosales, F. Arturo. *Chicano!: The History of the Mexican American Civil Rights Movement*. Houston: Arte Pùblico Press, 1996.

Rose, Robert A. *Lonely Eagles: The Story of the American Black Air Force in World War II*. Los Angeles: Tuskegee Airmen, Inc., Los Angeles Chapter, 1976.

Ross, Caroline Ross, and Ken Lawrence. *J. Edgar Hoover's Detention*

Plan: The Politics of Repression in the United States, 1939–1976. Jackson MS: Anti-Repression Resource Team, 1978.

Rothschild, Mary Logan, and Pamela Claire Hronek. Doing What the Day Brought: An Oral History of Arizona Women. Tucson: University of Arizona Press, 1992.

Ruiz, Vicki L. Cannery Women, Cannery Lives: Mexican Women, Unionization, and the California Food Processing Industry, 1930–1950. Albuquerque: University of New Mexico Press, 1987.

———. From Out of the Shadows: Mexican Women in Twentieth-Century America. New York: Oxford University Press, 1999.

Ruiz, Vicki L., and Ellen Carol Dubois, eds. Unequal Sisters: A Multicultural Reader in U.S. Women's History. New York: Routledge, 2000.

Ruiz, Vicki L., et al. Created Equal: A Social and Political History of the United States. Vol. 2, From 1865. New York: Longman, 2002.

Ruppel, John Louis, Jr. "Urban Community Participation in Federal Grant Programs for the Phoenix Metropolitan Area." Master's thesis, Arizona State University, 1971.

Savage, Sherman W. Blacks in the West. Westport CT: Greenwood, 1976.

Scott, Daryl Michael. Contempt and Pity: Social Policy and the Image of the Damaged Black Psyche, 1880–1996. Chapel Hill: University of North Carolina Press, 1997.

Scott, Lawrence P., and William W. Womack. Double V: The Civil Rights Struggle of the Tuskegee Airmen. East Lansing: Michigan State University Press, 1998.

Servin, Manuel P., ed. An Awakened Minority: The Mexican Americans. Beverly Hills CA: Sage, 1974.

Shaw, Stephanie. What a Woman Ought to Be and to Do: Black Professional Women Workers during the Jim Crow Era. Chicago: University of Chicago Press, 1996.

Sheridan, Thomas E. Arizona: A History. Tucson: University of Arizona Press, 1995.

Sitkoff, Howard. A New Deal for Blacks: The Emergence of Civil Rights as a National Issue. Vol. 1, Depression Decade. New York: Oxford University Press, 1978.

———. "Racial Militancy and Interracial Violence in the Second World War." Journal of American History 58, no. 3 (1971): 663–83.

———. The Struggle for Black Equality, 1954–1980. New York: Farrar, Straus and Giroux, 1981.

Skidmore, Thomas E., and Peter H. Smith, Modern Latin America, 3rd ed. New York: Oxford University Press, 1992.

Smith, Gloria. Arizona's Slice of Black Americana. Tucson AZ: Gloria Smith, 1976.

Smith, Ronald G. E. *The Death Care Industries in the United States.* Jefferson NC: McFarland, 1995.

Smith, Susan M. "Litchfield Park and Vicinity." Master's thesis, University of Arizona, 1948.

Smith, William and Valida Smith. *A History of the First Institutional Baptist Church.* Phoenix: First Institutional Baptist Church, 1985.

Sowell, Thomas Sowell. *Preferential Politics: An International Perspective.* New York: William Morrow, 1990.

———. *Race and Culture: A World View.* New York: Basic Books, 1995.

Steele, Shelby. *Content of Our Character: A New Vision of Race in America.* New York: Perennial Press, Reprint, 1998.

Stoker, Joseph. "Phoenix: City Growing in the Sun." *Arizona Highways,* April 1957, 36–39.

———. "What Happens When Segregation Ends?" *Look,* February 23, 1954, 25–28.

Stone, Eddie. *Jessie Jackson: An Intimate Portrait.* Los Angeles: Holloway House, 1981.

Sugrue, Thomas J. *The Origins of the Urban Crisis: Race and Inequality in Postwar Detroit.* Princeton NJ: Princeton University Press, 1996.

Sullivan, Leon. *Moving Mountains: The Principles and Purposes of Leon Sullivan.* Valley Forge PA: Judson Press, 1998.

Sullivan, Patricia. *Days of Hope: Race and Democracy in the New Deal Era.* Chapel Hill: University of North Carolina Press, 1996.

Summerville, James. *Educating Black Doctors: A History of Meharry Medical College.* Birmingham: University of Alabama Press, 1983.

Takaki, Ronald. *Debating Diversity: Clashing Perspectives on Race and Ethnicity in America,* 2nd ed. New York: Oxford University Press, 2002.

Taylor, Quintard, Jr. *The Forging of a Black Community: Seattle's Central District from 1870 through the Civil Rights Era.* Seattle: University of Washington Press, 1994.

———. *In Search of the Racial Frontier: African Americans in the American West, 1528–1990.* New York: W. W. Norton, 1998.

Taylor, Quintard, Jr., Lawrence B. de Graaf, and Kevin Mulroy, eds. *Seeking El Dorado: African Americans in California, 1769–1997.* Seattle: University of Washington Press, 2001.

Taylor, Quintard, Jr., and Shirley Ann Wilson Moore, eds. *African American Women Confront the West, 1600–2000.* Norman: University of Oklahoma Press, 2003.

Teall, Kaye M. *Black History in Oklahoma: A Resource Book.* Oklahoma City: Oklahoma City Public Schools, 1971.

Terborg-Penn, Rosalyn. *African American Women in the Struggle for the Vote, 1850–1920*. Bloomington: Indiana University Press, 1998.

Terrell, John Upton. *Estevanico the Black*. Los Angeles: Western Lore Press, 1968.

Thomas, Richard W. *Understanding Interracial Unity: A Study of U.S. Race Relations*. London: Sage, 1996.

Tobin, Gary A., ed. *Divided Neighborhoods: Changing Patterns of Racial Segregation*. Beverly Hills: Sage, 1987.

Tolson, Arthur L. *The Black Oklahomans: A History, 1541–1972*. New Orleans: Edwards Printing, 1974.

Trelease, Allan W. *White Terror: The Ku Klux Klan Conspiracy and Southern Reconstruction*. Baton Rouge: Louisiana State University Press, 1995.

Trennert, Robert A. *The Phoenix Indian School: Forced Assimilation in Arizona, 1891–1935*. Norman: University of Oklahoma Press, 1988.

Trimble, Marshall. *Arizona: A Cavalcade of History*. Tucson AZ: Treasure Chest, 1989.

Trotter, Joe William. *Black Milwaukee: The Making of an Industrial Proletariat, 1915–45*. Urbana: University of Illinois Press, 1985.

———, ed. *The Great Migration in Historical Perspective: New Dimensions of Race, Class, and Gender*. Bloomington: Indiana University Press, 1991.

Trotter, Joe William, Earl Lewis, and Tera W. Hunter, eds. *The African American Urban Experience: Perspectives from the Colonial Period to the Present*. New York: Palgrave MacMillan, 2004.

Turner, Frederick Jackson. "The Significance of the Frontier in American History." American Historical Association, *Annual Report for the Year 1893* (1894).

Tushnet, Mark V. *The NAACP's Legal Strategy against Segregated Education, 1925–1950*. Chapel Hill: University of North Carolina Press, 1987.

Twine, France Winddance. *Racism in a Racial Democracy: The Maintenance of White Supremacy in Brazil*. New Brunswick NJ: Rutgers University Press, 1997.

Tyson, Timothy B. *Radio Free Dixie: Robert F. Williams and the Roots of Black Power*. Chapel Hill: University of North Carolina Press, 1999.

Universal Memorial Center, Inc. *A Celebration and Worship Service Honoring the Life of Dr. Lincoln Johnson Ragsdale, Sr.* Phoenix: Universal Memorial Center, 1995.

———. *A Celebration and Worship Service Honoring the Life of Mrs. Eleanor Dickey Ragsdale*. Phoenix: Universal Memorial Center, 1995.

———. *Ragsdale Family History in Funeral Service*. Phoenix: Universal Memorial Center, 1999.

Upton, James N. *Urban Riots in the Twentieth Century: A Social History*. New York: Wyndham Press, 1989.

Van Deburg, William L. *New Day in Babylon: The Black Power Movement and American Culture, 1965–1975*. Chicago: University of Chicago Press, 1992.

VanderMeer, Philip R. *Phoenix Rising: Making of a Desert Metropolis, 1940–2000*. Carlsbad CA: Heritage Media, 2002.

Van Petten, Donald, *The Constitution and Government of Arizona*. Phoenix: Jahn and Tyler, 1952.

Wade, Wyn Craig. *The Fiery Cross: The Ku Klux Klan in America*. New York: Oxford University Press, 1998.

Walker, Curtis. "The Influence of Culture and Demography on the Colored People of McNary." Master's thesis, University of Arizona, 1975.

Washington, Booker T. *The Negro in Business*. Boston: Hertel, Jenkins, 1907.

———. "The Race Problem in Arizona." *Phoenix Independent* October 1911, 909–13.

———. *Up from Slavery*. New York: Double Day, 1901.

Webb, Walter Prescott. "The American West: Perpetual Mirage." *Harper's Magazine*, May 1957, 25–31.

Weisiger, Marsha L. *Land of Plenty: Oklahomans in the Fields of Arizona, 1933–1942*. Norman: University of Oklahoma Press, 1995.

———. "Mythic Fields of Plenty." *Journal of Arizona History* 32, no. 3 (1991): 241–66.

Wells-Barnett, Ida B. *Crusade for Justice: The Autobiography of Ida B. Wells*. Ed. Alfreda M. Duster. Chicago: University of Chicago Press, 1970.

West, Cornel. *The Cornel West Reader*. New York: Basic Civitas Books, 1999.

———. *Race Matters*. New York: Vintage, 1994.

Whitaker, Matthew C. " 'Creative Conflict': Lincoln and Eleanor Ragsdale, Collaboration, and Community Activism in Phoenix, 1953–1965." *Western Historical Quarterly* 34, no. 2 (2003): 165–90.

White, Deborah Gray. *Too Heavy a Load: Black Women in Defense of Themselves, 1894–1994*. New York: W. W. Norton, 1999.

White, Richard. *"It's Your Misfortune and None of My Own": A New History of the American West*. Norman: University of Oklahoma Press, 1991.

———. "Race Relations in the American West." *American Quarterly* 38, no. 3 (1986): 396–416.

White, Walter. *A Man Called White: The Autobiography of Walter White.* Athens: University of Georgia Press, 1995.

Whitfield, Stephen J. *A Death in the Delta: The Story of Emmett Till.* Baltimore: Johns Hopkins University Press, 1991.

Williams, Armstrong. *Letters to a Young Victim: Hope and Healing in America's Inner Cities.* New York: Free Press, 1996.

Williams, Patricia J. *The Alchemy of Race and Rights.* Cambridge: Harvard University Press, 1992.

Wilson, William Julius. *The Declining Significance of Race: Blacks and Changing American Institutions.* Chicago: University of Chicago Press, 1978.

———. *The Truly Disadvantaged: The Inner City, the Underclass, and Public Policy.* Chicago: University of Chicago Press, 1987.

———. *When Work Disappears: The World of the New Urban Poor.* New York: Alfred A. Knopf, 1996.

Wolfe, Edward N. *Top Heavy: Increasing Inequality of Wealth in America and What Can Be Done about It*, rev. ed. New York: New Press, 2002.

Woodson, Carter G. *The Negro Professional Man in the Community.* New York: Negro University Press, 1934.

Woodward, C. Vann. *Reunion and Reaction: The Compromise of 1877 and the End of Reconstruction.* New York: Oxford University Press, 1951.

X, Malcolm. *The Autobiography of Malcolm X.* With the assistance of Alex Haley. New York: Ballantine Books, 1964.

———. *The End of White Supremacy: Four Speeches by Malcolm X.* New York: Arcade, 1989.

Young, Andrew. *An Easy Burden: The Civil Rights Movement and the Transformation of America.* New York: Harper Collins, 1996.

Zarbin, Earl. *All the Time a Newspaper: The First 100 Years of the Arizona Republic.* Phoenix: Arizona Republic, 1990.

Zellmer, Al M. "Welcome Stranger!" *Arizona Highways*, August 1943, 20–25, 59.

# INDEX

Page numbers in italics indicate illustrations.

Action Citizens Committee (ACT), 15, 166–67

activist groups: advocating nonviolent resistance, 155–57, 161–62; black nationalism and, 175–76; early, 14–15; during the Great Depression, 59–60; Mexican American, 208–9, 214–16; militant, 18, 172, 173–74, 186–88, 274; in Oklahoma, 38; in Phoenix, 93–95, 117–18; police responses to, 177–78; prior to the Civil Rights Act of 1964, 17–18, 154–57; protesting retailers, 90–91, 150–51; radical *versus* traditional, 186–88, 228; sit-ins by, 148, 160–61; successes of, 163; women in, 38–39, 102–3, 188–89, 193, 196–97; working against employer discrimination, 82; working against lynching, 41; during World War II, 83–84

Adams Hotel (Phoenix), 157

Advisory Committee on Small and Minority Businesses (ACSMB), 241–42

African Americans: and the abolition of slavery, 25–26; alliances with other groups, 4–5; and the black freedom struggle, 4, 8–9, 19, 129–30, 173–74, 269, 274, 281–82; and the Black Power movement, 187–88, 189, 324n4; class conflicts among, 19–20, 275, 276; coalitions with Mexican Americans, 15–16, 171, 199–200, 208–9, 218–21, 271–72; community activism groups, 14; compared to other people of African descent, 57–58; economic self-determination by, 43–44, 175–76, 240–42; employment of, 32–35, 72–83, 80–81, 81, 85–86, 143, 146–48, 179–80, 235–36, 307–8n106; funerals and death rites of, 34, 101; involved in politics, 43; leadership in Phoenix, 5–6, 155–56, 194–96, 229–30; legislation affecting, 17, 25–26; manhood and identity of, 112; middle-class, 19–20, 189, 197, 212, 225, 227–30, 240, 273, 276–77; migration into the American West, 9–13, 64, 80–81, 85–86, 129; migration out of the South following the Civil War, 28; in the military, 44–45, 47, 63–79; morticians, 32–35; negative labels on, 56–57; neoconservative, 214, 225–26, 253–54; political involvement of, 86, 120–21, 128–29, 137–38, 164, 166–67, 191–92, 194–96, 227, 254–55; population in the Phoenix metropolitan area, 111, 136, 226, 239, 264–65, 285, 286; poverty among, 19–20, 58, 175–76, 197, 198, 225, 235–38, 251, 255–56; as professional athletes, 242–43; religious life of, 136–41, 180–81; subjected to social Darwinism, 11, 13, 27, 35; tensions between Mexican Americans and, 209–11, 213–14, 272–73; violence against, 29–30, 31, 36–37, 40–41, 76–77, 81–82, 85, 176–77, 249–50; voting by, 17, 133, 167–68, 190, 192, 194–95; working in defense industries, 72–73; during World War II, 63–79. *See also* Phoenicians, black; professional class, black; women, African American

Alden, Robert L., 166, 171

Alexander, Paul, 155

American Civil Liberties Union (ACLU), 95

American Federation of Labor (AFL), 72

Anderson, C. Alfred, 68

Anderson-Ragsdale Mortuary, 100

Andrews, Judis, 195–96, 230–31, 233

Angelou, Maya, 267

antimiscegenation laws, 13–14

Arizona Club Board of Trustees, 289

Arizona Coordinating Committee for International Women's Year, 290

Arizona Council for Civil Unity (ACCU), 118

*Arizona Democrat*, 116

Arizona Federation of Colored Women's Clubs (AFCWC), 14, 16

Arizona Historical Foundation, 289, 290

*Arizona Informant*, 191, 194

*Arizona Republic*, 135, 152, 156, 162, 165, 166, 217, 234, 244, 250, 278

*Arizona Republican*, 105, 113

Arizona State University, 72, 217–18, 252; Alumni Association, 289

*Arizona Sun*, 90, 93, 98, 99, 126, 127, 137, 153, 157; coverage of George B. Brooks, 140; on Mexican American and African American relations, 199–200, 201

Arizona Voter's League (AVL), 93

Armstrong, Louis, 43

Armstrong, Samuel Chapman, 46

Asians and Pacific Islanders: employed in defense industries, 72; population in Arizona, 286

Association of Southern Women for the Prevention of Lynching, 41

*The Autobiography of Malcolm X*, 173

Babbitt, Bruce, 256, 257

Baker, Ella, 59, 174

Baker, Lori K., 110, 124, 153

bankers of Phoenix, 141–43

Bank One of Arizona, 142

Barber, John, 59

Baron, Harold M., 237–38

Bates, Ruby, 60

Bayless, Samuel, 14, 116

Bell, William, 191

Bentley, Leon, 244

Bernstein, Charles E., 121

Berry, Mary Francis, 226

Bethune, Mary McLeod, 43

Black, Claude, 219

Black, Hugo, 155

Black, Joe, 188, 196

Black Board of Directors Project, 249

Black Codes, 26

*Black Enterprise Magazine*, 1

"black flight," 227–30, 277

black freedom struggle, 4, 8–9, 19, 129–30, 173–74, 269, 274, 281–82

Black Panther Party, 175–76, 188, 190–91

Black Political Action Association of Arizona, 192

Black Power movement, 187–88, 189, 324n4

Black Women's Task Force, 275, 290

Blair, Ezell, Jr., 148

Blue, Gene, 261

Booker T. Washington Life Insurance Company, 137

Boozer, Mary, 259

Bostrom, William, 155

Bowman, Junius A., 186, 240

Boyer, Sylvanus, 119

Brinkley-Rodgers, Paul, 250

Broadway House Apartments, 188, 196

Brooks, Benjamin, 195

Brooks, George B.: activist work of, 1, 5, 7, 138–48, 150, 155, 162, 167, 168, 174, 177, 182, 188, 196, 248, 256; and Mexican Americans, 213, 214

Brotherhood of Sleeping Car Porters, 72–73

Brown, Hallie Q., 106–7

Brown, Trevor G., 121

*Brown II*, 134

white supremacy (*continued*)
African Americans, 175–76; Lincoln
Ragsdale's early experiences with,
40; in Phoenix, 5–6, 270–71; in the
South following the Civil War, 26–27,
29–30; in the West, 81–82. *See also*
discrimination; racism
Wilburn, Zenothia, 193
Wilcox, Earl, 209
Wilcox, Mary Rose Garrido, 227
Wilkins, Roy, 92–93
Willey, Keven, 244
Williams, Armstrong, 214, 226
Williams, Cody, 261
Williams, D. W., 101, 136
Williams, Emily Crump, 90
Williams, Fannie Barrier, 241
Williams, Fred, 90
Williams, Hazel, 100
Williams, J. T., 114, 116
Williams, Jim, 186
Williams, Tolly, 121
Williams, Travis, 136, 147, 261
Williams Air Force Base, 71
Wilson, H. F., 45–46
Wilson, William Julius, 236, 238
Wirth, Lewis, 93
Woman's Christian Temperance Union
(WCTU), 54

women, African American: activism by,
38–39, 102–3, 188–89, 193, 196–
97; education of, 48–49, 51–54, 56;
race, 2, 3; racism against, 17; social
obligations of middle-class, 49–50,
52–53
Women's Army Corps (WAC), 77
Woodruff, Hale, 126
Woolworth's stores, 90–91, 117, 150–
51
Wooten, Duane, 250–51
Works Progress Administration (WPA),
59
World War II: African Americans in the
military during, 63–80; changes in
attitudes during, 83–84, 269; employment of African Americans after, 81;
impact on African American population in the West, 80–81; migration
of African Americans during, 85–
86; political involvement of African
Americans after, 86

Young Socialist Alliance (YSA), 209
Young Women's Christian Association
(YWCA), 60, 103, 290
Youth Corps, 179

zoot suit riot, 81–82